Dr. Jack Pastor is coordinator of the Department of Jewish History at Oranim-the University of Haifa where he teaches the history of the Second Temple period. He has written articles on economic and social issues of the Second Temple, and co-authored a unit of the Open University on the economy of the Hasmonean State.

LAND AND ECONOMY IN ANCIENT PALESTINE

LAND AND ECONOMY IN ANCIENT PALESTINE

Jack Pastor

London and New York

First published 1997
by Routledge
11 New Fetter Lane, London EC4P 4EE

Simultaneously published in the USA and Canada
by Routledge
29 West 35th Street, New York, NY 10001

© 1997 Jack Pastor

Typeset in Garamond by Keystroke, Jacaranda Lodge, Wolverhampton
Printed and bound in Great Britain by Creative Print and Design (Wales),
Ebbw Vale

British Library Cataloguing in Publication Data
A catalogue record for this book is available from the British Library

Library of Congress Cataloguing in Publication Data
Pastor, Jack
Land and economy in ancient Palestine / Jack Pastor.
p. cm.
Includes bibliographical references.
1. Land tenure—Palestine—History. 2. Palestine—Economic conditions.
3. Land use—Palestine—History. 4. Jews—History—586
B.C.–70 A.D. 5. Palestine—History—To 70 A.D. I. Title.
HD129.P37 1997
333.3'095694—dc20   96–41705
ISBN 0–415–15960–1

To my parents and my sister Magda, an innocent victim of man's selfishness.

CONTENTS

vii

PREFACE

This work originated as an investigation into the economic crises of the Second Temple period of Jewish History. My kibbutz was mired in a morass of problems with which it seemed incapable of dealing. While listening to an interminable lecture on what had gone wrong with our economy, I realized that I had heard all this somewhere before. I then decided that my research would deal with economic crises. At first I cast my net as wide as can be, because I thought that the number of sources available was very limited. I feared that this supposed dearth of material would be a serious hindrance to any meaningful inquiry. I therefore included every aspect of economy and society in my search and I expanded my field of inquiry from crises to problems. After writing hundreds of pages I realized that I had made two serious mistakes. First, there are far more sources dealing with all the aspects of the economy than I estimated. Second, there was no single unifying factor in my plan of inquiry. It was set up as a ramble through different problems, different periods. I suddenly realized that while economic crises can indeed be studied individually, and then strung together in a narrative, that approach would not provide a core to focus on. Upon further contemplation I saw that economic problems and crises can be studied through different facets of society, the facet becoming a prism through which a spectrum of problems, responses, and theories can be examined. The more I studied the more apparent it became that land is one factor of the economy that is related to almost every aspect, problem, and crisis that the ancient society encountered. I therefore chose to chart the landownership of the Jews in Palestine throughout the Persian, Hellenistic, and Roman periods, and examine developments and problems related to landownership: debt, taxation, famine, and others.

ACKNOWLEDGMENTS

I would like to express my gratitude to Professors Uriel Rappaport and Akiva Gilboa for their guidance and assistance over the years.

I owe a special debt to all the teachers, colleagues, and students who helped and encouraged me in this project.

I am grateful to the Memorial Foundation for Jewish Culture, and the Center for the Study of Eretz Israel and its Yishuv of Yad Izhak Ben-Zvi and the University of Haifa for the aid they provided.

Above all, I wish to thank my wife Ronit and my children Dan and Daphna, whose patience, sacrifice, and encouragement supported me for so long.

ABBREVIATIONS

Full information on all entries is provided in the bibliography.

AB	*Anchor Bible*
ADAJ	*Annual of the Department of Antiquities of Jordan*
AJPh	*American Journal of Philology*
ANRW	Temporini and Haase, eds, *Aufstieg und Niedergang der römischen Welt*
Ant.	Josephus, *Jewish Antiquities*
APOT	Charles, *The Apocrypha and Pseudepigrapha of the Old Testament*
BA	Biblical Archaeologist
BAR	British Archaeological Reports
BASOR	*Bulletin of the American Schools of Oriental Research*
BASP	*Bulletin of the American Society of Papyrologists*
BJ	Josephus, *The Jewish War*
BJPES	*Bulletin of the Jewish Palestine Exploration Society*
B.M.	Tractate Baba Metzia
BT	Babylonian Talmud
CA	Josephus, *Against Apion*
CAH	*The Cambridge Ancient History*
CBQ	*Catholic Biblical Quarterly*
CHJ	Davies and Finkelstein, eds, *The Cambridge History of Judaism*
CIJ	Frey, *Corpus Inscriptionum Judaicarum*
C.Ord.Ptol.	Lenger, M.T., *Corpus des Ordonnances des Ptolémées*
Cowley	Cowley, *Aramaic Papyri of the Fifth Century BC*
CPJ	Tcherikover and Fuks, *Corpus Papyrorum Judaicarum*
Diod.	Diodorus Siculus
DJD	Benoit, Milik, de Vaux, eds, *Discoveries in the Judean Desert*

EJ	Roth, ed., *Encyclopedia Judaica*
ERE	Duncan-Jones, *The Economy of the Roman Empire*
ESAR	Frank, ed., *An Economic Survey of Ancient Rome*
GLAJJ	Stern, M., *Greek and Latin Authors on Jews and Judaism*
HCJ	Tcherikover, *Hellenistic Civilization and the Jews*
Hev.	Nahal Hever
HTR	*Harvard Theological Review*
HUCA	*Hebrew Union College Annual*
ICC	*International Critical Commentary*
IDB	*The Interpreter's Dictionary of the Bible*
IEJ	*Israel Exploration Journal*
IGLS	Jalabert and Mouterde, *Inscriptions Grecques et Latines de la Syrie*
IMJ	*Israel Museum Journal*
JBL	*Journal of Biblical Literature*
JCS	*Journal of Cuneiform Studies*
JESHO	*Journal of the Economic and Social History of the Orient*
JJS	*Journal of Jewish Studies*
JNES	*Journal of Near Eastern Studies*
JQR	*Jewish Quarterly Review*
JRS	*Journal of Roman Studies*
JSOT	*Journal for the Study of the Old Testament*
JSS	*Journal of Semitic Studies*
JStJ	*Journal for the Study of Judaism in the Persian, Hellenistic and Roman Period*
KAI	Donner and Röllig, *Kanaanäische und aramäische Inschriften*
Ket.	Tractate Ketuboth
Kleine Pauly	Ziegler, Sontheimer, Gärtner, *Der Kleine Pauly Lexikon der Antike*
KS	Alt, *Kleine Schriften Zur Geschichte Des Volkes Israel*
LCL	Loeb Classical Library
Liddell and Scott	Liddell and Scott, *A Greek–English Lexicon*
M	Mishnah
Macc	Maccabaeorum liber
MGWJ	*Monatsschrift für Geschichte und Wissenschaft des Judentums*
NEAEHL	Stern, E., ed., *New Encyclopedia of Archaeological Excavations in the Holy Land*

NTS	*New Testament Studies*
OCD	*Oxford Classical Dictionary*
OGIS	*Orientis Graeci Inscriptiones Selectae*
OSSA	International Journal of Skeletal Research
OTP	Charlesworth, *The Old Testament Pseudepigrapha*
P.Col.	Westermann and Hasenoehrl, *Zenon Papyri: Business Papers of the Third Century* BC *Dealing with Palestine and Egypt I*
PCZ	Edgar, ed., *Zenon papyri, catalogue général des antiquités égyptiennes du musée de Caire*
PEQ	*Palestine Exploration Quarterly*
Pes.	Tractate Pesahim
PJB	*Palästina-Jahrbuch des deutschen Evangelischen Instituts*
P.London	Skeat, ed., *Greek Papyri in the British Museum*, vol. VII, *The Zenon Archive*
PSI	*Pubblicazioni della Societa Italiana, Papiri Greci et Latini*
PT	Palestinian Talmud
P-W	Pauly-Wissowa, eds, *Real-Encyclopadie der classischen Altertumswissenschaft*, Stuttgart, 1903ff.
P.Yadin	Lewis, *The Documents from the Bar Kochba Period in the Cave of Letters, vol. 2, Greek Papyri*
RB	*Revue Biblique*
RC	Welles, ed., *Royal Correspondence in the Hellenistic Period*
REA	*Revue des études anciennes*
REG	*Revue des études Grecques*
REJ	*Revue des études Juives*
RIDA	*Revue internationale des droits de l'antiquité*
RTP	Briant, *Rois, tribute, et paysans*
SB	*Sammelbuch griechischer Urkunden aus Agypten*
SBL	Society of Biblical Literature
SCI	*Scripta Classica Israelica*
SEG	*Supplementum Epigraphicum Graecum*
SEHHW	Rostovtzeff, *The Social and Economic History of the Hellenistic World*
SEHRE	Rostovtzeff, *The Social and Economic History of the Roman Empire*
Shebi	Tractate Shebiit
SIG	*Sylloge Inscriptionum Graecarum*

T	Tosefta
TAPA	*Transactions of the American Philological Association*
TDNT	*Theological Dictionary of the New Testament*
T.Men.	Tractate Menahot
Vita	Josephus, *The Life*
VT	*Vetus Testamentum*
YCS	*Yale Classical Studies*
ZNW	*Zeitschrift für die Neutestamentliche Wissenschaft*
ZPE	*Zeitschrift für Papyrologie und Epigraphik*

NOTE ON QUOTATIONS, TRANSLATIONS, AND TRANSLITERATIONS

Quotations and translations are from the editions listed unless otherwise noted. Full details are listed in the bibliography.

Hebrew biblical texts = the Jewish Publication Society translation of the Bible.

Ecclesiasticus (Ben-Sira) are from the Revised Standard Version, or translated by me as noted.

Books of the Maccabees are from the edition prepared by S. Zeitlin.

Greek and Latin texts are usually from the Loeb Classical Library editions.

Dead Sea Scrolls are from the edition by G. Vermes.

All other translations are from the editions referred to in the endnotes, or made by me as indicated.

Transliterations
Transliterations are according to the system of the *Encyclopedia Judaica*.

1

INTRODUCTION

LAND: ITS ROLE IN THE ECONOMY AND SOCIETY

The problem facing Judean society, as indeed all societies, was how to
feed its population. This problem hinges on a number of underlying
factors: the physical environment, the demographic conditions, and the
social and political framework. In essence, the society has to find a way
to deal with a finite amount of natural resources; of these, the land is
pre-eminent.[1] Of six possible policies to prevent food crisis four entail
ownership or use of land: expansion of territory, extension of cultivated
areas, intensification of cultivation, colonization. The last two are
development of alternative livelihoods which will enable people to
trade for foodstuffs, or internal regulation which will control how the
available food is distributed in the society.[2]

The land is the major factor of production and as such it is both
property and capital. Early in human society it became evident that
political power and privilege were linked to the control of land.[3] Land
is still one of the most important aspects of the economy, but in the
pre-industrial age it was certainly the pre-eminent source of wealth and
prestige.[4] Being vital to security and wealth land had a concomitant
political value.[5]

Finley succinctly summarized the varied nuances of landownership
in a seminal paragraph.[6] He determined that land is a special sort of
property, having attributes not shared by any other types of property,
e.g. it is permanent and it is the major source of livelihood. As a result,
landownership holds great importance in all societies. The state is interested in landowners because of the fiscal aspects. He who owns land
pays taxes. The society is interested in landownership because civic
privileges such as citizenship and the right to vote often derive from it.
Furthermore, the obligation of military service is often derived from the
status of landownership. Additionally, landownership has judicial

1

aspects, for instance, whether land can be alienated, or encumbered. Finally, land has administrative aspects, such as who determines land use, and what are the community interests in a parcel of land.

We have indicated that landownership determines to a great extent the social and political framework of society. We therefore must ask what was the system of landownership in the Land of Israel during the period of the Second Temple? Specifically, we want to determine as best we can who owned land and how he came to own it. How large were landholdings? What were the privileges and liabilities entailed by landholding? These questions must be examined over the entire chronological length of the Second Temple period in order to determine if the landholding system remained stable and consistent or whether there were any changes and developments. Moreover, we intend to see if there is any correlation between developments in the landholding structure and other aspects of the society.[7]

Finally, Finley intended to emphasize the importance of landownership records, but his paper in fact pointed out most of the social and political aspects of landownership. However, he left out one very important subject, the use to which land is put. In economic theory the use of land is determined by its rent. Rent, in the strict economic sense, is the monetary value of the surplus left after the costs of production and of capital have been met. Where there is a monetary price for rent it acts as a rationing device for land use. Ideally, land will be used for the most productive purpose. But sometimes social and political concerns will dictate land use.[8] We will discuss land use in conjunction with landownership as we deal with specific cases. However, the obviously preponderant use of land is to produce food. The nutritional needs of people, as individuals and as society, determine many of the aspects of landownership. To understand the one we must be familiar with the other. We shall begin our study with a discussion of the physical basics of the cultivator's life.

The farmer in the Land of Israel had to raise a minimum crop despite a climate whose precipitation pattern is unstable.[9] In order to grow wheat at all a minimum of 300 mm of rainfall are needed, and in order to obtain a minimally decent crop 400 mm are necessary, and these have to be distributed correctly.[10] The climatic record shows that droughts, although not frequent, do occur from time to time.[11] In addition to drought the farmer was threatened by a battery of other natural disasters. These could be climatic phenomena such as hail[12] or wind, or pests such as the locust,[13] rodents, or birds, or weeds such as the darnel, or crop diseases such as wheat rust.[14] The ancient cultivator was also faced with the requirement to leave part of his crop-land fallow in order to replenish the fertility of the soil. Finally bandits, public disturbances, revolts, and wars could and did diminish the productive capacity of the farmer or deprive him of his hard-earned crop.

FAMINE AND LANDOWNERSHIP

When a confluence of destructive and disabling factors come together the result is famine. We see an organic link between the landholding system and the complex of economic and social factors which together result in famine. The landholding system, while never solely responsible for famine, is determinant in such factors as plot size, choice of crops, use of water resources, and development of alternative livelihoods. Starvation and famine are functions of what famine specialists now call "entitlements." These are not to be confused with any moral concepts, rather they are the legal control of commodities or resources: the control of these will determine whether a person will eat, or not. These may be consumed, or exchanged for other items. In our period the most significant entitlement is land. It can be used to grow food, or cash crops, it can be rented or leased. However, if something occurs to limit the size of the entitlement the person may starve. The landholding system and the superstructure of society determine how large entitlements will be, and who will control them. Furthermore, food crisis relief measures are often tangent to the landownership structure.[15]

In this study we will deal with famine particularly as a result of natural and economic factors. Famine as a result of war, although frequent, is a situation that we feel has little to teach us about the general workings of society and the economy. Nevertheless, we shall use illustrative instances from war-time famines when they can help us understand the behavior of individuals and society in famine circumstances.

We define famine as a serious food shortage resulting in a high mortality rate over a brief period of time.[16] One must differentiate between (1) starvation, (2) food crisis, and (3) famine. Regrettably the first is always with us and is the condition of being starved, i.e. when someone suffers severely and perishes from hunger. It exists in many primitive societies today, and sometimes in societies generally not thought of as primitive. Food crisis is a situation in which greater numbers of people than the usual suffer from starvation, but the impact of the shortage does not have a mass effect. The last is a "dramatic" and "catastrophic" increase in the numbers of people affected by a food shortage.[17] It is both quantitatively and qualitatively the most severe of the food crises. The terminological differentiation is not quite clear today, and was even less so in the Hellenistic and Roman worlds.[18] Therefore, the phenomenon cannot be explored solely by the philological method.

There have been relatively few attempts to investigate the occurrences of famine in the Hellenistic and Roman world, and almost nothing has been done to examine famine in Second Temple Judea.[19] The latest and most comprehensive attempt to probe the occurrences of famine in the Greek and Roman periods is by Garnsey.[20] He suggests a method entailing (1) use of proxy-data on climate and food production[21] and (2) analysis of the famine narratives according to ten different aspects of the food crises in an attempt to "construct a profile of a particular food crisis and locate it roughly on the spectrum leading from mild shortage to disastrous famine."[22] The aspects which Garnsey suggests should be checked are:[23]

Immediate causes
Geographical range
Location
Duration
Price movements
Incidence of disease
Response of authorities
Behavior of the people
Categories of victim
Mortality

These subjects focus attention on a range of interrelated aspects of the society and the economy. We shall see that price movements have a lot to teach us about the usual levels of income and expenses. The response of authorities often teaches us about alternative sources of livelihood, and the transport infrastructure. Categories of victim have a direct correlation to the landholding structure. Hence, we propose to analyze the food crises in the Land of Israel during the Second Temple era as we analyze the landownership situation and other related problems. The crises will be dealt with in chronological order, from first to last, in the sections relevant to their historical milieux.

DIETARY NEEDS

The primary function of land in human society is to provide food. This prosaic fact underlies much of the social and political dynamic which makes up all human history. The diet of human beings differs from culture to culture and from period to period; however, it must always include certain various basic ingredients that sustain life.[24] Among these ingredients are a minimum amount of calories which provide the energy to power the organism, proteins to replenish the cells, and minerals and vitamins which make certain vital processes possible. In proportional terms of one dietary component in relation to another, the greatest needs are for calories and proteins, this demand dictating the choice of the major staple in the diet.[25] In pre-modern cultures (before the Industrial Revolution) field-crops were the greatest source of proteins and calories.[26] Of all the different field-crops wheat and barley were the most important in the Mediterranean area in the period of our study.[27]

Wheat was, and still is, the preferred grain for human consumption.[28] It contains a large proportion of the nutrients human diet demands, consisting of 60–80 percent carbohydrates, 8–15 percent proteins which have adequate amounts of almost all the essential amino acids, 1.5–2 percent fats, 1.5–2 percent minerals, and vitamins such as the B complex and E. Additionally the sticky nature of the gluten protein entraps the CO_2 formed during yeast fermentation, enabling a leavened dough to rise.[29] This in turn makes wheat bread more palatable and easy to chew. Also wheat provides more nutrients per volume of grain than does barley.[30] We have found that wheat was consistently priced much higher than barley. In fact wheat is associated with the well-to-do, while barley is the poor man's fare.[31] Barley has two major advantages over wheat: it needs less water,[32] and it ripens earlier. Being less desirable for human consumption, but more likely to survive in drier climes, barley is present everywhere as a fodder, and as a staple in arid areas.[33]

Estimates as to the proportion of grain in the diet in the Greco-Roman period vary from 53 percent to 75 percent.[34] But, in addition to his immediate dietary needs, the farmer had to grow enough of a surplus in order to meet other demands. He had to sell or barter part of his crop in return for those necessities that he could not grow or make. He had to pay his debts and his taxes to his landlord, ruler, and Temple. He had to store some food against hard days in the future.[35] In order to obtain his needs the farmer had to have a crop of at least 250–350 kg per person annually of wheat or its equivalent value in another crop.[36]

POPULATION

Of all the basic questions on Second Temple society perhaps the most vexing is what was the size and composition of the population. Unlike ancient Greece and the Roman Empire, ancient Judea did not leave enough information in the literary or the archaeological record for a well-grounded estimate of population size.[37]

Scholars have been struggling with the problem for decades, having to rely on a number of approaches, none of which are certain. The first estimates were based on the literary sources.[38] Later attempts to estimate population size were made by extrapolating population size from the size of an area and the assumed population density, multiplied by the number of archaeological sites.[39] More ingenious attempts at population estimation are based on the water supply or the food production capability of the land.[40] In brief the scholar is faced with a wide range of approximations arising from greatly varying systems of reckoning. To illustrate, we have on the one hand Applebaum, who believes that "the Jewish population of Herod's kingdom numbered no less than one and half million Jews"; while Ben-David suggests that number for Judea alone.[41] Baron believed that Palestine had about 30 percent of the Jews of the Roman Empire in Claudius' time, i.e. about 2,300,000 Jews.[42] In contrast to these, Broshi's figure for the total population of Palestine west of the Jordan is about one million at its maximum; keeping in mind that Second Temple Israel was not the period of maximum population.[43]

In the end, after gazing at the demographic forest, we will have to suggest which "tree" best answers the question, how many Jews in Eretz Israel? Broshi is the most convincing because he bases his proposition on fairly well authenticated data, i.e. the role of grain in the diet, and the maximum potential grain-producing capacity of the country. However, the problems with his system are many. First, by necessity, he can only give the approximate average consumption, his figure being 200 kg per person per annum; however, he rounds out this figure to 250 kg. The result would mean the difference between one million people or 1,250,000 people. The addition of a quarter of a million people would make a tremendous difference in the economic life of a community. Second, his figure is the maximum number, so we are left guessing as to the difference between Herodian Israel, or any other era of Second Temple and Byzantine Palestine. Third, and more importantly, we cannot judge how much of the population was gentile or Jewish.

An important aspect of population size is population growth. One of the basic claims made by scholars regarding landownership problems is that the demographic pressure created by the population growth of the Jews in the Land of Israel was so acute that it found release in conquest, emigration, or, failing these, it created social–political tensions inducive to revolt.[44] These assumptions have to be examined; however, because of the lack of data, we are forced to use comparative information. Our conclusions must perforce be accepted with caution.

There are a number of aspects of the problem that have to be considered. First, the average population growth in pre-industrial societies is 0.5–1 percent per annum.[45] This factor should be qualified by the work of Broshi and Finkelstein who found that in the period from 1000 BCE to 750 BCE the natural growth of the Jewish population in Palestine was an average of 0.4 percent per annum. This figure, representing a period not too dissimilar in many facets from the Second Temple period, and drawn from the same physical and climatic environment, strengthens the assumption that the factor of population growth is closer to 0.5 percent than to the higher figure.[46]

This factor of growth would result in higher population than we proposed, if it were not for wars, famines, epidemics, and other vectors which would reduce the population.[47] Even assuming a reduced population growth, we are nevertheless faced with the question if the natural increase still was sufficient to create insupportable demands for land. This would happen if the following conditions were extant: life-expectancy was so long that a number of generations had to coexist at the same time, and the size of families was large. However, regarding the first condition, it can be demonstrated that life-expectancy was probably low. Brunt estimated a life-expectancy of between 20 to 30 years of age for Roman Italy.[48] This figure may perhaps be compared to Ottoman Palestine in the late nineteenth century, where the life-expectancy was no longer than 44 years.[49] Brunt came to the conclusion that the growth of the Roman population was not sufficient to reproduce itself. However, as he points out, his conclusions are relevant to a society that practiced abortion and infanticide. In a society that forbade these practices one might expect different findings. Brunt relates that from 1725 to 1850 Japan had a stable population, when these practices were allowed, but Japan's population soared steeply after they were outlawed.[50]

Since these practices were outlawed in Jewish society, as remarked on by ancient authors, one can conclude that the Jewish population did have a natural increase.[51]

The other factor pressing on land hunger would be the size of families. Goodman asserts that the requirement to divide property among all the sons created plots too small to support the families living off them.[52] We have already shown that life-expectancy was low, so many generations would not exist at one time.[53] However, a large number of children in a family would create the situation anticipated by Goodman. Regarding this case, however, we would have to state that the indications are that families were small, i.e. four to five persons.[54] On the one hand, considering that part of the population was female and would not necessarily inherit a plot, and part of the male population would predecease their fathers, or would for some reason leave the area, the conclusion would be that family properties would not be split between a large number of heirs. On the other hand the average size of a family reflects an arithmetic value that includes large as well as small families, and over a long period of stable population growth, plots would have to be divided between an average of more than one heir.

We would conclude that population growth in the Jewish population increased steadily but moderately. The pressure would be felt after a prolonged period of relative security, without significant vectors to decrease the population. The gradual but continuous process of leaving inheritances to more than one heir would lead to the diminution of the plot sizes. Hence, while Bar-Kochva and Goodman may be overstressing their case, in principle they are correct.

THE SIZE OF PLOTS

Some scholars feel that the Land of Israel was more agriculturally productive in the ancient past than in anytime up to the introduction of modern technology.[55] There is no doubt that the country was considered fertile and productive by the standards of the region and the time.[56] Nevertheless, two questions are of immediate concern in dealing with economic and social problems. Was the country able to feed its population? How much land was necessary to feed a person?[57]

The literary sources are few, and not necessarily illustrative of the common situation. However, Brunt used information provided by Cato and Polybius on ration needs of slaves and soldiers, demonstrating that two *iugera* were needed to support one adult.[58] This has been confirmed by the work of White and Hopkins.[59] Some modern works quote Eusebius' anecdote about the sons of Jesus' brother. These two men lived off a farm of 39 *plethora* (Alon claims that equals 34 *dunams*).[60] Oakman tried to compare the figures from Italy derived by Hopkins, and the figures from Eusebius, while taking into consideration that some land had to be fallow. His conclusion was that a "subsistence plot in antiquity was, then, about 1.5 acres" (6 *dunams*).[61] Feliks notes that the Talmudic literature mentions plots of a few *dunams* to plots of 23 *dunams* which are considered generous.

Shimon Dar working on the basis of archaeological surveys in north-western Samaria reached a conclusion for the Roman–Byzantine era that a family holding averaged 39–45 *dunams*.[62] Admittedly the evidence is drawn from a limited geographical area, but another survey in the western Hebron Mountain region found the average size of farms to be 30–50 *dunams*.[63] Comparative figures for other Mediterranean areas are 40 *dunams* for Attica and 5–25 *dunams* for Italy.[64]

Dar contends that the average Jewish farmer lived on a smallholding worked by himself and his family.[65] It is difficult if not impossible to determine what the average size of an agricultural unit was. The Mishnah recognizes the minimum size of a field to be nine "*kabs*."[66] The Tosefta mandates 9.5 *kabs* as the minimum size of a field.[67] Dar notes that deeds from the Nessana area in the late Roman–Byzantine period show small plots of only 1–4 *dunams*.[68]

Applebaum, working from the archaeological research in Samaria, maintains that 25 *dunams* may have been the average figure of a holding. He quotes Ben-David, who working from talmudic sources suggests 40 *batei seah* as the average holding needed to support a family, which he computes as 31.3 *dunams*. These figures of Ben-David are derived from the Mishnah.[69] Orman based on a survey of the Golan region found an average settlement comprised 20 *dunams*.[70] Golomb and Kedar found enclosed fields in the Galilee were about 16 *dunams*, although individual plots may vary between about 4 *dunams* to even 60 *dunams*.[71]

However, not only subsistence farms draw our interest. As we shall demonstrate one of the recurring problems of the landownership system of Israel was the tendency to concentrate large areas of land in a few hands; with all the concomitant ills of debt, starvation, and social unrest. Fiensy, basing his work on Dohr, claims that most "gentlemen landowners" owned "medium-sized estates of 80–500 *iugera*."[72]

Most people lived in villages during our period.[73] Portugali, working with an average population density of 45 persons per *dunam* in a settle-ment (village, town, city), multiplying that figure by the number of sites for each period, comes to the conclusion that the western portion of the Jezreel Valley had a population of 13,000 in the Persian period, 18,000 in the Hellenistic period, and 34,000 in the Roman period.[74] Of course these numbers could be wrong. There is no guarantee that all the settlements have been discovered. Furthermore, the supposed size of a settlement is dependent on how well the survey really revealed the site. Finally how sure can we be that 45 persons per *dunam* is always the average density? Nevertheless Portugali's figures give us an approximate figure from which we can judge the minimum nutrient needs of an area.

LAND USES

It should be self-evident that the choice of crops is dictated by a complicated variety of considerations. First in importance is the ability of the crop to flourish within the natural environment of soil, water, and temperature; second, the potential contribution of the crop to the livelihood of the grower. The farmer has to choose between growing cash crops, i.e. crops which are mainly intended for sale, their sale price providing the farmer with the means to buy staples, or raising staples. Third, local traditions and technical ability lead the farmer to choose a crop that he knows how to grow.

The Jewish farmer of the Second Temple period was limited in most cases to a limited range of endeavors which are commonplace for most of the Mediterranean region. He grew grains, olives, grapes, and a small herd of beasts, usually sheep and goats, with an additional few head of cattle.[75] Recently, Sanders, while dealing with *BJ* 6.420–7, where Josephus claims that 255,600 sheep were sacrificed for Passover in Jerusalem before the war, arrived at the conclusion that in reality 30,000 lambs were necessary every year for Passover sacrifice in Jerusalem.[76] He draws this conclusion by pure speculation as to how many people with sacrificial lambs could fit into the space of the Temple. But it raises the question, what would have to be the livestock population in order to maintain a consumer rate that high?[77] On the basis of talmudic literature Z. Safrai claims that the land devoted to grazing before the destruction of the Temple was considerably greater than in the post-destruction period.[78]

Dar suggested a family farm with about 52 percent grains, 22 percent vines, 25 percent olives, ten to fifteen head of sheep and goats, and one or two head of cattle.[79] These suggested proportions are by their nature very schematic, yet there is some supporting evidence from literary and other sources. The rabbinical sources have some comment to make on the ideal mix of crops. While keeping in mind the nature of the source as a halachic text compiled and edited much later than the period of our study, we must also recognize that there is no evidence that the basic elements of the agricultural economy changed from one century to the next in the ancient world.[80]

Dar also suggested that the small plots of the average farmer drove him to develop intensified agriculture with two to three yields a year.[81]

The balsam was the most profitable of the crops of the land and the income derived was out of all proportion to the land used.[82] However, the balsam groves of Ein Gedi and Jericho were royal property and would not serve as an example of the usual cultivators' crop. A better example of the choices made by cultivators would be the date groves of the Dead Sea region. The Murabba'at and Babatha archives present repeated evidence of the economic interest of landowners in the raising of dates. We know that the date was an export item, perhaps even reaching the Emperor's table.[83]

Another crop which was prominent in Judea was the grape. Dar believes that Hellenism developed side by side with the distribution of vine cultivation. As the area of the Hellenistic culture expanded, so did the amount of land devoted to vineyards. He suggests that the Ptolemaic economic and political policy encouraged the development of vineyards both in Egypt and in Judea.[84] On the basis of the archaeological finds in Samaria he believes that in the Hellenistic period regional vine growing and wine production were organized by governmental methods on an unprecedented scale.[85] Based on a complicated and doubtful computation, Dar comes to the conclusion that 1.5–3 *dunams* of vineyard sufficed to feed a family.[86] An ancient, non-Judean source claimed that it was five times more profitable to grow grapes than to grow grain.[87]

The olive was a cash crop and a mainstay of the economy of Palestine.[88] It is native to the area and has grown here since time immemorial. The olive is rich in nutrients, and the oil is important for lighting, perfumes, soap, medicines, and it was used in religious rituals.

Land was used for agriculture, unless it was within the precincts of a city. Agricultural land was of necessity sacrificed for housing and purposes such as shops, workshops, and public buildings. However, we find that even in a burgeoning city such as Jerusalem, which grew steadily from the Hasmonean period till its destruction, value was still put on the agricultural use of land. The eastern slope of the City of David in the Hasmonean and Herodian periods was covered by stepped terraces used for agriculture. "It is certain that close to the base of the slope along the Kidron Valley very intense agricultural activity took place, in which the different farming tracts were supplied by irrigation channels, some hewn in the rock, which brought water from various sources."[89] The terraces and irrigation system were destroyed by the

Romans during the Great Revolt. Josephus relates that around the walls of Jerusalem, every fence and palisade with which the inhabitants had enclosed their gardens and plantations was swept away, and every fruit tree within the area felled (*BJ* 5.57,107).

The hilly regions of Judea were terraced to make use of as much land as possible.[90] The rocky fields of Samaria were cleared of stones so that crops could be raised. Even desert areas were exploited for agriculture: "The floodwater farmers of the Judean Desert selected their farm sites wisely, taking advantage of accumulated fertile alluvium transported from the western highlands."[91] They were able to grow modest stands of wheat and barley as well as legumes by harnessing floodwaters and raising the water yield well beyond that supplied by direct rainfall. Desert farmers did not have to interrupt their production cycle with fallow periods. The soils were renewed and enriched each winter by "fertilizers" deposited by the floodwaters. Unlike most types of irrigation which eventually produce saline soil, floodwater farming left the fields of the Buqe'ah (a large plain in the Judean Desert southwest of Jericho) virtually salt free because of the annual leaching by fresh water.[92]

Keeping in mind the basic needs of the population and the physical characteristics of the country we will now review the history of the landowning structure of the Jewish people in Palestine.

2

THE PERSIAN PERIOD

THE RETURN

The Persian period opens the era under our consideration. For our purposes it provides the advantage of coming after a clear and decisive break in the routine life of Judean society: the Babylonian Exile. While the landownership system in First Temple Judah is beyond the purview of this work, it is thought that the land was then owned by an increasingly small aristocracy and much of it was crown land.[1] There were, however, also small landholdings of a free peasant class.[2]

Did the landholding system change with the fall of the Judean monarchy? The sources for the period indicate that the aristocracy of Judah was deported and the land left to the poor.[3] The period of exile lasted at least two generations and would have served to deepen the link between the formerly landless and poor, and their new possessions. Perhaps Ezek. 11:15 gives expression to this link.[4]

בן-אדם אחיך אחיך אנשי גאלתך וכל בית ישראל כלה אשר אמרו להם
ישבי ירושלים רחקו מעל יהוה לנו היא נתנה הארץ למורשה

O mortal, [I will save] your brothers, your brothers, the men of your kindred, [the exiles] all of that very House of Israel to whom the inhabitants of Jerusalem say, "Keep far from the Lord; the land has been given as a heritage to us."

The return from Babylon provides the next crucial turning point in the history of the landownership system in the Land of Israel. The formerly exiled aristocracy now returned, creating one of two possible scenarios: (1) they entered a devastated and "empty" country, and resettled their lands;[5] (2) they returned to the land and found people living on their possessions.[6] In this case the question arises who were the "squatters"? The first scenario echoes the Jewish sources; however, according to the archaeological evidence the Land of Israel was in no way empty.[7] If so, who were the people living on the land? The traditional view was that gentiles had exploited the Exile in order to move into the Land of Israel.[8] We suggest a different view.[9]

We suggest that the returnees found their lands settled by the Jews who had not been exiled from Judah. These were Jews who had been left in Judah by the Babylonians, joined by Jews who had temporarily fled the country, but had returned at the earliest opportunity.[10] The returnees from Babylon were endowed with money, position, and royal support. They repossessed their patrimonies, forcing the residents to either pay rents as tenants, or alternatively move to marginal farming areas.[11] This new situation created a tenant-farmer class.

The literary sources in the Bible substantiate the view that the aristocracy was exiled and their lands distributed to the lower socio-economic classes. Furthermore, the lists of returnees in the Books of Ezra and Nehemiah consist of some people distinguished by place names, while others are identified by family relationship (בית אב). It has been suggested that the former are in fact not returnees at all, but descendants of those who remained in the Land of Israel.[12]

The returnees came back to Judah as the lords of the land. It has been demonstrated that they were of the elite of the First Temple society. They are referred to as members of the tribes of Judah and Benjamin, perhaps indicating that they were people taken originally from Jerusalem or its immediate vicinity.[13] Cyrus sent them on their way with money and gifts.[14] More significantly, it is clearly stated that they were to return each to his own city (עירו).[15] It may be understood that "each to his own home" was the intention of the command.[16] Because the Persian monarch frequently purchased service by the gift of land, it would stand to reason that he provided the returnees with titles to their former landholdings.[17] If this is true, the conflict between the exiles and the "people of the land," which is presented as a religious issue, would in fact have stemmed from a clash over landownership. Membership in the cult community carried some sort of claim to the land, as Ezek. 11:15, 17 seems to show. Those excluded from the cult would also have been perceived as lacking landownership rights. The people left out of the cult would oppose the establishment of a Temple, because the establishment of a Temple would put a seal to their exclusion, particularly if the cult-temple had royal support for its claims.[18]

The return to Zion engendered conflict over landownership.[19] The returnees became the large landholders at the expense of those who were already in the country. The new landlords owed their advantageous position to the crown, a situation that would predominate throughout the Second Temple period.

THE FOOD CRISIS

The first economic crisis mentioned in the sources on the period of the Second Temple is briefly described in Haggai 1:6–11; 2:16–19 and in Zechariah 8:9–12. The description is very schematic, leaving most of even the important questions of fact unanswered. The verses relate that as a result of the inaction of the returnees in building the Temple anew, God punished the Judean community with drought, which in turn led to a famine.[20] The famine was accompanied by social and economic dislocations such as unemployment and the insufficiency of wages to pay for needed goods. Because of the dearth of details, we can only note that the interrelationship between drought, famine, poverty, and unemployment is well documented, and will be analyzed in greater detail when we deal with reports of famines and food crises which were recorded with a wider array of particulars for the historian to work with.

THE DEBT CRISIS

The food crisis, such as it was, passed, leaving no trace of any significant change in the economic and social structure of Judea. As best as we can tell the returnees remained the major landowners.

The wealth and power of the large landowners is evident in the major socioeconomic crisis that is described in Chapter 5 of the Book of Nehemiah, and which took place in 444 BCE.[21] The chapter relates that the people cry out that they have had to mortgage their children, their fields, vineyards, and houses, and as a result, these have been taken over by others.[22]

In order to determine who the debtors are we should examine why they came to be in debt. The reasons for taking loans are (1) to have enough food to feed themselves and (2) to pay the royal tax.[23] Regarding the first, it is evident from their complaint that they were landowners, growing the staple crops of grain, wine, and oil. If so, why were they unable to feed themselves without borrowing? There are a number of possible answers which come to mind: (1) famine, which is the answer suggested by verse 3;[24] (2) the plots were unproductive because they were marginal lands; (3) the plots were too small to supply sufficient food; (4) too much of their crop was spent on rents, debts, and taxes.

One additional cause not specified as such by Nehemiah is suggested by scholars. There are those who propose that the building of Jerusalem's defensive wall was accomplished by forced labor. The enforced presence of small landholders in Jerusalem during the agricultural season led to a decline in income for the already poor farmers.[25] But Nehemiah began his wall building immediately on arrival in Jerusalem, and it lasted only 52 days (Neh. 2:11; 6:15). The economic distress of the farmers was probably a pre-existing situation. The building of the wall in the time frame given would have hurt the in-gathering of summer fruits and the grape harvesting, but would not necessarily have infringed on the in-gathering of the olives, depending on when Elul occurred in that year.[26] However, if the farmers who were working on the wall were those who had already lost their land, then the work would have been a blessing rather than a curse, since public works would have provided a subsistence income to the workers.

One of the recurring aspects of famines is that land is mortgaged or sold to obtain food. However, we would suggest that in this particular case the word רעב refers to a famine which occurred sometime in the recent past, but is no longer current.[27] In support of our view we would point out that (1) there is no other mention of a food crisis in Nehemiah's memoirs, although Nehemiah goes into quite a bit of detail regarding these times; (2) Nehemiah's measures against the socio-economic crisis do not include any famine relief;[28] (3) one of the salient grievances of the people is that their sons and daughters are being taken as dependent labor, while famine conditions generally lead to the dismissal of dependent labor. The hunger referred to in verse 5:2 probably stems from overpopulation. The food crisis mentioned in 5:3 was one more contributing factor to the widespread debt situation. We suggest that the debtors were forced to borrow money and food because of their inability to produce enough on their plots. This situation may have arisen from the conditions enumerated above, i.e. plots too poor, too small, or overburdened by obligations. Gallant has shown that in an agricultural society an expanding population will lead to an increase in agricultural output. At first this will be obtained by extension of the cultivated area, then group splintering, i.e. emigration if possible, then intensification of the cultivation by changing the fallow system.[29]

The population of Judah had been expanding since the return.[30] First, the return itself brought a sudden infusion of population. Second, the Jewish culture was noted for its fecundity and its devotion to the raising of offspring.[31] The alternative of extension of agriculture was limited because the amount of arable land in Judah is limited by such factors as rainfall and topography. We may assume that whatever land could have been brought into cultivation by irrigation and terracing had already been utilized.[32] Land outside Judah's borders was settled by gentiles who did not take kindly to Jewish settlement. Nevertheless there were some Jews who were forced to take advantage of this option.[33] Their numbers would have been limited by the opposition of their gentile neighbors. Therefore the only option was intensified cultivation. As Gallant pointed out this entailed considerable capital to pay for the seeds, fertilizer, and labor of man and beast;[34] capital that only the wealthy would have. Small farmers would have had to borrow against future crops, providing surety with their holdings and with their children. The vagaries of the climate made the possibility of crop failure very great. A string of bad seasons would make it impossible for the farmer to repay his debt.[35] Finally, the royal and religious taxes overstrained an already overburdened peasantry.[36] It has been suggested that the policy initiated by Darius to exploit the empire for maximum revenue and its emphasis on taxation in coin, led to the impoverishment of the small farmer.[37]

Nehemiah's history indicates that it is חורים and סגנים (*horim* and *seganim*) who are responsible for the foreclosures.[38]

Morton Smith and others have suggested that the assimilationists were the *horim* ("the local gentry"), and that these were descendants of those Jews who had not been exiled to Babylonia. Their syncretism stemmed from the more pluralistic atmosphere that existed in Judean society till the coming of the Yahweh-only party partisans who made up the returning exiles.[39] A further development of this idea is the view that the Jubilee was a priestly solution to the problems of the exiles who had lost the land.[40] However, it was the returnees who were given royal protection, large gifts, while the remnant had been described as דלת הארץ ("poorest in the land"). Are we to believe that the returnees lost all their wealth and influence, while the "poorest in the land" became a class of influential landowners? If M. Smith is correct how did the rich, influential, and propertied returnees become impoverished farmers? If they had returned to empty lands they should have had no problem in maintaining their wealth, having no reason to become indebted to those who had remained. If they returned to settled lands it seems more likely that they would be the landowners, rent receivers, and eventually creditors.

As we examine the identity of the *horim* it becomes obvious that they are nobles, and are a separate class from the priests and high priests.[41] Furthermore, they share in the governing of the province.[42] An example of a family of *Horim* might be the Tobiads. The Tobiads are definitely Jewish aristocrats. At the time of the First Temple they owned lands, they were among the exiles who returned, and at the time of Nehemiah they owned a large estate.[43] The *seganim* are officials of the Persian administration.[44]

This ties in with other aspects of the situation described by Gallant. First, the best lands were in the hands of the wealthy, leaving the marginally productive lands to the poor. The wealthy farmers would need to cultivate their own land to its maximum productive level, hence they would need more labor. This labor could be obtained by using day laborers, or slaves, or bondsmen.[45]

The wealthy also would need an investment outlet for their wealth. Land purchase or loans would be the major avenue for the use of their available wealth.[46] Despite the strong cultural value that land possession had in Jewish society, economic pressures would force poor Jews to sell their plots.

This ties in with the second major reason for borrowing, to pay the tax. It is evident that the Persian Empire had developed a money economy and as a result taxes were no longer paid only in kind, but also in cash.[47]

Another indication of the growth of a money economy is the presence of a significant number of craftsmen in Jerusalem. These were of sufficient importance to rate their own mention among the builders of the wall.[48] Similarly, the market operations of the Tyrians reflect a market economy (Neh. 13:16, 20).

Now we should examine Nehemiah's actions and policies and their origins. Nehemiah appeals to the *horim* and *seganim* to cancel the outstanding debts and return the properties acquired by foreclosure (Neh. 5:11). The צעקת העם ("outcry by the common folk") does not refer to violation of the commandments forbidding usury.[49] Note that nothing is said about interest, because there was no interest.[50] The whole question, which has been endlessly examined by scholars, hinges on the interpretation of the words משא and מאת.[51] Notice that the narrative never mentions נשך ותרבית (interest).[52]

Nehemiah's solution was to force the creditors to return the foreclosed properties and waive payment on the loans.[53] Nehemiah called a special assembly in which he castigated the nobles, set a personal example by foregoing his debts, and appealed to the creditors to do likewise. They agreed (Neh. 5:7–12).

It is not clear exactly how Nehemiah accomplished what he did. The record does not show that he used his authority as Governor to order the implementation of his reforms. Yet it is difficult to believe that the creditors simply acquiesced to his preaching. The answer may lie in the קהילה גדולה (great assembly) which Nehemiah called.[54] Freund suggested that it was a special mass meeting at which many of the poor were present. We suggest that this mass of resentful people in a situation pregnant with violence, did much to convince the nobles of the truth of Nehemiah's preaching on brotherly love. Nehemiah's prestige, and the possibility that he could command that, which for the time being he was just suggesting, added to the effectiveness of his words.

We must also take into consideration the general atmosphere in Judah during Nehemiah's time. He arrived in Judah as a self-proclaimed, but royally appointed reformer. One of his major aims was to bring about an unpopular religious reform. It was to his benefit to enroll as much support as possible, especially among those circles already opposed to his rivals, the *Horim*.[55] Consequently, unlike Smith, we do not feel that Nehemiah made overtures to the poor because they were Yahwehists, but rather, that by enlisting them in his cause he ensured that they would become Yahwehist. Likewise, the building of the wall can be seen not as a burden on the poor, but as a public works program that aided those who were otherwise at the mercy of the wealthy. One may ask whether the wall was actually built by the wealthy, or whether the wall was built by the poor, the wealthy paying for the work.[56] We can see the increase of population in Jerusalem (Neh. 11:1), and the consolidation of Levites and priests there (Neh. 12:27–9; 13:10), as additional projects that concentrated people in Jerusalem who shared Nehemiah's point of view.[57] All these people needed housing, a fine source of employment for the landless (*Ant.* 11.181). Josephus states that Nehemiah at his own expense built houses for those moving to Jerusalem, a detail not found in scripture.

Where did Nehemiah get his ideas for reform? Smith has proposed that Nehemiah fits the pattern of the Greek tyrant.[58] He suggests that as a Persian Governor, he may have been aware of the methods used by tyrants in the Greek cities of the Persian Empire in dealing with problems similar to his own. Freund has rejected identifying Nehemiah with tyrants because his motivations were religious and not personal or familial ambition.[59] Yamauchi compared Nehemiah to Solon.[60] Indeed, the apparently unique actions of Nehemiah invite far-reaching comparisons. It is true that the Pentateuchal instruments for dealing with the economic and social crisis were ineffective. But there are other possibilities besides the Greek example.

Nehemiah may have drawn on the *misarum* acts of the ancient mid-eastern rulers. These were often ad hoc cancellations of debt and the liberation of debt-enslaved persons.[61] As a Persian official he would be at least as familiar with the customs of the ancient Near East as he would be with those of the Greek poleis.

Finally, the most important question is the one we know the least about. What was the final situation of the landowning system after Nehemiah? We may assume that the *Amana* which promised to uphold the laws of the Torah, was intended to cover the social and economic laws as well.[62] Nehemiah may have hoped that this would prevent future developments from degenerating into crisis. In any case Hecataeus at the beginning of the Hellenistic period relates that there existed a law in "Judea prohibiting private individuals from selling their estates in order to prevent the wealthy from concentrating land in their hands" (Diod. XL 3, 7).[63]

3

THE EARLY HELLENISTIC PERIOD

ALEXANDER THE GREAT

Our knowledge of the landowning system of the Hellenistic period is clouded because of the scattered and sparse evidence that has come down to us. Additionally, the changing political conditions, varied ethnic and religious communities, and different types of topography make an accurate description of the landownership system throughout all Palestine very difficult. To illustrate this point by example, consider that ethnically, parts of Palestine were Jewish, others belonged to other Semitic peoples such as the Idumeans and the Itureans. Did all these peoples have the same methods of land distribution? How did the Phoenician coastal cities organize their lands? Was it in the same manner as the inland cities such as Beth-Shean or Samaria? Did the change from Persian to Hellenistic political forms also change the landholding forms in these places? In order not to over-extend our limits we will attempt to deal principally with the landownership system of the Jewish-controlled areas. We will of course examine evidence from the gentile-controlled regions of Palestine when that evidence seems to be useful. Furthermore, as our discussion progresses chronologically through the Hellenistic period we will see that the geographical extent of the Jewish-controlled area increases with the expansion of the Hasmonean state.

We will demonstrate that the pre-eminent characteristic of the landholding system in this period, and of the succeeding periods in the purview of this volume, is that much and probably most of the land was controlled by the crown.[1] This land was sometimes settled by towns, or villages, or it may have been given as a grant to favored servants of the regime, or allocated to *kleruchs* (settlers who received land in return for military service), but it was controlled by the crown. We cannot doubt that alongside the crown land there also existed privately owned property, but it is not evident that this land was a major part of the total land available.

The era opens with the coming of Alexander the Great to Palestine. His presence in the coastal areas is well documented, while his visit to Judea and Jerusalem is an open issue.[2] His presence in Palestine left its mark on the landholding situation in the following ways: (1) by claiming the title and prerogatives of the Great King he gained control of all royal land already in the country;[3] (2) his punishment of the Samaritans certainly included the expropriation of their land, or parts of it, both as a penalty and in order to establish the military settlement Samaria;[4] (3) it is possible that he transferred the three nomes of southern Samaria, Lydda, Ephraim, and Ramathaim, to Judea.[5] Otherwise nothing is known of his rule in the country, and indeed he was soon busy with other matters in other places.

Alexander left Perdiccas in charge, and in his period of rule, and in the following years, whatever changes and developments occurred are clouded from our view because of a lack of sources. It is held by some that the first Greek settlements and poleis were established in this period.[6] We may also assume that the destruction concomitant with the number of military campaigns that passed over the country had its effect on the landholding situation.[7] Large numbers of people were probably taken into captivity, resulting in abandoned homesteads.[8] Simultaneously, the establishment of new settlements or the expansion of existing communities by the addition of new colonists also resulted in changes among the landowners, it being inconceivable and unexampled that new settlers did not receive some land.

THE PTOLEMAIC PERIOD

The major change in landholding patterns came with the final capture of Palestine by Ptolemy I in 301 BC. This opened up a period of just over a century, during which a relatively stable, consistent, and highly active administration was able to leave its imprint on the society and economy of Palestine.

In the realm of landownership we have claimed that the lion's share of the land was royal land. Yet Hecataeus, Ptolemy's contemporary, wrote that the Jews observed laws which prevented the alienation of the land. This suggests that in his time a significant portion of the land was in private hands.[9] If so, how did the concentration of land in royal hands come about? We suggest that it came about in two ways. First, in Palestine the Great King certainly owned estates; as stated above

Alexander and the Diadochi "inherited" the crown property of the Persian kings.[10] Second, in theory all the land conquered by the Hellenistic king was his by right of conquest (δορίκτητος γῆ = "spear-won land"). This theoretical right was supposedly invoked by Ptolemy when justifying his claim to Egypt.[11] However, a recent work has claimed that in theory the Ptolemies had no right to claim spear-won land in Egypt because they did not win it by the spear and that privately owned land existed in Egypt throughout the Ptolemaic period.[12] However, the case of Palestine leaves no doubt that it was conquered territory. Tcherikover has ably reconciled the conflicting stories about Ptolemy's treatment of the Jews in Judea by showing that the version in Agatharchides reflects the fact that he was forced to take Jerusalem violently.[13]

The principle of spear-won land was that the conqueror now totally owned the entire country and all its resources, and could dispense them as he wished.[14] Bingen has shown that Hellenistic political and economic practice was not necessarily the reflection of a well-planned program, but was the result of momentary initiatives and sporadic responses to situations.[15] Nevertheless, we feel it would be a mistake to underestimate the pervasiveness of Ptolemaic economic control. Certainly in Egypt the crown tried to maintain control of as much land as possible. The Ptolemaic land policy in Egypt has been much researched and commented upon, so that an in-depth treatment of the subject here would be superfluous and impractical.[16] We will simply give an overview of the main points of their policy.

The Ptolemaic king ruled Egypt as his personal property; all the soil, the subsoil, and ultimately the products of the soil were his.[17] There were essentially three kinds of land in Ptolemaic Egypt: (1) royal land (γῆ βασιλική) managed directly by the king; (2) land granted (γῆ ἐν ἀφέσει) or released to the management of others; (3) city land (γῆ πολιτική) – land assigned to the cities and their citizens.[18] Granted land had various categories: γῆ ἱερά temple land, land to servants of the state (γῆ ἐν συντάξει), land to soldiers (γῆ κληρουχική) and gift estates to highest officials (γῆ ἐν δωρεᾷ), and finally land held in private ownership (κτήματα or γῆ ἰδιόκτητος).[19] We should note that the gifts of land in Egypt never included villages, but only areas of land.[20] Furthermore, the lots of land were contingent on military service, and upon rank and arm of service.[21]

The most obvious and important question is how much of the Ptolemaic economic policy in Egypt, especially relating to land-ownership, was applied to Palestine? Rostovtzeff found no satisfactory answer to the question as to what extent the Ptolemies applied to their provinces the principle of a planned economy which was the foundation of their economic policy in Egypt.[22] However, he surveyed the provinces and it is evident that royal presence and control were very widespread.[23] Hence one might ask why would the landownership policies be very different from all other aspects of the economy? Indeed, Rostovtzeff finally assumed that except for the building of cities, Palestine was "reorganized on much the same lines as Egypt."[24] Since Rostovtzeff's milestone work nearly half a century has passed, and research into the Ptolemaic rule has not led to any major revision of his assessment.

In a detailed footnote on the antecedents of the Herodian land regime, Schalit accepted the schema posed by Rostovtzeff.[25] Hengel, cleaving to the argument of spear-won land, believes that the Ptolemaic land policy in Palestine was basically same as for Egypt.[26] Bagnall recently examined Ptolemaic policies in the areas outside Egypt and came to the conclusion that "there was a close resemblance between the two areas in administration. This is especially true in the relationship of king, city, and *chora*. Had we more evidence the similarities might be more or less striking."[27]

So the direct evidence we have for Ptolemaic landownership practice (and policy) is from outside of Judea, originating in Egypt, the Galilee, the Beth Shean valley, and other parts of the Ptolemaic empire. Yet, in light of the research done by others and quoted above, we believe that it is reasonable to assume that Ptolemaic policy, which was remarkably consistent comparing the empire with Palestine, would not suddenly be dissimilar for Judea.

It should be noted that whatever similarities there were between the Egyptian land policy and the program in Palestine, there were some obvious differences. First, in Egypt the settlers were scattered over the whole country, usually in already existing native villages.[28] In Egypt the villages themselves were not given as a grant, while in Palestine we know of at least one case in which villages are part of the grant. Most importantly, Tcherikover pointed out that a major difference between Ptolemaic land policy in Egypt and their land policy in Palestine was that in Egypt the only Greek cities were Alexandria, Naucratis, and Ptolemais, while in Palestine there were a host of Greek cities founded by them.[29] Let us now examine the various types of landholding in Palestine. We shall begin with the royal land. It should be noted at the outset that the existence of royal land in Palestine is an accepted fact, except for the reservations of A. Alt who held that the area of Judea was considered the land of an ethnos.[30]

The first source of royal land was the Persian king's property. Some hints of the existence of such properties can be distinguished in Ezekiel 45:7–8; the prince has a portion of country, and will no longer abuse the people who will have their own possessions. This obviously hints at a situation in which the crown was usurping the patrimonies of the population. The question is whether this source is referring to traditions from the period of the First Temple, or to events in the Persian period.[31] Further in Ezekiel (46:16–18) the prince can give land to his sons, from his own patrimony, and it remains that of his sons. If he gives land to his retainers it returns to the prince in the Jubilee (*shnat ha-deror*). The prince shall not take from the inheritance of the people. Here we have a clear reference to the granting of estates to royal servants, with the proviso that the land never really leaves the ultimate ownership of the crown. Another hint of large tracts of royal land prior to the Hellenistic period might be II Chron. 26:10, which relates that King Uzziah had lands in the deserts, the Shephlah, the Plain, and on the mountains and in Carmel.[32] Furthermore these lands had flocks, farmers, and vinedressers.[33]

Another indication of large tracts of land which belonged to the crown is the Eshmunezzer inscription which refers to the lands of Dor and Jaffa and the Sharon given to the king of Sidon by the Persian king.[34]

From the early Hellenistic period we have the evidence of Theophrastus on the balsam plantations which he calls *paradeisoi*, a term used to describe estates of the Persian king.[35] These estates were probably in the region of Jericho and Ein Gedi.[36]

To these we should add those places for which seal impressions have been found bearing the name of a location or other indication that the place had a royal estate, e.g. Motza, Gibeon, and Jerusalem.[37]

The seal impressions bring us to the evidence from the Ptolemaic era for royal estates. Seal impressions have been found at Gezer which are credited by scholars as signifying a royal estate.[38] If Avigad is right, we can consider Ramat-Rachel, Tell en-Nasbah, and Motza as royal estates, noting also that there is a continuity of existence for royal estates from the Persian period into the Hellenistic period.[39] There are other archaeological indications for royal estates, although they are not for the most part from Judea. Dar surveyed large areas of western Samaria. He found remains of concentrations of many small farms in the proximity of a large and elaborate main building. These areas are characterized by an extensive agricultural infrastructure, i.e. towers, wine presses, oil presses, threshing floors, cisterns, and terraces. Furthermore, these finds are dated to the third century BC.[40] Applebaum, based on these findings, has postulated that these are the remnants of royal estates, and are the fruit of the Ptolemaic attempt to develop the area.[41] The remains at Kalandia are in Judea and may perhaps reflect a Ptolemaic royal estate.[42] Another hint of royal estates is found in the Zenon Papyri. The itinerary of Zenon's group took them from one place to another, at a number of stops the travelers were issued wheat-flour. It might be that since the party was an official or at least semi-official delegation of the Ptolemaic minister Apollonius, they received their rations at royal estates.[43] Other evidence for Ptolemaic estates can be deduced by assuming that the Seleucid royal estates were originally Ptolemaic. So Klein argued that the town of Arethusa was a Ptolemaic estate on the site of *Etam* (*Artas*).[44] He further claimed that *Har ha-Melech* originated with the Ptolemaic landholdings in the mountainous region near Jerusalem.[45]

Regarding royal land granted as estates we have two well-documented examples. The first is Apollonius' estate of Beth Anath. The second example is the estate of Ptolemy son of Thraseas. Before we discuss them in any great detail we should note that neither of these estates was in Judea itself, nor is there any proof that they were inhabited by Jews.[46]

Beth Anath is mentioned as one of the way-stops of the Zenon party.[47] Furthermore the Zenon archive contains a number of documents reporting on conditions there.[48] It was apparently a gift-estate of the *dioketes* Apollonius and as such under the general supervision of Zenon. Since the discovery of the Zenon archives no new information has been discovered regarding the estate although an important papyrus has only recently benefited from publication.[49]

This papyrus reveals that the estate grew grapes for wine.[50] It had at least 80,000 vines, which would entail about 25 workmen, which Hengel calls a small village. He should have explained that to the workmen one must add their wives and children; this much larger population justifies calling Beth Anath a small village. The area required just for the vines is somewhere between 168 and 400 *dunams*.[51] To that area must be added the living quarters, community facilities, and the land used to produce other crops and the private vineyards of the farmers.[52] The letter stresses the high quality of the wine produced, and the preparation of an infrastructure of living quarters and water supply.[53]

In the case of Beth Anath one might wonder about the effects of a long-distance administration on the efficiency of the estate, as well as on the farm workers inhabiting it. Not only is the owner an absentee landlord, but the primary manager is also far-removed. Apollonius' choice of wine and raisins, especially quality wine, is most thought-provoking. There are those who have characterized this as conformity with some central mercantilistic policy.[54] That is to minimize the expenditure of currency on imported wine, the Ptolemies encouraged domestic production.[55] Another way of looking at this same situation is to conceive of Apollonius as a perspicacious businessman who realized that better grapes, wine, and raisins could be raised in the Land of Israel than in Egypt.

This care for the vine-growing branch can best be understood if we note that vine-growing property in Egypt was worth five times other crop-growing lands.[56]

The first question that concerned the scientific world when the papyri were first published was the location of Beth Anath. Various theories were propounded, but the most prevalent current view places Beth Anath in the upper Galilee.[57] All the attempts to locate the place depend upon dubious similarities between Arab place names and the name mentioned in the papyri, plus the fact that Beth Anath lay on the route between two places whose identification is also doubtful.[58]

More significant than its location is the nature of the landholding. Tcherikover made a very strong case for it being royal land given in grant.[59] His conclusions were criticized by Rostovtzeff, who claimed that they were too far-reaching for the scanty material.[60] Hengel sprang to Tcherikover's defense, but focused his argument on the question whether the word κτῆμα means a privately owned vineyard or could be royal land.[61] We would suggest stressing some additional points. Most important is the fact that the land was farmed out by a functionary called a κωμομισθωτής. Rostovtzeff claimed that the κωμομισθωτής was a tax-farmer for a whole village.[62] Tcherikover interpreted the position as that of a "royal official farming out lots."[63]

Hengel, caught in the cross-fire, suggested that these κωμομισ-θωταί could be both.[64] Yet, Rostovtzeff himself admitted that these κωμομισθωταί are general farmers of revenue

> charged with the duty of making contracts for the cultivation of the king's land with the individual *laoi* in the same way as in Egypt. In this case we must assume that the λαοί (natives) of Phoenicia were treated like the λαοὶ βασιλικοί (royal peasants) of Egypt, as free tenants of the parcel of land which they rented from the crown through the κωμομισθωτής. If this be correct,

the *chora* of Phoenicia tilled by the *laoi* had the same status as the crown land (χώρα βασιλική) in Egypt.[65]

Another point regarding Rostovtzeff's view of the κωμομισθωταί needs examination. He considered the κωμομισθωταί hinted at in the Rainer Papyrus (lines 17–20) as general farmers of revenue, out-ranking the village chiefs.[66] But Westermann, who wrote a detailed examination of this papyrus, rejected this interpretation and proposed that the lines in question are concerned with the lease of royal lands.[67] Another revealing point is that the farmers apparently refer to a petition (ἐντευκξις). The addressee of the petition is not known, but for it to have had any value at all, it would have had to be directed to a person higher in the Ptolemaic world than Apollonius.[68] Hence, we suggest that it was directed to the king. Furthermore, while all subjects could appeal to the king for justice, the request for a lessening of their burden of payments would be more reasonably directed to the ultimate recipient of those payments, in this case the king.

Yet one more point stems from Rostovtzeff's own works. Hengel suggested that Beth Anath was a development–settlement area, much like Philadelphia in Egypt.[69] Rostovtzeff noted that settlements like Philadelphia that were settled by Greeks received Greek names, but that settlements peopled by crown-peasants, the *basilikoi georgoi*, had purely Egyptian names. It is revealing that Beth Anath has such a Semitic name, and has been identified with places mentioned in the Bible.[70]

We should also remember that Apollonius received a gift estate in Egypt of 10,000 *aroura* and he rented out land there too.[71]

Finally, the Hefzibah inscription, which was unknown to Rostovtzeff, and which we will analyze in greater detail further on, clearly demonstrates the dependent nature of the *laoi*.

The Hefzibah inscription is a limestone stele discovered near Beth Shean in 1960. It consists of a number of orders and memoranda dating from 202 BCE to 195 BCE and sent from King Antiochus III to Ptolemy son of Thraseas who was strategos of Syria and Phoenicia, and to other royal officials. The inscription contains information elucidating the administrative practices of the Seleucid regime.[72] More importantly, it contains information relevant to landownership. Although the documents stem from the Seleucid period, it is generally held that much of the situation referred to is a continuation of Ptolemaic practice.[73] This is indicated by the continued use of the name "Syria and Phoenicia" instead of the later Seleucid term "Coele-Syria." Likewise, the position of the *dioiketai* as financial officers of the crown resembles Ptolemaic practice. The continuation of Ptolemaic practice may simply be a result of the brief time that passed from the conquest of Palestine till the exchange of correspondence which is the source of the edicts on the stele.[74]

Ptolemy son of Thraseas was a senior official in the Ptolemaic regime who turned traitor and went over to the Seleucids.[75] He apparently was rewarded for his efforts by receiving confirmation of the lands previously granted to him by the Ptolemies, and by the grant of other villages.[76] Landau describes him "as the owner of various villages, which were in part his absolute property (ἐγκτήσει), partly leased to him (by the Crown) as hereditary tenure, and partly assigned to him by the king, possibly as endowment, from the King's Land."[77] Fischer agrees that we are dealing with these three types of property.[78] Furthermore, when Ptolemy son of Thraseas refers to claims between villages which are in his territories, and other villages which are not in his territory, we may infer that these latter may be crown land, because there is reference to the *oikonomos* and the official in charge of them.[79] It is difficult, perhaps impossible, to determine which of the properties belonged to the strategos prior to the Seleucid conquest. The tendency is to see the first named as possibly the original landholding. The second suits what we know of granted land for Seleucid times, and we will discuss it later. The third clearly refers to lands that the current king assigned to him.

The last sort of gift land we will deal with is the *kleroi*. There is substantial proof of the existence of *kleroi* in the Ptolemaic province of Syria–Phoenicia. The Rainer papyrus specifically refers to soldiers and military settlers (*kataoikoi*) who took wives there.[80] We have even more specific evidence from the Zenon Papyri regarding the area east of the Jordan.[81] The papyrus is a bill of sale drawn up at the Birta of Ammanitis, mentioning two cavalrymen who are designated *kleruchs*.[82]

The questions that arise are numerous. To whom did the land belong prior to the granting of the *kleruchy*? What were the conditions according to which the *kleruchy* was granted? What was the size of the *kleruchy*?

One interpretation of the situation is that the soldiers, who are under the command of Tobiah, are also settled on his land.[83] This assumes that Tobiah was granted an estate in an area called Birta of Ammanitis, and from this estate plots were further allocated for settlement for royal troops. The key to this question is to locate Birta of Ammanitis and understand its relation to the *kleruchoi*.

One possibility raised in the literature is that the Birta of Ammanitis is really Iraq el-Emir, and that the lands given to the soldiers are from the immediate area.[84] That would mean that these lands which the family had owned for generations were in part confiscated.[85] But it is generally agreed that the Ptolemaic policy toward local aristocrats was one of conciliation, in an effort to coopt them to the regime. Tcherikover develops this idea, stating that Tobiah was a local sheikh, protecting the border from raiders.[86] But why then take land from his patrimony? Confiscating his land, and then handing it out to his own soldiers, would be a very illogical move. The solution is to see the patrimony of Tobiah as unviolated, the administrative headquarters may have been in the *birta* and the *kleruchies* were in another area, very likely near Amman.[87] The bill of sale does not indicate where the *kleroi* are, it just records where the deal was registered. With time the area of the *kleruchies* and the lands of the Tobiads were interchangeably called the land of the Tobiads and the land of Ammon.[88] The area was certainly important strategically, as it is the eastern flank of the Land of Israel.[89] It stands to reason that the Ptolemies would wish to settle the area between the ancestral lands of the Tobiads and Philadelphia with military settlers. Significantly, a military obligation was a condition for receiving a *kleros* under the Ptolemies.[90]

An interesting allusion to the presence of *kleruchies* in Palestine is a passage in the Letter of Aristeas in which the author relates that six hundred thousand men each became holders of 100-*aroura* lots.[91] He is probably referring to the number of men who went up from Egypt.[92] But the mention of "100-*aroura* men" is characteristic for the veterans of Ptolemy Philadelphus.[93]

While confiscation of land in Palestine was not unknown, attempts were made to settle areas previously unoccupied. Certainly the region of Transjordan was not overly settled. The tale of Joseph son of Hyrcanus, who was sent two days' journey from his home in order to sow some fields, illustrates the extensive nature of the lands in question (*Ant.* 12.192).

The subject of grant-land leads us to the question of grants of land to cities. Tcherikover dates four foundings to the period of Ptolemy II Philadelphus: Ptolemais, Philadelpheia, Philoteria, Arsinoe.[94] Fuks has dated the founding of Scythopolis also to the time of Philadelphus.[95] It is significant for the areas concerned that royal land was granted to the cities, converting royal land into city land. However, it must be noted that none of these foundations was in Judea, or for that matter in localities known to be primarily inhabited by Jews. These cities are relevant to this inquiry only if it might be demonstrated that these foundations were adjoining concentrations of Jewish settlement, and that these were now pressured, expropriated, or similarly affected. Regarding this, we will demonstrate that eventually the expansion of the Jewish population clashed with the desire of the poleis to expand their *chora*. However, this conflict occurred not earlier than the Seleucid era in Palestine.

Jerusalem was the only truly urban settlement in Judea. This possibly surprising lack of city foundations in Judea by the Ptolemies can be explained by examining the tenets underlying Ptolemaic city foundations in general. It appears that Ptolemaic urbanization was dictated by a desire to control the commercial routes from the Persian Gulf and the Arabian Peninsula passing through central and southern Syria to the harbors of the eastern Mediterranean located on the Egyptian and southern Syrian coasts. Hence, on the one hand this policy dictated the establishment of fortresses, colonies, and cities on the inland caravan routes, and on the other hand encouraged the development of the urban centers on the coast. Since Judea does not lie athwart any major commercial routes it would not have been necessary to develop new urban centers within her borders.[96]

The lack of Hellenistic foundations in Judea protected the Judean peasant from expropriations for the sake of citizens of new poleis, and his taxes were paid to Jerusalem.[97]

Determining Jerusalem's status is a problem. On the one hand, it was not a polis, or at least there are no indications that it had such a status. It did not receive a dynastic name, and there were no colonists that we know of. In fact, the tale of the Tobiads relates that King Ptolemy, enraged by the refusal of the High Priest to pay the tribute, threatened to expropriate the land and hand it out to colonists.[98] This threat makes no sense at all if the land had already been expropriated.

In this connection we would note that the evidence of Hecataeus on the situation in Jerusalem weighs against any idea that the city and its lands had been taken over as crown property. Hecataeus relates how Moses distributed land and that the Jews' land is inalienable. He stops there and does not relate any major change made by Ptolemy I. If the king had confiscated all of the land, and settled new owners, Hecataeus would have had to note it in the context of the story.[99]

The Letter of Aristeas would also be incomprehensible if Jerusalem was a Ptolemaic colony.[100] Verses 112–13 describe the prosperous state of the agriculture, and are a continuation of verses 107–11. The whole point of the narrative is to highlight the diligence with which the Jews in Judea work their land. The inference is that the Jews are cultivating their own lands, not that they are dependent labor on the lands of Ptolemaic settlers.

Therefore, Jerusalem was the city of the ethnos of the Jews in Judea. It was semi-autonomous, living according to the traditional laws, having a city-territory, and living under the authority of the High Priest. At the same time it probably had a Ptolemaic military garrison, and royal officials.

It had no control over areas outside Judea and certainly did not function as a capital city for the province of Syria–Phoenicia. Zenon wrote to all sorts of local officials in order to arrange his various customs, slave, and debt problems, but to no representative in Jerusalem.[101]

On the other hand it was not a temple state, because the Ptolemaic military presence in the city would militate against it. The idea of Jerusalem as a temple state is an analogy to the temple states of Asia Minor and the Seleucid Empire, but it is an inappropriate analogy.[102] It has nothing more to support it than an over-reaching interpretation of Hecataeus and Aristeas.[103] Polybius as quoted by Josephus also lends credence to this misconception (*Ant.* 12.136). Rostovtzeff referred to Judea as a sort of temple state, notwithstanding his own definition that stipulates ownership of territory and state organization.[104] Hengel also claims that Judea was a temple state, ignoring his own evidence that the Ptolemies hardly would have tolerated such a situation. He points out that Egyptian temples had a royal officer to supervise their finances, and their land was under royal administration.[105] In that case what justification is there for claiming the existence of temple states? Receiving privileges such as *asylia* and tax exemptions does not necessarily make a temple a temple state. Likewise, the obligation of the worshipers to pay tithes or other sacrifices does not define a temple state, otherwise practically all temples would be temple states. Moreover, if Judea was a temple state, why was the Temple so dependent on royal grants, the half-shekel contribution, and special privileges granted by the kings?[106]

I fail to find any proof that the Temple in Jerusalem "owned" the territory of Judea, unless we consider the biblical expressions of God's ultimate ownership of the Land of Israel as an expression of the Temple's ownership of the land by extension.[107] This latter possibility seems a forced interpretation of the scriptures.

The remaining type of land is private land. The earliest evidence for it is literary. The Book of Judith relates that "Manasses had left her gold and silver, and menservants, and maidservants, and cattle, and lands, and she remained upon them."[108] Although the Judith tale is probably fictional, and somewhat fantastic, and attempts to use it as a historical source invite failure, it should still be noted that the details of the story had to be sufficiently rooted in realia so that the readers would find the story believable. Therefore, we assume that the following points were at least credible: that Jews lived near the valley of Esdraelon, and that a widow could inherit enough property, including land, to live on comfortably.[109] Does the story in question have anything to say about Judea and the Ptolemaic period? The fact that Judith's husband owned and managed his own property, and his wife carried on doing so, is treated so matter-of-factly, that it leads us to believe that this was a situation which the readers accepted as commonplace. Furthermore, if the story indeed originated in Persian times, and was reworked over the generations, it would have had to pass through the Ptolemaic period. During the latter, the editors would have eliminated any material which was obviously unrealistic. Since they chose to leave in the landholding relationships, we assume that they were in existence then.

The next evidence of landholding is the Tale of the Tobiads, which we have had occasion to discuss previously. The Tobiad clan had extensive lands in the Transjordan area, probably around Iraq el-Emir. Tcherikover, and others, see the continued existence of ancestral estates, as exemplified by the Tobiads, as a deliberate policy of the Ptolemies. Ostensibly this policy aimed at coopting the local aristocracy of Palestine to ensure tranquillity in a strategically sensitive province.[110]

The impressive ruins at Iraq el-Emir surely indicate something of the wealth that this clan had.[111] Recent excavations in the area reveal that the heart of the Tobiad estates, Iraq el-Emir, was a *paradeisos* of at least 2,000 *dunams*, including terraces, irrigation works, and supporting and enclosing walls. Researchers have also come to the conclusion that there was an animal-breeding farm on the estate.[112] The papyri mention wheat, donkeys, and horses, provided by Tobiah, as well as grooms for the Zenon party.[113] Similarly, the correspondence between Tobiah and Apollonius, the king's minister, and even between Tobiah and the king, demonstrate the prominence and therefore probably the wealth of this family.[114] In summary, it is significant that an area, undefinable as it may be, was referred to as "belonging to Tobiah" (ἐν τῆι Τουβίου).[115]

Other indications of private landownership are tenuous. The papyri mention one Jeddous, who owed a debt to Zenon. When Zenon's representative called on him in order to collect the debt, the collector was driven out of the village.[116] Tcherikover suggests that, judging by the name, Jeddous was a Jew, and that the incident probably took place in Judea, or in Idumea.[117] Furthermore, he postulates that Jeddous was "one of those native 'sheiks,' who owned vast areas of land in the country."[118] Moreover, "probably the whole village was on his land."[119] While this view of the text would suit our purposes, we cannot accept it at face value. Any number of scenarios could explain who Jeddous was and why he was able to throw them out of the village. In fact, the text proves nothing more than that Zenon had difficulty in collecting a debt.

Zaidelous and Colochoutos are also described by Tcherikover as "wealthy sheiks."[120] These two men are attested in *PCZ* 59015 as harboring runaway slaves belonging to Zenon. From the same papyrus it is clear that they trade in slaves, but nowhere is it demonstrated that they are landowners. Since the purchase took place in Marissa (cf. *PCZ* 59006), a large and prosperous community with a Sidonian settlement on the trade route to Gaza, there is no reason to conclude that anyone who was a slave dealer there was also a landowner. It is possible that a community of Marisa's sort could serve as a base for merchants, including slave dealers.

One last hint of private ownership of land can be inferred from the Rainer Papyrus.[121] One may postulate that the owners of herds, who employed shepherds to care for their flocks, also had agricultural investments besides livestock. They may well have employed shepherds in order to free themselves for other jobs, such as taking care of crops and groves; moreover, they must have had land on which to graze their flocks.

This then covers the evidence for landholding in Ptolemaic Palestine. What evidence do we have for a crisis?

The crisis

We intend to demonstrate that the rigorous economic policy of the Ptolemies created a situation in which elements of the population could not stand up to the pressures either of taxes or of a money economy gone sour. As a result a significant number of people lost their land, or were forced into slavery or dependent labor.

It is noteworthy that from the period of Onias II (Ptolemy III Euergetes) till the final defeat of the Ptolemies by Antiochus III, there is a steady erosion of support for the Ptolemaic regime in Judea. The Ptolemaic economic policy, which has been likened to a money-making machine, eventually eroded the prosperity which it needed to thrive on.[122]

This view of affairs, hinted at first by Rostovtzeff,[123] and affirmed lately in the recent edition of the *Cambridge Ancient History*,[124] finds expression in the political and military history of the period, as well as in the economic record. As we follow events in Ptolemaic history we note that there is a decline in the effectiveness of Ptolemaic rule from the period of Ptolemy II Philadelphus through Ptolemy III Euergetes and continuing to Ptolemy IV Philopator. During the Third Syrian War Euergetes attacked Syria. The campaign was at first successful, but then Euergetes was forced to return to Egypt. Jerome and Justin explain the retreat by a sedition in Egypt.[125] The ensuing Seleucid counter-attack almost conquered Coele-Syria. It has been suggested that the troubles in Egypt that drew Euergetes back were connected to a famine.[126] A famine is mentioned in the Canopus Decree which is from March 238 BCE, just a very few years after the conclusion of the Third Syrian War (*OGIS* 56). Furthermore, recent studies indicate that the Nile inundation was disastrously low in 240 BCE.[127] On the other hand Turner asserts that the Nile and the poor harvests are only one factor, and not the most important, in a complex of economic and political errors committed by Philadelphus. These errors led to an "oppressive exploitation" throughout the 250s, which caused the "explosion of the 240's BCE."[128] One can only speculate what effect these events had on Judea. But it is a fact that to curb the famine in Egypt the Ptolemies brought grain at high prices from Syria and Phoenicia (*OGIS* 56). In Egypt people were required to register the amount of grain in their possession.[129] We suggest that the landowners and government officials in Judea would have done their utmost to wrest as much grain as possible from the population in order to meet the demands of the Egyptian rulers. The practice of stockpiling grain for export, when landowners and merchants place personal profit before local interest, is a well-documented development of famine situations.[130] In such cases the speculation causes deficiency in an area that in fact has plenty. If we further accept Turner's contention, which is well substantiated by papyrological studies and deals with the evidence cumulatively, we are confronted by a situation of economic oppression under Ptolemaic rule.[131] This suggestion, although speculative, may help to explain the strange behavior of Onias II, the High Priest in Jerusalem. According to the Tale of the Tobiads, he refused to forward the tribute to the Ptolemaic rulers (*Ant.* 12.158). The reason for this, according to the Josephean version, was that he was greedy. Stern suggested that the apparently imminent victory of Seleucus II, coupled with the possibility of linking Palestine to the great centers of Jews in the Seleucid Empire, may have motivated Onias' actions.[132]

Hengel blamed "general weariness in face of constant regimentation by the Ptolemaic administration" as well as the hope of a change of regime.[133] We suggest that while these motivations existed, the underlying motivation may have been antagonism to the oppressive regime.[134]

The Samarian raids against the Jews have been explained by Rappaport as a punishment for the refusal of the High Priest to pay the tribute.[135] Let us note that the depredations of the Samarians against the Jews are mentioned before the refusal. The actions are described as cutting up the country, and carrying off slaves.[136] But the definition of the first verb used to indicate their activities is "laying waste the country by cutting the corn." The second verb which is translated by Marcus as "carrying off slaves" is defined "to plunder."[137] Is it reasonable to believe that the Ptolemaic regime would permit the wanton destruction of crops when all other evidence indicates how much effort was put into raising and gathering crops? Likewise, the abduction of persons was strictly forbidden in the Rainer Papyrus.[138] There the enslaving of free persons on private initiative was banned; however, the crown could enslave persons in cases where taxes were owed to the government. Therefore, it is more reasonable to assume that the Samarians were expropriating crops, and taking into slavery those who could not fill the demands of the regime. The Tobiad story censored that aspect of the affair because the author was writing a pro-Ptolemaic tract in which tales of Ptolemaic oppression were out of place.[139]

Another indication of the situation in Judea is perhaps expressed in the biblical book of Ecclesiastes. The composition is very abstruse and lends itself to different dating and theories about its provenance.[140] Because we subscribe to the judgment of Bickerman and Hengel that it is a Hellenistic–Jewish work, we will not enter into an examination of the work as a whole, or into literary and philosophical points. We will concern ourselves only with those verses that can shed light on economic and social tensions of the period.

Rostovtzeff points out that verse 10:20 relates to the ubiquity of spies and informers in Ptolemaic Judea.[141] He considers this a cry of the oppressed rural population, whereas the city population "was satisfied."[142] In this connection it is appropriate to recall that the Rainer Papyrus provides rewards for informers who receive a third of the value of property confiscated to the crown.[143] These informers are encouraged to report people who did not honestly declare the size of their herds, or those who keep slaves illegally. We can see in this policy the determination of the Ptolemaic regime to maximize its income.

Qohelet's (3:16) complaint that "the place of judgement is the place of wickedness" may be a cry against oppression administered through the courts.[144] It is repeated and amplified in 4:1–2, which specifically cries against "all the oppressions," protesting that the oppressed have no comfort, and the oppressors have power on their side, so that the dead are better off than the living. The verse (5:7): "If you see in a province oppression of the poor and suppression of right and justice, don't wonder at the fact; for one high official is protected by a higher one, and both of them by still higher ones" clearly describes an oppressed land, burdened by a hierarchy of officials.

To what oppression could Qohelet be referring? We would exclude religious oppression from the sins of the Ptolemies, except for the very problematic possibility that Philopator pursued a pro-Dionysian religious policy.[145] By the same token, we would eliminate political oppression.[146] This leaves economic oppression. Unfortunately, Qohelet does not speak in specific terms that can be related to historical events or personalities. But the description of an oppressive, hierarchical, omnipresent system fits what we already know about the Ptolemaic administration. Moreover, it describes the reaction of the governed to the actions of the government. The aspect of landownership is difficult to demonstrate. But we should keep in mind that land is the basis of the economy, it employed the vast majority of the population. When perverted justice is referred to one thinks of the expropriation of plots through the use of the judicial system. Two more verses may also be revealing: 5:8 (ויתרון ארץ בכל היא מלך לשדה נעבד) is difficult to interpret but might read: "Thus the greatest advantage in all the land is his: he controls a field that is cultivated."[147] This verse perhaps refers to the king's interest in all the land. Verse 6:1–2 is particularly revealing:

יש רעה אשר ראיתי תחת השמש ורבה היא על האדם : אשר יתן לו
האלוהים עשר ונכסים וכבוד ואיננו חסר לנפשו מכל אשר יתאוה ולא
ישליטנו האלהים לאכל ממנו כי איש נכרי יאכלנו זה הבל וחלי רע הוא

There is an evil I have observed under the sun, and a grave one it is for man: that God sometimes grants a man riches, property, and wealth, so that he does not want for anything his appetite may crave, but God does not permit him to enjoy it; instead a stranger will enjoy it.

In other words, an evil which Qohelet has witnessed is a rich and wealthy man whose wealth is consumed by a "איש נוכרי." According to the usage of the word נכרי the intention is definitely a foreigner.[148]

Similarly, the all-encompassing fiat of the Hellenistic king is hinted at in 8:4, "inasmuch as a king's command is authoritative, and none can say to him, 'What are you doing?'"

Simultaneously, with the increasing oppression of the royal government, there must have been an increase in the oppression of the poor by the rich. Qohelet is rife with criticisms of the wealthy.[149] We can only postulate that in the period in which Qohelet was writing, there was an ever-increasing concentration of wealth (land) directly in the hands of the crown, and persons who received gift estates confiscated from Judeans.

Whatever the situation in Judea in the time of Ptolemy III, the relationship between the crown and the population must have become more onerous and less effective. An indication of this is manifest during the reign of the following Ptolemy (IV Philopator). Then, until the surprising turn-around at the Battle of Raphia, the Seleucid, Antiochus III, was very successful in his campaign to conquer the area of Coele-Syria. This campaign was noticeably marked by the disaffection of leading Ptolemaic commanders (Theodotus, Panaitolus, and their friends, Keraias, Hippolochus, Nicias).[150] Unfortunately, we have no record of Judean attitudes to that war. However, after his victory, Philopator and his queen deemed it necessary to spend four months in the border province of Syria–Phoenicia.[151] This is the period supposedly described in III Maccabees and perhaps alluded to in Dan. 11:10–11.

From 217 BCE till 200 BCE the Ptolemaic kingdom degenerated.[152] In 205 BCE Philopator and Arsinoe died. In 202 or 201 Antiochus III again tried to invade Syria–Phoenicia, now, except for Gaza, with even more success. In this period an anti-Ptolemaic (pro-Seleucid) party tried to take over in Jerusalem (Dan.11:14). But when Scopas counter-attacked he apparently punished those Jews who had supported the Seleucids.[153] When he was forced to withdraw he took pro-Ptolemaic aristocratic Jews back with him to Egypt.[154]

In this period of fluctuating fortunes, two points are clear. First, the Seleucids made an effort to win the allegiance of the inhabitants. The Hefzibah inscription shows Seleucid effort to win support. We will discuss it later in greater detail, but at this point we note that its earliest provisions include protection for the villagers.[155] Second, there were members of the Jewish and non-Jewish leadership who were anxious to see a Seleucid victory. Ptolemy son of Thraseas is probably the best example of the non-Jewish leadership. While the Jewish support for the Seleucids was apparently widespread, it was no doubt led by the High Priest and other priests.[156]

What were the developments, in landownership, which brought about the active support of the Judean community for the Seleucid monarchy? Why did some Jewish aristocrats support the Ptolemaic regime to the extent of having to be evacuated from Judea?

As we have maintained above, we suggest that the last score of Ptolemaic rule in Judea was characterized by increasing economic pressures which led to the loss of land by more and more inhabitants.

First, this period is marked by an inflation in Ptolemaic currency.[157] In Egypt, taxes were collected according to the new price levels, but wages were paid at the old rates. A class of moneylenders exploited the situation, lending money to help families meet their immediate needs and then foreclosing on the land.[158]

In Judea the period from Ptolemy II till the beginning of the Fifth Syrian War is marked by a steadily decreasing number of Ptolemaic coin finds. Hengel suggests that an additional levy of taxes might have decreased the amount of currency in circulation.[159] That also fits the situation in Egypt, where taxes went up while wages remained low.

This also is the period when a wealthy class of Jews, having economic interests in the Ptolemaic regime, drew closer to Hellenistic culture.[160] Hengel dates the service of Joseph son of Tobiah to the years 239–217 BCE.[161] He maintains that Joseph became increasingly wealthy, but at the same time his office made it possible for him to protect his people from exploitation. Moreover, he accepts the summary in Josephus which credits Joseph with bringing prosperity to his countrymen.[162] Yet, at the same time, Hengel develops the idea that the aristocratic class, which identified with the Ptolemaic conquerors, enriched itself through the use of the system to the chagrin of the poor.[163]

The "Wisdom of Ben-Sira" is our chief literary source for the period just before and after the Seleucid conquest of Palestine.[164] Because the composition is of the "wisdom literature" genre (much like Qohelet), and neither a historical narrative nor an economic report, it is difficult to reconstruct the economic life of its era. With all wisdom literature one must be careful not to assume that aphorisms which are valid for all times are in fact evidence of contemporaneous events. Nevertheless, we consider that some of the verses divulge problems that concerned Ben-Sira and his contemporaries.[165]

It is evident that the rich are portrayed as exploitative and oppressive (13:9): "When a powerful man invites you, keep your distance."[166] It is also clear that other verses (13:8) relate to the estrangement between the rich and the poor: "What peace is there between a hyena and a dog? And what peace between a rich man and a poor man?"

However, the verses that concern us have to do with debts and debtors, and the hard-hearted attitude of the rich toward the needy. We assume that repeated adjurations toward a certain action or code of behavior indicate that people are not behaving in that desired manner, or otherwise why bother encouraging it? Ben-Sira exhorted his son to "support his neighbor in his poverty" (22:23). This message is repeated and amplified in great detail in verses 29:1–20. But, besides serving as evidence that many people needed loans,[167] it also shows that many people were failing to pay their loans and lost their property as a result (29:18): "Being surety has ruined many men who were prosperous . . . , it has driven men of power into exile."

The problems of lost livelihood and lost land are apparent in some passages which specifically relate to those eventualities. Verse 4:1 adjures "אל תלעג לחיי עני." The text is problematic, but one of the more frequent interpretations is "defraud not the poor of his sustenance."[168] This idea is echoed in a later verse which teaches that הורג רע לוקח "מחיה" (34:23). In other words, the seizure of a man's livelihood is tantamount to killing him. The verse prior to this criticizes persons who offer sacrifice from the goods of the poor (34:21). All these passages relate in one way or another to the loss of one's source of livelihood. The inference which we draw is that the livelihood stems from land. We base this on the fact that most of the population drew its livelihood from the land. The sacrifices made in the Temple are in great part offerings from the family soil. Therefore, land is the property that is being taken from those who cannot withstand the economic pressures created by the demands of the Ptolemaic system.

The wealthy aristocrats who cooperated with the Ptolemaic rulers, and were in part, like Tobias and his son Hyrkanos, agents of the government, profited by the system, and probably enlarged their holdings.[169] The majority suffered impoverishment and expropriation. When the Seleucid juggernaut came south these people rallied to what they hoped would be a better regime.

4

THE LATE HELLENISTIC
PERIOD

THE SELEUCID PERIOD

The Seleucid period is characterized by a sea-change in relations between the imperial government and the Judean society. Under Seleucid rule a crisis developed which in its progress touched aspects of life and religion so deeply that its effects are of world historical importance. One result of the crisis was a series of changes in the landholding structure of Judea. These changes mirrored the developments in the relations between the Jewish people in Judea and the Seleucid rulers.

The Seleucids finally conquered Coele-Syria, including Palestine, from the Ptolemies in 200 BCE.[1]

At first the Seleucid administration was probably welcomed by the majority of the inhabitants of Judea as a relief from the onerous Ptolemaic rule. This assumption is supported by the willingness of the Jews to aid Antiochus III in his campaign against the Ptolemaic defenders of Jerusalem.[2] Among the Jews, the High Priest Simon II correctly read the political–military situation, while others who had profited from the Ptolemaic rule remained loyal to the King of the South. As a result the right of *prostasia* reverted to Simon, while the pro-Ptolemaic Hyrcanus lost his power.[3]

How did the shift to Seleucid rule affect the landholding system in Judea?

We suggest that the immediate effect of the change of regime was the departure of leading pro-Ptolemaic Judeans who withdrew along with the Ptolemaic army.[4] What happened to their lands, their houses, their debtors? The sources do not answer that question. The only specific case known to us is that of Hyrcanus, son of Joseph of the Tobiads.

Hyrcanus, according to the Tobiad tale in Josephus, withdrew to the area east of the Jordan River.[5] This supposedly was a result of his conflict with his brethren. We do not know the exact time frame for this clash, but as Tcherikover states, it is reasonable to assume that it occurred sometime before Antiochus' conquest, or even at the same time.[6] Two things are clear, Hyrcanus once maintained a domicile in Jerusalem, and now built his home outside of Judea; and he had some kind of social and economic presence in Judea during the reign of Seleucus IV. We would suggest that at first Jerusalem was too hot to hold him, but with the passing of time, and the king, he was able to renew his contacts. Yet he did not return to Jerusalem to live.

In general we can assume that the fugitive members of the defeated Ptolemaic party suffered a fate similar to that of other losers in the Hellenistic wars. They were forced to leave their homes, either permanently, or until such time as the political climate made it possible for them to return. Some examples come to mind of fugitives defeated in political struggles departing Judea, not to return: Onias IV who went to Egypt and Jason who also fled to the Transjordan area.[7]

The disposition of the property of the fugitives, and all of the land in Judea, depends on the crucial question of the status of Judea after the Seleucid conquest. If Judea was treated as belonging to a polis (Jerusalem),[8] its land was γῆ πολιτική, "city land." In a polis the property of fugitives and banned persons became κοινὸς τόπος, the "common property" of the polis, which could be redistributed among the remaining citizens.[9] Of course, we do not know if these rules applied in Judea or whether the biblical and traditional idea of *nahala* was in effect, i.e. the land of a fugitive would pass to some other part of the family.[10]

Alternatively, we have to consider the options that Judea was either γῆ ἱερά or χώρα βασιλική.

Was Judea temple land under the Seleucids? The same considerations mitigating against Judea as a temple state in Ptolemaic times (see previous chapter) are in effect for the Seleucid period.[11] We should also keep in mind that temple land could be disposed of at royal whim.[12] For example, on the island of Failaka in the Persian Gulf Antiochus III specifically handed out patrimonies on land ostensibly belonging to the local temple.[13]

Was Judea royal land? In the previous chapter we endeavored to demonstrate that Judea was treated as *chora basilike* by the Ptolemies. Indeed, Applebaum tries to maintain that even under the Seleucids this was the case.[14] Based on the Hefzibah inscription, and on the tax relief granted by Demetrius I and II, Applebaum felt that much of the land was already royal land before the Maccabean Revolt. He ignored the fact that the Hefzibah inscription is from an area far removed from Judea. Also, the taxes do not necessarily indicate that Judea was *chora basilike* before the decrees. They may have reflected the later punitive measures of the crown against the rebellious Jews.[15] For that matter, it is yet to be demonstrated that city land or private land automatically paid tax at lower rates than royal land. Rostovtzeff, while admitting that the high taxes are similar to the taxes paid by βασιλικοὶ γεοργοί (royal peasants) in Egypt, rejected the idea that the high taxes were a punishment. He rightly pointed out that taxes varied from place to place.[16] There is no doubt that the Seleucids maintained large areas as royal land, and that such land was sometimes given as γῆ ἐν δωρεᾷ.[17] The Hefzibah inscription is proof of the existence of gift land and royal land under Seleucid rule in Palestine. However, some thought must be given to the special circumstances of Jerusalem and Judea.

The Seleucids were materially assisted by the population and its leadership. In fact the Judean sympathy with the Seleucids stands in bold contrast to the attitudes of Hellenistic cities of Palestine.[18] The Seleucid conquest restored the primacy of the High Priest, and established the members of the *gerousia* in a favored status. It would seem self-defeating and uncharacteristic of the new royal administration to turn all of Judea into royal land.[19] Additionally, we should consider that in two other cases cities which had come to an accommodation with Antiochus III retained their territory.[20] Moreover, the indications from Samaria suggest that the Seleucid conquest encouraged the development of local centers.[21] If anything, we may consider that some of the land now lost to pro-Ptolemaic elements was allocated to those who had been of service to the Seleucids in the recent struggle. The example of Ptolemy son of Thraseas, who was rewarded for his services by gifts of land, comes to mind. Those who were useful to the Seleucids would have included the High Priest, other priests (such as Johanan father of Eupolemos), some of the Tobiads, and other leading citizens whose names we unfortunately do not know.[22] These unnamed citizens are almost certainly members of the *gerousia*. This is singled out for mention twice in the *prostagma* of Antiochus III to the Jews. First, it is mentioned in connection with the splendid welcome the king received on coming to Jerusalem (*Ant.* 12.138). Then it is also mentioned in connection with the special exemption from poll, crown, and salt taxes.[23] Stern pointed out that in this period the *gerousia* was perceived as the leadership of Judea.[24] The High Priest had not yet attained the pre-eminent position reached in the Hasmonean period. This suggestion of Stern's is supported by the fact that Johanan, the father of Eupolemos, and not Simon the High Priest, is singled out as the obtainer of the privileges of autonomy from Antiochus. Additionally, in the period before the decrees we witness the relative access of prominent Judeans to members of the royal administration and the king himself. That this favored position is intended more for the aristocracy than for the people at large is evident from the tax exemption which is granted to those in Jerusalem and not in Judea at large.[25]

Kreissig suggested that the Land of Judea was the land of an ethnos with Jerusalem being the main city.[26] His proofs were the conclusions he drew from the taxes levied on the Jews, and a process of elimination. However, the land in Judea remained private land, παγκτητικὴ κυρεία, except for traditional royal estates such as Jericho.[27] If this were not so, then part of the punishments enacted by the Seleucids, such as expropriation and transferring land to their supporters, would not make any sense. Likewise the relief promised in the conciliatory decrees would have been valueless if the land was not in private ownership.

Bickerman also held that Judea was the land of an ethnos.[28] He based his conclusion on interpretation of *Ant.* 12.141 which speaks of trees from Judea καὶ ἐκ τῶν ἄλλον ἐθνῶν, and later texts. He admitted that we have very little information on ἔθνη in the Seleucid Empire.[29] We also conclude that Judea was considered the land of an ethnos, Jerusalem being the capital city, its Temple enjoying privileges. *Ant.* 12.142 clearly states that all the members of the nation (ethnos) will have a government according to their own laws.

The land, except for royal estates, belonged to private owners. In *Ant.* 12.144 the king orders that the property of people who were carried away and sold as slaves be restored to them. The aristocratic circles probably owned a large portion of the land, and as always were interested in increasing their wealth.

THE HELLENISTIC REFORM

This idyllic state of affairs continued till the Hellenistic reform, when the next major change in landownership took place. Then the party led by Simon, Jason, Lysimachus, and finally Menelaus, was able to obtain a charter from the Seleucid king for the establishment of a polis in Jerusalem. The Hellenistic reform in Jerusalem has been examined frequently and thoroughly by many scholars. It is not in the purview of this volume to re-examine the questions so often debated by others.

In general, we accept the reconstruction of events as described by Tcherikover, Hengel, and Stern.[30] There are of course differences among the three versions, but they all agree that the Hellenistic reform had its source in the economic ambitions of members of the Tobiad family, allied with some elements of the Oniads. Tcherikover and Hengel both emphasize the commercial aspirations of the reformists. We, however, wish to raise some heretofore unasked questions about the supposed commercial orientation of the reform. Specifically we should start with the question "cui bono?" Then, in what manner did the preferred group actually benefit? What did they gain that they did not have before, or could not acquire without the establishment of a polis? After all, the autonomy provided them with local rule, they were the leaders in any case. Did the polis suddenly open up commercial vistas previously closed to them?

Judea did not become a commercial power until Simon's day at the earliest, if at all. The territorial expansion which brought Jaffa, and later other ports, into the Judean sphere of control was concomitant on the Maccabean wars, and was a serendipitous result of those wars. Certainly, Jason and his ilk did not plan to acquire large areas of territory and seaports. Yet Tcherikover bases his case against the Hellenizers on two primarily mercantile points.[31] First, the alleged slogan of the Hellenizers in I Macc. 1:11: "Πορευθῶμεν καὶ διαθώμεθα διαθήεκην μετὰ τῶν ἐθνῶν τῶν κύκλῳ ἡμῶν, ὅτι ἀφ᾽ ἧς ἐχωρίσθημεν ἀπ᾽ αὐτῶν, εὗρεν ἡμᾶς κακὰ πολλά." ("Let us go and make a treaty with the heathen around us, because ever since we separated from them, many evils have come upon us.") This supposedly indicates that the Hellenizers realized that they had been depriving themselves of trade advantages by not being from a polis. Second, the alacrity with which the Hellenizers sent delegates to the festival in Tyre ostensibly demonstrates the ambition of the Hellenizers to create cultural ties that would yield economic advantages.[32] Furthermore, Tcherikover deals extensively with the verses in Ben-Sira which deal with a developing commercial class.[33] Yet he himself pointed out that "The secular aristocratic group in Judea, therefore, was based economically on two sources of livelihood, both generally characteristic of the nobility of the ancient world, namely income derived from agricultural holdings and high posts in the administration."[34] Likewise he points out that the secular aristocracy and part of the priestly class dwelt in Jerusalem, but had country estates, the Jerusalem priests being a wealthy landed group.[35]

The land provided a respectable income, judging by the reports of

Simon to the Seleucid authorities on the money in the Temple bank.[36] The proposed raid on the private deposits succeeded in exciting the population of Jerusalem, a situation which may indicate that there was more than widows' pensions involved.[37] We suggest that the money belonged to the well-off aristocracy of Judea. The Temple bank in Jerusalem did not increase the deposit by interest, but just guarded it.[38] The wealth that accumulated may have derived from the pressure of wealthy landowners who were slowly squeezing the small farmers, as Applebaum suggested.[39] This situation would also fit the descriptions of Ben-Sira, and would be more in keeping with the actual nature of Judean society than an emergent and aggressive mercantile class.

We have already noted that the royal administration during the Ptolemaic period oppressed the Jewish farmer. But in the period prior to the Hellenistic reform it was the large estate owners who would have found their ambitions to expand their holdings blocked by the traditions embodied in the "Laws of the Fathers." These certainly included the *Amana* and the provisos for protection of the *nahalot* and these were in force regarding the Jewish society and endorsed by the royal charter.[40]

It is assumed that the High Priest Onias II clashed with Simon the *Prostates* over some mercantile question.[41] But Tcherikover also has suggested that the *agoranomos* may have had jurisdiction over the police or "it may have been a juridical and administrative post."[42] Onias II is described as "hater of wickedness" who preserved the Laws most perfectly.[43] He is further described as one who was concerned for his fellow countrymen and zealous for the Law.[44] Is it not possible that the issue between Onias and Simon concerned some action or abuse of privilege which contravened the Law and customs? In that case one solution for the wealthy landowning classes was to eliminate whoever stood in the way of their ambitions. An even better solution would be the abrogation of the Laws as the constitution of the community, and the simultaneous establishment of a polis.

The accompanying benefits of citizenship in a polis included the option of dividing up the common lands among the citizens, as well as other financial, tax, and land manipulations which certainly outraged those excluded from the benefits of citizenship.[45] This is evident from a number of indications. First of all future membership in the polis would be limited to those who could afford to be educated in the Gymnasium and the Ephebia.[46] II Macc. 4:19 relates that 300 silver drachmas were sent by the Antiochians of Jerusalem to the games in Tyre. The citizens of the polis may have decided to send the money, but where did it come from? Menelaus could not make the payments due to the king, and was forced to take sacred vessels from the Temple.[47] Does this not indicate that he had wrung as much money out of the residents as was possible?[48] Another incident that might illustrate the attitude of the populace to the polis occurred when Jason thought that the king was dead. He led an attack on the city, pressing Menelaus into the fortress, but then the people revolted against Jason.[49] Why? He had no part in the sacrilegious expropriations of Temple vessels. His earlier innovations in the cultural life of the city had not provoked a violent response. It remains then, that he was identified with the establishment of the polis. As such he incensed the population.

THE EVIL DECREES

The rebellion of the Judeans against the polis in Jerusalem provoked the king to draconian actions against the city population (II Macc. 5:11–14). He established a military government in the city in order to defend the polis and its citizens (II Macc. 5:22–6). The presence of the soldiers, gentiles of course, led to an exodus of people fleeing both from the contamination with idol worshipers and the depredations of the soldiery.[50]

As a result of these events there was a change in the landownership structure. Our understanding of the measures enacted by Antiochus IV in Judah determines how we reconstruct these phases in the landowner-ship history. It is accepted and clear that gentile troops were introduced into Jerusalem, and especially the Akra.[51] Moreover, it is fairly clear that much of the indigenous Jewish population fled Jerusalem.[52] Further-more, it is also apparent that land was allocated by the royal government to some elements. However, the following questions bedevil all attempts at reconstructing developments. Who precisely were the elements to whom land was allocated? Was it to the gentile troops, who are then to be considered military settlers? Was it to the Hellenizers who made up the polis Antioch-in-Jerusalem? Was the land expropriated and as a result many Jews fled the city? Or did many Jews flee the city, and as a result their land was reassigned to other owners? Or was it a vicious circle, some land being expropriated, others fleeing from the unwelcome new situation, and their land being seized in turn? Was the land sold at a price, or handed out as a payment? How much land was taken? Where was it?

First let us recapitulate the major points of view in the scientific literature.

Of all the scholars who have dealt with the subject Applebaum is the most confusing. On the one hand, he accepts the view that Judean territory was turned into holdings for military settlers.[53] On the other hand, he also accepts Bar-Kochva's interpretation of Dan. 11:39 that the confiscated lands were sold to Jewish Hellenizers.[54] He rejects the view that there was a polis in Jerusalem, while at the same time maintaining that much of the land was taken by the Hellenizers in Jerusalem.[55] These contradictory and confusing positions serve only to demonstrate the ambivalent nature of the evidence.

Bar-Kochva takes the view that Jerusalem was never converted into a military settlement, but rather, that confiscated land was transferred to the ownership of the Hellenizers.[56] His reasoning is very convincing. First of all, assuming that Jerusalem was a polis, there is no example of a polis ever being reduced to the level of a *katoikia*. Second, the Seleucids would not have risked placing a military settlement in a dangerous border province which could one day fall to the Ptolemaic enemy, consequently losing Macedonian soldiers precious to the realm. Third, the soldiers themselves would have hardly been willing to accept allotments of land in a highly dangerous and unstable environment such as Judah c. 167 BCE.[57]

In total contradiction to Bar-Kochva's point of view is the belief of a large number of scholars who claim that the land was handed out by the king to military settlers and to the Hellenizers. The leading exponent of this view is Tcherikover. He states that I Macc. 1:35–6 shows that Antiochus settled in Jerusalem "people of pollution," as a result of which the inhabitants of Jerusalem abandoned the city, and it became an abode of aliens. Tcherikover asserts "*I Maccabees* (3:45) again speaks of Jerusalem as having become a waste and of the 'sons of aliens in the Akra.'" He interprets this verse as further evidence supporting his position. Similarly, he construes Dan. 11:39 as more proof that the land was given to the military settlers.

Another, yet similar point of view, is that of Bickerman and Stern. They maintain that the royal government settled gentiles in the land, but not necessarily military settlers.[58]

As Bar-Kochva has shown, other scholars come to the same or similar conclusions as Tcherikover, based on the same interpretation of the same texts.[59] He claims that they misunderstood the intention of the underlying Hebrew. In brief, he maintains that *katoikoi* does not refer to military settlers, but that in the translation from Hebrew to Greek of I Macc. the Hebrew word was mistranslated to *katoikoi*. The intention of the Hebrew was not to indicate military settlers, but rather residents.[60] No one denies that there were gentile soldiers dwelling in Jerusalem; but simply put, the question is whether the Jewish Hellenizers, or gentile military settlers, or a combination of both, received the land.

Let us review the sources, and briefly comment on them, to see if we can recover the actual chain of events.

1 Polis in Jerusalem (I Macc. 1:14; II Macc. 4:7–12). Discussed above.

2 Jerusalem is plundered, its walls destroyed, the cattle are taken, the Akra built (I Macc. 1:29–33; II Macc. 5:24–6). This action is interpreted by many as signifying the conversion of Judah into royal land.[61] Moreover, it reveals that the agricultural class suffered from the action.

3 The Akra is garrisoned by gentiles and Hellenizers (I Macc. 1:34). The text refers to ἔθνος ἁμαρτωλόν, ἄνδρας παρανόμος (sinful people, lawless men). The question is whether these two phrases refer to one, or to two groups. The first inclination is one group, but then we have to choose between Hellenizers or gentiles. If this one group is made up only of Hellenizers, then we have to account for the gentile soldiers who were with Apollonius; and their sudden reappearance in I Macc. 1:38. If the reference is only to gentiles, then "lawless men" is inappropriate because this generally refers to violators of the Law (Torah), and these by definition cannot be gentiles. The solution is to accept that there are two groups referred to in the sentence. The former are the gentiles because I Macc. 2:10 demonstrates that ethnos refers to other nations, and not the Hellenizers.[62] The latter group is clearly the Jewish Hellenizers.[63]

4 The Jewish inhabitants flee the city because of the pollution (I Macc. 1:37–8). The Jewish inhabitants of Jerusalem apparently left their land in protest at the pagan environment introduced to the city: καὶ ἐμόλυναν τὸ ἁγίασμα. καὶ ἔφυγον οἱ κάτοικοι Ιερουσαλημ δι᾽ αὐτούς ("and polluted the sanctuary. And because of them the inhabitants of Jerusalem fled"). But it is also possible that their departure was a protest reaction to the diminished status to which they had been reduced by the punitive actions of the crown.[64] One might call their action a form of *anachoresis* (fleeing the land in protest).[65] Some scholars are of the opinion that the non-Hellenized mass of residents were transformed from free peasants to *laoi*, i.e. dependent farmers on royal land.[66] While popular, this *laoi* theory has nothing to support it in the sources.[67] I would suggest another possibility, that they were not royal "serfs," but had become second-class citizens, at the mercy of the

polis.[68] This suggestion stems from the belief that the land of Judea could not have been *chora basilike* because it belonged to a polis. Jerusalem and its *gerousia* are evidently held responsible for the affairs in Judea as late as 164 BC as indicated by Antiochus IV's letter to the *gerousia*.[69]

The inhabitants of Judea were now under pressure from the citizens of the polis who enjoyed the advantages of the polis laws. In either case, royal serfs, or non-citizens of the polis, disestablishing the Mosaic constitution meant that the legal protection of family holdings, the abolition of debts, etc., were no longer binding; especially since the Laws of the Fathers included the *Amana* and the reforms of Nehemiah.[70]

5 The Edicts of Persecution (I Macc. 1:41–64; II Macc. 6:1–12).

6 More Jews fled the city (I Macc. 2:29). The source indicates that the refugees went to the wilderness "to settle there." Also they came with their whole families and their cattle (2:30). The period of flight to the desert can be fixed to after the decrees, because the issue was the profanation of the Sabbath (2:34). The land that was abandoned became royal land.

The crown had no reason to confiscate private lands of those who did not flee the decrees. In fact, these people were criticized for going along with the government.[71] Their homes and villages became the first targets of Maccabean operations.[72] The land abandoned by those fleeing the decrees became attached to the *chora* of the city and was sold to members of the polis.[73] This procedure would fit with Seleucid policy: confiscation of lands in unstable areas, and their distribution for a reasonable price, in return for loyalty.[74] The land was sold to the Jewish Hellenizers, the military contingent did not receive land.[75]

The military settlers did not receive the land because the Hellenistic polis had not ceased to exist. As Bar-Kochva rightly pointed out there is no example of a polis losing its status to a military settlement. The fact that there was a polis is clear from the title of Antioch-in-Jerusalem.[76] Applebaum's cavil that the lack of any coins rules out the existence of a polis in Jerusalem willfully ignores the fact that there were other poleis in Palestine in the second century BCE which also did not leave any coins.[77]

To summarize the landownership situation as of the end of 167 BCE, the land belonged to those who had at least passively acquiesced to the rule of the Seleucids and their creatures, the Hellenizers. Those who made trouble, fled their lands, or refused to obey the decrees, lost their land. The land lost to them was taken by the crown and redistributed to loyalists.

Let us now adduce some proofs for this picture of the situation.

The example of Mattityahu the Hasmonean is instructive. He left Jerusalem in disgust with the religious developments there and settled in his patriarchal village.[78] When he is accosted by the Seleucid officer it is clear that Mattityahu is an influential member of the community (I Macc. 2:17). He is definitely not one of the *laoi*. Lest it be said that as a priest he had no lands and his status derived solely from his ecclesiastical position, we should note the following. I Macc. 2:28 indicates that he left his possessions in the town of Modein. He also evidently had a family burial plot there.[79] Mazar proposed that the Hasmoneans were descendants of the people who built Ono and Lod and other villages in the area.[80]

One can see that the Hellenizers profited, at first, from the situation. Dan. 11:39, והמשילם ברבים ואדמה יחלק במחיר ("He will make them master over many; he will distribute land for a price") indicates that the king sold plots of land to those who supported his policy.[81] As Bar-Kochva has claimed, the word במחיר always indicates a sale for money.[82] Moreover, he stated that "The Books of the Maccabees do not explicitly report the confiscation of land and its distribution to the Hellenizers, but probably the later despoilment of their estates and [I Macc. 6.24 and 7:7] should be understood against that background."[83] We would add that in the first source the expression used is αἱ κληρονομίαι. This word, although principally indicating an inheritance, lends itself to interpretation as property distributed as a reward. In a previous verse the same word is used to designate the land allocated to Caleb for bearing witness.[84]

The recurrent demands of the Hellenizers for assistance from the Seleucids, and their repeated complaints against the Maccabees, lend credence to the idea that they were losing valuable property and advantage. Early on in the struggle I Macc. 2:44 relates that the Hellenizers fled to the heathens in face of the wrath of the army of the Maccabees. But this was at a stage when the rebels could not attack Jerusalem, so the Hellenizers must have been holding properties outside the metropolitan area. Furthermore, these were not simple farmers enamored of the Hellenistic lifestyle: for them to be dyed-in-the-wool Hellenizers they would have to have come from the leading circles in society.

Other evidence that the lands of the opponents of the king were confiscated is II Macc. 11:29 which refers to the desire of the Jews to return to their homes and personal affairs (βούλεσθαι κατελθόντας ὑμᾶς γινεσθαι πρὸς τοῖς ἰδίοις), and the following verse which uses the word καταπορευμένοις ("return home").[85] The *idiois* are the private holdings which the farmers lost because of the banishment.[86]

5

THE HASMONEANS

THE MACCABEAN REVOLT

With the intensification of the Maccabean struggle and its successes, the pendulum swung the other way. While in the period of the decrees and the supremacy of the Hellenists the Seleucid supporters gained land at the expense of the rebels and their sympathizers, so during the ascendancy of the insurgents the rebels gained land at the expense of the Hellenizers.[1]

The end of this process is clear: the Hellenizers flee, and the lands formerly owned by them are divided among the victorious rebels. We will demonstrate that the Hasmonean family significantly increased its estates, probably gaining control of the former royal lands. We also propose that leading figures in the rebel camp also acquired lands they had not previously owned, thereby creating a new aristocracy.[2]

By the end of 164 BCE the insurgents were able to drive off the Hellenizers. Certainly no later than 162 the insurgent hold on the area of Judea was strong enough to justify an attack on the Akra itself.[3] Following the attack, the Hellenizers complained to the authorities in Antioch that the rebels had seized their αἱ κληρονομίαι (I Macc. 6:24).[4] There is no doubt that the displaced complainants are Jews because they claim that they have become estranged to their own people (6:24). They stress that not only are they under attack, but all that is in their borders is also taken. This verse (25) is difficult and has created problems for translators and commentators.[5] But there is a parallelism between 6:24 and 25:

24 killed us / plundered our property
25 raised hands against us / also against all our borders

Let us remember that the Greek word τὰ ὅρια is used to denote the borders of land, of estates, as well as the borders of a region.[6] The meaning may have been the rule of the Hellenizers within Judea, inferring their control of the land, or it might actually refer to the borders of the estates themselves.

The dislodgement of the Hellenizers and the corresponding return of rebels and refugees to their former lands prevailed until Alcimus and Bacchides restored the Hellenizers to power (I Macc. 7:16–22). Verse 7:22 indicates that the Hellenizers gained the mastery (κατεκράτεσαν γῆν Ιουδα) over Judea. But Judah prevented the Hellenizers from leaving Jerusalem and establishing themselves on their properties. This interpretation is the only one that makes sense of verses 7:23–4: "Accordingly, he [Judah] went around the entire territory of Judea, punishing the turncoats so that they shrank from going out into the countryside."[7] Note that no mention is made of gentiles, but only of "deserters" (τοῖς αὐτομολήσασι) who can only be Jews. If the Seleucids had granted lands to the gentile garrison of Jerusalem they too would have been prevented from benefiting from their lands, but only the apostate Jews are mentioned. So we have another indication that in fact the confiscated lands were granted to the Hellenizers and not to the garrison.

A further indication that under Judah's leadership the lands had returned to the control of the Jewish farmers, is the description of the final defeat of Nicanor's forces on the 13th of Adar. I Macc. 7:45–6 states that from "all the surrounding villages" people came out to attack the fleeing army.

The rebel control of Judea lasted until Demetrius sent Bacchides to restore order (I Macc. 9:1–57). This period saw the death of Judah and the defeat of the rebel forces. As a result of these developments the Hellenizers once again controlled Judea (I Macc. 9:25). Applebaum believes that "It is highly improbable that the Hellenizers were in a position to resume their estates in Judaea."[8] Furthermore he, with reservations, suggests that Bacchides evicted Jewish farmers and settled gentiles in their place.[9] We reject this suggestion because I Macc. 10:12–13 makes it clear that the gentiles garrisoned the fortresses, and as soon as their situation deteriorated they abandoned the country. The narrative does not fit the behavior of military settlers.[10] Contrary to Applebaum, we hold that the Hellenizers were the ones that benefited from any changes in the landholding situation. We can only conjecture what these changes were. No doubt, those who were directly associated with the Maccabean camp were punished and probably disinherited from their lands (I Macc. 9:26). By the same token, there is no reason to assume any new large-scale displacement of landholders for political reasons. However, a major contributing factor to the supremacy of the Hellenizers was the famine (I Macc. 9:24). We can only surmise what effect the famine had on the landholding structure of the country. The evidence from famines in other places and times suggests that land was encumbered, sold, or even abandoned in order to obtain food.[11] This situation may lie behind Demetrius' generous offer: "Whoever shall flee to the Temple in Jerusalem, or to any of its precincts, whether because they owe money to the king or for any other debt shall be released, with all they possess in my kingdom (I Macc. 10:43)." This offer may be only rhetorical, in that it echoes the usual cancellation of debts that characterize the philanthropia of Hellenistic monarchs. But, considering the difficult times, war, famine, and political instability, it is more likely that this concession answered a real need of the Judean farmers.

THE FAMINE OF 160 BCE

I Macc. 9:23–4 is our primary source for this famine.[12] It is also described in some slightly greater detail by Josephus in his version of the Maccabean history (*Ant.* 13.2–3).[13] On the one hand, this episode has been ignored for the most part in the historical literature on the period.[14] On the other hand, translations and commentaries have dealt with the passage. We will briefly survey the main works.

Oesterley presents a different text than the one found in the Rahlfs or Göttingen editions.[15] Basing himself on Torrey, he proposes that λιμὸς (line 24) is a misreading of the original Hebrew which had רעם ("murmuring") not רעב ("famine"),[16] thus denying there ever was a famine. The rest of his interpretation is intended to buttress this assumption. Naturally we cannot proceed further discussing a famine which may never have happened unless we dispose of Oesterley's reading. Suffice it to say that none of the alternative readings in Rahlfs and in Kappler justify his proposal. He has neither any textual basis for such an extreme emendation, nor has he any historical evidence that would justify it. Oesterley's emendation obviously did not gain acceptance as we can see by the rest of our survey.

Kahana is next in chronological order of the commentators who dealt with the passage.[17] His translation reads: בימים ההם היה רעב גדול מאד ותשלם הארץ אתם ("In those days there was a very great famine and the land came to terms with them"). He justifies this by using the only example of αὐτομόλεω ("to desert") appearing together with μετά in the Septuaginta (LXX II Sam. 10:19), a use rejected by Oesterley, but certainly justified by the methods used in reconstructing the Hebrew text underlying the LXX. However, he interprets χώρα as referring to the followers of Judah, and although he ostensibly bases this claim on the Syriac version and on Josephus' paraphrase, he has no real substantiation for his interpretation in these texts. Whoever, or whatever, the *chora* is, Kahana is clear that the famine forced them to accept the rule of the faithless and lay down their arms. He does not say why this should be so.

Abel understands our passage to mean that the famine caused the country (he doesn't explain who is meant) to desert to the other side.[18] He presents two other instances in I Macc. in which a famine tipped the scales against one side or the other, and in this case he infers that the famine put the finishing touches on the decaying situation of the rebels since the defeat at Bir-Zeit (Elasa).

Zeitlin's translation gives the same import as does Abel's, although in his brief comment he qualifies matters by claiming that the death of Judah was a causative factor, as well as the famine. He also does not explain why the famine should have led "many to go over to the Hellenizers and Bacchides."[19] Dancy's commentary claims that the grain harvest failed unexpectedly and that the "mass of the people" deserted to the enemy.[20] While we suspect that something of that nature occurred, Dancy presents no basis for his explanation.

Goldstein's translation does not differ from those above, i.e. the famine caused the land (the people) to go over to the enemy.[21] However, his commentary is unique, because he infers that the famine is an excuse "to explain away" the fact "that most Jews readily accepted the local regime around Alcimus." In other words, Goldstein is suggesting that there was no famine at all, but that it is a literary invention devised by the Hasmonean chronicler to cover up the fact that the Hasmoneans did not have mass popular support at this time. This suggestion has no corroborative support.

Schunck, the most recent major translator of I Macc., translates the passage in the same way as most of the former scholars have, i.e. the famine caused the people to go over to the enemy.[22] He presents no commentary or discussion on this event.

Before proceeding further let us deal with the two major reservations against the authenticity of the events. First, the view that there was no famine because the passage has its roots in a scribal error is untenable since, as stated above, there is no textual basis of any sort to support such an argument. Second, the theory suggested by Goldstein assumes that I Maccabees presents outright lies when necessary to cover unpalatable facts. However, as far as we know, there are no bald lies and fabrications in I Maccabees, excepting those fables that have a theological basis, such as Antiochus IV's repentance. Moreover, there are a number of instances in which unpleasant facts relating to the Maccabees are revealed, without lies to mitigate the truth, e.g. the dwindling away of Judah's army (I Macc. 9:5–7), and the willingness of the Hasidim to make peace (I Macc. 7:11–13).

We therefore accept the most prevalent reading, i.e. there was a famine and consequently the masses of the Jewish population deserted the fight against the Hellenizers and the Seleucid regime.[23] Based upon this, we feel this episode highlights various aspects of the economic structure of Judean and Hellenistic society and the interrelationship between the economy and the political structure.

Until the death of Judah, his party had apparently held sway in the Judean countryside and amongst the people. Otherwise one is hard put to explain the need to send Nicanor to Jerusalem, or Judah's victory over Nicanor, or especially the purpose of Bacchides' second expedition.[24] Something had to cause the sudden massive loss of allegiance suffered by the Maccabean party. Moreover, this loss of allegiance was only temporary, for within a few years Jonathan and Simon were able to successfully resist another attack by Bacchides (I Macc. 9:60–72). We suggest that an ever-worsening food supply situation reached its peak, and that the extremity of the famine forced the masses to turn to the only institution capable of large-scale famine-relief: the central government and its representatives in Judea.

It is possible that the indications of a worsening food supply situation can be found in I Macc. 6:49–54. There we read that the defenders of Beth Zur surrendered because they had no sustenance as a result of the Sabbath Year. Further on in the text we learn that there was a dearth of provisions in the Temple, also because of the Sabbath Year, and also because the refugees had eaten up the supplies. Moreover, a lack of supplies also threatened the besiegers (I Macc. 6:57).

We suggest that under normal circumstances there should have been sufficient food for the defenders of Beth Zur and Jerusalem. We have already mentioned that farmers were known to regularly store part of their crop against the possibility of hard times in the future. Agricultural societies plant, harvest, and store in a manner so that a harvest will provide for two years at least.[25] Governments in the ancient world also stored part of the crop which they received in taxes or in rents. Moreover, Jewish society in the Land of Israel also had to consistently make preparations for the Sabbatical Year.[26] It was a recurring practice, and so the Jews would have planned for the periodic renunciation of a harvest. Furthermore, the year following the Sabbath Year would not yield its harvest till the next spring, hence that period of lack would also have been taken into consideration in the planning.

Therefore the siege should not have materially changed the food supply situation in the fortresses because in any case the population would have had to live off stored provisions, new provisions not being available during a Sabbatical Year. Finally, we must dismiss the claim that the refugees ate up the stores. The text refers to those who fled to Judea for safety. If the Jews rescued by Judah and Simon are meant, then they can only have been few, otherwise how could they have been transplanted?[27] If, for argument's sake, the text intended the Judean population fleeing to its center and stronghold, then we should recall that the population would normally flee to the local fortresses in the event of war. Such an eventuality should not have diminished the potential of the fortress since provisions for a siege would have been on hand. We propose that the lack of provisions resulted from a period of poor harvests that occurred just prior to the Sabbatical Year. This might also explain why the besieging army also felt the pinch of declining supplies.[28]

There is some other evidence to suggest that there had been a difficult period. A recently discovered inscription from Iamnia (Yavneh) records the request and grant of philanthropia and tax waivers to the city by the crown.[29] The inscription does not include the reasons for this request, but we suggest that slim harvests may have been the cause. Chronologically the inscription fits the period before the Sabbath Year. It records a document from the summer of 163 BCE. The difficulties that led to the actions recorded in the inscription would have had to occur some time before this date, in order to allow time for the request to be forwarded and answered.[30] The Sabbath Year which is mentioned in our source lasted from the autumn of 164 BCE till the autumn of 163 BCE.[31] As we have noted above, the food shortage should have been before the Sabbath Year, i.e. spring 164 BCE. We do not know when exactly the troubles hinted at in the Iamnia inscription occurred, but there can very well be an overlap.

This brings us finally to the famine in question. It happened following upon Judah's death, which was sometime shortly after April 160 BCE.[32] This means that the crop of spring 160 BCE had failed.[33] However, there should have been a reserve from the previous year, spring 161 BCE. If there was a famine then we can assume the previous crop had also been poor. Postulating from our information above we can suggest the following scheme: spring 164 had a poor crop; spring

163 was the end of the Sabbatical Year, no crop; spring 162 perhaps a decent harvest, but we don't have any information on it; spring 161 a poor crop; spring 160 a failed crop.[34] Under these circumstances the population had to turn to some factor that could provide it with the food necessary to survive. What were the alternatives?

Jewish society had a number of institutionalized responses to poverty and need, e.g. לקט, שיכחה, מעשר שני along with a general emphasis on charity which is variously expressed throughout the Bible.[35] We, however, have not found any indication of a prepared institutionalized response to catastrophic situations such as famine. The forms of aid normally in use would have been ineffective when there was very little food to hand out, and no crop to be left for the gleaners.

Meanwhile, as the most thorough study of the subject has shown, the alleviation of food crises in Hellenistic society, although differing in its details from locality to locality, was performed by local men of wealth, who on the whole controlled food production and distribution, and dominated local government.[36] These persons were often honored in civic inscriptions as *euergetes*.[37]

This response, even if it existed in Judea, and there is no evidence that it did in this period, would have entailed turning to the Hellenizers. The rebels of the Maccabean party were not in possession of the grain stocks of the Temple, as small as they may have been by this time. Moreover, as far as the Jewish population was concerned, the Hellenizers were the only ones in position to import the grain that was necessary to relieve the famine. Importation presupposes the ability to make unobstructed purchases, use funds without hindrance, and move goods along the commercial routes. In the period immediately following Bacchides' arrival in Judea, until a number of years later, the Hellenizers seated in Jerusalem, and not the rebels hiding in the desert, were the ones in a position to exercise those operations needed to bring and distribute large amounts of food.

The only alternative left to the population if, as we suppose, it lacked its own infrastructure for famine relief, was to rely on the royal government which operated through its local minions. In Maccabean terms this would be prima facie desertion, and indeed that is one of the meanings of αὐτομόλεω.[38]

Hellenistic kingship ostensibly entailed an active interest in the welfare of the people.[39] There are a number of cases in which Hellenistic kings came to the aid of stricken areas, or expressed a willingness to do so if the need arose. Antigonus wrote to the city of Teos that if the need for grain arose it could be supplied from his own nearby sources.[40] The

Hellenistic monarchs competed with each other in aiding Rhodes after the disastrous earthquake of 227 or 226 BCE (Polybius V 88–9). One should also note the Canopus inscription praising Ptolemy III and Berenice (238 BCE) for importing grain into Egypt in order to relieve a famine (*OGIS* 56,17). While we have as yet no concrete examples of a Seleucid monarch rescuing a starving subject population, we can suppose that they would have acted in the manner expected of Hellenistic kings. We can take some support for this inference from the actions of Seleucus IV in Phocea. Although there he used the existence of a famine in order to interfere in favor of his faction, it was a situation somewhat analogous to that in Judea. A slightly similar case of royal aid might be the material assistance Antiochus III provided the residents of Jerusalem after the city and populace had suffered from the vicissitudes of the Fifth Syrian War.[41]

In the specific case of our episode we should note Bacchides' actions in detail. Upon driving Jonathan out of Judea he built fortified cities and put troops and stores of food in them (I Macc. 9:50–2).[42] Now based on the researches of Briant we know that in the Achemenid monarchy the governor of a province was responsible for the welfare and protection of the farmers, as well as levying taxes on them.[43] Furthermore, the fortresses served as a link between the government and the local population. One of the functions of these fortresses was to serve as a refuge for the peasants.[44] If so, we must assume that they had enough provisions stored in order to supply the populace of the surrounding countryside.[45] These provisions, if sufficient for periods of siege, must have been sufficient for periods of famine. Finally, it has been demonstrated that the relationship between the crown, the local ruler, and the population of the countryside that existed in the Achemenid period continued and carried on into the Hellenistic period.[46]

In consequence we suggest that Bacchides' system of forts served to control the population, not only by their presence as strongpoints, but also as centers from which famine relief could be supplied to the countryside. Furthermore, since Alcimus and the other pro-Seleucid Jews had been placed in control of the country (I Macc. 9:25), they would have been in charge of the import and distribution of the provisions. The famine relief effort would have been an obvious way to garner the support of the people for the pro-Seleucid elements, *vis-à-vis* the now defeated, but popular Maccabees.

Concern for the economic well-being of the people was one of the common ways to gain loyalty, as is evidenced both by the attempts to seduce the Maccabees made by the various Seleucid rivals, and by the importance placed on Simon's contribution to the prosperity of the country as a justification for his leadership.[47] Now in summary let us try to place what we know and what we infer into the framework of Garnsey's ten points. It immediately becomes obvious that in the case of this particular famine we have to admit that we don't know most of the facts. However, analysis, deduction, and some imagination based on what we know about famine situations in general, may help fill out the picture.

The immediate causes of the famine are unknown, although a period of successive drought years is the most likely cause of a massive crop failure. At the same time, we should not rule out the cumulative and deleterious effect of the years of strife on the production and storage of food crops. While admittedly this is purely speculative, as we lack any quantitative evidence, it is also a predictable result of the disarray of the society. Large numbers of farmers either fled their land or were disabled or killed by the punitive actions of the government or their local allies. We would venture to assume that this had a deleterious effect on the agricultural base of the economy.

The geographical range of the famine is also unknown. There is no reason to assume that the famine struck Judea only. Moreover, the characterization of the famine as very great suggests a wide impact. If it had been only a local famine then aid could have been extended from locality to locality, and there would have been no reason to turn to the government.

Palestine's location is a factor in the ease with which famine relief can be extended. This point will be discussed at length later on. Suffice to say that the Land of Israel lies athwart the major land and sea routes connecting the southern and northern parts of the Eastern Mediterranean basin. Additionally, its hinterland is not over-distant from its sea-coast. Also, one should note that to the south lies Egypt, whose grain supply is not dependent on the vagaries of climate that affect Palestine, although in this period one may assume that Egyptian grain was unavailable to Judeans for political reasons. Yet, notwithstanding that, Judea was part of a still very large empire, with diverse agro-climatic conditions. Grain could be supplied to Judea from other parts of the realm.[48]

The famine lasted two years at most. It began in the spring of 161 BCE. A year later Alcimus was still sufficiently sure of himself to order renovations in the sanctuary (I Macc. 9:54). We conclude from this that the populace may still have been dependent on the Seleucids for their needs. When Alcimus died in the spring of 160 BCE, Bacchides left Judea and there was quiet for two years (I Macc. 9:54, 56–7). These two years may comprise the period needed to recover from the effects of the famine, although an alternative explanation could be that the harvest of 160 BCE was also poor. In any event, two years later Jonathan and his supporters became powerful enough to warrant a new expedition by Bacchides with a large force.[49] Moreover, the rebels were able to provision their fortress well enough in order to successfully withstand a siege (I Macc. 9:64–8). Hence, we conclude that either the harvest of spring 159 or of 158 BCE was successful and put an end to the famine. The year 159 seems more likely, because the rebels would have needed time to get organized and become a threat to the Hellenizers.

The price movements are unfortunately not indicated and we have no information on any diseases that struck at this time.

The response of the authorities puts us in touch with the landownership question. We do not know the specific details of the response but it included putting the Hellenizers in charge of the country (I Macc. 9:25) and establishing centers of authority and stocks of food (I Macc. 9:50–2). We may also deduce that they provided seed, otherwise one cannot guess from where the next crop sprung.

The people in response to the famine abandoned the war against the Hellenizers, but apparently only for the duration of the famine.

We do not know who were the victims, other than our ability to draw comparative information from the studies of famine in agricultural societies. The same is true for rates of mortality.

In terms of the landownership situation we can assume that the famine had resulted in a temporary cancellation of the advances which had been made under Judah.

JONATHAN

The rule of the Hellenizers lasted for two years (I Macc. 9:57), but then Jonathan was able to withstand a renewed onslaught by Bacchides. The latter, enraged at the constant frustration of the Seleucid policy, abandoned the Hellenizers to their own resources. Jonathan was powerful enough to control the countryside, but as yet incapable of imposing his will in Jerusalem or on the fortified places of the Hellenizers. This changed when the internal struggle in the Seleucid dynasty forced Demetrius to woo Jonathan with concessions.[50] Then we read, "The foreigners who were in the strongholds that Bacchides had built fled; each one left his place, and went back to his own country" (I Macc.

10:12–13). Jerusalem now became untenable for the Hellenizers except for those in the Akra. The rebels now had the upper hand, and at least in terms of landownership never lost it. With the ascendancy of Jonathan we can begin to chart the course of the Hasmonean state. We can assume that from this point in time till the coming of the Romans, it is the Hasmoneans who will determine the pattern of landownership.

From the outset we must separate the different strands of policy and practice that characterized developments in landownership. We feel that a delineation must be made between land in pre-Hasmonean Judea, and land in the territories that accrued to Judea as a result of concession and conquest.

In Judea, land remained in the hands of the original Judean owners, i.e. the נחלות returned to their traditional proprietors. This was true except for the lands the extreme Hellenizers lost. The Hasmoneans now had these lands at their disposal, as well as the former royal lands.

In the territories that Judea gained there were three types of land-holding: first and foremost, lands owned by gentiles; second, royal lands; third, land held by Jews who were resident in some of these areas prior to their political annexation to Judea. The landholding pattern in these territories would change according to whatever policy was initiated by the Hasmoneans.

Having made these general distinctions, let us now try to establish what we can as to the specific developments. The Hasmoneans themselves were the greatest beneficiaries of the changed circumstances. They received lands formerly belonging to the crown, they were appointed to high imperial positions, which certainly were accompanied by gifts of land, and they acquired land by right of conquest.

We have already shown that in Judea the Hellenizers were dislocated from their lands. We can assume that these were split up among the pro-Hasmonean forces, since that policy had already been implemented in Judah's day (I Macc. 6:24; 7:6) and there is no reason to think that Jonathan would have reversed that policy.[51] We do not know who specifically received these plots, but according to the laws and usages of Hellenistic warfare, the higher ranks would get larger shares of the spoils. It is impossible to corroborate whether that policy was followed in the Hasmonean army. The latter Hasmoneans did seem to reward their higher officers with estates,[52] but it is a pertinent question if that was the policy from the beginning, or a development reflecting the gradual Hellenization of the Judean state.[53] The Hasmonean army had its hierarchy of command and high officials[54] and it should be expected that the commanders filling the positions below the Hasmonean leaders would gain some material reward.[55]

As for the rest of the Judean population, the great aggrandizement in land was a result of the expansion at the expense of the gentiles. At first the expansion was into areas already partially settled by Jews (the three *nomoi* (districts) of Samaria, and perhaps the Perea),[56] but with Judean expansion into the coastal region, Samaria, Galilee, Golan, and the Decapolis, Jewish settlement profited at the expense of the gentile population.

Now returning specifically to the step-by-step examination of developments, Jonathan was proclaimed High Priest by Alexander Balas (I Macc. 10:20) and later designated "Friend of the king, general and governor" (I Macc. 10:65). We have seen repeatedly that favored officials in the Hellenistic kingdoms, certainly in the Seleucid Empire, received estates as part of their emoluments.

Jonathan's major personal acquisition was Ekron, which he received, in the best Hellenistic tradition, as a reward for defeating Alexander Balas' enemies (I Macc. 10:88–9). It is noteworthy that the territory was not awarded to Judea, or to the Temple, or even to the High Priest, as such, but was a κληροδοσία.[57] This meant that there was a substantial increase in the personal fortunes of the Hasmoneans, and moreover those who would receive lands in the new territory from the hand of Jonathan would then be especially beholden to him.

The question of how the land in Ekron and the three districts of Samaria were used obligates us to discuss the theory of Bar-Kochva.[58] He proposes that Judean society suffered from land hunger as a result of a burgeoning population. This lack of land is, according to Bar-Kochva, behind Demetrius I's offer to enroll 30,000 Judeans in his army.[59] Applebaum accepts the basic assumption of landlessness, but diverging from Bar-Kochva, he suggests that the lands made available in Ekron and Samaria were now open to Jewish settlement.[60] Contrary to both Bar-Kochva and Applebaum is the position of Shatzman that there is no reason to assume either an unusually large Jewish population, or a lack of land.[61] We accept Shatzman's view that the figure of 30,000 does not necessarily represent the landless of Judea. There is just not enough evidence to support that contention. However, we cannot agree with Shatzman's skepticism as to the existence of Jewish population pressure. It is true that there is no hard data, but it is also true that from Hecataeus to Tacitus there is a gap of a few centuries and yet the claim of Jewish prolificacy remains constant.[62]

Another outgrowth of Jonathan's acquisition of Ekron is suggested by

Applebaum. He notes that Strabo describes the area of Yavneh as densely populated by Jews.[63] He connects that statement with Jewish settlement in the Ekron region, stemming from Demetrius' grant to Jonathan. He fails to distinguish what that information signifies. Yavneh had a Jewish population which was threatened with extinction (I Macc. 12:8–9). After that we hear of it only as a base for gentile operations against Judea.[64] M. Stern hinted that Strabo used the name Yavneh very inaccurately, and that the intended reference may be to "the Sharon and the toparchy of Lydda."[65] However, assuming that the area of Yavneh is really intended, at sometime between the incursions of Cendebaeus and the time of Strabo's source the area became Jewish. Applebaum would have us believe that it was a result of an earlier settlement of the Ekron region. But Cendebaeus operated during the time of Simon, after Jonathan's rule; so the Jewish settlement of the Yavneh area is not directly connected to Jonathan's acquisition of Ekron.

However, we may still learn something from the fact that Cendebaeus fortified Kedron in order to use it as a base against Judea (I Macc.15:40–1). Kedron is identified as Katra, southwest of Ekron according to Zeitlin, placed northwest of Ekron by Goldstein.[66] We assume that Ekron is Tel Mikne, or in its close vicinity,[67] and so in any case Kedron was west of Ekron. Then we have a situation in which the area of the coastal plain was held by gentiles, while the Shephela was already well in Jewish hands by the end of Simon's reign. This would have to be the case or Cendebaeus would have moved his base of operations further east, into Judea, as previous Seleucid commanders had tried to do. In summary we can assume that there was Jewish settlement in the region of Ekron. Unfortunately, this does not help us a whit in determining what Jonathan did with his land, how much he assigned to others, and on what terms.

While we do not doubt that Ekron was granted personally to Jonathan, we hold that the three districts of Ephraim, Lydda, and Ramathaim were added to the land of Judea. Demetrius II's letter to Jonathan, and to the Jewish people, states that the *nomoi* are added to Judea "for the benefit of all those who offer sacrifice in Jerusalem" (I Macc. 11:30, 34). The question remains what effect this grant had on the landownership situation in the now enlarged Judea. Applebaum, based primarily on Dar's extensive surveys, has proposed that these areas were now settled by Judea's land-hungry population, now grateful to the Hasmoneans for the opportunity they had obtained.[68] It is a gratuitous assumption that the lately acquired region was now flooded by new settlers brought in from old Judea. First, there is no literary proof for such an assumption. Second, the archaeological finds do not provide evidence for the origin of the inhabitants of the area. Third, the prevailing assumption in much of the scholarly literature is that these three districts were already occupied by Jews.

A further point stemming from Jonathan's gains may be the first documented rejection of Maccabean leadership by Jews who were loyal to the Torah.[69] Pesher Habakkuk has a section about the wicked priest who "robbed and amassed the wealth of the apostates . . . and the wealth of the peoples he took. . . . "[70] According to Hengel this refers to Jonathan.[71]

SIMON

When Jonathan's political control of all four regions was confirmed by Antiochus VI (I Macc. 11:57), his brother Simon was appointed governor of the coastal region (I Macc. 11:59). This office must have provided Simon with estates, and the legal power to provide lands to whomever he wished, for we have sufficient examples of Seleucid governors who received land, and granted land themselves.[72] However, did Simon, at that stage, make use of his powers in order to assign land?

In that period Simon conquered the citadel of Beth Zur, and expelled the garrison (I Macc. 11:65–6).[73] What did he do with the inhabitants? Apparently he also expelled them, for in the tribute to Simon (I Macc. 14:7) it is clear that Beth Zur is free of gentiles, and his actions there are associated with his actions at Gezer and the Akra, also places where the gentiles were expelled (I Macc.13:47, 49–50). Yet we should not be quick to assume that Simon used his authority to settle Jews in previously gentile areas in this period. In Jaffa he only placed a garrison (I Macc. 12:33–4), the actual occupation of the city by settlers occurred later (I Macc. 13:11). He built Adida and fortified it, yet there is no mention of settlement (I Macc. 12:38). In fact Gezer was the first case in which a previously gentile settlement was expelled and Jews put in their stead (I Macc. 13:47). However, that happened after Simon was ruler in his own right (I Macc. 13:41–3). It is possible that until Simon felt strong enough he did not expel gentile inhabitants from their own areas, or settle Jews in gentile regions. The case of Beth Zur is not an exception. I Macc. refers to it as part of Judea, in contrast to Gezer and Jaffa (I Macc. 14:33–4).[74]

When Jonathan was entrapped and then executed, Simon began an eight-year period of rule which is summarized in the encomium in I Macc. 14:4–15. This paean to Simon certainly represents the "official line" of the Hasmonean house.[75] Furthermore, it is rife with biblical motifs of "the good king's reign," and as such may justifiably be called a "topos" of the rule of a blessed leader.[76]

Nevertheless, it would be ill-advised to totally discount the evidence of this section, just because it fits a literary pattern.

The description can be analyzed and divided into any number of categories, but for our purposes let us first note that there are statements of specific facts, and there are descriptive general phrases. On the one hand, for example, verse 7 states that Simon reigned over Gezer, Beth Zur, and the Akra. That is a statement of fact, even with some supportive evidence.[77] On the other hand, verse 12 is purely descriptive, echoing a well-known topos.[78] Regarding the "facts" it is evident that Simon undertook a policy which improved the economic base of Judea. One of the first acts praised by the tribute is the annexation and operation of the harbor of Jaffa (verse 5). We have already noted the conquest of Gezer, hence we see that the plaudits for "expanding the borders of the nation and ruling over the land" are based on fact.[79] Under Simon's rule the extent of Jewish settlement was enlarged.[80]

The description of the purification of the land and the successful stand against foreign threats fit the facts as we know them. So we now have to decide what to admit of the claims that Simon provided food for the cities and supported the poor.[81] However, before we address this issue we should point out that in the decision of the *Knesset HaGedolah*, Simon is also praised for arming and paying the nation's forces out of his own pocket (I Macc. 14:32–4).[82]

These two claims are similar in content and purpose; they describe Simon as a rich and powerful benefactor. One must ask if indeed he did the acts ascribed to him, and if he did, where did he get the money to do so?

Applebaum dealt with this question very elegantly. He suggested that the poor were resettled in the newly "liberated" areas, and in the best Hellenistic tradition were provided with aid and benefits until they could establish themselves into viable settlements.[83] Goldstein assumes it is from "the booty from his succesful warfare" that Simon provided for the army.[84] Bar-Kochva is skeptical about the value of this information. He maintains that this claim fits the paradigm of the Hellenistic ruler.[85] Applebaum accepts that plunder provided a part of Simon's wealth, but he suggests that Simon drew the greater part of his resources from land that now was in his possession. He enumerates the personal properties of the Hasmoneans, the royal estates of Judah, and most of all, the three Samarian provinces.[86]

Regarding the first point – whether Simon did arm Judean forces out of his own pocket – we would note the following. Simon was personally wealthy, as explained above, and had access to large sums of money and sources of military equipment because of his position as a high Seleucid official. Let us add to that the fact that he had spent the last twenty-five years as one of the leaders of a rebel army which he had help form, an army largely owing personal loyalty to him and his brothers. We would say that "arming the forces out of his own pocket" is a generous version of the truth. He probably contributed much out of pocket and organized and channeled whatever other funds he could find.

Once in power Simon could take care of the needs of his supporters, and of the country at large. The song of praise summarizes his eight-year rule. He received broad powers in the third year of his rule (I Macc. 14:27).[87] Applebaum suggests that verse 42 might be interpreted to mean that Simon had authority over the countryside, i.e. he had authority over the land.[88] In short, Simon had about five years to allocate lands and estates.

One of the outgrowths of Simon's position as heir to the Seleucids and other kings before them was personal control of royal estates. Gezer was under the governorship of Hyrcanus (I Macc. 13:53; 16:1,19).[89] We would suggest that the fact that his son-in-law was the governor of the fortress of Dok may be tied in to the proximity of Dok to Jericho. The latter, as we have noted previously, was probably a royal estate. Simon would have entrusted it to a loyal manager, such as a member of his family.[90] Unfortunately for Simon, family ties were not a guarantee of loyalty in this case.

JOHN HYRCANUS I

The period of John Hyrcanus I is relatively well documented by the sources.[91] However, they focus on primarily three aspects of his reign: the relations with Antiochus VII Sidetes, the conquest of large areas of Palestine, and the alleged conflict with the Pharisees. Strife and conquest are the main themes of the sources for John's reign. Consequently, on the most superficial level of examination, it appears that we have little to learn about the landholding structure of the nation, or about any problems which may have developed in that aspect of the economy. Nevertheless, a number of deductions can be made from the available evidence. But first let us review in brief the political and military developments of his reign.

His first years were taken up with the struggle against Antiochus VII Sidetes and his henchman Ptolemy Abbus. After coming to terms with Antiochus, and returning from the latter's ill-fated Parthian expedition, Hyrcanus embarked on a series of campaigns of conquest. The motivation for these campaigns, their chronological framework, and method of accomplishment, are not definitely known or understood.[92] The generally accepted view is that Hyrcanus first attacked the area of Transjordan, annexing Medeba. Then Shechem and Mount Gerizm were conquered, followed by Idumea. These last two waves of conquest may have included Apollonia, Jamnia, and Azotus.[93] The next campaign was directed against Samaria, and also brought Scythopolis into the realm.[94]

As we noted in the discussion of Simon's expansion, a Jewish ruler had little leeway to change landholding rights in areas already settled by Jews, because of the societal strictures against depriving families of their *nahala*.[95] However, the more the Hasmoneans captured lands not settled by Jews, the more possibility they had to allocate lands according to their own policies and needs. As a result, the conquest of new areas had three different effects on the landownership structure: (1) some of the gentiles were forced to emigrate, thereby vacating lands which were now available to Jews; (2) some of the gentiles converted to Judaism and were able to acquire land abandoned by emigrating gentiles; (3) the ruling family increased the amount of land it owned directly.

The sources, unfortunately, do not provide details of the exact disposition of each and every addition to the Hasmonean state. However, a number of specific details do enlighten us.

The primary issue is the famous (or infamous, depending on the point of view) accusation that Hyrcanus gave the gentile inhabitants of the conquered territories the choice between conversion to Judaism, or expulsion from their territory.[96] A point to consider is whether the gentiles were actually expelled from their lands, or whether they stayed on as tenant farmers. If the charge of expulsion is established, the changes in landownership in the conquered territories hinge on how much land was "liberated" from the gentiles.

The only source for Hyrcanus' policy of "conversion or expulsion" is *Ant.* 13.257–8. Actually the offer of conversion is noted only in regard to Idumea. In other areas no such condition is laid down.[97] Yet historians assume that Hyrcanus made the same offer everywhere.[98] In Idumea we can assume that much of the Idumean population converted and stayed, but that the Hellenistic residents departed. These were the descendants of the Greeks who had settled in Idumea in the

Hellenistic poleis of Marisa and Adorra, and those natives who had assimilated with them.[99] In support of this assumption we should note the large colony of expatriate Hellenistic Idumeans in Egypt,[100] the appointment of Idumean aristocrats to leading positions in the province,[101] the fact that Pompey left Idumea in Judean hands when his policy was to sever from Judea those areas whose ethnic character was not Jewish,[102] and that recently published archaeological evidence indicates that the city of Maresha was damaged and went into decline after 113 BC.[103] In summary, in Idumea, at least, part of the population emigrated, and the rest probably acquired some land from the abandoned plots.

What evidence is there for movement of Jews from their previous borders in order to occupy "new" lands in the areas conquered by Hyrcanus? Remains of rural settlement in western Samaria confirm that the area called *arei Nebrakhta* was not settled by Jewish colonists till the time of Hyrcanus.[104] Another indication of Hyrcanus' settlement policy may perhaps be found in *Ant.* 13.275 which states that the Samarians attacked the Marisans who were settlers and allies of the Jews.[105]

Bar-Kochva suggests that the large Jewish population in areas such as the coastal plain in the first century AD, and the populousness of the Galilee, are evidence enough of an "intensive" settlement policy during the reigns of Hyrcanus and Yannai.[106] One must accept Bar-Kochva's suggestion because there is no period between the end of Yannai's reign and the first century AD that could be characterized as conducive to mass Jewish settlement in these regions. Certainly there is no evidence of such an event; yet the large Jewish population is a fact, and unless we have a case of population growth ex nihilo, this demographic fact must have its origin in the period of Hasmonean conquest and rule.

Who received the land? First, let us keep in mind that ostensibly much of the demographic pressure on landownership should have been relieved in the days of Simon. There is no evidence for a landownership crisis in the days of John Hyrcanus. There are no records of complaints about debt or famine.

It may be that the Hasmonean ruler allocated lands in a way that gave advantage to certain groups while others gained little or nothing from the wars. This may be the underlying cause of the rift between the Pharisees and Hyrcanus. Levine suggested that the Hasmoneans realized that they needed to base their administration on the socioeconomic elite which generally formed the political elite in Hellenistic states and coopted them into the administration of the kingdom.[107] As we have demonstrated above, the ruling elite of Hellenistic states, and Oriental states as well, received land grants. So a new class of landowners arose which especially benefited from the conquests of gentile areas.

Levine's position would lead us to believe that the Pharisees were opposed to the expansionist campaigns. In contrast, Bar-Kochva demonstrates that the Pharisees were also in favor of the expansionist policy.[108] He asserts that the land settlement satisfied the land hunger of all sections of the Jewish people, but most especially for those who really lacked land, the poorer classes.

The Hasmonean conqueror had no specifically Jewish rule to follow in handing out the new lands. As we said before, it would have been clear that family plots would be returned to their patrimony, but the last Jewish precedent for mass conquest of land was in the period of the Conquest, or in the days of David and Solomon.[109] These were obviously no longer viable patterns of land distribution.

Yet the Hasmoneans already had a pattern they had personally benefited from: the Hellenistic ruler's right to do as he wished with spear-won land. The Hasmoneans, as we have shown above, had received royal lands in Judea. Now lands such as those referred to in the Hefzibah inscription devolved to them as the new rulers of the area.

Unfortunately, we cannot determine what John did with these lands. However, an indication that the tracts were acknowledged as primarily belonging to the Hasmoneans is to be found in Julius Caesar's decision that "as for the villages in the Great Plain,[110] which Hyrcanus and his forefathers before him possessed, it is the pleasure of the Senate that Hyrcanus and the Jews shall retain them with the same rights as they formerly had."[111] We postulate that much of the land taken by conquest was now ostensibly "crown land" owned directly by Hyrcanus or given by him for settlement by Jews (including converts) who paid some sort of rent to the Hasmoneans.

In this vein Applebaum proposed, following Luria, that land in Idumea became crown land, and was leased to tenants. He further suggested that the first abrogation of *Yohanan Kohen Gadol* was issued in order to spare tenants the need to make a false declaration. This edict (*takkana*) (M. Ma'aser Sheni 5:15) canceled the usual declaration by farmers that the tithes had been paid to the Levites (Deut. 26:13).[112]

This interpretation of ours that the conquered lands of Palestine were owned by the Hasmoneans or released to Jewish settlement in return for payment receives some confirmation from *Ant.* 13.273. "[Hyrcanus'] government progressed and flourished greatly during the reign of Alexander Zebinas and especially under these brothers [Cyzicenus and Grypus]. For the war between them gave Hyrcanus leisure to exploit Judea undisturbed, with the result that he amassed a limitless sum of money."[113]

This would help explain the statement in *Ant.* 13.288 that "the envy of the Jews was aroused against him by his own successes and those of his sons," which is followed by the tale of the alleged split between the Pharisees and Hyrcanus. As Schwartz noted, there is no apparent connection between the "envy of the Jews" and the rift as it is described.[114] The Pharisee–Hasmonean breach is beyond the purview of this volume, but it is sufficient to note that from the days of Hyrcanus on there is a pattern of discontentment in the Jewish body politic with the Hasmoneans. For example, could the change of slogan on the Hasmonean coins from the words יוחנן כהן גדול וחבר היהודים ("Yohanan High Priest and the Commonwealth of the Jews") to יוחנן כהן הגדול וראש חבר היהודים ("Yohanan High Priest and the Head of the Commonwealth of the Jews") represent another step in accumulation of power in the hands of the Hasmoneans? An accumulation of power whose economic aspect is the acquisition of large tracts of land and tenants beholden to the ruling house.

JUDAH ARISTOBOLUS I

The period of Judah Aristobolus is both brief and in great part unknown.[115] His reign lasted only a year, and in this time he may have managed to add the Galilee, or some part of it, to the Hasmonean realm. Perhaps more significantly he may have been the first Hasmonean to wear a royal crown. The landownership aspects of his reign are tied in to these two problematic political achievements of his rule.

By converting the Hasmonean house into royalty, Aristobolus laid the basis in Judah for the adoption of the Hellenistic view of the land as the personal possession of the ruler. Schalit states that in their complaint to Pompey (*Ant.*14.41) the people's delegation was referring to the attempt by the Hasmoneans to convert the land into royal land. He lays the charge primarily against Alexander Yannai.[116] Indeed, there can be no doubt that in the brief period of one year, which included a war of expansion in the north, a vigorous foreign policy regarding the poleis, family feuds, and possibly this major constitutional change, it would have been difficult for Aristobolus also to bring the landownership structure of the nation under another form of rule.[117] Yet it is to the constitutional change we must look as the legal and political step which made possible any attempt by the ruler to seize control of the land.[118] Aristobolus' policies earned him the appellation *philhellene*. Scholars are divided as to the reason for this "honor." The new Schürer claims that he favored Greek culture.[119] Kasher explains the title by claiming that Aristobolus' foreign policy favored the Greek coastal cities in their struggle against Iturean expansion.[120] Shatzman credits Timagenes' description of a good ruler as the basis for the praise of Aristobolus. Yet in any case no matter what the specific reason, a Hellenistic tendency on the part of Aristobolus would lead to a concentration of power in the ruler's hands, and, more to the point, a concentration of land under his control.

ALEXANDER YANNAI

The reign of Alexander Yannai is long and eventful in the domestic and foreign spheres. Of all the Hasmonean dynasty he is probably the most well-documented figure, and perhaps the most problematic for the historian. His historical record has given growth to totally divergent appreciations of the man and the ruler. He has been portrayed as a despot and as a national hero.[121] Despite the temptation to discuss the many facets of this Hasmonean, we will try to limit ourselves to those issues relevant to the problem of landownership during Yannai's reign.

Landownership in the Hasmonean kingdom during Yannai's reign is bound up part and parcel with two larger issues. First, his wars against neighboring territories, and second, the nature of Yannai's kingship.

Regarding the wars it is evident that Yannai added extensive areas to the Judean kingdom. However, the question remains as to what use did Yannai put, or intend to put, the conquered areas?[122] Were they to be royal property, or to be granted, leased, or sold to the Jewish population? What was to become of the indigenous residents and their lands? Was he a complete Hellenistic monarch, enjoying the privileges of spear-won land? Or did he in essence remain a Judean king, limited in his powers by the strictures of the Law, the Prophets, and ancient custom?

Some may think that the targets of Yannai's expansion may, by their very nature, suggest the reason for his conquests. Yet his first attempt at expansion already confuses rather than clarifies an understanding of his program. He attacked Acco-Ptolemais.[123] Various reasons have been proposed for this offensive. Some think that Yannai attacked Acco in order to bring to an end the influence of that city in its Galilean hinterland.[124] Others hold that Judean irredentism regarded Acco as one more area that had to be returned to Jewish rule.[125] Finally, there are others who suggest that Yannai wanted Acco as the natural outlet to the sea for the northern part of the kingdom.[126] In fact all of these motives can fit comfortably together. The rest of Yannai's conquests also lend themselves to various interpretations. Schalit, Kanael, and Kasher in their wake believe that Yannai wanted to gain control of international commercial routes which passed through southern Palestine to Gaza, Transjordan, and the northern routes leading from Damascus to the ports of Acco, Tyre, and Sidon.[127]

In fact the purpose of Yannai's policy of conquest is unknown. This much is clear, there is a consistent effort to clear the kingdom of paganism, but that does not demonstrate that all pagans were expelled.[128] It may be that only the public glorification and official religious standing of the pagan cults were discouraged.[129] It is yet to be demonstrated conclusively that a settlement policy was the driving factor behind Yannai's belligerency.

The literary and archaeological evidence has to be sifted for indications, however slim, that Jewish settlement was introduced. Then the question is whether the settlement was on king's land, or whether some other settlement policy was followed. In fact, we must try to determine if any planned and directed policy was followed at all. The simple fact of Jewish settlement is not in itself an indication of a "policy."

The indications for Jewish settlement in the newly conquered territories are all retrospective, i.e. one assumes that a later situation could not have arisen unless Jews had been settled in these areas by Yannai. The most common example of this sort of thinking is the interpretation of Pompey's settlement of Judea.

Josephus writes: καί τὸ σύμπαν ἔθνος, ἐπί μέγα πρότερον αἰρόμενον, ἐντὸς τῶν ἰδίων ὅρον συνέστειλεν.[130] It is the consensus of all works that Pompey tore from Judean control some of the areas conquered by the Hasmoneans.[131] Furthermore, he returned those areas to the gentile population which had lived there previously. Yet large areas which had indeed been taken from the gentiles by the Hasmoneans nevertheless remained under Judean rule. The fact that Pompey left them under Jerusalem's government is considered an indication that, from the time of the Hasmonean conquest till the coming of the Romans, these areas had become predominantly populated by Jews. Galilee and eastern Idumea had become Jewish, else Pompey would have torn them from Judea. The large Jewish population of the Galilee during the first century CE is cited as further evidence of a considerable settlement drive during the Hasmonean sovereignty.[132] In Idumea, Adorra disappeared, indicating that its resuscitation as polis was no longer feasible. In other words the eastern part of Idumea had also been heavily settled by Jews.[133]

Gamla, which was conquered by Yannai, appears to have been consistently inhabited by Jews after its capture.[134] Its fate in the Pompeian settlement is problematic. On the one hand, the city is not mentioned as a reestablishment by Pompey or Gabinius. On the other hand, its geographical location places it in the so-called Decapolis.

Another ex post facto indication of the presence of Jewish settlers is the activity of Hezekias along the northern border of the Galilee. It has been suggested that the bandits led by Hezekias were Jewish farmers who had settled on lands taken from the gentiles by the Hasmoneans and were in turn dispossessed by Pompey.[135]

In addition to these examples, we have Strabo's evidence that the area of Iamnia (Yavne) and the Sharon was able to furnish 40,000 armed Judeans. This source is considered to represent the situation after Yannai conquered the coastal area, but before Pompey tore it from Judean control.[136]

Yet another indication of the possible existence of Jewish expansion during Yannai's reign is the presence of Jewish communities in gentile areas in the first century AD. We have examples of Jewish inhabitants in Dor, Caesarea, Scythopolis, Gerasa, and Iamnia.[137] These areas probably had no Jewish population after the first wave of Jewish–gentile warfare during the early Maccabean period. Therefore, the Jewish population in them was a result either of settlement during Yannai's (or his successors') time, or of internal Jewish migration in Herod's expanded kingdom.[138]

In support of the latter conclusion we have Josephus' statement, that the Syrians claimed that before Herod's time, there "had not been a single [Jewish] inhabitant" in Straton's Tower.[139] In rebuttal one might claim that Yannai initiated Jewish settlement in these areas only to have it undone by the mandate of Pompey, and renewed yet again by Herod.

In summary, up till now, Jewish settlement in the conquered territories appears to have been a fact. Perhaps Avi-Yonah first made the claim, since reaffirmed by other scholars, that the Hasmoneans for the most part did not destroy Hellenistic cities in the physical sense, but instead reinhabited them with Jewish settlers.[140] This has received some confirmation from archaeological findings.[141] However, there are some perplexing anomalies which make it difficult to draw firm conclusions. Strabo mentioned Gaza as a city ruined by Yannai.[142] But the Hellenistic city of Gaza has never been sufficiently excavated to prove or disprove the assertion that it was destroyed. In any case the argument that Gaza was needed by Yannai as a port militates against the physical destruction of the city; as does the rapid recovery and settlement following Pompey's arrangements.[143] Ashdod does show evidence of destruction.[144] Apollonia continued to exist and shows no destruction layer and no significant change in its settlement pattern; although Josephus (*BJ* 1.166) claimed that it was repopulated by Gabinius.[145] Gerasa on the other hand does not show a destruction layer. Shikmona shows a destruction layer from c. 130 BCE. The area is mentioned as a viable landing area during the campaign of Ptolemy Lathyrus against Yannai, although this does not necessarily prove that the city was extant.[146] There is no indication that Yannai made any effort to develop Shikmona, and Strabo lists it as a no-longer existing town.[147] The conclusion must be that there was no single policy for all conquered cities, but that the fate of the polis was determined by a number of different factors. These factors might have been the nature and time of the campaign to take the city,[148] or the cultural environment of the city,[149] or the economic possibilities of the polis. We have seen that Maresha was ruined after Hyrcanus conquered it, while at the same time Beit Govrin began to develop. By the same token one might claim that the port cities of the coast were not kept up in order to encourage the development of Jaffa.[150] The case of Tel Anafa is instructive. According to the archaeological findings the city was prosperous, productive, and a locus of trade on the regional routes of commerce. Nevertheless, the city's existence came to an abrupt halt, probably at the hands of Alexander Yannai.[151] Why weren't its commercial and production facilities put to use by the king, who, we have been told, put such stress on obtaining these very advantages? Since the city was in an agriculturally fertile area we suggest that the city as such was not the focus of interest but its agricultural land.

A similar case may have occurred in Geba (Tel Abu Shusha). According to one interpretation of the archaeological evidence, the site was a Hellenistic polis up till the time of Yannai, when it was destroyed.[152] The area certainly became part of the Hasmonean kingdom.[153] If the polis was ruined and no urban center grew up in its stead, then perhaps we can assume that the area was exploited as an agricultural region. It is intriguing to speculate where the local government and market center was during the period that this Geba was out of use. The nearby Hellenistic fortress found at Kibbutz Shaar Haamakim no longer functioned as a strongpoint. Part of its tower was converted into a ramp, its underground tunnel became filled with debris, while its spring became a regular water-storage cistern, and finally four iron plow shares were found in a storage cache.[154] These findings all are dated between the end of the second century BC and the beginning of the first century BC. In other words about the time that Yannai was on his way to Akko. The discontinuance of the fort probably indicates that there was no longer a threat of hostilities in the immediate area. On the one hand, the border apparently moved, most likely north or northwest. On the other hand, if the area's inhabitants were hostile to the new rulers, then the fort would probably have remained in use. Since it fell into disuse we can conjecture that the population of the vicinity was at least passive if not actively in favor of the new rulers.

One might speculate that Shaar Haamakim served as an agricultural center. Perhaps the findings in Shaar Haamakim and Tel Abu Shusha, and the lack of any nearby urban center, strengthen the argument that the area was converted into a royal agricultural estate. On the one hand, the existence of separate large farms is a general phenomenon of the Hellenistic period.[155] For the same period we have indications of manor farms at Tel Mevorakh and Tel Zeror.[156] On the other hand, in the area of the western Emek the prevalent form of settlement is the village. The area shows no significant increase in the number of settlements in the Hellenistic period, although many settlement locations fell into disuse while others were started. In short, there is no evidence in this region of a vast settlement policy and only a portion of the area may have been royal land.[157]

The questions still remain as to who received the land, and under what conditions. Was there a policy?

Despite the efforts of scholars the fact remains that there is no substantive evidence that all of the conquered lands became royal land. The closest thing to direct evidence is a Delphic statement in one of the Dead Sea documents, Pesher Habakkuk.

Pesher Habakkuk criticizes the evil priest and the last priests in Jerusalem for gathering wealth and plunder from the peoples (8:8–13; 9:4–6):[158]

> Interpreted, this concerns the Wicked Priest who was called by the name of truth when he first arose. But when he ruled over Israel his heart became proud, and he forsook God and betrayed the precepts for the sake of riches. He robbed and amassed the riches of the men of violence who rebelled against God, and he took the wealth of the peoples, heaping sinful iniquity upon himself. And he lived in the ways of abominations amidst every unclean defilement.
>
> Interpreted this concerns the last Priests of Jerusalem, who shall amass money and wealth by plundering the peoples. But in the last days, their riches and booty shall be delivered into the hands of the army of the Kittim.

The problem of identifying historical personages in the Dead Sea documents is notorious, but this is the closest instance of a criticism of what is certainly the Hasmonean dynasty, for personal greed in contravention of biblical strictures.[159] The statement while certainly critical of the Hasmonean greed does not specifically relate to land, and moreover is suspect because of its polemical nature. Despite the generally critical tone of Josephus' narrative, it is clear that Yannai had support among some not inconsequential numbers of the population. The fact is he was greeted with a warm welcome by the "nation" upon his return from the conquests in the Golan and northern Transjordan.[160] Even the Dead Sea documents provide a balance to the negative views of Pesher Habakkuk. Yadin reinterpreted Pesher Nahum and demonstrated that Yannai's actions against the rebels met with approval.[161] Another document found in the Judean desert even has a prayer for the welfare of the king.[162]

Even the proven existence of royal land does not cancel out the possibility that private land existed alongside, or even surrounded by, the former. We have seen that in previous periods private plots existed in the kingdom while at the same time there were also royal lands. This prosaic fact should not be forgotten when dealing with Yannai.

In the same vein, one of the most prevalent theories concerning the Hasmoneans is that they handed out land in return for military service, somewhat like *kleruchies*.[163] This theory although attractive has no substantiation in the sources. The archaeological data are also inconclusive. While it may be demonstrated that some areas received an infusion of new settlers, other areas show the opposite. For example, the area of Tel Michal knew a Hasmonean presence which could only be from the time of Yannai, yet the population of the area decreased.[164] In any case the evidence for settlement does not prove or disprove the contention that the lands were parceled out in return for military service.

Some recent archaeological findings may at last shed light on the question of Yannai's policy in the new territories. The area of the Upper Galilee was probably added to the Judean state by Yannai, certainly it was annexed no earlier than the days of Judah Aristobolus. The Rehov inscription which describes the most expanded borders of the Judean state is thought by some to reflect the situation in the days of Herod the Great. We would suggest that it probably reflects the period of Yannai.[165] This is further substantiated by the findings in Hirbet Tefen, which show that the border of the northern Galilee moved north during the later Hasmonean period.[166] Lately, it has been shown that in the Upper Galilee the gentile inhabitants were replaced by Jewish settlers, that these newcomers settled only in villages, and that they brought with them on a large scale the technology of olive oil agriculture.[167] The olive was a staple crop and a mainstay of Judean export commerce. It would have been logical to expect that the royal government would encourage the spread of a profitable industry to its new areas. Alternatively, we might speculate that the influx of new settlers was not orchestrated by the crown, and that the introduction of a new crop, the attendant processing technology, and infrastructure were all the fruit of individual or group initiative. The second alternative is less likely because private initiative on a large scale is just not a characteristic of Jewish society in this period. Let us also recall other areas of Hasmonean expansion. From Beit Zur, through Gezer, Jaffa, and northeastern Samaria, all the Jewish expansion was managed by the Hasmonean rulers.

In summary up to this point, Yannai settled Jews in the conquered lands, no poleis were established, some urban centers were destroyed, the land becoming agricultural. Only part of the area was allocated as royal land. We do not know what portion became king's land, but the large number of villages, the tie to the land, and the popular support of some of the people favor the conclusion that Yannai encouraged settlement of private lands as well as royal estates.

The problem of landownership under Yannai is not limited to the areas which were conquered by him and added to the kingdom. We must also seek to determine if there was any special policy regarding the lands already under Judean control. This question is tied into the greater question of the civil war of Yannai's reign. Much has been written on the subject, and much of what has been written is logical, sensible, predictable.

In brief, the oft-mentioned reasons for the hostility are: the High Priesthood of Yannai was objectionable because the Hasmoneans were not of the Oniad branch. Likewise a warlike and bloody High Priest offended religious sensibilities.[168] Similarly, there are those who claimed that the secularization of the state was a disappointment for which Yannai must be blamed. The many wars with their concomitant casualties, cruelty, and costs are thought to have been the cause of resentment; as was the presence of gentile mercenaries within the Jewish state.[169] The supposed abolition or curtailment of the Sanhedrin might have been another reason for the strife.[170] Then there are those who suggest that the cooption of the Sadducees into the ruling circle was the source of the problem.[171] Finally, the monarchy itself is thought to have been at fault.[172] Yannai is alleged to have raised a host of enemies because he usurped the Davidic title. Furthermore, his kingship was allegedly extremely Hellenistic, rife with symbols and policies in direct contradiction to the religious–political norms of Jewish society in Judah.[173] All these reasons have been used either individually, or often in conjunction with each other.

Unfortunately, most of these reasons have not been sufficiently substantiated. Reliable sources simply do not provide a cause for the hostility against Yannai. This lacuna has provided an opportunity for scholars to raise speculations about the "real" source of the conflict.

In this regard the issue is related to the question of Yannai's monarchy. The prevalent view is that of Schalit, who has been supported by Applebaum. In brief, Schalit's theory is that Yannai, while creating a Hellenistic kingship, also attempted to enforce the concept of royal land on the country. He claimed all the land as his, took the best lands for royal estates, gave lands to deserving servants of the crown, and tried to convert the free farmers into royal tenants.[174]

The evidence to support this contention is tenuous at best. It is based on the following points in the sources. First, alongside the delegations representing Aristobolus II and Hyrcanus II, which appeared before Pompey in Damascus, there was a third group representing the "people." This group complained that they wished not to be ruled by a king, and that the Hasmonean brothers were trying to change the form of government and turn them into slaves.[175] This incident has been discussed by scholars who use it to justify various theories regarding the political and social framework of the late Hasmonean dynasty.[176]

The other major support for the view that Yannai tried to apply the concept of royal land to his kingdom is found in the rabbinic traditions about הר המלך = *Har ha-Melekh*, also translated as "King's Mountain Country."

Applebaum is the leading exponent of the idea that *Har ha-Melekh* was an area primarily from Lydda to Tulkerem-Shechem, and perhaps the border of the Hefer Valley that was created by the Hasmonean conquests. "The first mention of *Har ha-Melech* is in connection with Yannai (BT Gittin 57a)." Although he notes that most of this area was conquered by Yannai's predecessors, he maintains that Yannai's conquests led him to espouse the idea of Hellenistic conquest and motivated him to claim ownership of the conquered areas. Furthermore, the name *ha-Melekh* indicates to Applebaum that the land belonged to a king and that since Yannai was the first and most important king of the dynasty, this shows that he somehow tried to organize the land in a new way.[177]

Applebaum repeats the basic points raised by Luria who uncritically accepts the talmudic sources and has spent much effort in trying to reconstruct the exact borders of *Har ha-Melekh* in Yannai's day.[178]

Bar-Kochva, while not delving into the question, also accepts the connection between *Har ha-Melekh* and Yannai. He too appears to lay the emphasis on the coincidental name *ha-Melekh*.[179]

Avi-Yonah thought that the area was Judah, based on the coincidence that there is a toparchy called "Orine," which means mountain, and that the Orine is in Judah.[180] This runs into the problem that there is no evidence whatsoever that Yannai expropriated the area surrounding Jerusalem to himself. Furthermore, if any credence is at all given to the rabbinic traditions, *Har ha-Melekh* is never listed as Judah.

Goodman subtly denies the value of the sources and then accepts their evidence. He writes, "The evidence is in fact tenuous . . . According to an early third-century AD . . . text portions of the Judaean hills were known colloquially as the 'Mountain of the King'." He notes that "The only explicit evidence to link royal ownership with the late Hasmoneans is, however, a quite fantastic tale about King Yannai preserved in a collection of boastful stories about the distant past that is quoted in the fifth-century AD Babylonian Talmud (BT Gittin 57a)." Nevertheless he concludes that "there is no evidence of Herodian or imperial Roman land in this area, so the name probably derives from an earlier period."[181]

Klein was a pioneer in maintaining that the *Har ha-Melekh* traditions changed over a long period of time, refer to different areas, and that the "ha-Melech" probably originally referred to Ptolemaic estates.[182] Later, Alon also noted that the expression *Har ha-Melekh* is not at all clear, and that scholars are divided on the issue. He argued that it may sometimes refer to a specific place, but then at other times to an area.[183]

However, it was Efron who demonstrated that the whole framework of Yannai–*Har ha-Melekh* is nothing less than late traditions used to illustrate points irrelevant both to Yannai and to the question of royal land.[184]

We think that in light of the late provenance of the *Har ha-Melekh* traditions, their fantastic nature, and the lack of any corroborative material, they cannot be used to reconstruct Yannai's policy on landownership.

In summary on Yannai, there is no provable connection between landownership and domestic problems during his reign. Likewise there is no indication of indebtedness or exploitation. It would be convenient if we could tie Yannai's rocky relations with the Jewish society of his day to some sort of landownership policy, perhaps excessive taxation leading to loss of *nahalot*. However, the unpalatable truth is that there is nothing, but nothing to support any allegations of that sort. On the other hand, we can confirm that Jews did settle in large new areas, and that there is a likelihood that just as the general Jewish population acquired new lands, so did the crown.

SHLOMZION

Shlomzion (Salome) Alexandra replaced her husband as the ruler of the Judean kingdom.[185] Her reign is remembered in Jewish tradition as a period of peace and prosperity.[186] In her realm the only discordant note was the enmity between the Pharisees who were now the leading royal advisers, and those commanders who had been Yannai's henchmen.[187] To protect them from the vendetta waged by the Pharisees, the queen gave these men her fortresses.[188] We suppose that these responsibilities carried with them gifts of land. The sources do not support a firm conclusion, but the Hasmonean kingdom was much Hellenized, and the precedents for gift land are strong.

The queen's reign ended in civil war, but nothing about that war indicates that it was about landownership. Both her sons had supporters who were large landowners, and it is conceivable that both brothers had supporters among the small farmers (*BJ* 1.153). Nothing of significance occurred in the landownership relations in Judah until the Roman conquest. However, there was a food crisis with the accompanying price rises of grain. This food crisis demonstrates the direct link between natural disasters and the price of basic foods.

The famine

During the last days of Shlomzion there was a civil war between the Hasmonean brothers Aristobulus II and Hyrcanus II. A food crisis is mentioned by Josephus in connection with this war.[189] He relates that while Aristobulus was besieged in Jerusalem his opponents tried to have him cursed by Onias (Honi HaMaagel). When the holy man refused he was stoned to death. Later on, the besiegers thwarted the attempts of the besieged to conduct the Passover sacrifices. For these impieties the crops of the entire country were destroyed (*Ant.* 14.25–8).

We should mention in passing that Amusin and Dupont-Sommer suggested that the drought referred to in the Honi HaMaagel tales is identical with the famine mentioned in 4QpHos[a] (4Q166).[190] However, the Honi story is a miracle-worker fable, the point of the story is that the holy man averts the drought, and saves the day; it cannot therefore be a famine story. Furthermore, the drought that Honi ended had to have occurred at some time previous to the war, while 4QpHos[a] 2:12–13 suggests that the famine occurred after the Jews had called for help from the gentiles. That can mean either the Nabateans, or the Romans, but must refer to a time during the war. We conclude that the Honi story is irrelevant, other than its demonstration of how greatly drought was feared.

Nevertheless, some sort of food crisis occurred during the time of the civil war, or Pompey's conquest of Judea. We have already cited Josephus' evidence and we will examine it further, but first let us also note the other evidence indicating that there was a food crisis. A number of texts from the Dead Sea Scrolls mention famine, and also allude to the Romans.[191] Likewise the Psalms of Solomon may refer to a famine around the time of Pompey's invasion.[192] The Dead Sea Scrolls are notoriously difficult to date, nevertheless there is a significant body of opinion which dates these texts to the second half of the first century BCE.[193] Taken as a whole, all these indications justify accepting Josephus' basic claim that there was a food crisis.

The famine was caused by a πνεῦμα πολὺ καὶ βίαιον ("a mighty and violent wind") sent by God which destroyed the crops of the entire country (*Ant.* 14.28). The wind is a punishment for the bad faith shown by the supporters of Hyrcanus. Since we are not concerned here with theology or the history of religions we will ignore the last mentioned aspect of Josephus' tale.[194] What concerns us is if a wind could have destroyed the crops of the entire country, or a significant portion of them.

Let us state categorically that strong winds can and do damage crops severely. Fruit trees are very adversely affected because the fruit is blown to the ground where it rots. The effect on grain is to flatten the stalks before the grain can ripen fully, thus preventing further development of the plant. Barley is harvested earlier than wheat. In fact, the barley in Palestine was harvested in time for the bringing of the Omer at a time when the wheat, although well advanced, was still not ripe.[195] The wind described by Josephus came just after or during Passover, during the period when strong winds can do the most damage to both crops.

What wind would have such a powerful effect? On this question we flutter between the realm of possible meteorological conditions and the world of faith and theology. Josephus has used the word *pneuma* which has a connotation of spirit as well as wind. In fact we found only one instance in which Josephus uses the word to indicate wind in the sense of the natural movement of air without any suggestion of supernatural interference (*BJ* 3.422). He may have been influenced by the Hebrew term רוח (*ruah*) which also has the meaning of spirit, and has been used to indicate the wind as God's agent.[196] The Bible records strong destructive winds, but calls them סופה (*supha*) or סערה (*sa'ara*). The former is considered by Baly to be the whirlwind, however investigation shows that whirlwinds only occur close to the seashore, and in the beginning of the rainy season.[197] *Supha* is never translated as *pneuma*,[198] *sa'ara* is also a poor suspect as the culprit. It is often used in conjunction with *supha* or with *ruah*, giving it a literary effect rather than a description of a weather phenomenon. Also it is rarely translated as *pneuma*.[199]

Lacking any other evidence we propose that some powerful wind out of the eastern deserts may have damaged the crops of spring 65 BCE causing a food shortage.[200] The wind would not have been powerful enough to destroy the crops of the whole country, that is obviously an embellishment by Josephus, but severe damage around Jerusalem or in the Judean countryside would be enough to skyrocket prices.

We may perhaps assume that since the shortage was caused by wind damage and that after all grain was available, the area affected was not wide. The story centers around Jerusalem and we may surmise that the eastern areas of Judea were most involved.

Since the damage was probably limited in range of impact, and was by its nature singular and not repeated the next year, and there was grain available so that a seed supply was ensured, we suggest that the crisis did not last for more than a year.

Josephus states that the people had to pay eleven drachmas for a modius of wheat (*Ant.* 14.28). The drachma in use in Judea was the Tyrian drachma.[201] Josephus is probably referring to a basic or Italian modius, since by the time he wrote the *Antiquities* he had more than enough opportunity to learn the common weights, thus we are dealing with 8.62 liters of wheat for 66 obols. Jeremias estimates that the price increased by about sixteen times its normal level.[202] He, like the others who have tried to deal with wage and price levels, has resorted to a mixed bag of information coming from literary sources that represent different origins in time and circumstance.[203] Were we to blindly accept these figures we would also have to accept that the daily wage and the basic price of bread retained their original levels from the end of the Hasmonean kingdom c. 63 BCE until the canonization of the Mishnah c. 200 CE, i.e. in an interval of more than a quarter of a millennium which included significant and wide-reaching developments in politics, society, and economics.

The only evidence we have so far for prices or wages from the first century BCE in Judea is a list of daily wages inscribed on the lid of an ossuary.[204] The wages there run from a low of one obol to a high of four drachmas.[205] Hence the lowest paid man could buy only c. 130 g. of wheat while the highest paid could buy c. 3.13 kg. Naturally, these numbers are theoretical and only illustrative, first because we have no way of confirming Josephus' figures, and second, wages would decrease in time of famine.[206] However, if we examine the caloric value of the amount of wheat one could buy even under these circumstances we see that we are dealing with a food crisis and not a famine.[207]

We suggest that the damage to the crops was local, that food was available in the stocks, and that more food could be brought from other areas not over-distant from the scene of the shortage. The fear of real famine drove prices up, an effect documented time and again in many places and times, but food was available to those with means. Note that in the spring of 65 BCE immediately following the alleged destruction of crops, Scaurus did not entertain any illusions about his ability to conquer Jerusalem, for he chose to scare away the Nabateans rather than try his strength with the fortress (*Ant.* 14.31). Had the Judeans been starving they could not have withstood a siege. There is also no mention of food supply problems with relation to Pompey's invasion of Judea and the siege of Jerusalem in 63 BCE, and by 62 BCE Hyrcanus was sending grain to Scaurus (*Ant.* 14.80).

Unfortunately, we have no information on the other parameters of the food crisis, i.e. the incidence of disease, the response of the authorities, the behavior of the people, or the number and categories of victims.

Nevertheless, we should consider what effect a steep rise in grain prices might have. The freeholding farmers would probably manage quite well. Those farmers who had large reserves could speculate, hoarding grain and then selling it at the highest prices. Josephus refers to this practice and, as we noted, reports a food crisis price of eleven drachmas. A predictable result of this situation is that some land-holders, especially the large landholders who had large reserves from previous years, would realize a large profit. However, what about the small cultivators? Despite the popular consensus that small freeholders, lessees, and tenant-farmers would now be forced into debt, or slavery, because they could not meet their obligations (rents, religious dues, taxes), we believe that their situation would not be significantly changed.[208] The practice of storing grain for a reserve year would be a buffer against immediate starvation, and would also provide enough for seed. The rents would only affect the lessees, who undertake to pay a fixed amount. The tenant-farmer (*aris*) was obliged to pay a percentage of the crop: if his yield was low, so was his payment.[209] We shall return to this question in a later chapter.

6

THE EARLY ROMAN PERIOD

THE CONQUEST

Pompey's great expedition to the east brought the Hasmonean kingdom to an end. Pompey reduced the borders of Judah to encompass Judah, Idumea, the Galilee, and the Jewish Perea. The Hellenistic cities of the coast, the Jordan Valley, Golan, and Samaria were liberated from Judean rule and reestablished as poleis. Aristobolus II was removed from his throne, and Hyrcanus II reinstated as ruler, but only as the High Priest, not as a king.[1]

How did this turning point in Jewish history affect landownership and related questions? The answer lies in three aspects of the Pompeian settlement: first, the status of Judea within the Roman Empire; second, the direct effects of Pompey's changes of Judea's borders; third, the internal changes in the Jewish society resulting from the war against the Romans.

It is not precisely clear what Judea's status was within the framework of the Roman Empire. The majority of scholars avoid the issue entirely, others see Judea as a conquered client state, while others suggest that it was somehow part of the Province of Syria.[2]

Sherwin-White pointed out that in fact Rome had not conquered Judea in war.[3] If she had there was a possibility that Judean land would have become *ager publicus*,[4] although Roman policy did not mandate the confiscation of land. Cicero claimed that the Romans very frequently restored their property even to foreign enemies whom they had conquered.[5] Instead one may propose that the Judean situation was closer to that of Pontus. There some of the land was granted to local dynasts, such as Archelaus, who received the priesthood of the temple state of Comana with a great accession of land. The rest of the land was assigned to the new city territories.[6] In Judea also, Pompey granted lands to the rehabilitated Hellenistic cities and left the Jewish area to the control of Hyrcanus the High Priest.

Judea was burdened with a tribute to Rome,[7] but we know of no indications that there were any other taxes.[8] How was the tribute collected? One possibility is that the revenue-collecting infrastructure of the Hasmonean state gathered the money as in the past. Another possibility is that the Roman publicani offered their services.[9] This would fit the usual pattern of events in countries conquered by Rome. The publicani would try to gain the right to raise the money. In order to pay the publicani the locals would mortgage their property, and if they failed to raise the requisite amount, the publicani would foreclose.[10]

Our evidence for the activities of the publicani in Judea comes from a contemporary account by Cicero:[11]

> Iam vero publicanos miseros . . . tradidit in servitutem Iudaeis et Syris . . . Statuit ab initio, et in eo perseveravit ius publicano non dicere; pactiones sine ulla iniuria factas rescidit; custodias sustulit; vectigalis multos ac stipendiarios liberavit.

> Then, too, there are those unhappy revenue-farmers . . . he handed them over as slaves to Jews and Syrians. . . . From the beginning he made it a rule, in which he persisted, not to hear any suits brought by revenue farmers; he revoked agreements which had been made in which there was no unfairness; removed guards; released many imposts or tribute.

This well-known diatribe is directed against Gabinius, whose rule we will presently discuss. It assumes that until Gabinius' rule the publicani were operating freely.[12] Two items mentioned, the *vectigalia* and the *stipendia*, were payments for which the publicani were responsible. Unfortunately, we do not know what the difference between the *vectigalia* and the *stipendia* really was.[13] It is possible that the term *vectigalia* designates taxes of various kinds derived from public lands and other properties such as mines or salt works.[14] *Stipendia*, according to a tentative suggestion of Rostovtzeff, might have been payments of "a certain quantity of grain and money calculated probably on the normal yield of the Hellenistic and Hasmonean land-tax and other taxes."[15] If this is so, then the *stipendia* would probably have been based on the *phoros* of the Hellenistic and Hasmonean rulers, since this was the basic tax on land.[16] The *pactiones* were the agreements between the city (or state) which was under obligation to pay taxes, and the publicani who collected the taxes and acted as surety for their payment.[17]

We can assume that all the accusations relate to Syria, which was a province, with all the taxes that status entails. But the speech also specifically mentions Judeans, but we cannot know which of the complaints is relevant to Judea. Rostovtzeff was convinced that the *stipendium* was the *phoros* which Pompey levied on Judea.[18] However, we believe that the publicani had not fully come into play in Judea. We suggest that Hyrcanus and the Judean nobles loyal to him were able to organize the payment of the *phoros*, or most of it. Let us note that in the administration of Scaurus it is Antipater who acted as the surety for Aretas' payment, it was not the publicani (*Ant.* 14.81). Schalit believed that the publicani were not very interested in Judea at first because the country had become impoverished during the civil war and the Roman conquest.[19] This seems far-fetched because Pompey had not looted the country; and despite the civil war it was capable of rapid regeneration as the repeated exactions of later Roman governors demonstrate. Likewise, Hyrcanus and Antipater were able to furnish the needs of Scaurus' army.

We can only speculate why the publicani did not become a major presence in Judea in the years following the Roman conquest. Perhaps the sudden opening of so much territory (Syria and Judea) delayed the full effect of their operations. Similarly, the re-birth of many Hellenistic cities in the fertile and commercially valuable regions which were now sundered from Judea and assigned to Syria, made those areas more attractive to the publicani than the relative backwaters attached to Judea.

This leads us to the second effect of Pompey's arrangements, tearing away large areas and liberating Hellenistic cities from Judean rule.[20] This had at least two effects on the land tenure situation. Large numbers of Jews were now landless and possibly homeless. For example, Jews had resided in Straton's Tower since Yannai's conquest of the city, but years later the gentiles would claim that there were no Jews in the city until after Herod's foundation of Caesarea (*Ant.* 20.173). This indicates that the Jews of Straton's Tower departed, probably because of the polis' re-birth in the wake of Pompey (*BJ* 1.156–7). Likewise, Pompey's actions may have created the conditions which spawned the activities of Ezekias.[21] Similarly, some Jews may now have found themselves resident in gentile-controlled areas. Strabo mentions that the Carmel, the Forest (the Sharon), and Iamnia once belonged to the Jews. Yet although these areas were cut off from Judean control the Carmel provided Jewish supporters to Antigonus.[22]

Another significant result of Pompey's order must have been a drastic diminution in Hasmonean revenues.[23] Hyrcanus lost a large part of his territory so that income from taxes on agriculture had to have declined. Similarly, he lost control over all his port cities, and his caravan cities of the eastern borders. Thus, he must have been deprived of duties levied on trade and commerce.

In addition Hyrcanus, although "pro-Roman" in the context of the struggle between Aristobolus and Pompey, lost personal territories. The area of Lydda, Ekron, the Jezreel Valley, all ended up outside his domain. Thus, personally, he may have become poorer.[24]

How did these losses affect the land tenure situation in the lands still under Jewish rule? We can only hypothesize that the financial burden on the landholders became heavier. Did the financial pressures created by Pompey's actions contribute to the rebellions of the 50s? We assume so, but lack the sources to prove our supposition.

Another aspect of the landholding situation was created when Aristobolus' initial war failed. The leaders of the revolt were executed (*BJ* 1.154; *Ant.* 14.73). We assume that they were punished by expropriation of their property.[25] It is reasonable to assume that some of the executed nobles owned estates in the areas now torn from Judean rule. These estates were simply lost, probably passing to the reconstructed Hellenistic centers. The estates in Jewish-ruled territory of executed rebels had to go to some other owner. One likelihood is that the lands went to some other member of the family who was not stained by anti-Roman or anti-Hyrcanian actions. Another prospect is that some loyal noble, such as Antipater, benefited from the change. Yet another possibility is that the estates devolved to the High Priest Hyrcanus. There is no indication that any land went directly to Roman ownership.

GABINIUS

We suggest that the period of Gabinius, the Roman governor of Syria (57–55 BCE), was a major step in the development of the basic framework of landownership and taxation that existed until Herod's accession to the throne. Most studies of the period emphasize the rise of Antipater and his sons. However, in many respects the period is characterized by the rule of elements of essentially the same Hasmonean aristocracy that had existed prior to the coming of the Romans. True, Antipater and his sons became the dominant personalities, but as late as 43 BCE a major Judean aristocrat such as Malichus could still entertain hopes of displacing the Idumean nobles.[26] We maintain that although the adherents of Aristobolus had been defeated, and the more extreme opponents of the Romans had been executed in the wake of the Roman conquest (*BJ* 1.154; *Ant.* 14.73), yet many of the native aristocrats had remained alive and in positions of influence. This native aristocracy gained importance as a counterweight to the revolutionary elements of the Judeans, and as an acceptable administrative alternative to the otherwise necessary publicani.

In the years following the Roman conquest the publicani had tried to get their talons into the economic body of Judea.[27] At first, the *negotiatores* were evidently not strongly entrenched in the economy because Scaurus needed Hyrcanus and Antipater to provide grain to his army (*BJ* 1.159; *Ant.* 14.81). But by 57 BCE the Roman presence in Judea had become sufficiently strong to prevent Alexander from capturing Jerusalem. This Roman presence was able to withstand one attack, but it might also have been responsible for provoking the outburst of violence. The increasing presence of the publicani in Judea was possibly the trigger which set off Alexander's revolt. On the one hand, this rebellion provided ample incentive to the Romans to strengthen the pro-Hellenistic base in Palestine.[28] On the other hand, the Romans also needed a native Jewish leadership which would counter-balance the forces urging revolt. This counter-balance existed in the Hyrcanian party. For example, the force which defeated Alexander included Jewish soldiers led by three prominent nobles of the Hyrcanian party: Peitholaus, Malichus, and Antipater. The existence of a native aristocracy amenable to Roman rule provided a new option for dealing with the situation in Judea.

After this victory Gabinius divided Judea into five districts called *sanhedria*. This reorganization is a subject which raises more questions than answers.[29] Its purpose, detailed operation, and duration are all problems that await solution.[30] However, the *sanhedria* are relevant to two aspects of interest to us: taxes and land tenure.

Based upon the previously quoted passage by Cicero, it has been suggested that Gabinius abolished the tax-gathering of the publicani and substituted direct taxation by Jewish authorities.[31] Specifically, he was accused of revoking agreements made by the publicani, removing guards, canceling taxes and tributes, and generally preferring the Jews to the publicani.[32] Smallwood saw that the collection of taxes directly by Jewish councils may indeed have been one of the tasks of the *sanhedria*.[33] She suggested that the direct collection of taxes would have mitigated any bitter feeling resulting from the new organization.[34] Furthermore, she noted that Julius Caesar's order of 47 BCE assumed that the Jews collect and hand over their own taxes.[35] Braund tried to refute these views by claiming that Cicero did not specifically accuse Gabinius of expelling the publicani.[36] That observation is valid but does not refute Cicero's explicit and bitter attack on Gabinius for limiting the activities of the publicani in Judea and Syria. Stern cogently noted that Gabinius' reform may have brought relief from the more extreme depredations of the publicani, whose excesses were commonplace. He stated that this would have been in keeping with the generally humane rule of Gabinius, who did not execute any of the Hasmonean rebels.[37]

Gabinius created the *sanhedria* after the rebellion and defeat of Alexander. The *sanhedria* are described as ruled by an aristocracy. This has been interpreted to mean that the *sanhedria* were run by priests.[38] This view appears to us too limiting. Indications of who or what this aristocracy was can be inferred from the fact that Peitholaus was ὑποστράτηγος in Jerusalem.[39] Peitholaus was also one of the major figures among the Jewish leaders who helped defeat Alexander. We suggest that the aristocracy which ruled the *sanhedria* was composed of the social–economic elite which had supported Hyrcanus. Certainly it included priests, but it also included secular leaders who filled political and military positions. Shatzman has pointed out that the faction of Aristobolus II had "widespread loyalty" from those who had benefited from the Hasmonean state in the past, and who now had lost their wealth. However, it may be significant that in the rebellion of 56 BCE Aristobolus only managed to recruit some 8,000 armed men and that many[40] of his supporters were unarmed.[41] From this we conclude that many of the wealthy landowning elements were loyal to the new regime, but significant numbers of the poorer strata were willing to support the former ruler. We have noted above that Pompey's reorganization of Palestine led to wide-scale displacement of Jews. The contribution of this landlessness to the support of the abortive rebellions of the 50s has been widely discussed. However, we suggest that the other side of the coin has not been sufficiently stressed. The Romans had intervened in a civil war on the side of one of the participants. The Hyrcanus faction also included aristocrats and simple farmers (*BJ* 1.153). The five *sanhedria* all had a veteran Jewish population, which essentially was not dislocated by the Romans. The actions of the publicani may have begun a corrosive process, which Gabinius diverted by limiting the publicani's activity. What could Cicero mean by his accusation other than that Jewish elements were filling the roles the publicani usually played? For example, when Gabinius made his excursion to Egypt, once again Antipater and Hyrcanus were major suppliers for the army. We do not hear of the activities of the publicani who generally supplied Roman armies.

An indication of the measure of Gabinius' success, and the effectiveness of the Jewish aristocracy of the *sanhedria*, can be gained from Alexander's second rebellion (55 BCE). In general terms it is stated that Alexander was killing Romans in the country, but the only specific concentration of Romans mentioned are those who took refuge on Mount Gerizm (*Ant.* 14.100). This could be an indication that Romans were present in the country, but not concentrated in the five Jewish *sanhedria*. Next, it is noted that Antipater succeeded in dissuading elements of the population from joining Alexander. This could be discounted as Nicolaus' hyperbole, but if Antipater had not succeeded in being of some major use there would have been no reason for Gabinius to appoint him ἐπιμελητής of the Jerusalem *sanhedrion*.[42]

The existence of this position also demonstrates that the publicani were neutralized in the Jewish districts. Because the *sanhedria* ostensibly had the political power, then the ἐπιμελητής was a financial office.[43] Henceforth, we see that the Jewish aristocracy remains responsible for tax collection in Jewish territory. Gabinius' policies made it possible for the Hyrcanian party to survive as the arbiters of Judea's political and economic life.

JOHN HYRCANUS II

Crassus

Crassus, the triumvir, came to Syria as governor in 54 BCE. To prepare for his adventure into Parthia he seized the money of the Temple.[44] The money in the Temple treasury had attracted greedy hands before, and would so again.[45] Josephus states that 2,000 talents were commandeered by Crassus.[46] Curiously, this is the same amount that was supposedly in the Temple when Pompey magnanimously did not loot the Temple (*BJ* 1.152; *Ant.* 14.72). After a period of nine years the amount had remained the same; this despite the large amounts of money that should have poured into the sacred treasury.[47]

There is no way to ascertain why the fund did not grow. We would suggest that there were heavy expenses involved in repairing the damage to the Temple and Jerusalem brought about by the Roman siege and conquest. According to the Mishnah these funds could be used for such purposes.[48]

Josephus claims that there was no public treasury besides God's (*Ant.* 14.113). This is probably hyperbole to blacken Crassus' image and to strengthen the impression that the Jews are a holy people. Indeed, there can be no doubt that the Jewish state had some sort of governmental funds, although it has even been claimed that the Temple treasury was part of the revenues of the state.[49] This is probably wrong. While we do not know the details of the state treasury, we can assume that even the Hasmonean priestly rulers kept the Temple monies separate from state monies. The effort and importance attached to the Judean desert fortresses spring also from their importance as treasure-stores.[50] Shlomzion Alexandra kept her treasures in Alexandrium, Hyrcania, and Machaerus (*Ant.* 13.417). Aristobolus raised an army with the money he found in the fortresses (*BJ* 1.117). Herod also used fortresses for his money (*BJ* 2.17; *Ant.* 17.223). Certainly, Herod had a separate treasury from the Temple's. In any case, Crassus' only known depredations in Judea fell on the Temple.

Crassus led his forces to one of the more notorious defeats in Roman history. Cassius, his quaestor, survived the debacle in Parthia in time to return to Syria and put down a revolt led by Peitholaus. Incidental to this, he supposedly sold 30,000 Tarichaeans into slavery. This figure is extremely large for a small fishing town. We can assume that it is either an exaggerated figure, or represents inhabitants of the surrounding region, or both.[51] In any case one can only wonder how the loss of so many men affected the economic life of the region because we have no further information on this episode.

Julius Caesar

The next major change in the land tenure situation of the Jews in the Land of Israel was the return of large areas of the country to Jewish control. Julius Caesar rewarded Hyrcanus and Antipater with a series of decisions and decrees regarding personal and political privileges.[52] The texts are problematic. Nevertheless, there are aspects relating to land and taxes that interest us in these documents. In general, the edicts guaranteed the security of the possessions of the Jews against arbitrary depredations and exactions.[53] The port city of Jaffa was returned to Jewish control.[54] It is possible to read *Ant.* 14.206 so that one understands that the inhabitants of the territory of Jaffa were to pay tribute to Hyrcanus and his sons.[55] In Schalit's view, the people of Jaffa were tenants of Hyrcanus. He further argued that if this was so, then *Ant.* 14.202 should be understood to state that the people of Jaffa will pay tax to the "city of the people of Jerusalem."[56] As Schalit noted, some scholars interpret section 206 to mean that Hyrcanus was required to pay a tax for Jaffa in Sidon to the Romans.[57] Heichelheim rendered a different translation indicating that Hyrcanus had tribute of 20,675 modii from Jaffa for the land and for what they export to Sidon.[58] Smallwood accepts that Hyrcanus must pay a tax for the recovery of Jaffa.[59]

Accepting Marcus and Schalit's translation, the explanation of the text is that Jerusalem (all of the country under Judean control) must pay tribute every year, except Sabbatical years. The tribute was probably 12.5 percent of the crop.[60] However, Jaffa was excluded from this arrangement and other demands were imposed as payment for her return. Hyrcanus had to pay a fixed tribute of 20,675 modii every year, except once again the Sabbatical Year. Why the different arrangements regarding Jaffa?

It has nothing to do with Pompey's program since Caesar declares that Jaffa belonged to Judea (*Ant.* 14.205). He also recognizes that the Jezreel Valley once belonged to Judea, yet he makes no special tax demands for that area (*Ant.* 14.207).[61] The only characteristic which makes Jaffa stand out is her being a seaport, Judea's only seaport. Taxes on agriculture as we have pointed out can be percentages of yield or fixed amounts. The former is certainly fairer in regions in which the yield is relatively unpredictable. However, the traffic passing through a port is probably generally constant.[62]

Among the questions arising from Caesar's enactments is whether the area of Lydda was the private estate of Hyrcanus, or whether the decrees simply restored it to Jewish control. Rosenfeld claims that the Lydda–Gezer area was a Hasmonean estate since the time of Simon. He maintains that the grants by Julius Caesar are based on Roman recognition of the Hasmonean claims to Gezer in the days of Hyrcanus I.[63]

Furthermore, in the document by Caesar, Gezer is not mentioned, but Lydda is, so that Rosenfeld asserts that Lydda was a Hasmonean property which simply eclipsed Gezer. J. Schwartz readily grants that Gezer was a Hasmonean estate, but he categorically rejects any administrative connection between the two places.[64] However, he adds a new theory. He maintains that the sentence on Lydda should be read as parallel to the sentence on the Jezreel Valley. There he reads that the "villages were returned to the Hasmoneans and Jews according to the rights which they had previously possessed." He draws the conclusion that the edict thus deprived the Hasmoneans of their personal possession of these villages and returned them instead to Judea or to the Jewish nation in general.[65]

The texts also guarantee the payment of the tithes to Hyrcanus and the other priests (*Ant.* 14.203).[66] Although there is some problem in understanding the intention of the word "tithe," on the face of it the priest's "first tithe" is meant. However, Bar-Kochva has pointed out that Caesar's edict includes another clause (208) which promises the priests their traditional rights, thus the latter paragraph would contradict the former paragraph. He suggests that the intention of paragraph 203 was to guarantee the Hasmoneans the income from the *dekate*, i.e. the "main land tax under the Seleucids."[67]

The revenues generated by the lands returned to Judean control must have been considerable because Josephus notes that "the leading Jews saw Antipater and his sons growing so great through the goodwill of the nation and the revenues which they received from Judaea and Hyrcanus' wealth."[68] Shatzman has pointed out that this indicates that Antipater and his sons had control of the regular tax revenues of the regions which they administered, with the addition of Hyrcanus' private revenues.[69] This conclusion while inescapable in light of the accumulated evidence, i.e. the statement itself and the probable significance of the appointments of Antipater to the positions of ἐπιμελητής and subsequently ἐπίτροπος, raises very difficult questions as to the administration of revenues in Judea.[70] It is reasonable to assume that Antipater was considered more dependable and efficient than Hyrcanus and so he had the disposition of revenues and hence the responsibility of ensuring that the client state stayed solvent and paid its tribute. However, why would Hyrcanus' personal patrimony be channeled through his minister? We suggest that no such situation existed and that this is merely an attempt to present the Antipater group as the puppeteer pulling the strings of Hyrcanus. Later we see that in spite of the interests of the Antipater group Hyrcanus makes good the debt incurred by Malichus.

Cassius (44–42 BCE)

During the civil war between the loyalists of Julius Caesar and his assassins, Cassius, who was governor of Syria, demanded 700 silver talents in tribute from Judea.[71] We do not know how this sum was divided between the various districts, except that the Galilee had to pay 100 talents. Malichus failed to raise his due, but was rescued by Hyrcanus who donated 100 talents.[72] Gophna, Emmaus, Lydda, and Thamna did not raise the amount necessary so the officials of these towns were sold into slavery. Schalit suggested that Malichus was the governor of the district comprising the towns that did not meet their quota.[73] In that case the area in question, like the Galilee, had to raise 100 talents. The sum of 700 talents is enormous if one takes into consideration that Hyrcanus II ruled a territory smaller than that of Herod, who raised about 1,000 talents annually from a much larger area.[74]

The action of Cassius must have included confiscation and sale of lands of those who were sold as slaves. It seems unrealistic to assume that the persons were sold, but their property was not. Affirmation of this assumption comes from *Ant.* 14.304 in which Hyrcanus asks that Antony free "Jews who had been taken captive by Cassius" and "restore to them the territory of which they had been deprived in the time of Cassius."[75] This suggestion is further strengthened by Antony's answer which refers to his enemies and those of the Roman people sparing neither cities nor temples and disregarding sworn agreements.[76] These phrases do not properly describe or relate to Marion. Similarly, it is not likely that Antigonus would have sold his fellow Jews into slavery, and certainly not out of Judea. Additionally, in *Ant.* 14.313 Antony states that people sold at auction by Cassius are to be released. In *Ant.* 14.320–1 the edict describes how Cassius behaved; it is noted that "whatever was sold belonging to the Jews, whether persons or possessions, shall be released." Once again these fit Cassius' actions in Judea.

At the same time these texts do indicate that the Tyrians had expropriated lands belonging to the Jews. *Ant.* 14.314, 317 determine that the Tyrians hold land belonging to Hyrcanus and order them to restore to Hyrcanus any places which belonged to him. More significantly for our understanding of the problems of the period is this demonstration of the almost constant competition for the border lands, an indication of the value of land and the pressure to control as much as possible of it.[77]

Finally, it is evident that the gathering of taxes was the responsibility of the local officials, who were in turn answerable to regional governors.

7

THE HERODIAN PERIOD

HEROD

The Herodian period, for our purposes, will be defined as commencing with the Parthian invasion of 40 BCE and ending with the dismissal of Archelaus in 6 BCE. It encompasses the struggle of Herod to gain mastery of Judea, his reign, and the reign of his son, Archelaus.

Herod was a complicated and dynamic figure, and so history's assessment of his personality and his motives is still not final.[1] His reign was conspicuous for initiatives in every aspect of government and society. His life and reign arouse criticism, anger, admiration, and even pity. His personal and family life are the raw material for a soap opera. His attitude and policies regarding the Jewish religion provoke debate. His foreign relations are variously described as self-serving or cynically brilliant. However, of all the debates provoked by this complex personality, perhaps none are so polarized as the evaluation of his economic policies.

There are basically two opposing points of view. The first and perhaps more commonly held interpretation of the historical record is that the Jews under Herod suffered terribly from economic oppression.[2] This oppression is usually presented as the result of three factors: (1) the concentration of land in the hands of the king and his henchmen so that the average Jewish cultivator was a tenant paying excessive rents, or a poor freeholder on marginal soil, or totally landless and without means of support;[3] (2) exorbitant taxes supposedly impoverished the population; (3) lavish spending on the court, gifts to patrons and allies, and, most of all, on an expansive building program, drained the wealth of the people. The rival perception is that Herod's economic policies were not harsher than those of his predecessors or contemporaries.[4] In fact, according to this version, Herod's economic policies contributed to prosperity and progress for most of his kingdom. This point of view maintains that the criticism of Herod in the sources arises from religious and social resentments, biased reporting, and the inability of ancient sources to judge the economic reality accurately.[5]

In light of the debate on Herod's economic policies, we intend to review the landholding system, taxes, and public spending. It is our view that Herod's policies were initiatives in a few practical areas, not innovations. He operated in a manner commensurate with the Hellenistic monarchical tradition already embarked on by his Hasmonean predecessors, and like them he was limited by the Jewish religious–legal norms. Herod did not change the landholding system. The granting of estates to loyal subjects and military colonists, for which he was famous, was not an innovation, rather Herod was simply treading a path well laid out in the Hellenistic and Judean world. In addition his settlement policy probably opened up solutions to the landlessness created by Pompey's settlement. Furthermore, although the Romans gave Herod political and military support, and also provided Herod with examples of cultural and administrative policies, yet none of the land tenure changes in his reign was a Roman initiative, or even a Roman innovation.

Yet while Herod's management of the landholding structure was not original in terms of policy it was still a significant achievement in terms of accomplishing the aims of his administration. Through efficient use of standard policies, well known in the Hellenistic and Roman worlds, Herod was able to maximize his political and social power, incidentally providing solutions to some of the economic and social ills of his society.

Landholding structure

Despite the scattered nature of the evidence let us first describe the landholding structure in Herod's kingdom.[6] It is evident that the basic structure of landholding is the same as that of the Hellenistic monarchies as we have outlined above, i.e. royal land, gift land, private estates.

Herod's personal properties

Herod had private estates which he obtained from three sources: his own inheritance, his wife Miriam's inheritance, and estates which he acquired on his own prior to his coronation.

Herod's grandfather was governor of all Idumea and was described as having a large fortune (*Ant.* 14.8, 10).[7] His father Antipater was rich: he lent money (*Ant.* 14.372; *BJ* 1.276). He also was guarantor for 300 talents to Scaurus (*Ant.* 14.81; *BJ* 1.159). An indication of the family wealth may be found in *BJ* 1.483 which relates that Herod's brother Pheroras enjoyed an income of 100 talents from his private possessions, exclusive of the income he received from the region bestowed upon him by Herod. Both Schalit and Applebaum claim that the grazing land which Herod rented to the Nabateans was a family inheritance.[8]

Herod's wife Miriam was one of the last linear descendants of the Hasmonean rulers. We have shown in the story of Judith that women could inherit land. Furthermore, and with all due caution in using later sources, we know that Herod left Iamnia, Azotus, and Phasaelis to his sister Salome (*BJ* 2.98), and Berenice, the daughter of Agrippa I, had estates in the Galilee (*Vita* 118). Similarly, there are documents from the Babatha file demonstrating that a woman could inherit lands (*P. Yadin* 3, 16, 19, 20). Hence, we suppose that Herod inherited the lands of his deceased wife, or at least had their usufruct.[9]

Personal land that Herod obtained till 40 BCE

Josephus (*Ant.* 14.163) relates that Antipater and sons received revenues (πρόσοδος) from Judea, during the period that Hyrcanus was still ostensibly the ruler.[10] Herod was at one point governor of the Galilee, then governor of Coele-Syria and Samaria (*Ant.* 14.180; *BJ* 1.213). Regrettably, we can only speculate that these positions endowed him with some estates in keeping with the prevalent practice of the period. But in summary we can see that Herod probably had large assets of his own, even without those accruing to the crown. His lands would have been worked either by a permanent staff of servants, or by tenant farmers, or leased. In any case there could have been nothing like a newly oppressive system in the ownership of these estates.

Royal land

Herod certainly also had royal lands formerly held by the Hasmoneans who ruled immediately before him. We have seen how the Hasmoneans claimed land in the Ekron region, in Gezer, and in the Jezreel Valley. By the same token Herod owned estates in Jericho, Ein Gedi, and other portions of the Jordan Valley, such as Phasaelis and Ein Boqeq.[11] Augustus increased the number of territories ruled by Herod and thereby the amount of land directly in his possession. After Actium,

Augustus bestowed cities on Herod (Jericho, Gaza, Anthedon, Joppa, Strato's Tower, Samaria, Gadara, and Hippus).[12] In at least some of these Herod had property.[13] Jericho was the site of a large palace and estate complex.[14] We may assume that some of the famous palm groves were in Jericho, in any case there is evidence that Herod owned palm groves.[15] In Samaria Herod had a palace (we noted above his past as strategos there). During his reign he not only rebuilt the city, but he handed out parcels to veterans whom he settled in the vicinity. It may be assumed that if he gave them the land it belonged to him.[16] By the same token Herod probably owned the areas around Gaba and Antipatris, before he established cities there. The lands he granted to the Idumeans and Zamaris were state land granted to him by Augustus.[17] Whatever the relationship of the settlers to the crown, it is fairly certain that the land was royal land.[18] In Perea, Herod must have had some estates, because upon his death we hear of the activities of Simon, a slave of the king (*BJ* 2.57); and of others who burned the royal palace at Beth Ha-Ramatha (*BJ* 2.59; *Ant.* 17.277).[19]

Gift land

The existence of gift land in Hellenistic and Hasmonean Palestine has already been demonstrated. We assume that prior to 40 BCE gift lands were in the hands of the Hyrcanus party, when Antigonus took control it seems fairly certain that this party was punished. Those who had supported Hyrcanus now had to throw their support to Herod. We hear of the local inhabitants who rallied to Herod; some of these supporters lived in the Galilee, where they were attacked by the cave-dwelling partisans of Antigonus (*BJ* 1.293, 304). Later, the nobles in the Galilee were murdered by pro-Hasmoneans opposed to Herod.[20] The presence of the nobles indicates that there probably were estates in the Galilee occupied by pro-Herodians.[21] For a brief time, some of the land may have been taken by supporters of the old Aristobulian party that had been repeatedly defeated since Pompey. However, Herod's victory resulted in a redistribution of the lands in the Judean state. Some of the leading aristocrats were killed by Herod and their properties were forfeited to the crown. For example, after conquering Jerusalem, Herod confiscated the estates of forty-five opposing nobles (*Ant.* 15.5–7), a policy which he supposedly continued throughout his reign (*Ant.* 17.305, 307). Herod distributed land to loyal ministers, supporters, and military settlers. During the period in which he struggled with Antigonus he had attracted support from those who expected to be rewarded for their help (*BJ* 1.293). Now, he redistributed the land to them, a new elite, in place of the old Hasmonean aristocracy.[22] Ptolemy, an adviser to Herod, was given an estate near Samaria.[23] Similarly, Herod bestowed lands on family members and royal favorites (*Ant.* 17.147). For example, Antipater was assigned a territory that produced 50 talents annually.[24] But as we have seen the Hellenistic world considered the punishment of opponents and the reward of supporters through land allocation as a legitimate exercise of political authority.

Herod also disposed of gift lands by placing military settlers on them. We have mentioned the settlement of 6,000 veterans in Samaria (*Ant.* 15.296; *BJ* 1.403). He placed 3,000 Idumeans in Trachonitis (*Ant.* 16.285), put a colony in Batanea (*Ant.* 17.23–5), settled veterans at Gaba (*Ant.* 15.294; *BJ* 3.36) and also at Heshbon (*Ant.* 15.294).[25]

Regarding the royal lands and the gift lands, there is a widely held belief that "the best lands became part of the royal possessions, either through confiscation or because their owners could not meet the heavy taxes which Herod exacted from the country people."[26] Applebaum suggests that the Greeks, civil-servants, administrators, and soldiers were rewarded by properties farmed by Jewish tenants. This development ostensibly led to the "breaking of long-standing allegiances and subjection of numerous Jewish tenants to hellenized administrative machines and to non-Jewish landlords."[27] To this claim we would answer that there is almost no evidence of specific grants to non-Jews within the Jewish area of settlement. If Herod had confiscated so much land why don't we hear of the establishment of veterans on lands in Judea?

Safrai and Lin are convinced that Gaba Hippeon, on the border of the Jezreel Valley, was settled by gentile veterans, probably Phrygians, who were allocated royal land on the borders of the town.[28] Moreover, they claim that the (Jewish) villagers who had lived on these lands now became tenants. There are two problems with this version of events. First, if the lands were royal estate before the establishment of the veterans, then the farmers who lived there were already tenants, henceforth they would have had to pay rent to the veterans, and not to Herod, but they had been tenants and they remained tenants. Second, it is demonstrated that the earlier residents of Gaba were gentiles who had lands and houses of their own. However, there is no reason to assume that all the land of Gaba was in private hands.[29] Safrai and Lin note the town is called a χωρίον, i.e. an estate, probably a royal estate. Even if Gaba was a polis at this time, the king could take some of its land and allocate it as he wished, but Gaba was not a polis then.[30] In brief, Gaba was a royal estate with a gentile population and Herod decided to place a colony of veterans in the area to keep an eye on the neighboring Jews. Nothing here indicates that the Jews became tenants of the gentiles.

The areas of Jericho and Perea which Applebaum cites as focuses of resentment bursting into violence and disruption were all, by his own statement, "under direct administration as crown domains."[31] If these were crown domains then the cultivators were not tenants of the gentiles. Moreover, royal tenants were accustomed to the status and situation of tenancy under Hellenistic administration. These estates were not an innovation.

If there were so many confiscations and expropriations, why is it that the crowds who later demanded reform from Archelaus did not demand restitution of property? Why did they not demand land reform? Who were the people who presented the complaints to Augustus?[32] We have no answers to these questions, but they should be considered before accepting the usual model of events.

Private land

Gabba asserts that "There is no doubt that the king and royal household were the biggest landowners in the country and that they had at their disposal what was often the most fertile land in all parts of the kingdom."[33] Quoting Otto he points out that "It is frequently assumed that either a half or two thirds of the land of the kingdom were Herod's private property."[34] We cannot prove or disprove that quantitative allegation. The sources specifically mentioning personal, royal, and gift estates do not add up to anywhere near that magnitude. We know that land was owned by private persons outright. Some of these were probably pre-Herodian aristocrats who had inherited family estates. For example, Costobar had his own estates (*Ant.* 15.264).

The New Testament is replete with examples of rich landowners.[35] In fact the New Testament version of economic life is that of a society split between a few wealthy men and many poor people.[36] The New Testament relates episodes in which people sell their lands, a fairly certain indication of privately owned property.[37] The Mishnah also has rules regarding the sale of land. These are not tenants, or enjoying gift land, because it is clear that they can sell the land.[38] The Mishnah also deals with religious obligations on the bringing of first fruits to the Temple. These obligations apply only to freeholders.[39]

If we analyze the above information a number of interesting points come to light. None of the areas or estates which were owned by Herod were new to royal control. The royal estates which were owned by him were also owned by the Hasmoneans, or other rulers. They had been royal land and the tenants were not dispossessed freeholders, but royal tenants. The areas which were given by Herod for settlement were either royal land previously, or unsettled land which now came under Judean control. Those lands which were expropriated were taken from rebels and political opponents. We do not have a record of specific expropriations. None of the estates mentioned as Herodian is specifically in Judea proper, the heartland of the Jewish people in Palestine. Finally, freeholders continue to exist throughout the Herodian period.

Another common claim made about the landholding structure is that most of the farmers were tenants. According to this view a Jewish tenant class was created by the "displacement of the Jewish population from the coastal plain and Transjordan under Pompey." This was compounded by Herod's confiscations and grants to gentile supporters as well as veterans.[40]

Two types of argument are used to substantiate this assertion: literary sources and archaeology.

Applebaum claims that a process was at work in the country in the first century BCE: "the growth of large estates which assimilated complete villages in tenancy."[41] For example, he writes that Philip son of Jacimus owned villages in the vicinity of Gamla.[42] However, considering that Philip was the army commander of Agrippa II, it would not seem unusual for him to have villagers as tenants. We may assume that Demetrius, the strategos of Gamla in Yannai's day, might have also had the same reward (*Ant.* 13.394). Ptolemy, the dioketes, apparently owned the village of Arous. But, once again, this is no different than the Ptolemy who owned the villages mentioned in the Hefzibah inscription. In fact, we know of no written source establishing that Herod converted free farmers into tenants.

The archaeological record is used to demonstrate the ubiquity of tenant farming in this period. The argument is based on finding many small fields well defined by the remains of stone fences, and often marked by field towers. In the vicinity of these fields there are the remains of large houses or an elaborate mausoleum or family burial cave. The assumption is that the inhabitants of the large houses were lords of the estate and indeed it is difficult to see that they farmed all the surrounding plots themselves. Alternatively, it is also hard to imagine that the owners of these lavish homes owned only the small adjoining plots. We are willing to stipulate that the lavish homes were the houses of the estate owners and that the surrounding farms were probably worked by tenant farmers of one sort or another. However, these same findings are also found for the Hasmonean period. There is no concrete proof that the number of estates burgeoned in Herod's time.[43] We, too, believe that estates with tenant farmers were common. However, because there is no supporting evidence to prove otherwise, we are not convinced that the tenant farming system expanded outrageously during Herod's rule.

Taxation

Those who view Herod's rule as an economic catastrophe for the Jewish people in Judea, generally blame high taxes, rents, and religious dues for the situation. Of the three major ills which supposedly afflicted the society, over-taxation appears to be the easiest to prove. Taxation is a corollary of landownership; the assumption is that high taxes would force freeholders into debt, and then into tenant farmer status. Extreme cases of tax failure ostensibly led to the loss of land, i.e. the creation of a lumpenproletariat in the cities. Judea saw at least two cases in which the tax burden led to crises: during Nehemiah's term as governor and during the last stages of the Ptolemaic rule in Palestine. Those who argue that the high taxes and rents were a major contributing factor in the disequilibrium of the Jewish society usually base their case on the extraordinary expenses that characterized Herod's administration, the argument being that he could not have paid for all the projects and gifts without squeezing the population. However, one must examine other sources of income to judge if the tax burden really had to be so high.[44]

Sources of tax revenue

Herod's main source of tax revenue was from the products of the earth. When his kingdom was struck by a catastrophic drought he found himself without adequate income for his needs (*Ant.* 15.303). This point is brought out more clearly if we compare the situation of Herod's kingdom in the fall of 37 BCE to the situation in the fall of 31 BCE. When Jerusalem fell to the Romans, Herod was in dire straits. He had to pay off Antony and the conquering troops, so he sheared the wealthy (*Ant.* 15.5). Costobar was even tasked with the arrest of all those people who owed money to the king (*Ant.* 15.264). Herod's funds gone, he converted his valuables to money in order to pay Antony (*BJ* 1.359). It was the Sabbatical Year and the kingdom had no way of paying taxes on the produce. We have seen that even Julius Caesar recognized that without a crop there was nothing to collect taxes from. The same point was made decades later by Petronius, the governor of Syria, when he was faced with a "strike" of the Jewish population. He predicted that the tribute could not be paid if the populace did not work the soil (*Ant.* 18.274). In brief, Herod's situation in 37 BCE was very poor indeed. However, at the time of Actium we find that "Herod, whose country had been yielding him rich crops for a long time, having procured revenues and resources, enrolled an auxiliary force for Antony and furnished it with the most carefully chosen equipment" (*Ant.* 15.109). This source obviously credits the country's agricultural base as the mainstay of Herod's prosperity. To further emphasize the relative importance of his agricultural base to the prosperity of the realm, let us remember that for much of the period between 37 BCE and 31 BCE, Cleopatra managed to gain control of significant parts of the kingdom.

We have seen how despite the loss to Cleopatra of major revenue-yielding areas such as the ports and harbors, and the obligation to pay her 200 talents for the balsam-producing territory, Herod profited handsomely from the agricultural resources of his kingdom and his own lands (*Ant.* 15.109).[45]

On at least two occasions Herod saw fit to reduce taxes.[46] In 20 BCE Herod remitted a third of the taxes. Josephus asserts that this was only ostensibly to help the people recover from a period of low yields (*Ant.* 15.365). He claims that the real reason was to defuse the resentment that greeted Herod's cultural policies. We can detect the obvious anti-Herodian bias. If Herod felt that he had angered the populace on religious–cultural grounds, why would he try to remedy that problem by cutting taxes?

It is impossible to give an accurate description of the effect of the tax cut because we do not know what the tax rate on farm produce was.[47] Those who assume that the Roman system of taxation was in effect are probably right.[48] The Roman tax on field produce was 12.5 percent as we have explained above. However, there are indications that different crops had different rates of tax.[49] If Herod's taxes were much lower than Roman taxes there would have been no point in complaining to Caesar about the oppressive level of taxation under Herod. If the taxes were much higher than Roman taxes then the Roman taxation under the provincial administration would have seemed a blessing, and not a cause for complaint.

In addition to the tax on produce we know that there was a sales levy which apparently angered the populace since it is prominent in their complaints to Archelaus.

Herod may have had a tax income from overseas: "The enumeration of the debts and taxes discharged by himself would be endless; it was thus, for instance that he lightened the burden of their annual taxes for Phasaelis, Balanea, and various minor towns in Cilicia" (*BJ* 1.428). The usual interpretation is that Herod was being generous, for political reasons. Gabba sees a pattern of involvement in tax-collecting activities such as being associated with the procurators of the province of Syria (*BJ* 1.399; *Ant.* 15.360) or dealing with the Nabateans for Cleopatra (*Ant.* 15.107).[50]

Among the taxes which Herod levied we must count the customs duties. We can assume that all the ports that Herod controlled levied duty: Caesarea, Jaffa, Iamnia, Gaza. We do not have any documentation of the level of customs in Herod's kingdom but some comparative material might be edifying. In 399 BCE a 2 percent customs duty in the harbor of Piraeus brought in 30 talents a year.[51] The authorities of Cyparissia in the third or fourth century BCE levied a 2 percent import–export tax.[52] These examples from hundreds of years before Herod should be compared to the customs law for the province of Asia in the first centuries BCE and CE. There the rate was 2.5 percent on all exports and imports.[53] It appears that about 2 percent was an accepted customs rate.[54] It is also not surprising that there is a general conservativeness in tax rates.[55] Herod had the largest harbor in the Eastern Mediterranean, except for Alexandria: how much was it worth? In 170 BCE Rhodes complained that the harbor dues used to bring in one million drachmas, but because of the diversion of commerce to Delos she was now making only 150,000 a year.[56] Rhodes was once a leading port, but when she fell on hard times she was still earning 25 talents annually just from harbor dues. Another way of estimating the income from customs is to consider the 20,675 modii paid by Hyrcanus at Jaffa, an indication of how much could be raised in just one bureau of customs.[57]

Beyond the usual forms of taxation, every now and again Herod could draw on punitive fines. Before he succeeded in capturing Jerusalem, Herod punished the towns in the Galilee for renewing the revolt, with a fine of 100 talents (*BJ* 1.314–16; *Ant.* 14.433). Likewise, the Pharisees who refused to take an oath of allegiance were punished with a fine (*Ant.* 17.42).[58]

When judging whether Herod's expenses forced the small farmer into poverty, we should take into account the other sources of income that Herod could draw on.

Other sources of income

Herod apparently also lent money at interest. In *Ant.* 16.279 it is related that he was angry with Obadas, the Nabatean king, because of 60 talents which the latter avoided repaying. In *Ant.* 16.343 the sum of 500 talents is the reason for the feud. Most scholars simply ignore the difference, some explain it as a copyist's error.[59] However, we would point out that 60 talents is 12 percent of 500; this arithmetic relationship suggests that the loan was 500 talents and the interest on the loan was 60 talents.[60]

Not only did the Arabs refuse to pay back the money which they owed, but they refused to pay for the grazing land which they had rented and used (*Ant.* 16.291).

Additional sources of income were the areas previously underdeveloped, which Herod brought under cultivation. He built Phasaelis.[61] Although it has been demonstrated that Herod's efforts in the development of desert settlements were preceded by the Hasmoneans, it is clear that he greatly expanded the installations. He repaired, completed, and expanded the irrigation infrastructure in order to maximize the cash crops which grow in the region.[62] Salome, Herod's sister, inherited Phasaelis, as well as Iamnia (Yavneh) and Azotus; her income was 60 talents from these places alone (*BJ* 2.98): compare that revenue to that of Archelaus, who received Judea, Samaria, Idumea, and the cities of Jerusalem, Sebaste, Jaffa, and Caesarea which yielded 400 or 600 talents (*BJ* 2.97; *Ant.* 17.320). We see in proportional terms how Salome's income from Phasaelis must have been high.

We should also remember the copper mines of Cyprus which Herod managed for 300 talents.[63]

The income of Herod is generally estimated at 900 or 1,000 talents annually. It is difficult to know what this number represents.[64] It could be the revenue from taxation, but without the various enterprises that Herod operated such as the mines, the rental of grazing land, or the income from the royal balsam plantations.[65]

In 14 BCE Herod remitted a third of the taxes for the past year (*Ant.* 16.64). He did this upon his return from Ionia, probably in the fall, since he had departed to Asia Minor the previous spring. The source indicates that he cut the past year's tax. Since it was the fall it must have been the past agricultural year, i.e. this was after he had an impression of the season's crop. Herod probably judged that his income was sufficiently high that he could afford to be generous.

Judging by Herod's cash bequests, his fortune was enormous. He left Salome 500,000 pieces of coined silver (drachmas), to Caesar ten million pieces of coined silver (drachmas), and to Julia and some others, five million pieces of coined silver (drachmas).[66] To get a perspective of how rich Herod was in contemporary terms, we should note that to qualify for senatorial rank it was necessary to hold property worth 1,000,000 sestertii, which equals 50 talents; Herod bequeathed 1,550 talents.[67]

Expenses

Having reviewed Herod's income it remains to explore his expenses. Perhaps the major question about Herod's expenses is whether he had to pay tribute to Rome. The basic text is in Appian:[68]

ἴστη δέ πη καὶ βασιλέας, οὓς δοκιμάσειεν, ἐπὶ φόροις ἄρα τεταγμένοις ... Ἰδουμαίων δὲ καὶ Σαμαρέων Ἡρῴδην ...

He set up kings here and there as he pleased, on condition of their paying a prescribed tribute: ... in Idumaea and Samaria, Herod ...

It relates that Antony set up kings as he wished, just as long as they paid tribute. Herod paid for Idumea and Samaria. The text raises the question whether Judea was included in the original grant, and left out of the text by a copyist's mistake, or whether the Romans bestowed Judea on Herod free of tribute, but were less generous with Idumaea and Samaria. M. Stern suggests that Herod probably paid tax for Judea. He explains that Appian implied that Samaria and parts of Idumea were not included in Hyrcanus' ethnarchy, because they were an addition to the territory granted in 40 BCE.[69]

Regarding Appian, the text does not say that Herod had to pay tax for Samaria and Idumea, it says that Herod was set up as king in Samaria and Idumea upon paying a prescribed tribute. Moreover, the suggestion that there is a haplography involved is attractive because of its simplicity.[70]

Applebaum, following upon Momigliano and Schalit, is also of the opinion that Herod paid tax to Rome. Their argument is that "there is no basis for supposing that Antony released Herod." Furthermore, they ask why would Augustus release Herod from taxes if Julius Caesar did not release Hyrcanus II?[71]

To this point there are a number of rebuttals. First, Herod was a king, not an ethnarch. Second, Appian's testimony need not necessarily refer to a regular payment of tribute. Third, there is no conclusive evidence that client-kings paid tribute.[72] Indeed, the major support of those who claim that Herod did not pay tribute is comparative information on client-kings.[73] Both Braund and Sands examined the information on the status of client-kings and came to the same conclusion, that client-kings did not pay a regular tribute, and that Judea probably paid tribute until 40 BCE, but not during Herod's reign.[74] One might also add that an indication that Herod did not pay tribute is the antagonism aroused by the census (*BJ* 2.118; *Ant.* 18.4–7). It appears to demonstrate that the Judeans were unused to paying tax directly to Rome.

One can take the middle ground, maintaining that Herod paid tribute to Antony, but not to Augustus. Antony's greed was a by-word; it seems unlikely that he would have excused Herod from any payment. When summarizing Herod's financial obligations we must remember the burden placed on him by Antony. We have noted that after conquering Jerusalem Herod collected all the valuables in the kingdom and when he had amassed a great sum of silver and gold, he made use of all this to make gifts to Antony and his friends (*BJ* 1.359; *Ant.* 15.5). Herod later gave 800 talents of silver to Augustus, and supplies to help him cross the Sinai desert.[75]

In comparison, Augustus gave Herod a great deal of leeway and bestowed lands, privileges, and honors on him. It is possible that the large fortunes spent by Herod throughout the empire were in lieu of tribute.[76]

Herod's economic policies

Up till now we have examined the landholding and taxation in Herod's kingdom. Now let us examine the descriptions of Herod's economic policies and their impact as they appear in the ancient literature. We shall then compare that to whatever we can learn of Herod's activities from an objective analysis of the sources.

Herod's reign reportedly began with a bleak economic start. Josephus writes that Herod, being in need (of money), plundered the population, while on the other hand the Sabbatical Year came around at that time, forcing them to leave the land unsowed (*Ant.* 15.6–7).

The source blatantly reveals its biases. Herod is described as being greedy (πλεονέκτικός). The people, despite his greed, and the troubles that have come upon them, will obey their religion's strictures. One may wonder if Herod is not being negatively compared to Julius Caesar who considerately moderated his demands during the Seventh Year. We, however, can learn from the preceding paragraph that Herod's actions were not motivated by greed, but by the necessity of bribing the Romans (*Ant*. 15.5; *BJ* 1.358).

Josephus states that Herod had expenses greater than his means, spending the money on some, while oppressing the many. Herod supposedly understood the situation he had created, but chose to be hated rather than cut his revenues (*Ant*. 16.154–5).

In *BJ* 1.520–5 a rogue called Eurycles relates to Herod complaints and criticisms allegedly made by Alexander. He supposedly said that he would "proclaim to the world the sufferings of his nation, bled to death by taxation, and then go on to describe the luxury and malpractices on which the money obtained by its blood was lavished, the characters of the men who had grown rich at his and his brother's expense, and to the motives which had led to the favouritism shown to particular cities." This criticism of Herod is presented to the reader as a lie, not as the actual criticisms voiced by Herod's son. Moreover, Herod is enraged at the accusation. If he himself thought that he was bleeding the country dry while living in lavish splendor at the expense of the blood of the country, why would he fly into a rage?

A famous appraisal of Herod's effect on the economy of his kingdom was delivered to Augustus by Jewish envoys supposedly representing the nation.[77] After the usual generalities, the envoys claimed that people lost their property (305). Herod adorned neighboring foreign cities until cities in his own kingdom were ruined and disappeared (306). He had reduced the entire nation to helpless poverty after taking it over in as flourishing condition as few ever knew, and he was wont to kill members of the nobility upon absurd pretexts and then take their property for himself; if he let them live, he would condemn them to be stripped of their possessions (307). In addition to the collecting of the tribute that was imposed on everyone each year, lavish extra contributions had to be made to him and his household and friends and those of his slaves who were sent out to collect the tribute because there was no immunity at all from outrage unless bribes were paid (308).

If we organize the complaints according to subject we get the following: confiscation of property; excessive foreign spending; the nation is impoverished; execution of the nobility; additional levies; corruption.

How much truth is there in these accusations? Let us remember that coming as they do from the pen of Josephus, they are suspect. It is true that Josephus relied heavily on Nicolaus of Damascus, but it is difficult to credit such a bitter condemnation of the king as the work of Herod's close friend and biographer.[78]

Herod was hated. No doubt he had his supporters, but the literary record retains the opinion of his opponents.[79] Regarding the above accusations we have already dealt with the question of confiscations. There is no doubt that Herod spent fortunes overseas, but the accusation is not that he spent the money, but that the spending led to the ruin and disappearance of cities in his kingdom.

Not only is there no evidence for this accusation, but the opposite is true. During his administration Herod established new cities or greatly expanded existing communities. He founded three cities: Caesarea, Sebaste, and Antipatris, and he contributed greatly to the development of Jerusalem. In Jerusalem alone he built many public buildings, fortresses and towers, monuments, and of course the Temple. One might claim that these do not necessarily indicate the growth of the city, but rather Herod's megalomania. However, the city itself had an area of about 90 hectares at the end of the Hasmonean period, but by the time of Agrippa I it enclosed about 170 hectares.[80] The growth of the city is also indicated by the improvements in the water-supply system of the city.

Applebaum maintains that a Jewish tenant class was created by the "displacement of Jewish population from the coastal plain and Transjordan under Pompey."[81] The evidence seems to show that Herod's reign opened opportunities for Jewish settlement in areas that had been lost to it by Pompey's settlement.

Of the three cities he founded, Sebaste did not provide any solutions to Judean problems. However, as an indication of what Herod's policies did to the country's cities it is enlightening to observe that on the basis of coin finds, Z. Safrai suggests that Samaria/Sebaste's situation improved in Herod's day, although it did not exceed the economic level of the Seleucid period.[82] Moreover, after Herod there are indications of a downturn in economic activity and probably in the population of the city.

Caesarea became a major Jewish center, to such an extent that the conflict between the Jewish element and the gentile is a recurring problem in the decade or so before the Great Revolt. Suffice it to say that the gentiles of Caesarea claimed that until Herod's day there were no Jews in the polis. However, in the years just before the Great Revolt the Jews in Caesarea drew confidence from their wealth (*Ant.* 20.175) and some of them had large sums of money (*Ant.* 20.177). The community was able to raise 8 talents in order to bribe Florus (*BJ* 2.287).

Antipatris was established by Herod in the area of the plain of

Kephar Saba. The ruins of the city lie on the upper reaches of the Yarkon River, below the last ridges of the Shephela. One may assume that this area was included in the regions torn from Judea by Pompey. Applebaum claims that the environs of the city had many Jews in villages, who had remained after the Pompeian "liberation" of the city from Hasmonean rule.[83] He bases his assumption of the Jewish nature of the city on *BJ* 2.513–14, which relates that Jews had gathered in Migdal Aphek. But there is no reason to assume that the tower was in the city, or that the Jews were city residents. Certainly there is nothing to show that they had remained in the area from Pompey's time on. There is no doubt that at the time of the Great Revolt Jews lived in the area; but the city itself was Greek: in 66 CE Gallus found refuge there (*BJ* 2.554). Josephus claims that Vespasian "restored order in Antipatris and then laid waste the neighborhood" (*BJ* 4.443). If the *chora* of Antipatris wasn't Jewish then this operation would have caused undeserved damage to an allied population. When did the Jews arrive in the area? It is more likely that they used the opportunity presented by Herod's development of the zone than that they had avoided Pompey's settlement.

Herod's reign is probably the occasion when Jews returned to Yavneh, Dor, Beth Sean, and other areas that had been cut off from Judean control by Pompey. It is interesting to note that in the blood-bath which featured at the beginning of the Great Revolt, Jews were found in many gentile cities of Palestine, but aside from some Greeks in Tiberias, gentiles were not found in the areas with a dense Jewish population. Apparently the Jews used the opportunities that Herod's reign gave them.

The list of complaints against Herod includes the accusation that he impoverished the country. Actually he probably enriched the country by developing unproductive areas. An example of this policy is the settlement in the Trachonitis which introduced a permanent Jewish agricultural presence into an area which was formerly a haven for bandits and outlaws. Likewise, Herod developed agriculture in the Jordan Valley to a greater extent than had previously been accomplished.

Probably more significant than the development of admittedly small desert areas as viable agricultural centers was the massive building program which certainly provided employment. It is probably impossible to prove that Herod's building mania was not a mania at all but a deliberate program to provide employment for the population.[84] We might not be able to prove intentions, but we can demonstrate the results of the program.

It would be redundant to list all of Herod's building projects.[85] Shatzman cogently pointed out that it took an enormous amount of work to build the large range of buildings, forts, monuments, waterworks, temples, monuments, and the Temple in Jerusalem.

The Temple provides a good perspective on the economic effect of Herod's program. The work on the Temple started in 20/19 or 23/22 BCE and lasted eight years or possibly nine and a half years, although apparently there was work on the entire complex that lasted into the sixth decade of the first century CE.[86] According to Josephus (*Ant.* 15.365) in 20/19 BCE Herod remitted one-third of the taxes, allegedly under the pretext of letting the people recover from a period of dearth, but really in order to defuse resentment against him. It is intriguing to wonder if the sudden decision to embark on a massive building program is not one solution to an economic crisis. Admittedly this is only a supposition, which as yet has no basis in the sources.

Recently two engineers from the Technion Institute of Haifa attempted to analyze the building of the Temple in terms of workforce and costs.[87] They concluded that the entire Temple project involved 50,000 man-years of labor. A permanent work crew of 7,000–8,000 men was kept employed, but with supporting projects, transportation, and the like, they believe that the total force employed was approximately 10,000 men.

The Temple certainly cost a fortune to build.[88] However, rather than being a burden on the economy, a burden that would have resulted in oppressive taxation leading to massive dislocation from the land, we feel the Temple provided solutions to some problems. First, the building itself provided employment for hard-pressed cultivators.[89] Despite the impression that farmers might not make good stonemasons, there is a body of empirical evidence that off-season farmers do work in the building trades. Furthermore, not all the working men, and probably not even the majority of the labor on a building project like the Temple, need to be craftsmen.[90] Second, a not insignificant part of the population of Judea was supported by the income of the working men. Ten thousand men can provide for a population of forty thousand or more people.[91] The Keynesian law that for full employment and prosperity it is sufficient to have one-half of the population dig holes and the other half fill them in was operative even in Herod's day.[92] Some of the people involved in the building lived quite well, judging by the tombs found in Jerusalem.[93]

Recognizing that the Temple was just one project, we see that Herod found employment for large sectors of the population. If we adopt

Thornton's conclusion that Roman emperors apparently planned their public works so as to always have some project under way, [94] and we compare that to the list of projects built by Herod, we see that for much of Herod's reign public works were under construction.[95]

A corollary effect to the building of the Temple was the influx of donations and pilgrims. The donations helped offset costs, and provided employment. Some salient examples are the donation of money for the paving of the Temple; and the building of a permanent synagogue and hostel for pilgrims.[96]

The development of a vibrant economy may have had a salutary effect by providing employment in commerce.

Cotton and Geiger suggest that "The jar inscriptions (*tituli picti*) in both Greek and Jewish characters reflect the prominence of Jews in trade and agriculture in Herod's kingdom."[97] Likewise, the Herodian economy may have generated increased employment in manufacturing. There are a large number of *tituli picti* bearing the notation καλόν κεράμιον (literally: "fair pottery"). The καλόν κεράμιον may be the translation of a Hebrew expression indicating the quality of pottery jars.[98] If so, it is further evidence for a series of jars of Jewish origin and hence for Jewish manufacturing. The fact that the quality is marked in Greek might indicate a desire to expand the economic activity of the manufacturer beyond the borders of the Hebrew/Aramaic settlement.[99]

Decades after Herod we find a wealthy Jewish community in Caesarea, competing with the gentiles for control of the city. A Jew is a prominent tax collector, and we can assume that many of the Jewish inhabitants are involved in commerce. The lands of the city were probably already owned by the gentiles, hence it appears to us that the commercial opportunities attracted the Jews.

A recent survey of Second Temple history sums up the situation with regard to Herod thus:

> it is often asserted how much the people hated Herod the Great and how hard he made life for the Jews, yet the available data can and, in some cases, probably should be synthesized in a completely different light. There are reasons to think that the average Jew in Palestine was better off in the later part of Herod's reign than before or after.[100]

The famine

An interesting example of Herod's concern for his subjects is the food crisis of 25/24 BCE (*Ant.* 15.299–316).[101] Our source is a very flattering tale about Herod (*Ant.* 15.315–16), probably by Nicolaus of Damascus.[102] Nevertheless, there is no reason to suspect that this is not a reliable and accurate description of a serious famine.[103]

Continual droughts are stated to have been the primary cause of the famine (*Ant.* 15.300). We have already presented some information about the precipitation pattern in Palestine. Since drought is given as the major factor let us add a few points about it.

Not all droughts lead to famine; the timing and geographical extent of the drought are the determining factors. Grain crops can survive some lack of rain if they receive water in the critical periods of sprouting and final ripening.[104] Furthermore the southern parts of Palestine are generally more prone to drought, but as long as the northern sections of the country get enough precipitation some crop will be harvested.[105] In this instance, however, the droughts are described as continual, which would lead to the destruction of the crop. Additionally, the drought lasted two years, which would lead to the consumption of the stores, and, more seriously, to a lack of seed to plant when the drought passed.

"Siege-induced food crises apart, the more geographically circumscribed a shortage, the more speedily it could be relieved, and therefore the less serious its effects were likely to be."[106] In our case the drought extended beyond the confines of Palestine (*Ant.* 15.305) so that the neighboring countries needed aid also (*Ant.* 15.311).[107] Josephus mentions Syria in particular, but does not specify further. However, it is clear that only Syria and Phoenicia are meant and not Egypt, because Herod turns to Egypt to buy grain. The two former areas share in some part the same climatic conditions.[108] We have no way of knowing in which parts of Syria the drought struck; however, during the so-called "Universal Famine" in the days of Queen Helene, the Christian community of Antioch sent aid to Jerusalem.[109] We may see in this evidence that northern Syria would not necessarily be affected by climatic conditions in southern Syria.

The location of an area struck by a food crisis can affect the efforts to aid the population. A recent and tragic example witnessed by millions on television was the starvation of many Ethiopians because of their location in remote regions. An oft-quoted example from the ancient world of the effect of location on famine is the case of Antioch. Finley blames transport difficulties for the delay in assistance, but Garnsey has called into question the validity of Finley's view.[110] Let us examine how Palestine's location may have affected a food crisis and how Herod made use of the advantages.

There are four geographic factors that are helpful in extending aid to

Palestine. First, it is close to Egypt. Second, it has a coastline the whole length of the country. Third, it is a land bridge between Asia and Africa. Fourth, it is a small country.

The agriculture of Egypt and Palestine are dependent on two separate and different patterns of precipitation. Egypt is watered by the Nile, Israel by western winter cyclones.[111] As a result Egypt can raise a successful crop while at the same time drought is devastating the agriculture of her northern neighbor. Egypt has served as the bread-basket of Syria and Palestine.[112] The opposite has also been the case when Egypt has been struck by famine.[113] Another advantage arising from Palestine's proximity to Egypt is that Egypt was a grain-exporting country whose political, social, and economic infrastructures were geared to supply wheat and barley.[114] Moreover, if we were to divide the problem of grain transport into three successive stages – getting the grain from the growers to the port of export, moving it from the exporting country to the importing country, and distributing it from its port of entry – we would see that Egypt had a tremendous advantage. Not only did the Nile water Egypt, but it also served as her major transportation artery. Additionally, Alexandria had an excellent port, so that many of the problems incurred in ancient commerce were avoided when buying grain from Egypt.

Seaborne commerce was significantly cheaper and faster than transportation of cargoes by land. Ships could carry larger burdens than pack animals or wagons could, and they made better time.[115] This came as an advantage to Palestine whose lengthy sea coast provides many landing opportunities for those who would supply her by sea. Stretched all along her Mediterranean seaboard were cities, large and small, with landing facilities of some nature. Some of these were barely usable (Shiqmona), others were major ports (Acco-Ptolemais). They all offered the possibility of a gateway into the hinterland for those who would wish to import grain.[116]

Palestine's geographical position and small size made the problem of distribution simpler to solve. Because the country was a bridge between the civilizations of Africa and Asia, a network of roads developed in Palestine from biblical times.[117] Later, the Romans improved and developed the road system. It is thought that the Roman contribution was made after Herod's day, but we can assume that in great part the Romans paved roads that had already been in existence.[118] In fact, we have evidence that cargoes of grain on pack animals were transported throughout Palestine in Ptolemaic times.[119] The distances within the country are not abnormal for transport of goods by camel and pack-mule. For example, necessities were brought to Rome from Ostia by pack-animals and grain was brought to the Nile for further shipment from the growing areas.[120] Furthermore the latest research maintains that there was land transportation of staple goods for short and intermediate distances.[121] Indeed, there is sufficient evidence that supplies were furnished to whole armies, in Palestine and elsewhere, to show that large stocks of food were moved by land when the government had an interest to do so.[122]

There remains the problem of moving the cargo from the ships to the shore. It is not enough to have a secure harbor, an efficient way has to be provided to disembark the shipment. Ideally, the ship should be able to tie up to a quay, otherwise the cargo has to be transferred to lighters and once more off-loaded to the shore. Ostensibly this should not have posed a problem. The praises of Jaffa as an entrance port are sung by I Macc., and *The Letter of Aristeas* praises Acco-Ptolemais.[123] However, the large and convenient ports of Acco and Gaza were not in Herod's realm. South of Acco the first coastal town of any consequence was Straton's Tower, which is described as only a landing-place, not a port.[124] Jaffa itself was not well suited for direct off-loading of ships.[125] From Jaffa south till Gaza, the coastal cities also seem to have either very small ports or only landing-places.[126] We do not know how this problem affected Herod's relief efforts, but it may have been serious enough to seed the idea of building a large deep-water port.

The misfortunes occurred in the thirteenth year of Herod's reign (*Ant.* 15.299), which according to the prevailing opinion is 25 BCE.[127] If Josephus intended to date the misfortunes from the beginning of the drought, then autumn 25 to spring 24 is the first drought year, and spring 24 is the first failed crop. But then the drought continued into the following year (*Ant.* 15.302), i.e. autumn 24–spring 23, which is when Herod turned to Petronius (*Ant.* 15.307). This is hard to credit because there was a food crisis in Rome that year and the following.[128] The Prefect of Egypt was hardly likely to sell large quantities of grain to Herod in a year when Rome was in the middle of a food crisis. Moreover, according to Westermann, Petronius sold Herod the "bumper crop" of May 24 BCE.[129] If so, we must conclude that perhaps Otto was correct in dating the beginning of the drought to autumn 26 BCE.[130] This suggests the possibility that Josephus began dating the troubles from the spring of 25, i.e. when the first crop failed.[131] Since the crop of spring 24 BCE failed also, but no further troubles are mentioned, we can assume that the crop of spring 23 BCE was successful, therefore in summary the food crisis lasted two years, 25/24–24/23 BCE.

There are two indications of price movement in our source. The first is a hint that food was available, but only at a very high price (*Ant.* 15.305). The second, while not mentioning prices directly, can be tied into price movements by comparison with known patterns of behavior in famines.

In the first case, a rise in food prices is expected in any food crisis. It is the natural result of the law of supply and demand. But one should bear in mind that even in the worst famine some people have food and these persons will either hoard it, or sell it at exorbitant prices.[132]

The second hint is that the people were in need of clothing and that their flocks had been slaughtered. What happened to their clothes and why were their herds slaughtered? The answer lies in two interesting consequences of famines. Concomitant with the rise in food prices is a drop in the price of non-edible possessions as people sell their goods in order to meet the rising costs of food.[133] Furthermore, famine has a very extraordinary effect on the price of meat, which drops relative to the price of other foods. This is because the farmers lack the grain to feed their livestock, and the animals are slaughtered for their meat. The sudden flooding of the market with meat leads to a plunge in that commodity's price.[134]

Josephus informs us that the drought led to crop failure, and the crop failure forced a change of diet, which led to illnesses, which in turn brought on plague (*Ant.* 15.300). The lack of medical care and nourishment increased the effects of the disease (*Ant.* 15.301). The link between drought and famine has already been demonstrated. It remains now to show the connection between change of diet and disease.

Galen observed that the change in diet stemming from famine conditions is a major cause of disease and death.[135] The interrelationship between disease and dietary deficiency is very complex. On the one hand, there are diseases that are not dependent on or affected by lack of nourishment. On the other hand, there are sicknesses which break out as a result of the weakening of the immune system which follows upon the malnutrition. Finally, there are illnesses which are not only caused by undernourishment, but which interfere with the patient's ability to eat any food, even if some becomes available.[136] The lack of food has one more unpleasant and significant side-effect. It decreases the willingness and ability to work, creating a sort of apathy.[137]

In summary, the empirical observations of modern cases of malnutrition, undernourishment, and starvation confirm Josephus' account as to the outbreak and effects of disease that accompanied the famine.

Faced with a catastrophic famine, Herod was handicapped by an empty treasury. We have already discussed the importance of the agricultural sector to Herod's income. Just when he needed money, his major source of funds literally withered on the vine. Herod gathered what funds he could (*Ant.* 15.306) and brought wheat by ship from Egypt (*Ant.* 15.307). He distributed grain to the able, and provided for bakers and baked bread for the feeble (*Ant.* 15.309). Then he furnished clothes to the needy population (*Ant.* 15.310) and harvesters to bring in the crop (*Ant.* 15.312). Finally, Herod aided the neighboring lands and cities, giving both land and seed (*Ant.* 15.311, 313).

These actions by Herod, while not unique, do not fit the prevalent pattern of famine relief in the Hellenistic world. As Garnsey has put it, "The key role in the resolution and alleviation of food crises was performed by local men of wealth."[138]

However, there is a model of food crisis relief that Garnsey apparently neglected, the Hellenistic king as *soter* (savior) and *euergetes* (benefactor). The ideal of Hellenistic kingship entailed the duty of the monarch to aid his subjects in their need.[139] We have already given the example of Ptolemy III (*OGIS* 56, 17), but a far more recent example existed for Herod: Cleopatra, who allegedly handed out corn to her subjects at a time of dearth.[140] Herod apparently also wished to be considered a *euergetes*. A stone weight from the thirty-second year of Herod is inscribed with the words "King Herod the Benefactor."[141]

Additionally, Herod had the Roman example to follow: the most recent was that of 28 BC when Augustus quadrupled the allowance of grain.[142] Herod had implied and explicit duties to his Roman rulers, among the most important of which was the obligation to maintain order. The Roman experience was that food crises often led to disorder. As Tiberius is alleged to have said, the neglect of the corn supply by the ruler could lead to the ruin of the state.[143]

Herod also had to contend with the memory of the Hasmonean rulers. Simon in particular is praised for his concern for the people's welfare (I Macc. 14:8–10).

Finally, we are left with an intriguing question: what was the Jewish component, if any, in his actions? Individual charity is frequently enjoined by the Bible and later Jewish writings. Royal intervention in economic crises is not a specifically defined commandment, nevertheless according to some eastern traditions of kingship the king is expected to care for the welfare of his people.[144]

In summary, we would point out that Herod's primary motivation as related by Josephus (Nicolaus?) is the requirement to defuse the resentment of his subjects (*Ant.* 15.304). If he felt any obligation to meet some philosophical or religious standard of kingship, it was secondary to his immediate political needs. This is well demonstrated by his action on receiving aid from Petronius. Our source states that the lion's share of aid came from Petronius, but that Herod garnered the credit for himself (*Ant.* 15.307).

Herod's famine relief actions entailed dealing with three different aspects of the crisis: food relief, provision of clothing, bringing in a crop. The first aspect involved locating a source of wheat, buying it, bringing it, and distributing it. He located wheat in Egypt. We will not repeat in detail what has already been said about Egypt as a source of grain independent of the vagaries of climate that affected Palestine. Buying the wheat comprised two separate problems: money and Roman consent to the purchase.

Josephus tells us that Herod was broke because he had spent his money on rebuilding cities and the famine had bitten deep into his revenues (*Ant.* 15.303).[145] To raise money Herod took silver and gold objects and made them into coinage (*Ant.* 15.306). This is a most intriguing statement, because it is clear from the verb used (συνεκόπτω) that Herod did not convert these precious items into cash by selling them, but coined them into money. We have no examples of Herodian coinage in precious metals. Nonetheless, there is sufficient evidence that throughout his career Herod paid and gave large sums of cash to various beneficiaries. It is not reasonable to assume that these payments were made in cheap bronze coinage, so that the question is in what coinage did he pay?[146]

It has been claimed that with the Roman conquest of Eygpt all the latter's grain became earmarked exclusively for Rome.[147] However, the more recent view is that Egypt had a large surplus which was not always needed in Rome, while Rome itself was more dependent for grain on the provinces of Sicily and Africa. In brief, grain was exported to other destinations besides Rome.[148] Moreover, Josephus does not imply that obtaining wheat from Egypt was an exception to policy. Rather he implies the opposite, the many demands made on Egyptian wheat can be inferred from the text (*Ant.* 15.307). Furthermore, and most important, Josephus states that Petronius gave Herod's shipments priority, implying that there were others. Therefore, the problem was not if Roman Egypt would sell grain at all, but in a period of high demand to whom would she sell it. Petronius' motives for favoring Herod are less clearly explained. It is said that he was a friend of Herod's and wished to aid his subjects. Josephus is the only witness to this friendship, nevertheless it fits the pattern of relationships Herod developed with the Roman ruling class. With regard to Petronius' desire to aid Herod's subjects, Gapp has postulated that Rome wished to ensure the stability of their client-king's throne, so the Roman Prefect in Egypt did what he could to help Herod.[149] Another, but related, reason could be tied into Herod's contribution to the expedition of Aelius Gallus to Arabia. Jameson's theory is that Herod sent troops by way of expressing his gratitude for the wheat.[150] It may well have been the other way around, with the Roman Prefect in Egypt rewarding a proven ally.

Herod brought the grain by ship (*Ant.* 15.307). Josephus gives us two indications of the amount; he claims that 10,000 *kor* were given to people outside the kingdom and about 80,000 *kor* were distributed among the inhabitants of the realm (*Ant.* 15.314).[151]

Therefore, Herod brought c. 35,550,000 – 41,850,000 liters of grain by ship and distributed them.[152] The number of shiploads necessary to move this amount depends of course on the carrying capacity of the ships. Ships of 150 tons were common in Hellenistic times, while the standard grain-ships on the Alexandria–Italy line were 340 tons.[153] Herod had to move about 28,000–33,000 tons, with ships of 150 tons: anywhere from 180 to 220 shiploads would be necessary. Egypt supposedly provided Rome with 135,000 tons annually.[154] Rickman claims that Rome imported the bulk of the 250,000 tons of grain a year she needed.[155] Garnsey, although more modest than Rickman in his estimates of the general level of imported wheat, states: "It is not inconceivable that import levels did occasionally reach 60 million modii."[156] In summary, the amount of grain that Herod had to move was not extraordinary, and if we take into account that Petronius allegedly arranged for the shipping, the transport problem was easily surmountable because the Alexandrian grain fleet shipped far larger quantities than Herod's.

How many people could be fed with the grain that Herod brought? The Roman grain distribution was 5 modii per month for men, 3 for women, and perhaps 1.9 for children.[157] Cato granted his field slaves 4–4.5 modii a month.[158] If we take 5 modii a month as an average consumption rate (43 liters) we find that Herod brought enough grain to feed c. 69,000–81,000 men for a year. Of these only about 90 percent were inhabitants of his kingdom.[159] However, if we base our calculations on 200 kilograms per head per annum the same amount of grain might support about 139,000 people.[160] But this is an optimum figure, because we do not know how much of the grain was used as food and how much used for seed.

Two passages in Josephus lead us to believe that part of the grain was used for seed (*Ant.* 15.309, 311). The seed had a critical value in preventing major changes in the landowning structure.[161] In famine situations freeholders are forced to buy their seed at exorbitant prices. The result is that they can be forced into a tenancy position. By distributing seed Herod operated in the most effective way to prevent wide-ranging drift into debt and tenancy.

A second related problem we have to face in order to accurately appreciate Herod's famine-relief effort is how large was the population of his kingdom? As we have seen, population estimates for the ancient world differ widely and those for Palestine are no better. The most conservative estimate is between one half to three quarters of a million people.[162] We see then that the grain provided by Herod could not have sufficed for the whole population.

Josephus suggests that there were other sources of relief. He states that peoples (δῆμοι), cities (πόλεις), and individuals (ἰδιῶται) found themselves in need because they had provided for too many others (*Ant.* 15.313). There is also another source which might indicate that Herod's efforts were not as successful or as all-encompassing as Josephus would lead us to believe. Flusser claims that 4QpHos^a 2:12–14 implies "the help received from Egypt was ineffective and could not supply sufficient provisions for the suffering population."[163] Furthermore, he suggests, based on 4QpPs^a 3:2–5, that the large storage facilities at Qumran provided the adherents of the sect, and others that took refuge with them, with the food they needed, implying that those who did not take refuge in Qumran starved.[164]

How much did the grain cost? Duncan-Jones has found that over a long period of time the official price of grain purchased from the Roman Prefect was 8 drachmas per artaba.[165] Therefore, at 2 Attic drachmas per 39 liters Herod may have paid between 1,800,000–2,100,000 Attic drachmas which are c. 300–50 talents. However, there were lower prices in Upper Egypt, as low as 2.5 drachmas per artaba, which would reduce our figures to a fourth, and at times of famine the price could go up to 16 drachmas, doubling our estimate.[166] Herod's annual income was c. 1,000 talents, so normally he could afford to buy this quantity of grain.[167] These were apparently abnormal times, but 350 talents were obtainable. In fact we do not know how much he paid, and we will probably never know, but the above figures are at least reasonable estimates of how much he might have paid.

Herod's famine relief included the distribution of food, seed, and clothing, the provision of bakers and baked bread, and the operation and maintenance of harvesters. We do not know how the distribution of food was handled. Hamburger suggests that a system of *tesserae* was employed, but while the idea is tempting there is not enough evidence to accept it.[168]

The seed distribution is self-evident. Under the pressure of the famine people consumed whatever grain they had, and they had also suffered the destruction of two sowing seasons. Seed was certainly very hard to come by, and could have been used as a lever to extract very unfavorable terms from the farmers. Therefore, Herod was very stringent and sparing of the seed, or so we interpret *Ant.* 15.309.

We have already explained the probable reason why Herod had to provide clothing to his people. In many places in the Greco-Roman world the recipients of grain had to grind it themselves or arrange to have it ground. On the other hand, there is a growing body of ostraca which indicate that bread was baked and then distributed.[169] It is quite possible that since Herod could not provide as much wheat as was needed, he minimized the wastage by using government-supervised millers and bakers.[170]

There is another explanation for the use of bakers and it ties in with the fifty thousand harvesters who Herod sent out to the fields. It is noted that he himself fed and cared for them and that he sent them into the country, i.e. they were not tenants on his land (*Ant.* 15.312). It might well be that these were the refugees who flock to the cities whenever a famine strikes, agriculturalists who can no longer live on the land. Herod's action could have been an attempt to deal with the widespread unemployment which studies demonstrate is an accompanying effect of serious famines.[171] Similarly, it may have been an effort to extend his personal patronage to otherwise unsupported people. Sen has demonstrated that the key to survival in a famine is "food entitlement," i.e. having the right position in the society. For example, the slaves of powerful and influential people will be more likely to receive food than free but unimportant people.[172]

In summary, Herod's actions in aid of the emergency are on the whole in keeping with what we know of such measures in his time and with his behavior as a Hellenistic ruler within the Roman Principate.

Josephus reports that the people consumed their stocks (*Ant.* 15.302), they were struck by malaise (*Ant.* 15.301), they resorted to famine foods (*Ant.* 15.300, 303), abandoned their occupations in an effort to find sources of food (*Ant.* 15.303), they turned their frustration on the authorities (*Ant.* 15.304), but changed their attitude in thankfulness for the aid they received (*Ant.* 15.308, 315–16). The actions of the people fit what we know about famines.

We have already given some explanation of these actions. The question of famine foods, abandonment of occupation, and resentment deserve a bit more elucidation.

Garnsey has categorized the foods into five groups: livestock not normally slaughtered, inferior cereals, animal foods, natural products not meant to be eaten such as leather, roots, and bark, and finally cannibalism.[173] This progression is not fully documented in our case. We only have three indicators: (1) the change of diet caused disease; (2) the want necessitated innovations; (3) and their flocks had completely been consumed (*Ant.* 15.310). Thus, we have evidence that at the very least the first category of famine food was consumed. The consumption of large quantities of meat should not be related to the sudden outbreak of disease since meat contains enough calorific and protein content to sustain life. Rather, we can assume that after having eaten their flocks the starving people turned to the lower categories of food. It is interesting to note that Josephus adds a detail to the tale of the famine in Egypt (Gen. 47:14–20). After paraphrasing the story more or less faithfully he appends that the people were driven to degrading means of subsistence (*Ant.* 2.190). This phrase is tied into another which has Thucydidean echoes.[174] Likewise, *BJ* 1.64 relates how the starving people of Samaria ate unheard of foods, which may very well be a tale inspired by the siege of Samaria in I Kings 6:25–9. So, also, the famine horror stories regarding the siege of Jerusalem during the Great Revolt (*BJ* 5.571). But rather than assume that we have a famine topos, based on the empirical knowledge we have of famine behavior we should realize that the famine-food pattern is probably true.[175]

Food riots are one of the attendant circumstances to food crises.[176] Yet Josephus makes no mention of riot or protest in connection with the famine. He only notes that "these misfortunes had brought upon him the hatred of his subjects, and when people do not get on well, there is always a tendency to blame those who rule over them." This is a curious lack of activity on the part of the population, considering that there were "disturbances" as a matter of course because of his other policies (*Ant.* 15.287). Perhaps the repressive measures conducted by Herod against the population had been so effective that no one dared to make overt protests.

Emigration is one of the usual responses to a food crisis.[177] But while we have evidence for Jewish emigration from Palestine for many varied reasons during the period of the Second Temple, we have no direct evidence for emigration due to famine.[178] Gapp believes that "many Jews had already fled to Egypt for food during the scarcity."[179] The text does not support that reading, because it does not specify Jews, but simply says that "not a few fled to him (Petronius) because of the need." Since the famine struck Palestine and Syria, including probably Phoenicia, there is no way to ascertain who the refugees were, their number, and their origin.

In summary, not only do we not have a record of wide-ranging expropriation with masses of small freeholders being left landless and homeless, but the major cause of dislocation, the debts resulting from natural catastrophes or prolonged dearth of crops, was actively combated by Herod through alleviation of taxes and famine relief. Furthermore, the extensive building projects provided by Herod must have had a salutary effect on the small landholder. They provided additional and alternative income for farmers who needed to supplement their earnings. The building projects needed working men, the large numbers of permanent building workers needed food supplies, thereby providing an outlet for those who had a surplus. The improved communications made it easier to bring produce to market and provided jobs in the transport and commercial spheres.

Herod's rule went far to ameliorate the effects of the period since Pompey. Pompey's dispositions caused mass dislocation because of the changes in land tenure. The intervening period saw further dislocations as the result of revolts and the Roman civil war. Herod's expropriation and gift of estates may not necessarily have improved matters, but his rule over the non-Jewish areas adjoining the coast resulted in the return of Jews to these areas, Jews who now prospered. His commercial program opened up new avenues of income. Finally, but certainly significant, was the building program that is so characteristic of Herod's reign.

Why the sudden violent outburst shortly upon Herod's death? Why did the unrest include two economic features: the demand for reduction of taxes and lower-class leaders prominent in much of the disturbances? Herod's economic policies might have been successful, but the attitudes of the general population did not stem from a reasoned analysis of the situation. To an untrained observer the blatant facts were that taxes were high. Moreover, the developing economy contained social and cultural elements that were regarded with distaste.[180] Indeed, Herod had been unpopular even before his reign. It took Roman spears to put him on the throne. He was perceived as a creature of the Romans, and his record prior to his coronation is replete with examples of oppression, especially tax-gouging. If these were not reasons enough to see Herod in a bad light, the first few years of his reign were marked by a struggle to overcome the effects of the conquest, the Sabbatical Year, and the limitless demands of Antony and Cleopatra. The first few years undoubtedly reinforced the negative image most of the people had of Herod. All they could see was the veteran lackey of the Romans who had milked them dry for Crassus, Cassius, and Antony. His attempts to improve his image were never successful. Although he probably succeeded in bringing his kingdom to unprecedented levels of prosperity, paradoxically this also hurt his image. The prosperity was tinged with cultural imperialism and associated with high taxes.

ARCHELAUS

The oft-encountered interpretation of the economic developments in Judea during the Herodian period is that Herod left a drained and oppressed populace. It is then related that his son Archelaus failed as a ruler and was deposed. We have tried to show that whatever surface impressions may have existed within some elements of the Jewish populace, Herod had successfully provided answers to various economic problems.

But Herod's death created the unavoidable problem of what to do with his kingdom. The questions regarding the validity of his will, the feuding within the family, and Augustus' political decision are not in the purview of this study.

However, in general terms the disposition of the kingdom was that Archelaus received Samaria, Judea, and Idumea, including Caesarea, Sebaste, Jaffa, and Jerusalem. Gaza, Gadara, and Hippus were detached to the Province of Syria. Antipas received the Galilee and the Peraea. Philip received Panias, the Golan, the Bashan, the Hauran, and Trachonitis. Herod's sister Salome received Iamnia, Azotus, and Phasaelis.[181]

Archelaus' reign lasted for a decade (4 BCE–6 CE) and then he was removed from his post and from Judea.[182] It has often been noted that Archelaus' dismissal is poorly explained by our sources, probably because Nicolaus was no longer on the scene while Josephus had no other reference.[183] To us it appears that though on the surface political ineptitude may seem the reason for his removal, in fact economic and social problems characterized his administration.

He began his rule with a riot ostensibly provoked by the "revolutionaries" who wished to revenge the men who had cut down the golden eagle from the gate of the Temple.[184] Yet in both versions of the events leading up to the riot, the crowds began their requests with increasingly vociferous demands for relief from taxes (*BJ* 2.4; *Ant.* 17.204–5). The taxes which Josephus mentions are the annual tax (εἰσφοραί) and the purchase and sales taxes (τέλη). Josephus relates that Archelaus consented to their request. There are a number of questions that arise from this incident. First of all, did the people really demand tax relief? Why these particular taxes? Did Archelaus grant their request? What were Archelaus' reasons, whatever his decision?

The demand for tax relief would have been expected in any case since such demands were *de rigueur* on any occasion on which the ruler would be likely to grant such requests. Such occasions might be after economic disasters, outstanding service, joyous events in the life of the crown, and when the ruler needed to improve his image.[185] We have seen that Herod granted tax relief on a number of occasions (*Ant.* 15.365; 16.64). By the same token Archelaus would feel social pressure to grant these requests. He would wish to appear at least as "philanthropic" as the late king. He would also wish to fit the mold of the euergetic ruler. Yet, when the delegates of the people appeared before Caesar, they repeated the complaint that the tax burden was too heavy (*Ant.* 17.307–8). It is possible that either the tax relief was suspended as a reaction to the riots, or it had been granted in proviso that Archelaus would be confirmed as the king by Augustus.

While Archelaus and his kin were feuding in front of Caesar, the violence in Judea had been rekindled by Sabinus, the *procurator Caesaris* (*BJ* 2.16; *Ant.* 17.221). It is unclear what specifically sparked the violent reaction to Sabinus.[186] He was Augustus' personal representative, and if there really was a "people's party" demanding direct Roman rule, then the rioting that occurred was counter-productive.[187] This reaction to his presence is even more puzzling when we consider that his activities should have been particularly offensive to Archelaus, who the people hated. He took possession of Herod's palace in Jerusalem, tried to enter the other fortresses, and to gain control of the deceased's treasures, so then why should the Jewish masses have taken such offence?[188] Perhaps they suspected that Sabinus intended robbing the Temple treasury; in fact, during the ensuing action the Romans looted the Temple, Sabinus taking 400 talents for himself (*BJ* 2.50; *Ant.* 17.264).

Sabinus was surrounded by soldiers who had deserted from the government side (*BJ* 2.52; *Ant.* 17.266). Meanwhile, two thousand veterans of Herod's army rebelled in Idumea.[189] What possessed these soldiers to rebel? No doubt the religious–national loyalties and resentments played a strong part.[190] However, on the one hand, one other betrayal by Herod's soldiers is recorded. The Arabs (Nabateans) feuding with Herod over the Hauran (23 BCE) had "won over those soldiers who were poor and hostile [to Herod], and were always hopefully inclined toward revolution, which is especially welcome to those who fare badly in life."[191] It is significant that after these events Herod had felt the need to settle more troops in the Trachon region, and these settlers benefited from extensive privileges (*Ant.* 16.285; 17.23–7). On the other hand, the Sebastenians remained loyal. They had many reasons for their loyalty: one of them might well have been the preferential conditions of their military settlements.[192] It is likely that not all soldiers received the same privileges, so that there may have been Jewish soldiers who were economically disaffected, as well as ideologically opposed to the Herodian house. Indeed, Nicolaus saw the conflict as one between the Jews and the Greeks.[193] The Greeks would include the cohorts raised from the Hellenistic cities.[194]

Those who would see an economic motivation for the rebellions base their view on the social–economic aspects of the rebel groups.

1 In the Galilee Judas, son of Ezekias, attacked the capital city of Sepphoris.[195] Judas was the son of a man whose actions were not unconnected to the loss of lands. Just a few decades earlier the "Galileans" had thrown the δυνατοί (nobles) into the Sea of Galilee. After attacking the palace and seizing all the arms, his followers stole the property there, and he continued to rob those he came across (*Ant.* 17.271–2; *BJ* 2.56).

2 In Perea, Simon, a royal slave, burnt down the royal palace, and other homes of the wealthy (*BJ* 2.57; *Ant.* 17.273–4).

3 Athronges, a shepherd, led a rebel band which attacked anyone from whom some gain could be obtained.[196]

In all these cases there was violence to property-holders and to property. However, is the conclusion inescapable that at the end of Herod's reign Jewish society had strong elements of economic and social rancor? Applebaum's assumption that these rebels were disgruntled tenants is simplistic.[197] If tenants' rights were at the heart of the uprising why did Judea not become a focus of revolt (*BJ* 2.73; *Ant.* 17.293)? Why was Sepphoris so rebellious that the city was sacked and the inhabitants sold into slavery (*Ant.* 17.289)? Why was the focus of the Galilean revolt in the region adjoining Acco-Ptolemais (*Ant.* 17.288) when most of the royal land in the Galilee was in the Jezreel Valley?[198] If the problem was tenancy, what future arrangements did the putative "kings" envision?[199]

Even under the Judean kings there was royal land and there were royal estates. Finally, why did the Samaritans remain passive, seeing that they too were tenants, who had not enjoyed immunity from taxation or rents?[200]

No one can doubt that the rebels included slaves and other disadvantaged elements. They resented the wealthy, especially those identified as the despised king's supporters.[201] There were sufficient religious, cultural, and political reasons to rebel without resorting to an unproved allegation that disgruntled and oppressed farmers were at the root of the War of Varus.

In short, Herod's reign had ended with a bang, but the explosion was not set off for economic reasons. The fact is that Augustus was unimpressed with the complaints of the "people's delegation." He appointed Archelaus, and his brothers, to rule in Palestine.

A decade after his appointment Archelaus was dismissed from his post. The reasons for Archelaus' removal are never made clear. It is claimed that he was cruel and oppressive; yet when we examine the complaints against him we find no actions of such substantial error that would justify the punishment he was given by Augustus. There are those who suggest that his rule was rife with flagrant violations of the Jewish Law: he appointed and deposed High Priests, and he married his sister-in-law. However, the Samaritans joined with the Jews in accusing him (*BJ* 2.111; *Ant.* 17.342). Why were they so sensitive to Archelaus' personal religious behavior? Apparently, the answer does not lie in the field of religion.

Augustus deposed him for failing to deal with his subjects with moderation, as he had been instructed to do (*Ant.* 17.342). What were the "brutalities" and the "tyrannies" which angered Jews, Samaritans, and Caesar? We read in Luke 19:12–28 that some great lord is very ruthless and oppresses his people. The pericope is about a man of noble birth who went to a far country in order to receive a kingdom, but his people sent after him saying they would not have him rule over them. This person is probably Archelaus. He is described as αἴρεις ὁ οὐκ ἔθηκας καὶ θερίζεις ὁ οὐκ ἔσπειρας (verse 21).[202] The behavior described could refer to usury, but also to abusive taxation, or even to expropriation.

Josephus also preserves indications of oppressive economic measures by Archelaus: diversion of water and forced resettlement under harsh conditions.[203] Archelaus established a date plantation and diverted half the water of a village in order to irrigate it. We have no way of knowing how large a plantation of dates was built by Archelaus.

However, by way of comparison the date plantation of Jericho is reported to have been 70×20 *stadia* (13×3.7 km) (*BJ* 4.467). The water resources of the area had already been exploited to the maximum by the Hasmoneans and Herod and the only way to obtain water for his interests was to expropriate it from the people of the region, which would have undoubtedly diminished their ability to raise a crop. An idea of the importance of water rights in these arid conditions may be obtained by considering a document from an albeit later period. In a gift deed from the "Babatha Archive," the time of irrigation is specified for one hour of one day in a week.[204]

He also built the village of Archelais.[205] The settlement became famous for the great number of palms and the high quality of the dates.[206] But it is in a hot arid region and it is safe to assume that the workforce for the plantation had to be brought in to the area. If they were indigenous then they would have had their own farms, which they now would have had to neglect.

We see a pattern of operation which suggests efforts to increase his revenues. His income had been diminished by Augustus when the latter cut the taxes of the Samaritans by 25 percent.[207] Moreover, he had only 600 talents revenue, compared to about twice that amount which his father enjoyed. He had lost the ports of Gaza, Iamnia, and Azotus. The income from the Galilee, Gadara, Hippus, and Phasaelis was no longer his to enjoy. By losing the Peraea, Panias, the Golan, the Bashan, the Hauran, and Trachonitis he lost the income gained from control of important lines of communication.

In order to compensate for this loss we suggest that Archelaus was forced to wring money out of his subjects. His personal wealth increased at the expense of his people. An indicator of Archelaus' amassed wealth is that Quirinius, the pro-consul of Syria, was instructed to sell the property of Archelaus.[208] This suggests that Archelaus had more than Augustus thought healthy.

HEROD ANTIPAS

Herod Antipas has left us a longer and perhaps better record than his older brother. His tetrarchy encompassed the Galilee and the Peraea. Because his territory and rule coincide with the activities of John the Baptist and Jesus of Nazareth, Antipas has benefited from the interest of historians.[209] Antipas' reign is further distinguished by two interesting features: he was the first Herodian to establish a Jewish polis in Jewish territory, and, unlike the situation of his father and his brother, there is no evidence of serious unrest or public dissatisfaction with his reign. There are those who claim that the repression by Varus removed any revolutionary core that may have existed in the Galilee, but Varus was no less ruthless in Judea and yet revolutionary movements continued there, and even blossomed within a decade.[210]

Antipas founded three cities, Sepphoris, Tiberias in the Galilee, and Livias in Peraea.[211] Sepphoris was really a refounding of an ancient city heavily damaged by Varus' operations. Livias was the refounding of the ancient city of Beth-haram, also damaged during the War of Varus.

Sepphoris had been the capital of the Galilee. It remained so for a short while under Antipas, although it lost this honor to the city of Tiberias. It regained its pre-eminence probably in 61 CE. Very little is known about the details of the refoundation. It is assumed that the citizens were chosen because of their loyalty to the Herods and their pro-Roman policies. During the Great Revolt the people of Sepphoris vigorously refused to be drawn into the conflict on the rebel side. This behavior is supposedly explained by the reluctance of the inhabitants to endure a repetition of Varus' punitive measures. Similarly, it is maintained that the citizens realized their vulnerability.[212] Yet the behavior of Sepphoris demonstrates above all that the population had not become disaffected. While admitting that all the conclusions are based on inference, it remains that on the one hand we have a chosen city population, in the leading city of the area, seat of the government, the archives, and the royal bank, "the ornament of all Galilee"; on the other hand, that same population is unwilling to revolt. We see a possible cause and effect relationship in these two factors. It is also likely that Sepphoris' pre-eminence gave its citizens economic preogatives vis-à-vis the rural inhabitants of the Galilee. This may in part explain the former's desire to keep the status quo, and the latter's desire to change it.

Livias provides nothing in the way of evidence on social and economic problems. Tiberias, however, provides a rich store of information on social and economic stresses. The city was a totally new foundation, as Josephus relates:

Ἡρώδης δὲ ὁ τετράρχης, ἐπὶ μέγα χὰρ ἦν τῷ Τιβερίῳ φιλίας προελθών, οἰκοδομεῖται πόλιν ἐπώνυμον αὐτῷ Τιβεριάδα τοῖς κρατίστοις ἐπικτίσας αὐτὴν τῆς Γαλιλαίας ἐπὶ λίμν τῇ Γεννησαρίτιδι. Θερμά τε οὐκ ἄπωθέν ἐστιν ἐν κώμῃ, Ἀμμαθοὺς ὄνομα αὐτῇ. σύγκλυδες δὲ ᾤκισαν, οὐκ ὀλίγον δὲ καὶ τὸ Γαλιλαῖον ἦν, καὶ ὅσοι μὲν ἐκ τῆς ὑπ᾽ αὐτῷ γῆς ἀναγκαστοὶ καὶ πρὸς βίαν εἰς τὴν κατοικίαν

ἀγόμενοι, τινὲς δὲ καὶ τῶν ἐν τέλει. ἐδέξατο δὲ αὐτοῖς
συνοίκους καὶ τοὺς πανταχόθεν ἐπισυναγομένους
ἄνδρας ἀπόρους, ἔστι δ᾽ οὓς μηδὲ σαφῶς ἐλευθέρους,
πολλά τε αὐτοὺς κἀπὶ πολλοῖς ἠλευθέρωσεν καὶ
εὐηργέτησεν ἀνάγκασμα τοῦ μὴ ἀπολείψειν τὴν πόλιν
ἐπιθείς, κατασκευαῖς τε οἰκήσεων τήλεσι τοῖς αὐτοῦ καὶ
γῆς ἐπιδόσει.

The tetrarch Herod, inasmuch as he had gained a high place
among the friends of Tiberius, had a city built, named after him
Tiberias, which he established in the best region of Galilee on
Lake Gennesaritis. There is a hot spring not far from it in a
village called Ammathus. The new settlers were a promiscuous
rabble, no small contingent being Galilean, with such as were
drafted from territory subject to him and brought forcibly to the
new foundation. Some of these were magistrates. Herod accepted
as participants even poor men who were brought in to join the
others from any and all places of origin. It was a question whether
some were even free beyond cavil. These latter he often and in
large bodies liberated and benefited (imposing the condition that
they should not quit the city), by equipping houses at his own
expense and adding new gifts of land.

(Ant. 18.36–8)

This text provides evidence for a number of interesting attributes of the
landholding system. However, first let us point out that whatever we
learn from this occurrence may indeed be relevant for the previous
period. The Galilee had been under Herodian rule since Herod's
victories in 37 BCE.[213] Since Tiberias was founded at the latest in
23 CE, only a generation had passed since his father's death.[214] The text
indicates that Antipas built the city in the region of Ginnosar, briefly
described here as the best region of the Galilee. In another place
Josephus describes in glowing terms the agricultural fecundity of this
area (BJ 3.516–21). One must ask to whom did the area belong?
Avi-Yonah claims that it was royal land. Although he provides no
definite proof of this assertion, he is probably correct. The support for
the inference comes from the text itself. Antipas had to bring settlers
in from the rest of his territory in order to populate the new city. If
the area already had an agricultural population this would have
been unnecessary. Among the new population he included people of
standing, who were forced to resettle in Tiberias. If there had been a
population of free large landowners already on the territory of Tiberias

they would have automatically become citizens, as was the case when poleis were founded. There is no record of any large settlements that existed in the immediate vicinity prior to the foundation of Tiberias, so that Harper's claim that Tiberias was a *synoecism* of local villages has nothing to stand on.[215]

The impression created by Josephus is that of a collection of different kinds of new settlers: Galileans, some of whom were forced to re-settle, aristocrats, and large numbers of impoverished people, perhaps even slaves.

We have no information on the population of the city, yet we read in Josephus that by the time of the Great Revolt the city had a council of 600 men (*BJ* 2.641; *Vita* 64, 284). We may assume that these all had a significant income, otherwise they would not have been councilors.[216] Some of the residents of Tiberias may have been quite wealthy in their own right. For example, during the Great Revolt, Crispus, one of the leading citizens, was absent on his estates beyond Jordan (*Vita* 33). We cannot know if the wealth of the leading citizens was theirs originally, i.e. they were descendants of the original aristocrats, or if they were granted wealth by the tetrarch, or if acquired riches through their own efforts during the decades leading to the revolt. Probably some combination of all factors would explain their status. There are a number of indications as to the economic activity of the wealthy class in Tiberias.

First, Justus, son of Pistus, who incited the Tiberians to attack Sepphoris, railed that Tiberias had been displaced as capital of the Galilee, seat of the royal bank, and the archives. I assume that these three elements must have had some value, or otherwise there would have been no point in harping on their loss as a reason to revolt (*Vita* 37–9).[217] Second, the Crispus mentioned above had been in the service of King Agrippa. Likewise, Justus served Agrippa II. Third, the Galileans hated the Tiberians, and specifically Justus and his family (*Vita* 99, 384). Once Josephus mentions that Justus' brother had his hands cut off for forging letters (*Vita* 177). Likewise, regarding Justus, the Galileans resented the miseries which he had inflicted on them before the war, would not tolerate him as their chief, and were embittered against the Tiberians (*Vita* 392).

The story about the forging of letters echoes familiarly from two other sources. First, many of the landownership documents found in the Dead Sea area are of the "double-tied" type. This technical form of preparing a document was intended to minimize the danger of forgeries.[218] Second, there is a talmudic story relating how farmers from

Betar lost their properties as a result of forgeries by rich city-dwellers.[219] We will deal later with the tensions in the Galilee just before the revolt.

We learn something about the extent and definition of poverty from the text. Josephus suggests that many poor people from all over were brought into the new city. They received both houses and land from Antipas. Their behavior contrasts with that of those who had to be forcibly brought in. We conclude that there must have been a class of small landowners who felt that their situation was worsened by the move, and a class of landless and possibly homeless people whose situation now improved.

Tiberias may have started out with land and homes for all but by the time of the Great Revolt the city had a large poor population (*Vita* 35, 66). It is curious that the fishermen are considered natural allies of the poor, indicating that the livelihood from land, and other occupations, was better than that of fishing.

We will deal with the economic problems of this region in greater detail when we discuss the period leading up to the Great Revolt.

8

JUDEA UNDER DIRECT ROMAN RULE

Archelaus proved incapable of properly governing the people and the land Augustus had entrusted to him. The emperor rejected alternative methods of rule, such as linking Judea to the tetrarchy of one of the neighboring brothers, or fetching another Herodian princeling to rule, or even placing the country under the rule of a High Priest. Rather, in 6 CE Augustus placed Judea under the rule of a Roman governor. Judea was now a Roman province of the category ruled by men drawn from the equestrian order.[1]

For the next six decades, with a very brief interlude for Agrippa I, it would be the Romans who had the responsibility for policies and administration that would determine the landownership structure in Judea. These sixty years would culminate in the Great Revolt. Let us from the outset state that we reject any deterministic interpretation of the economic events that led up to the Great Revolt.

In the historiography on the period, there are different approaches. One of the more prevalent views attributes the underlying reasons for the war to the weaknesses of the social–economic structure. The most extreme exponent of that view was the late H. Kreissig, an avowed Marxist historian.[2] In brief, he saw a struggle between a small group of rich landowners controlling the economy through their political position and their ability to undersell the small farmers, and the masses of small farmers who made up the majority. The large landowners exploited their power over wages and prices, while the tax burden became increasingly heavy. He believed "the masses of the people," forced into debt because of low prices, high taxes, Temple dues, and a dearth of alternative sources of income, "wanted renewal, that is the elimination of the old apparatus of state headed by the Sanhedrin composed of high priests and large landowners."[3] Much of what he wrote might be true, as we shall see. The clear-cut divisions into economically and socially conscious classes are, of course, part of the theology of Marxism.

Another "economic" point of view is that of Goodman, who claims that "much of the social tension in Judea lay in the growth and nature of the Judean economy, which fueled class hostility of increasing intensity." He explains that the causes of hostility between rich and poor lay in the widening gap between rich and poor as the economy of Judea was integrated into the wider Mediterranean world.[4] He elaborates that the economy was in his words "out of balance," because the wealthy had enormous amounts of money with no avenue for investment, while the poor were underemployed. The result was that the rich lent to the poor who were increasingly in debt.[5]

Recently, J. J. Price published a monograph on the Great Revolt of the Jews against Rome.[6] He rejects the "economic" explanation for the war. He states: "there is very little evidence for growing economic problems, even less for a general crisis, in first-century Judea. The best evidence for economic distress in Judea is the rebellion itself: the argument is circular."[7]

We agree with Price that the revolt was primarily caused by "general organized opposition to Rome, in which all classes participated, and which was based on both ideological and practical complaints; and also by violent conflicts with the gentiles." However, explaining that "A large poor and disadvantaged class is a common fixture in the Roman world" and "that before this war there was some degree of economic tension which may have contributed to individual decisions to rebel," is just too general and ignores the great body of evidence that there was acute discontent.[8] Why should economic tension contribute to a decision to rebel, unless the rebel perceives a causal connection between the economic tension and those against whom he rebels?

Rich landowners were always a feature of Judean society, as were high taxes and limited economic opportunities; nevertheless, there was not always rebellion. The situation had to become exacerbated, either because of a series of natural catastrophes, or because of political pressure, thus increasing the burden beyond what the farmer could bear.

Was Roman rule seen as the reason for economic problems? Did people believe that if Roman rule ceased (revolution) there would be a change for the better?

The first two decades of direct Roman rule are remarkable because of the little we know about them. They are illuminated primarily by their stormy beginning and end.

The beginning of provincial status was marked by two events which have significance for the landownership situation of Judea. First, the governor of the province of Syria was tasked by the emperor with the job of conducting a census, and second, he was instructed to lease the properties formerly belonging to Archelaus (*Ant.* 18.2, 26).

THE CENSUS OF QUIRINIUS

The provincial census raised the vigorous opposition of elements of the Judean population. The most significant of the opponents to the census were the adherents of the "Fourth Philosophy." This group was ostensibly founded by Judas the Galilean and Zadok the Pharisee (*BJ* 2.118; *Ant.* 18.4). This is not the appropriate forum to discuss the "Fourth Philosophy" other than in those aspects that shed light on the socioeconomic problems of Judea.[9] The census is relevant to our discussion because it relates to a basic point in assessing developments which led to the revolt. In brief, was the normative Roman taxation so high that it forced the people to revolt?

Taxation

The census was correctly perceived to be the preparation for direct Roman taxation. Up till then taxes were collected, except for the pre-Gabinius period, by agents of the king (*Ant.* 17.308). From the very beginning the census had the stamp of direct Roman rule. Until recently the mechanics of the census in Judea were unknown. With the publication of the Babatha archive we learn that, at least in 127 CE, the census was taken personally by Roman officials; Babatha's census was delivered to a cavalry commander. Furthermore, the tax census had to be attested at the local administrative center, an annoying bureaucratic burden.[10] Could it be that the Judean census of 6 CE was handled in the same manner, and was that what outraged Judas? Moreover, the census may have been handled by officers like Sabinus, lacking tact, or perhaps the many Greeks in the Judean administration were involved.[11] A provincial census caused an uprising in Pannonia in 10 CE.[12] Arminius' revolt may have been caused by Varus' decision to start taxing the region in 9 CE, although the area had been under Roman rule since 12 BCE.[13]

The tax and the census are characterized by the Fourth Philosophy as tantamount to slavery (ἄντικρυς δουλείαν). Some scholars have asked why this should be so, seeing that Judea had paid a tax before. The answer lies in understanding that Judeans had not paid a tax directly to a foreign administration since the Hasmoneans had liberated the nation. Even in the period following the Roman conquest the taxes had been collected by Judean officials. Now that they had to pay to Rome directly they may have been reminded of the words of Neh. 9:36:

> Today we are slaves, and the land that You gave our fathers to enjoy its fruit and bounty – here we are slaves on it! On account of our sins it yields its abundant crops to kings whom You have sent over us. They rule over our bodies and our beasts as they please, and we are in great distress.

No one doubts that the Roman tax burden was heavy. It has been reviewed time and again. There are those who collect lists of all the possible taxes listed in all of the sources, and include a few taxes which are not attested, but can be inferred.[14] We can substantiate: *tributum soli*, a tax on the produce of the land;[15] *tributum capitis*, a tax based on assets;[16] a tax on houses; a tax on sale of agricultural products;[17] customs.[18] We assume that there was a tax on salt, and a crown tax.

This approach is taken even further by the "double taxation" disciples. These, acknowledging their debt or otherwise, follow in the footsteps of F. C. Grant.[19] He claimed that the high Roman taxation was paralleled by heavy Jewish religious taxation. Grant believed that while one burden of taxes could somehow be bearable, the double burden made it almost impossible to survive.[20] The number and types of Jewish taxes are confusing. It is not clear how many tithes there were in a Sabbatical period. Josephus counted fourteen tithes (*Ant.* 4.69,205, 240); i.e. one tithe to the priests yearly, one tithe consumed by the farmer in Jerusalem every year, and one tithe to the poor every third year. In addition, there were first fruits and heave offering (*Terumah*) and *Hallah*, the Temple tax, and various sin offerings and purity offerings, such as after childbirth.[21]

This approach leads to the conclusion that the tax burden was so heavy that the small cultivator was forced to borrow money either to pay the tax or to make ends meet. Failing to pay the tax or to return his loan he became a landless proletarian ripe for revolution.

Recently, others have been more cautious and have come to the conclusion that the tax burden was not heavier in Judea than in any of the neighboring provinces.[22] It is also demonstrable that the two tax systems, i.e. Roman and Jewish, took account of each other.[23] In short, according to this view the regular taxes are not responsible for an economic and social crisis. We shall return to this subject later.

The property of Archelaus

The property of Archelaus was sold or leased (ἀποδόμενος). The land in question was probably the royal estates such as Ein Gedi, Jericho, and the Jezreel Valley. Some scholars hold that these were probably worked by tenant farmers now obliged to hand over a considerable portion of the harvest yield on their land to their landlords.[24] The question immediately arises, to whom were the lands leased? Were they leased to small freeholders who wished to increase the amount of land they had under cultivation, or were they leased to wealthy persons, perhaps Herodian relatives, or members of the High Priestly families, or just plain wealthy Jews who had the capital necessary to lease the land and then have it worked by sub-lessors, tenant-farmers, or hired laborers?

We know that all three forms of labor existed on what was now imperial land. The lands formerly owned by Archelaus were almost certainly worked by royal tenants and lessors or hired workers: probably all these forms of cultivation existed in conjunction. This fact must be taken for granted since the land could not have been worked by Archelaus and his family. The mere transfer of the ownership should not have made the conditions of the simple cultivator any worse than they had been. Therefore, we must identify the developments which led to the widespread and almost unceasing unrest.

THE PREFECTS

The establishment of the Province of Judea commenced a long period of almost constant unrest in the area. The litany of banditry, demonstrations, false Messiahs, and recurring bloodshed is familiar to all students of Second Temple history. We will attempt to demonstrate that the new province inherently contained the seeds of economic crisis. This crisis developed not because of the very existence of large estates, but rather because of the nature of the provincial administration. For comparison, it should be kept in mind that Herod had managed to rule for a number of decades without the situation deteriorating as badly as it did during the provincial period.

The deterioration of the economic situation of large numbers of Jews in the Province of Judea was the result of a provincial administration which was corrupt and extortionate. The difficult situation resulted in the readiness of many to heed calls for rebellion, calls which were couched in religious and national terms. These religious and national ideals were by definition antithetical to the ideological and practical methods which characterized the operations of the provincial administration.

Specifically, the Roman provincial administration created economic pressures by (1) extortion: the nominal tax system was high, but provincial governors and their staffs extorted sums much greater than were legally allowed; (2) corruption: in order for the Jewish sociopolitical elite to compete, and even to maintain their position, they needed large sums of money, which could only be obtained, within the limits of the Judean economy, by squeezing tenants, and lending money at high interest; (3) inefficiency: the Roman provincial administration did not deal successfully with natural crises, and it did not provide solutions to the problems of dislocation and unemployment. It may be edifying if we compare Herod to the procurators. He had sources of money they did not have: all the revenues from royal estates went into his purse while the procurators collected it for the imperial exchequer. Herod had foreign properties and investments to offset his expenses. Herod could call on foreign contributions. In terms of area, Herod had two to three times the tax and economic base that the procurators had. Herod was personally wealthy and although in need of money he was not out to get rich quick. Although he garnered fortunes in taxes and levies, he spent much of the money on building and development projects. These projects provided employment and lubricated the economy. The procurators, for the most part, did not engage in any serious public works, and if they did it is quite probable that they were corrupt, skimming money and taking bribes.

The corruption of the prefects

The writings of Josephus Flavius are replete with accusations against the prefects for corruption and oppression. Although his historiographic "Tendenz" excusing the mass of the Jewish people of culpability by blaming the "extremists" and the Roman procurators is generally acknowledged, there is no reason to assume that much of what he wrote is a fabrication. We have, after all, Tacitus and a wealth of comparative material clearly indicating that the Roman governors were as bad as they are described.[25] The equestrians did not receive high salaries for their efforts, and it seemed almost expected that governors would get rich at the expense of the governed.[26] If this were not so, there would be little point in Tiberius' tale regarding the flies on a wounded soldier or the epigram on the task of a shepherd.[27] Moreover, extortionate governors were responsible for rebellions in other provinces. Dalmatia in 6 CE is said to have complained about the financial officers as wolves preying on the province.[28] Gallic revolts in 12 BCE and 21 CE were both sparked off by opposition to extortionate officials.[29]

Not only Josephus and Tacitus report on the corruption of the Roman governors. Philo related that Capito, the procurator of Iamnia, came there as a poor man, but by his rapacity and peculation he amassed much wealth in various forms.[30] It may be significant that Philo refers to Capito as collector of taxes for Judea, but what is even more notable is Philo's expectation that the Roman official would by various forms of extortion enrich himself.

The first two decades of Roman rule are more or less an enigma. After the unrest of the census our sources dry up till Pilate's rule, but then we are indebted to Josephus for a chronological review of the remaining forty years. In that time there are specific complaints against almost all of the governors.

Pilate is the first governor about whom we have a detailed report. Certainly much has been said about the episodes of the insignia and the shields. His singular lack of sensitivity is evident from the pagan symbols on his coins, and the crucifixion story is a cultural landmark of Western civilization. However, he also used his position to squeeze money out of the populace. It is reported that Pilate took money from the Temple treasury in order to finance an aqueduct.[31] This episode has never been quite clearly understood because the money from the Temple can be used for the city's projects, including aqueducts.[32] We would suggest that the project was a boondoggle enabling Pilate to somehow line his pockets. Philo, when describing Pilate, launches into a very general but very acerbic attack on his administration: he mentions venality and his thefts specifically.[33] An indication of the mercenary nature of Pilate's custody is that Vitellius felt the need to remit all taxes on the sale of agricultural produce (*Ant.* 18.90). Moreover, during Tiberius' reign Tacitus relates that "About the same time . . . the provinces, too, of Syria and Judaea, exhausted by their burdens, were pressing for a diminution of the tribute."[34]

Agrippa I, the beloved last scion of the Hasmonean house, can teach us much about the ethos that placed pressure on prominent Judeans. In the period before his ascent to royal dignity, he had to make a living. This he accomplished by being in the good graces of various Romans. In order to be in their good graces he was forced to spend enormous sums of money which he borrowed from his friends, but also from his dependants.[35] In addition, he found some time for employment as a local government official. In these positions he was accused of taking bribes (*Ant.* 18.153–5).

Fadus' procuratorial period begins with a conflict between the Jewish inhabitants of the Perea and the Greeks of Philadelphia (*Ant.* 20.2–3). The conflict was about the borders of a village. The amount of arable land was a recurring problem, and has been explored in depth by a number of scholars. The last few years had seen Agrippa I as King of Judea, Petronius intervene on behalf of the Jews of Dor, and Claudius deal even-handedly with the Jews of Alexandria.[36] The Philadelphians posed a very good question: why did the Jews resort to violence rather than appeal for judgment to the Roman governor? No doubt the Jews of the Perea had no particular love for the Romans, but we suspect that the Jews knew that they could not afford the best justice money could buy when competing with the Philadelphians.

Cumanus, whose administration was studded with troubles, was finally relieved of his command when his incompetence and corruption became evident through an investigation by the Proconsul of Syria. Among other errors, it was found that he took bribes (*Ant.* 20.119, 127).

Felix, the Roman governor from 52 to 60 CE, is attacked both by Josephus and also by Tacitus for his venal government.[37] Josephus may be exaggerating when he accuses Felix of hiring the murderers who killed the High Priest Jonathan (*Ant.* 20.163), but the reason for Felix's anger is Jonathan's constant censure of a corrupt administration (*Ant.* 20.162). It is related that Felix also permitted his men to plunder the houses of some wealthy Jews in Caesarea (*Ant.* 20.177).

Albinus earns particularly harsh censure from Josephus (*BJ* 2.273–4). He is charged with using his official capacity to steal and plunder private property, and levying extraordinary taxes. Furthermore, he is accused of releasing arrested people in return for a bribe. The particular point that seems relevant to our inquiry is found in *BJ* 2.274–6. There Josephus relates that influential men paid Albinus bribes in order that he should turn a blind eye to their plundering of moderate citizens.

Florus is described as the worst offender by Josephus and Tacitus.[38] Josephus condemns Florus for robbery and violence; he says, "To make gain out of individuals seemed beneath him: he stripped whole cities, ruined entire populations, . . . all were at liberty to practice brigandage, on condition that he received his share." "His avarice brought desolation" (*BJ* 2.278–9). But what specifically can we say he did?

Corruption: Florus allegedly accepted a bribe of 8 talents in order to cease some construction that was troublesome to the Jewish community (*BJ* 2.285–8).[39] He took the large bribe and then failed to do what he had promised.

Embezzlement: he took 17 talents from the Temple treasury, supposedly for legitimate expenses of the Roman government.[40] We have seen how the populace reacted in Pilate's case when Temple money was concerned. Here also the confiscation was ostensibly for a legitimate reason. However, it was perceived that this was not government but greed. The revolutionary youth mocked "poor" Florus as a needy beggar.

Violence: it is charged that Florus went up to Jerusalem with the intention of fleecing the city (περιδύω) (*BJ* 2.296). He had the "upper city," the rich quarter, sacked (*BJ* 2.305). Josephus claims that he had an ear "only to profit accruing from the plunder" (*BJ* 2.311).

These examples of extortion must be considered along with the "tribute." It is a specific complaint which is repeatedly heard. Agrippa II in his speech (admittedly a Josephean composition) lists the nations under Roman rule and repeatedly stresses that they pay the tribute without problems.[41] Apparently the Jews refused to pay the tax (*BJ* 2.403–4). They owed 40 talents and the refusal to pay them was tantamount to a declaration of war (*BJ* 2.405; 5.405).

There is a connection between the tribute, the leading members of Jewish society (the rich), and the governor. When Agrippa finished his speech, he said, "pay the tax." The archons and councilors went to the villages to raise the arrears of the tribute amounting to 40 talents (*BJ* 2.405). In the meanwhile, Agrippa II sent the magistrates and principal citizens to Florus at Caesarea, in order that he might appoint some of their number to collect the tribute in the country (*BJ* 2.407).

We see that the tribute was collected by the leading members of the Jewish aristocracy, who were responsible to the governor. What effect did this have on the Jewish society and its economic life? An indication of how Jews may have felt may be gleaned from one of the holidays listed in Megilat Taanit: "On the 25th day of Sivan the tax-farmers were removed from Judea and Jerusalem."[42]

THE JEWISH ARISTOCRACY

If we keep in mind what we have learned about Jewish society in the period of the prefects, we will have noted that there was increasing violence as the years went on, especially after Agrippa I. We pointed out that the more powerful elements of the society bought impunity from the governor. A folk jingle preserved in the talmudic literature helps illuminate the behavior of the High Priestly families (BT Pes. 57a):[43]

אוי לי מבית ביתום   אוי לי מאלתן,
אוי לי מבית חנין   אוי לי מלחישתן
אוי לי מבית קתרום   אוי לי מקולמוסן,
אוי לי מבית ישמעאל בן פיאבי,   אוי לי מאגרופן
שהם כהנים גדולים ובניהן גיזברין וחתניהם אמרכלין
ועבדיהן חובטין את העם במקלות

Woe is me because of the house of Boethus, woe is me because of their staves!

Woe is me because of the house of Hanin [Hanan], woe is me because of their whisperings!

Woe is me because of the house of Kathros, woe is me because of their pens!

Woe is me because of the house of Ishmael ben Phiabi, woe is me because of their fists!

For they are High Priests and their sons are treasurers and their sons-in-law are administrators and their servants beat the people with staves.

These verses lament that the well-known High-Priestly families used their position to oppress the populace. Their sons-in-law are Temple treasurers and administrators (supply officers of the Temple). They are responsible for collecting tithes and obtaining the needs of the Temple. They use lies and "pens" to gain what they seek. However, sticks and fists and batons wielded by servants are also tools they have at their command.

Josephus relates that when Agrippa II appointed Ishmael ben Phiabi High Priest, enmity and warfare broke out between the High Priests and the priests and leaders of the populace of Jerusalem. Each of the factions formed and collected for itself a band. The High Priests expropriated the tithes from the threshing floors, depriving the priests of their rightful due (*Ant.* 20.179–81), while Costobar and Saul, members of the Herodian aristocracy, were plundering the property of those weaker than themselves. Moreover, during the fighting between factions, "Ananias, a former High Priest, used his wealth to attract those who were willing to receive bribes" (*Ant.* 20.213–14). Among those whom Ananias bought was Albinus the governor and the High Priest (*Ant.* 20.205). Josephus asserts that he was popular with the people, because he "was able to supply them with money."[44]

He could not have been popular with all the people because he was murdered in the first weeks of the revolt, his house burned by the same people who later burned the debt archives.[45] If we try to make sense of the conflicting stories about Ananias the High Priest, we note that the seizure of the tithes is also connected to him (*Ant.* 20.206–7). Although Josephus attempts to excuse Ananias from responsibility, it is not convincing. We surmise that "was able to supply them with money," is a half-truth. He provided funds to those of the elite who needed patronage to maintain their position. The money came from oppression, as in the case of the tithes. We know that grain was a monetary equivalent. There are at least two examples from the period of the war. The priests who accompanied Josephus to the Galilee made a point of collecting the tithes owed to them and returned to Jerusalem with a large sum of money.[46] A second indication that the grain had a cash value is demonstrated by the request of John of Gischala (*Vita* 71–3). He wanted to seize the imperial grain stocks in the Galilee in order to rebuild the walls of his town. Obviously he meant to sell the grain and use the proceeds to pay for the labor and material needed.

Up to this point we have provided a long list of depredations and oppressions and it is time to interpret them. We have demonstrated that the prefects generally expected bribes. These bribes purchased protection and privilege. The elite could be subject to violence if they did not pay the Roman governor. The elite also could fortify their position in the society by keeping in the good graces of the prefect. How did the elite get the money to keep their position? First through legal means – these people were rich. But they needed as much money as they could get, which meant moneylending, and increasing the ownership of the one major source of wealth that was available – land.

Most of the wealthy people in Jewish society owned land. The literary and archaeological record indicates farms owned by the wealthy. Josephus repeatedly refers to the raids of the *lestai* on the houses of the rich. In the days of Felix, brigands throughout the country looted the houses of the wealthy, murdered the owners, and set the villages on fire (*BJ* 2.264–5). During the war, Simon ben Gioras ransacked the houses of the wealthy in Acrabatene (*BJ* 2.652). Also during the war, the leading men of Gadara offered to surrender in order to preserve their property (*BJ* 4.414, 416). Tiberius Crispus, who was the son of the former prefect (ἔπαρχος) of Agrippa I, had estates beyond the Jordan (*Vita* 33). Finally, Josephus himself had land near Jerusalem (*Vita* 422), for which he was compensated by Titus after the war.

The New Testament contains many parables which relate that

wealthy people had large estates. More significantly, these parables often mention tenancy relationships and debt.[47]

Matthew 21:33–41 tells a story about a landowner (οἰκοδεσπότες) who fenced in a vineyard, built a tower, let it out to husbandmen (γεωργός), and then left. The rest of the story perhaps is more appropriate to our next point, but the tale ends with the owner letting out the vineyard to other farmers who will pay the rent. In another parable a vineyard owner goes in search of hired labor (Mt. 20:1–16). Landlords are often absent, one tale speaks about servants who increase their master's wealth in his absence (Mt. 25:14–28).

As the archaeological investigation of Palestine progresses, more and more large homestead farms (villas) are discovered.[48] Recently, work was done on the "palace" of Helkias, which is definitely dated to our period.[49] Ein Yael contains remains of a villa which may have been in existence in our period.[50] The southern tip of the Carmel has a farm which the excavators say existed in the pre-Revolt period and was probably owned by Jews.[51] North of Jerusalem there are remains of a farm which we mentioned in relation to the Hasmonean period: findings indicate that it was active in our period as well.[52] The ornate burial complexes such as that of the Goliath family may indicate a nearby family estate.[53]

Alongside the large estates, there were certainly small farmers who owned their own holdings. For example, the people of Gischala apparently were agricultural laborers (BJ 4.84) who worked their own plots because Titus promised them the secure enjoyment of their possessions (τῶν ἰδίων κτημάτων) (BJ 4.94).

Much of our argument depends on our ability to demonstrate that the small cultivator did indeed borrow money or seed or other foodstuffs. Evidence for this comes from the New Testament, some ancient documents, Josephus, and some comparative material. We have refrained as much as possible from using talmudic texts because of doubts regarding the dating of the information.

We have chosen four representative parables. Each one first demonstrates that credit and borrowing were considered commonplace, and, second, demonstrates some aspect of the credit transaction. In support of these parables we provide those few original documents from this period that can shed light on the subject.

In Lk. 7:41 there was a certain creditor who had two debtors; one owed 500 denarii, the other 50. The creditor extended credit to more than one debtor at a time; credit was not an infrequent affair. Moreover, the credit could have been extended in money, and large as well as small sums were involved.

A document from Nero's reign provides us with a glimpse of a loan transaction:[54]

[ ] .[ ] שנ[ת תרתין קסר. [ ].

בצויה איתודי אבשלום בר חנין מן צויה

בנפי מניה עמי אנה זכריה בר יהוחנן בר ה...] [

יתב בכסלון כסף זוזין עס[רי]ן [וכספא] מש[לם]

אנה. [ ] [ז] .[ ] . לא די זבינת עד זמ[נא]

דנה אפרוענך בחמש ואפשר בתמ[י]מותא]

ושנת שמטה דה והן כן לא אעבד תשלומ[תא]

לך מנכסי ודי אקנה לקובליך

[זכ]ריה בר יהוחנן ע[ל] נפשה

[כת]ב יהוסף ב[ר] .שהד

יהונתן בר יהוחנא שהד

יהוסף ב[ר י]הודן עד

the year two of the Emperor Nero

at Siwaya, Absalom, son of Hannin, from Siwaya, has declared in my presence that there is on account with me, me Zechariah, son of Yohanan, son H...[ ],

living at Cheaslon, the sum of twenty zuzin. The sum I am to repay b[y But if] I have not paid(?) by this

time, I will reimburse you with (interest of) a fifth and will settle in entirety,

even if this is the Year of Release. And if I do not do so, indemnity for you (will be) from my possessions, and whatever I acquire (will be) at your disposal.

Zechariah, son of Yohanan, for himself.

Joseph, so[n of], wrote (this), witness.

Jonathan, son of John, witness.

Joseph, so[n of J]udan, witness [Hebrew word].

The text provides a number of points: the sum is 20 *zuzin*, which are equal to 20 denarii. There is no way of knowing what the money was for, and how difficult repayment of the loan could be. The interest is 20 percent if the principal is not paid by a certain date (unreadable); does this mean that it was a loan without interest if repaid by that date? The money is to be paid despite the Sabbatical Year, and if not paid, all the debtor's possessions are at the disposal of the creditor. We understand that this means all the debtor's possessions are hypothecated until he pays the debt. Furthermore, the creditor will be able to seize as much property as needed to pay the principal, and the accrued interest.

Lk.16:1–6 recounts that a steward called in his master's debtors and renegotiated the terms. The loans were in oil and wheat, an indication that material in kind was also borrowed and returned in kind. We don't have a text that shows what the cost of loans in kind was, but comparative material from Egypt indicates that interest for the period between sowing and harvest could be as high as 50 percent.[55]

Mt.18:24–5 narrates that someone owed 10,000 talents, but when he could not pay, he and his wife and children were sold along with all that he had, in order to make the payment. Of course the sum is fantastic; larger sums were borrowed in the Roman world, but that class of people was not sold into slavery. It is apparent that the audience which heard this parable was familiar with the possibility that debtors could lose their property, as well as their liberty.[56]

In support of this there is an interesting text from 60 CE, the period of the Nabatean king Malichus II. It seems to be a document in which an heir pays off a debt and thereby recovers a garden which had been seized in default of that debt. The debt had been incurred by relatives who had then died. A survivor claimed the right to pay the debt, paid the principal and the outstanding interest, and recovered the property.[57] While we have to regard this text with due caution, coming as it does from the Nabatean kingdom and not from the Province of Judea, it does indicate that failure to pay one's debts could and did lead to expropriation.

In Mt. 25:14–28 a servant who did not increase his master's wealth is rebuked for not lending the money at usury. This is the first story that illustrates Goodman's thesis that the wealthy found no other outlet for investment for their money other than loans.[58]

According to Goodman, the wealthy had surplus money either from large landholdings which they already possessed, or "earned elsewhere."[59] Left with this money, they had no choice but to invest it in the only avenue open to them – land. Land, according to his view, was a source both of wealth and of prestige. However, he goes on to assert that Jewish society had no particular respect for money:[60] "Thus on the backs of the indebted peasantry, some of the priests, merchants and artisans of Jerusalem may have converted their profits from the pilgrimage business into real estate and become the natural rulers to whom Rome could turn."[61] It is a question of emphasis: was the land the ticket to power, or was it the money which the land provided?

According to Goodman's theory, the *prozbul* (M. Shebi. 10:3–7) was designed not for the poor, but for the rich, since they needed to lend. Howgego, in a wide-ranging investigation of money in the Roman world, found that there was evidence of lending in all corners of the empire. "Money lending was sufficiently widespread for it to be a requirement to declare money out on loan in the census."[62]

Why did the small farmer borrow? Why did the freeholder become a tenant? Goodman suggests that the pressures on the farmer arose from a growing population: in every generation the land would have to be split till plots were no longer large enough to feed a family.[63] The farmer might try and supplement his income by finding work elsewhere; however, while there were artisans and crafts, the ancient economy did not provide an expanding base of production and market for finished goods.[64] By the same token, the "service" industries were incapable of absorbing large numbers of desperate farmers. There certainly was some work to be had, but nothing with an expanding base.[65]

In addition to these problems, there are others that we can only surmise. There is reason to believe that there was a monetary crisis in the Roman Empire which may have pressed the Roman governors to extort even more from the population.[66] This pressure would have been felt at the lowest level, the farmer having to borrow to buy seed or to make the payments for taxes and rents. Unfortunately, we can only hope that more specific information on taxes and prices in Judea becomes available

Furthermore, following J. Schumpeter's theories of the business cycle (in which a major innovation generates a sharp boost to society; innovation then generates secondary and tertiary employment, slowly dying down as the original investment passes into history; depression follows),[67] in the wake of the boom we suggest that the Herodian era was the period of boom. We then can see that the period of direct Roman rule would be the depression.

Besides these general symptoms of economic malaise which were caused by the economic pressure exerted by the procurators, and by the lack of initiative they displayed, there were specific crises which affected the general welfare and created pressures on the landholding structure.

THE STRIKE

On the whole, the procurators failed to deal with crises, even though we have examples of successful crisis management. The threat that Caligula would place his statue in the Temple in Jerusalem provoked not only massive demonstrations, but also a "strike" during which the fields and groves were not tended.[68] The sources present some chronological problems, but the conclusion is inescapable that for one season much of the crop was lost because of the unrest engendered by Caligula's demand.[69]

Josephus explains that Petronius moved to Ptolemais intending to spend the winter there and be ready for war in the spring (*Ant.* 18.262). The delegations came immediately to Ptolemais; he then moved to Tiberias, and there the Jews protested for forty days, neglecting their fields, although it was time for sowing.[70] This would indicate that Josephus is consistent, i.e. sowing in autumn, after the first rains that come before the onset of winter. The negotiations continued, and Josephus notes that there was rain, while up till then there had been drought; another indication that it was the winter season (*Ant.* 18.284–5). This would also fit the time frame for fruit harvest.[71] It appears that the threat of harvest destruction was averted by Petronius' diplomacy. Nevertheless, some interference in the sowing schedule must have occurred, if massive demonstrations really kept people away from work for forty to fifty days.[72] The leading Jews claimed that the people had left their fields; as a result, the land was unsown and there would be a "harvest of banditry" because the tribute could not be paid (*Ant.* 18.274).[73]

The neglect of the fields was a problem demanding the attention of the leadership (*Ant.* 18.284), so the strike had the makings of a serious agricultural crisis. We can only speculate if the lost crops affected the prices of agricultural products, but it is intriguing that very shortly after these events Agrippa granted a tax break to the inhabitants of Jerusalem (*Ant.* 19.299).

In contrast to Petronius' understanding of the ramifications of an agricultural strike, we have the rather unresponsive behavior of Tiberius Julius Alexander to the famine which occurred during his tenure.

THE FAMINE

The last famine we know of in the period before the Great Revolt occurred during the reign of Claudius. There are some problems regarding the chronology which have led historians to postulate that either there were two famines, or that the famine occurred during the reign of Nero.[74] We shall discuss the chronological problems at greater length when we deal with the duration of the famine, but let us state at the outset that we assume that all the following sources refer to the same famine.

The main lines of the event are related in connection with Queen Helena of Adiabene. When she came to Jerusalem on pilgrimage she found the city suffering from a famine. Many were perishing because they lacked the money to purchase their needs. Helena brought grain from Alexandria, and a cargo of dried figs from Cyprus (*Ant.* 20.51).[75] These supplies were distributed among the needy (*Ant.* 20.52). Her son Izates also provided aid, sending a large sum of money to the leaders of Jerusalem. The money was distributed, and saved many from the famine (*Ant.* 20.53). From *Ant.* 3.320–1 we learn that the famine had already taken hold by Passover, when an *asaron* cost 4 drachmas. Seventy *kors* of flour were brought in (to Jerusalem) to help relieve the shortage. To this information provided by Josephus, we add that of Acts 11:27–30, which relates that during a great famine in Claudius' time, the Christians in Antioch sent aid to their brethren in Judea. Orosius (*Hist.* VII, 6, 12) adds the information that the famine struck in Syria.

We have no information on the reasons for the famine, although (as stated above) the most probable cause of a wide-ranging crop failure is drought. There is also some difficulty defining the range of the famine. *Ant.* 20.51–3 refers only to Jerusalem, but *Ant.* 20.101 refers to Judea, while *Ant.* 3.320 refers to "our country" (τὴν χώραν ἡμῶν). Orosius relates that the famine was all over ("per") Syria, while Acts 11:28 and the Chronicle of Eusebius claim the whole world was seized by famine.

We can dismiss the last claim quite easily, since it is an obvious absurdity. It can be explained in a number of ways. L. Feldman, quoting Torrey, suggests that the Aramaic source was mistranslated, i.e. "the land" interpreted as *oikeumene*.[76] Schürer and Gapp base their explanation on the fact that there were numerous famines in Claudius' reign. Schürer postulates that the various famines appeared to be a fulfillment of a prophecy of famine over the whole world. Gapp sees the statement more as a generalization or figure of speech indicating that there were many famines then.[77]

The famine probably affected Palestine and parts of Syria since, as we pointed out, the two areas share the same climatic conditions. Moreover, it is significant that Helena chose to buy supplies in Egypt and in Cyprus, but evidently she did not try to buy food in Syria.[78]

It should be added that the cargo of figs is evidence of the viability of supplying needed goods to the Land of Israel by ship. Additionally, one should note that the port of Caesarea was fully operational now. One can only speculate if four decades of direct Roman rule had contributed anything to the network of roads.

The duration of the famine can only be estimated after we determine whether our sources refer to two famines or one. Thackeray suggested that the famine recorded in *Ant.* 3.320–1 is separate from the famine in the rest of our sources. He drew his conclusion from two details. First, the source states that the famine occurred during the time of Claudius and the High Priest Ishmael. Second, it says that the famine occurred "shortly before the recent war" (τοῦδε τοῦ πολέμου μικρὸν ἔμπροσθεν). Since the only Ishmael who lived about that time is Ishmael ben Phiabi, and he is generally thought to have served in the period of Felix's procuratorship, "two or three years at the most around the year 60 CE," he could not be contemporaneous with Claudius.[79] However, why assume that the error is in the name of the emperor? It might well be that the name of the High Priest is an error, or that Josephus erred in recording the period of Ishmael's High Priesthood.[80] Likewise, one cannot base one's dating on the imprecise expression "shortly before the recent war."[81]

In favor of our identifying the two famine stories as one is the repeated use of the expression "import" (κομισθέντος).[82] Furthermore, while food crises are not uncommon, actual famines are rare, and it would seem strange that Josephus who lived through the period and documented its troubles did not devote some words to relate that two serious famines occurred.

When was the famine and for how long? Foakes-Jackson and Lake suggest 46 CE or 45 CE, based on textual grounds.[83] Jeremias states on the same grounds that it was only during the time of Tiberius Julius Alexander, i.e. that the "famine occurred in one of the years between 46–48."[84] Schürer maintains that it was during the procuratorship of Tiberius Julius Alexander "(AD 46–48?)" but may have begun as early as 44 CE.[85] Feldman quotes Gapp, i.e. 46 or 47 CE.[86] Gapp bases his argument on the assumption that there was a famine in Egypt in spring 46, and therefore Helena relieved the famine after the spring of 47.[87] We assume that Helena could buy grain in Egypt either before or after the food crisis there, but not during a food crisis. This assumption is based on the behavior of Roman authorities in two other Egyptian food crises: in 19 CE Germanicus handed out the grain stored for Rome in Egypt, and in 99/100 CE Trajan returned Egyptian wheat from Rome to Egypt.[88] It is difficult to imagine that in the period of the highest prices recorded in over a century, wheat would be exported.[89] Gapp notes prices for the fall of 45 CE, and hypothesized that the crisis lasted to the spring of 47.[90] But we have evidence that in November–December 46 CE prices were still at peak levels, indicating that prices could not have dropped till spring 47 CE.[91] Therefore, Helena either brought aid in the spring of 45 or the spring of 47. When she arrived,

Jerusalem was already in the grip of famine, hence the shortage had to begin during the previous harvest at least. If it began in the spring of 44 CE and lasted two years it would have extended from the time of Agrippa I to the time of Tiberius Julius Alexander.[92] This is very convenient for us because it substantiates the version of events in Acts 11, which tied the famine into the reign of Agrippa, and the version of events in Orosius, who said the famine occurred in the fourth year of Claudius (Orosius, *Hist.* VII, 6, 9). Furthermore, and with reservations as to the historical value of this source, T. Peah 4:18 relates that King Monobazus ביזבז אוצרותיו בשני בצרות ("wasted his treasures in two droughts"). This tale is generally accepted as referring to King Izaates' contribution to Jerusalem during this famine (*Ant.* 20.53).[93] The years 46 CE to 48 CE are less fitting in all respects; therefore, the famine lasted from 44 to 46 CE.

The famine affected prices drastically. We are told an *asaron* sold for 4 drachmas (*Ant.* 3.320). An *asaron* is 1/100 of a *kor*, i.e. equals 3.95–4.65 liters. We are therefore dealing with about 1 drachma per liter. As we have shown above, the "normal" price was about 1 drachma per 4.3 liters, hence the famine price is about four times the regular price.

The assumption that the 70 *kor* brought to Jerusalem during Passover were bought by Helena is totally unwarranted. We have no way of knowing how much grain Helena bought. The statement that she bought grain for large sums can mean either she purchased large amounts, therefore paying much, or that she paid high prices, although the amount was not large. The latter possibility has no connection with the Egyptian shortage. As there was a famine in Syria it is to be expected that purchasers would descend on Egypt, driving prices up. The phenomena of hoarding, speculation, and price rises are well documented for all food crises. Merchants would be able to bring their grain to the famine-struck areas and make a tidy profit. We infer that grain was available, but that the price was too high. This follows because the money that Izaates sent to Jerusalem was distributed to the needy, i.e. food was not distributed, money was. Therefore, we conclude that with larger sums one could buy food.

The absence of any mention of Roman authority in this crisis is intriguing. Josephus is not usually silent about the more pronounced failures and successes of the procurators. Yet in this case Josephus' silence suggests that the famine was not the concern of the governor. In fact there are very few cases anywhere in which the Roman governor personally directed the famine relief. The city authorities took charge, and their solution was to call on men of wealth and influence, who would either pay for corn stored by hoarders and speculators, or have corn shipped in.[94] In our case we know that the leaders of the Jerusalemites received money, which they in turn distributed. The distribution of money instead of provisions was one of the antidotes to a scarcity of grain.[95] The merchants and hoarders would sell grain from their stores if the price was right. Likewise, we know that Helena directly distributed grain and figs to the needy.[96] The actions of these two very much remind us of the *Proxenia* of the Greek cities. Goodman has claimed that the native-born Judaic aristocracy did not subscribe to the euergetism popular among the Romans, Hellenistic cities, and Diaspora Jews.[97] We do not have much evidence to prove or disprove his claim. We will deal with the reaction of the city fathers to the plight of the unemployed later (*Ant.* 20.220). There are traces of euergetism in the rabbinic legends about the pre-70 period.[98] In this case, however, evidently the leaders of the community organized the distribution of the monies sent by others.

More importantly, how was the grain purchased? We know from the great famine of Herod's day that Petronius had to personally intervene to help Herod buy and transfer the grain. In this famine, too, the same problems existed. We submit that Helena's prestige as an oriental queen from a kingdom in the Parthian sphere gave her requests added importance and perhaps gained her priority in the eyes of the Roman government of Egypt.

We also suggest that the appointment, or even the impending appointment, of Tiberius Julius Alexander to the position of Judean prefect might have had a salutary effect on any negotiations for Egyptian wheat. His family had position, connections, and much wealth. We know they had dealings with transport firms, just as we know that Tiberius Julius Alexander had been an *epistrategos* (district governor) in Egypt prior to his appointment to Judea.[99] However, in this crisis the Roman procurator does not provide leadership or solutions. The difference between Herod's action, and his inaction, is glaring.

The crisis passed and apparently it was managed by the leading men of the city, who included High Priests, but also a lay leadership based on wealth and family ties.

The traditions about fantastically rich men who could support the whole city of Jerusalem are obviously exaggerations.[100] Nevertheless, they indicate that within the Judean society, among the non-laity, there were individuals who attained very large fortunes. We have no basis on which to assume that these men were landowners, or for that matter merchants. The legends are a poor place to draw details from, and only reveal that these grandees would support the revolt with grain, oil, etc., not that they cultivated these products. But while the source of their wealth is a matter of conjecture, the influence of their wealth is not. Joseph ben Gurion shared command with Ananus the High Priest in the revolutionary government. His son Gurion ben Joseph was an associate of Simon ben Gamaliel, and a leader of the public (*BJ* 4.159). If these Gurions are somehow related to the Gurion ben Nicodemus (*BJ* 2.451) who negotiated with the Romans, and the Nakdimon ben Gurion recorded in the above mentioned traditions about the rich men of Jerusalem, then we have a clan of wealthy, influential men.

UNEMPLOYMENT

Ant. 20.219–23 recounts that the Temple had just been completed. The people saw that the workmen, numbering over 18,000, were out of work and would be deprived of pay, for they earned their living by working on the Temple. Moreover, owing to their fear that the Romans would take the money kept on deposit in the Temple, they urged the king (Agrippa II) to raise the height of the east portico. The king refused this request, but agreed to the paving of the city with white stone. The workmen received pay, even if they worked for but one hour of the day. The "people" chose to expend their treasures upon them, rather than risk having the Roman procurator take them.

This source substantiates a number of points we have been trying to make. First, it is obvious that the depositors in the Temple were men of means and influence.[101] They had money on deposit in the Temple, they had access to Agrippa, and they felt qualified to make suggestions regarding construction on the Temple complex. We may surmise that the initiative came from circles which included the priests. Second, they were afraid that the money on deposit would be seized by the Romans. This echoes the incident with Pilate. If the governor could have been trusted to use Temple deposits for honest public works, why did they not bring their suggestion to him? Third, the money consisted of the deposits of Jerusalemites, or, at the widest, Judeans; it was not the Temple treasury collected from the tithes. The sums must have been great, because they had to be enough to pay the daily salaries of thousands of workers for an indefinite period. Fourth, other than their fear of the Romans' avarice, it is clear that the initiators of the proposal were anxious about having thousands of unemployed men in the Jerusalem area.

It has been observed that stalled economic growth causes frustration.[102] Some have defined banditry as a social–economic phenomenon in which the lower economic classes, who are at a legal disadvantage, resort to the life of bandits in order to protect themselves from the establishment, while also earning a living.[103] Indeed, the period of the last procurators is well known for the banditry which characterized it. Although Price rejects this view, we believe the sources support this thesis unequivocally.[104] Horsley, and others, have gathered all the sources, but we may point out the salient examples. The robbery of a slave of Caesar on the Beth Horon road convinced Cumanus to order the neighboring villages pillaged (*Ant.* 20.113–14). He obviously suspected them of cooperating in the crime. Eleazar ben Dinai was a bandit for twenty years, and innumerable "common people" were convicted of complicity with him (*BJ* 2.253). When Festus arrived in Judea the villages were being plundered and set on fire by the lestai (*Ant.* 20.185, 187). Even the New Testament has evidence of rural banditry: Mk. 12:1–12 relates the hostility of the tenants to their landlord; they murdered every steward sent to collect the rents, and the landlord's son.

THE GREAT REVOLT

The Great Revolt was not a class war; but it did have manifestations of class conflict. The cavil that no demands were made for land reform fails to take into consideration that the revolution called for the establishment of society according to the rules of religion.[105] There was no need for a social program because the Torah, in its widest sense, contains a social program. We have no way of knowing if changes in the landholding structure would have been legislated, or how the government would have managed affairs. But there are a few assorted indicators that some of the rebels supported measures that would have had some effect on the landholding structure.

The most well-known example of these is the burning of the debt records in Jerusalem (*BJ* 2.425–9). The sicarii, who were kept out of the Temple by those opposed to the revolt, forced their way in along with some poor folk they had enlisted. Having gained the upper hand they burned the archives, "eager to destroy the money-lenders' bonds and to prevent the recovery of debts, in order to win over a host of grateful debtors and to cause a rising of the poor against the rich, sure of impunity." From this source it is possible to learn that the sicarii did not have a social program. The reason for the burning of the debt records was to win support from the poor. The alliance between the poor and the sicarii was a temporary bond that was born in the struggle to get into the Temple. The sicarii apparently hoped that the poor would identify their enemies with those of the sicarii. Goodman remarked that the burning of the archives might not have had any real effect on the debt records because most people kept "double documents," i.e. sealed copies of records that had legal standing.[106] However, *BJ* 7.60–1 relates that in Antioch people also burned the market-place and the public records, hoping to rid themselves of obligations. Isaac writes that double documents were often kept because someone did not trust the efficiency or the honesty of the documents kept as copies in the city archives.[107] Could the burning of the archives in Jerusalem be an indication that, once again, the archives contained falsified documents? Or, alternatively, Isaac explains that in Roman Egypt double documents were in disuse at this time, so people relied on the archives; hence, by burning the archive the debt record really was destroyed. In that case the double documents from the Judean desert would be a regional holdout against the prevailing routine.

After the struggles between the sicarii and their opponents ended with the removal of the sicarii from Jerusalem, the next we hear of anything remotely echoing a class conflict is the so-called murder of the nobles (*BJ* 4.168, 181). But as Price has shown these arguments are forced. The rebel camp included many nobles and High Priests until the very last days of the revolt.[108]

Similarly, the claim that Simon bar Giora was the Babeuf of the Judean revolt stresses that he liberated the slaves (*BJ* 4.508–10), but ignores the support he received from aristocrats.[109] Regarding the liberation of the slaves, the details given by Josephus are so sparse one wonders if this is not an attempt to blacken Simon's image by creating the impression that he led a slave revolt. Yet bar Giora does provide examples of a violent resentment against the wealthy, particularly against landowners (*BJ* 4.652). Certainly, the upper-class Josephus despised him more than any of the other rebel leaders.[110]

One other scene of the war provides material on economic and social relations: the Galilee. Josephus claims that the Galileans hated the people of Tiberias and Sepphoris.[111] In fact, the Galileans chopped off the hands of Justus' brother (*Vita* 177). In Gamla, Justus' brother-in-law was murdered. Josephus would have us believe that the inhabitants of Tiberias were split along class lines, i.e. the first faction of respectable citizens was for peace, the second faction, composed of the most insignificant persons (ασημοτατων), was bent on war. However, if Josephus is to be believed, there was a third faction which included otherwise respectable persons, but was also for the war (*Vita* 32–6). It is difficult if not impossible to draw schematic lines, with the rich for peace and the poor for war. It is easier to build a case for urban–rural tension, which may have had something to do with landownership and debt.

Justus argued against the king and Rome because Tiberias had been displaced as the capital of Galilee; it had lost the royal bank and the archives (*Vita* 37–9). We assume that these three elements must have had some value, else why did Justus harp on their loss as a reason to revolt? The archives had been in Tiberias; as had been Justus' brother. He was punished so severely because he had forged documents, while Justus himself was resented by the Galileans because of the miseries which he had inflicted on them before the war (*Vita* 392). It is possible that the urban wealthy of Tiberias and Sepphoris oppressed the rural hinterland in the matter of taxes and loans. Unfortunately, we do not have any other source, as yet, to support such a scenario.

The Great Revolt ended without any changes in the landownership structure of the country initiated by the revolutionary government. The changes that took place were the result of the devastation of the war itself, and the ad hoc measures enacted by the Roman commanders. In the next chapter we will discuss these changes more fully.

9

EPILOGUE: FROM YAVNEH TO BAR KOKHBA

YAVNEH

The war against the Romans created two factors which affected the landholding structure of the country. The first factor was the result of the impact of the war itself. Jews were killed, enslaved, or emigrated. The second factor was the disposition of the land by the Roman government.

There is no way to accurately measure the loss of life caused by the revolt. We cannot depend on the figures provided by Josephus and the other ancient sources. The latter may be more reasonable, but they also are not necessarily accurate.[1] We have no absolute record of where all the destruction took place, how extensive it was, and how soon it was remedied. Nevertheless, even without making a quantitative estimate, we can get a qualitative impression of the changes that occurred due to the devastation of the war. We can study the archaeological record, as well as gain an impression from the literary sources.[2] In this manner we discover that both large and small settlements were severely affected.[3] One result of the war was the removal of the Jewish population, in part or even in whole, from farms, villages, towns, and even cities. For example, findings at the settlement of Gamla indicate that the site ceased to be occupied after the destruction of the battle.[4] The villa at Hirbet el-Murak (the Villa of Helkias) was damaged and the site abandoned for some time. The archaeologist who excavated the site suggests that the villa was destroyed by raids in the spring of 68 after Vespasian captured Kfar Tov and Beit Govrin, and left forces to raid the area (*BJ* 4.447).[5] Regarding that campaign, Josephus relates that the Romans put more than 10,000 of the inhabitants to death, made prisoners of over 1,000, and expelled the remainder (*BJ* 4.448). In Gerasa, reportedly 1,000 young men were killed, the women and children enslaved, the property plundered, and the houses burned (*BJ* 4.488). The city of

Gabara and all its environs were burnt (*BJ* 2.132–4). Apparently the city of Narbatene was destroyed early in the war and not resettled.[6] In addition to information on specific sites reported in the sources, or evidence of abandonment in the physical record, we may assume that thousands of peasants from all over the country left their lands and made their way to Jerusalem, or some local city.[7] Even if these places were resettled after the hostilities (*BJ* 4.444) we cannot know how many of them were resettled by their previous owners.

Besides the changes that resulted from the dislocation of casualties and refugees, the Romans also initiated deliberate changes. Their motives were varied. In some places they had to solve logistic or security problems that came up during the campaigns; for example, Jewish deserters were settled in Perea (*BJ* 4.438). More frequently, the Romans were faced with the need to punish rebels, or to reward those who had remained loyal. Some illustrations of these situations: Titus promised to restore property after the war to prominent Jewish refugees who deserted from besieged Jerusalem (*BJ* 6.114–15).[8] Josephus is the best example of this policy; he was given land elsewhere to replace his original lands in the Jerusalem area. His situation reveals a number of points about the Roman policy.

From *Vita* 422 it has been claimed that the land in the vicinity of Jerusalem became legion territory. However, Isaac has reinterpreted the text, concluding that Josephus did intend not to say that his lands had been taken by the army.[9] Rather, Josephus explained that Titus was worried that the presence of a garrison in town might make Josephus' possessions unprofitable. In any case, it is clear the army had become a major presence in the former city, and its activities apparently limited the options of private landowners. It is also clear that the Romans bestowed land on whomever they felt deserving, but whose land did Josephus receive? He simply says it was in the "plain."[10] Was it royal land now belonging to the emperor, or confiscated land? If it was confiscated land, who worked it?

These questions bring us to the major point: did the Romans confiscate the land in its entirety? For years, historians claimed that Vespasian held all of Judean land as his private property, and that he leased it out to his own advantage.[11] But recently, Isaac refuted that reading; he pointed out that the Romans would not have confiscated the property of loyal subjects.[12] To illustrate this point, we have the example of Titus' promise to the deserters (*BJ* 6.114–15). Sepphoris is a good example of a settlement that remained loyal, and profited by its loyalty (*Vita* 411).[13]

Furthermore, Isaac showed that Vespasian did not farm out confiscated land, but had it sold. Who bought it? We can only speculate that some of the land was purchased by Jews who were Roman sympathizers. Possibly gentiles from the areas contiguous to the Jewish areas purchased land.

Besides the sale of the confiscated land, it is clear that the Romans settled eight hundred veterans near Emmaus.[14] In addition, other colonies were established at Caesarea, Samaria, and Jaffa.[15] Jerusalem ceased to be a city (*BJ* 7.3) and became the headquarters of the Tenth Legion, raising the unanswerable question, what happened to the Jewish inhabitants? In Caesarea and Jaffa one can conclude from Josephus' narrative that the Jewish population in Caesarea and Jaffa was massacred. But it is difficult to assume that all of the population of Jerusalem was massacred, especially since we know that some of them had left the city before the final stages of the battle. The Jewish inhabitants who left before the final stages of the revolt may have been allowed to return to the Jerusalem area, although we have no information to support that possibility. It is more likely that they relocated to areas such as Yavneh, as in the famous case of Rabban Yohanan ben Zakkai.[16]

In addition to the legion in Jerusalem, other places might have become temporary Roman installations. A few decades later in 124 CE, a site in Ein Gedi was occupied by a Roman camp.[17]

The establishment of a colony, the confiscation and sale of lands, and the presence of Roman camps have led some scholars to assign the problem of the *sikarikon* and the *matzikin* to the post-70 CE period.[18] The purpose of the *sikarikon* laws was to prevent Jewish-owned land from expropriation and sale without regard to the traditional rights of the original Jewish owners. In brief, they enjoin the purchaser of a plot, or the person using a plot, to compensate the original Jewish owner. Because these rulings are found in the Mishnah and the Tosefta it is impossible to date them accurately.[19] The Mishnah does provide a *terminus ad quem* so we can conclude that the problem of the *sikarikon* existed before 200 CE. However, the question arises whether these laws were promulgated as a result of the Great Revolt, or as a result of the Bar Kokhba Revolt.

In an exhaustive study of the talmudic literature, including the Midrashim, Applebaum came to the conclusion that large sections of Judea were confiscated from the rebels and distributed to Roman aristocrats and soldiers. According to this, the lands were administered by supervisors, some of whom were gentiles, but also included Jews.

These last are the people referred to as *matzikin*.[20] Applebaum's theory has much to recommend it, as we shall see, but to prove his point he relies heavily on late sources, i.e. the Jerusalem and Babylonian Talmuds, as well as the Midrashim. Since talmudic sources tend to build upon previous traditions in order to explain a current situation, one gets a worst-case impression of the landholding structure. The image we are seeing really reflects the agrarian situation of the third and fourth centuries CE.[21]

Applebaum observes that there were large tracts of royal land.[22] However, there was nothing new in that; we have seen that royal land always existed in Israel. He also held that the tenants on these lands were now subject to extraordinary demands from their landlord.[23] Applebaum further postulated that the situation of the Jewish agriculturist worsened upon the death of Agrippa II, when his lands were added to the imperial domain.[24]

Mor, in a review of the *sikarikon* and *matzikin* traditions, rejected Applebaum's theory.[25] Mor's criticism can be summed up in three points: (1) the sources are tendentious; (2) there is considerable evidence that large areas of the country remained the private property of Jews; (3) the tenancy arrangements of the Romans were in no way different or more onerous than all the other tenancy arrangements that were in effect throughout the Hellenistic and Roman periods. Mor asserts that if they did not provoke revolts, then there is no reason to expect that the Roman landlords would provide any greater provocation to revolt. Because some of the sources refer to the requirement to abrogate the *sikarikon* rules in Judea, but not in the Galilee, Mor is willing to concede that the *sikarikon* were a post-Betar phenomenon.[26]

In regard to the debate on the *sikarikon* and the *matzikin*, we believe two separate approaches should be followed. First, a critical analysis of the situation in Judea. This indicates that land was handed over both to gentiles and to Jewish sympathizers. This cannot be denied: the lands of Jaffa, Caesarea, and Motza were handed over to gentiles, Jews had lived there before, now many of them were dead. Likewise, the lands around Jerusalem had probably been farmed in great part by city residents, many of whom were now dead. Those who were alive probably did not occupy the city itself. In brief, some Jewish land was now owned by gentiles. Of these properties, some were probably worked by gentiles themselves, e.g. Caesarea. Other land was now owned by gentiles and worked by Jews. For example, it is quite possible that the *coloni* in Motza engaged Jewish agriculturists to actually work the plots. Furthermore, while royal lands belonging to Herod had been taken over by the

Roman emperors, large tracts of royal land had remained in the hands of the Herodian family; as these died out, their estates probably went to Roman control.

Second, the talmudic sources have to be used far more cautiously than they have been used till now. By the time the earliest sources were edited over a century had passed. In this time, the imperial and local situations had changed a number of times. Therefore, we cannot deny that some of the *sikarikon* and *matzikin* traditions indeed stem from the post-Great Revolt period, while we do not accept them as completely accurate versions of the landowning relationships of that era.

For example, M. Gittin 5:6 can fit the post-70 period better than the post-Betar period. It assumes that Jews live in Judea and are actively engaged in buying land, that the original owners are also alive and in the area, and that an illegitimate owner (either a Jew or a gentile) has the land in his possession and is willing to sell it. In the post-Betar period these conditions were less likely to exist. It is irrelevant, in our opinion, if another *sikarikon* source presents a different picture (T. Gittin 5:1). One cannot lump all the sources together and draw a conclusion for a whole century.

When trying to reconstruct the landownership structure of Jewish Palestine in the post-70 CE period we should not forget that along with confiscated and abandoned land there were many plots still owned by Jews.[27]

There is a brief anecdote related by Eusebius regarding the property of the grandsons of Judas, the brother of Jesus of Nazareth.[28] The temptation to accept this at face value is enormous. We could then extrapolate the monetary value of a *plethron*. However, how did Eusebius come by this story? He lived at the end of the third century CE, while the anecdote refers to a conversation that took place in Domitian's reign (end of first century CE). At best we can accept that there were traditions about Jews owning their own property at that time. Likewise, M. Gittin, discussed above, demonstrates internally that the Jews could and did buy properties, else there is no point to the ruling.

Finally, we have the documents from the Babatha archive. The documents are full of interesting and enlightening details. Unfortunately, as a source of information on landholding they suffer from two disadvantages. They are too limited to be truly representative of the situation in Jewish Palestine. We have what is basically one family's slice of the economy. Can we honestly claim that we should generalize from the details of landholding in the Judean desert region for the whole of the country? Moreover, for the most part the documents represent life in the Province of Arabia; even if we were able to generalize from them, we have no way of knowing if the same conditions prevailed in the Province of Judea.

THE REVOLT OF BAR KOKHBA

The last major revolt of the Jews against the Romans broke out in 132 CE. This is not the appropriate forum to discuss the many interesting questions raised by the revolt. With regard to landownership and the revolt only two questions will occupy us: did landownership problems contribute in any way to the outbreak of the revolt? Is there anything of interest that can be learned about landownership from the period of Bar Kokhba's administration?

Regarding the causes of the war, Applebaum attempted to show that the Judean farmer was prey to the greedy agents of the emperor, and other landlords.[29] Supposedly, the heavy oppression forced the Judean cultivator to join in the revolt. We have discussed this in greater detail in the previous section. Applebaum built his theory on the basis of talmudic legends and halachic rulings whose provenance throws suspicion on their accuracy about early second-century Judea.

Mor dismissed most of Applebaum's argument for the reason we mentioned above. It is significant that no source specifically blames landownership relations for the war. Even the legends about rioting peasants are too folkloristic, and indeed do not refer to landownership as a motivation for revolt.[30]

The documents reveal that some areas of land were controlled by Bar Kokhba in his capacity of Nasi.[31] In a place called 'Ir Nahas, an official of the administration leased land to a number of people. The leases were for five-year periods, and until the eve of the Sabbatical Year. The amount owed by each lessee was specified in amounts and not in percent of the yield. From their payment a percent was to be deducted to the treasury. The amounts of each lease differ: perhaps the lessor took into consideration the size of the plot or the richness of the soil. Although we can see that the lessees paid a fixed fee and not a percentage of the crop, we cannot establish whether the fees were high. We would have to know the size of the fields, and at least the type of crop (Mur. 24E – fine wheat) even to guess at the relative scale of the prices. Contracts B, C, D include a clause warning that if the farmer did not live up to his obligations, he would lose the soil.

The fact that the land was leased by Bar Kokhba as Nasi, and not as a private person, provokes all sorts of speculations. Milik suggested that these were royal lands, seized from Jews in the wake of the Great Revolt, and now devolved upon Bar Kokhba as the de jure (in Jewish eyes) ruler.[32] Alternatively, the land may have once been Herodian land, which, as the house of Herod died out, was inherited by the emperors. This would explain why no Jews came forth to claim it as their land. It is remarkable that the land remained "royal land" and was not handed out to the Jewish farmers as property, and not by lease. Did the Hasmoneans use the same landownership relations? Unfortunately, we cannot make determinations about previous periods from information gleaned from later periods.

Continuing the examination of the concept of king's land, one document has an intriguing statement which has only been used to illustrate national and religious aspects of the revolt:[33]

משמעון בר כוסבא לאנשי עינגדי
למסבלא]ו[ל]יהו[נ[תן ב[ר] בעין שלום. בטוב
אתן יושבין אכלין וש]ו[תין מן נכסי בית
ישראל ולא דאנין לאחיכן לכול דבר.

From Simon Bar Kosiba to the men of Ein Gedi
To Masabala and Yehonathan son of Be'ayia, peace. . . . In comfort
you sit eating and drinking of the property of the House of
Israel and do not take care of your brothers for all their needs.

What is meant by מן נכסי בית ישראל? Yadin suggested that it refers to wheat that should have been passed on to other forces of Bar Kokhba in Mahoz. But could it mean that the addressees were living well off the product of Ein Gedi, land which could be considered royal land, in the sense that all royal land is property of the nation?[34] In Julius Caesar's grant to Hyrcanus, the same identity is hinted:

As for the villages in the Great Plain, which Hyrcanus and his forefathers before him possessed, it is the pleasure of the Senate that Hyrcanus and the Jews shall retain them. . . . As for the places, lands and farms the fruits of which the kings of Syria and Phoenicia . . . were permitted to enjoy . . . these the Senate decrees that the ethnarch Hyrcanus and the Jews shall have.

(*Ant.* 14.207–9)

Furthermore, we have seen that Ein Gedi was a royal property, certainly in the decades just prior to the war. Ein Gedi also had a port (Mahoz) as indicated by the yet unpublished part of the text (pp. 59–60).[35] A port would be most likely in a spot which had to bring in supplies and ship-out products, and which would therefore have a customs authority, another aspect of the royal administration.

Besides the leasing agreements between Bar Kokhba and some farmers, there are copies of agreements relating to the leasing and the sale of private land.[36] These agreements are characterized by payments in cash, not in kind as in the Bar Kokhba leases. However, before we jump to conclusions, we must remember how slim our field of information really is. The most we can responsibly assume is that private land was available and exchanged under market conditions, and that a money economy existed.

With the end of the Bar Kokhba revolt, new questions arise and other problems need to be solved. These will have to remain for a later date.

10

CONCLUSIONS

The economy of the Jewish people in Eretz Israel throughout the Second Temple period retained certain constant characteristics. Most people lived by agriculture, so that land was the source of livelihood, wealth, and power. Much of the land was owned by the ruler, whoever he was. Royal lands were an integral part of the landholding structure from the First Temple period through the talmudic age. These lands provided the crown personal wealth, control over economically significant products, such as balsam, and a reserve of land to be allocated to whomever the ruler wished to advance. The actual work on the royal lands was performed by tenants who were either share-croppers or lessees.

Other lands were owned by notables who were usually favorites of the regime. All the rulers in the period we surveyed rewarded loyal retainers by allocating estates to them. In the Persian period the privileged returnees received lands. The Hellenistic rulers of both the Ptolemaic and Seleucid houses granted estates to their adherents. The Ptolemies bestowed estates on leading officials such as Apollonius and Ptolemy son of Thraseas. In the case of the Seleucids the granting of land and the expropriation of land were part and parcel of their policy in Judea. The Hasmoneans did not significantly differ in this respect from the Hellenistic kingdoms. Their contribution to the landholding history of Judea was to open lands to Jewish settlement that formerly belonged to the gentile population of the country. The Romans canceled the achievements of this policy, returning captured lands to the gentile population. However, within the borders of the Jewish areas they also bestowed lands on their supporters, while disenfranchising their enemies. Herod behaved in the same manner, raising a new elite, and providing lands for his veterans. We see, therefore, that the policy of land grants and expropriations is consistent throughout the period; the only change, albeit an important one, is who specifically benefited from the policy.

At the same time small freeholders also owned and lived on family plots. There was a basic conservatism in the ownership of land. This tie to the land was rooted in cultural traditions regarding the land as a patrimony belonging ultimately to the family in its widest sense. Yet the land was, on a more practical plane, the major source of livelihood for most people. When the land was unproductive, or external forces prevented the farmer from successfully drawing a livelihood from his property, the result was always economic and social disequilibrium, producing demands for remedies.

The disturbing factor might have been caused by a sudden and even brief and temporary event such as a drought, or an earthquake. We have seen that natural causes created or contributed to crises in the Persian period, both at its inception and in the days of Nehemiah's tutelage. We have postulated that the temporary collapse of the Maccabean forces may have been due to a prolonged crop failure. Invasion and war could also cause a sudden dislocation of the usual order of society. The Roman conquest created the problem of landlessness for all those Jews who were dislodged from the areas of Maccabean conquests.

Alternatively, the upset might have been caused by long-term problems such as over-taxation, overpopulation, and unemployment. We have sought to demonstrate that Ptolemaic economic policies created economic pressures on the Judean population. Their intensive taxation and monopoly of many incoming producing crops may have contributed to the lamentable situations of debtors described by Ben-Sira. Similarly, the pressures created by the extortionate demands of the Roman procurators contributed to the eruption of the Great Revolt. The growth of the Jewish population cannot be ruled out as a contributory factor toward the need for expansion to find land. While we suggest that the population size and growth were not as excessive as some scholars have claimed, they were sufficient to create economic and social pressures. One may also assume that many of these problems occurred concurrently.

When society entered into a crisis, the landholding structure also bore the marks of the disturbance. One might suggest that the destabilization of society developed in which the smaller land-holders became indebted, and then became either tenants on their own land, or were forced to meet their debts by extra labor on the creditors' behalf. If the crisis was extraordinary, mass starvation — famine — struck.

When these crises happen the society could best hope for leadership that was able to successfully remedy the problems and find solutions enabling a return to the routine and accepted patterns. However, if such leadership is lacking, then the crisis can contribute to the development of a historical turning point. In the case of Nehemiah, Judean society found the leader it needed. So Herod, although much hated, managed to initiate programs and policies that guaranteed domestic stability. The decades following Herod, although marked by scattered efforts to find solutions to problems, were more characterized by a lack of remedies than by a wealth of solutions. The result was the cataclysm of the Great Revolt. In the wake of the Jewish defeat gentile ownership of land was introduced within Jewish areas, albeit only to a limited extent.

The Bar Kokhba Revolt provides a glimpse into the conservative nature of landholding practices in Jewish society over the length of the entire Second Temple period. The ruler, although perhaps a messianic figure, still controls parcels of land which are worked by tenants and lessees. Others, holding private plots, also let out the land to farmers who will pay for the privilege. After nearly seven centuries we still find the same basic landholding relationships that were extant in the Persian period.

APPENDIX: WEIGHTS AND MEASURES

Area

  Modern:

	hectare	= 10,000 sq.m. = 10 **dunam**.

  Ancient:

Hebrew:	*beit seah*	= 625 sq.m.
Greek:	*aroura*	= 2,756 sq.m.
	plethron	= 1,262 sq.m.
Latin:	*jugera*	= 2,523 sq.m.

Volume

  Modern:

	liter of wheat	= c. 782.1 gr.
	bushel (US)	= 35.238 l.

  Ancient:

Hebrew:	*kab*	= c. 2.2 l. (180 *kab* in the *kor*)
	assaron	= 3.9 l. (one-hundredth of a *kor*)
	seah	= c.13 l. Opinions vary from c. 8.56 l. to c.15.5 l.
	kor	= 390 l. (depends on the size of the *seah*)
Greek:	*medimnus*	= c. 52 l.
Latin:	*modius*	= 8.6185 l.

NOTES

1 INTRODUCTION

1 P. Garnsey and I. Morris, "Risk and the Polis: The Evolution of Institutionalised Responses to Food Supply Problems in the Ancient Greek State," P. Halstead and J. O'Shea, eds, *Bad Year Economics: Cultural Responses to Risk and Uncertainty*, Cambridge, 1989, p. 99.
2 Ibid.
3 V. G. Childe, *Man Makes Himself*, New York, 1951, p. 107; idem, *What Happened in History*, New York, 1946, pp. 113–14; W. I. Davisson and J. E. Harper, *European Economic History*, vol. I, *The Ancient World*, New York, 1972, p. 48.
4 "Indeed the word *nahala* (נחלה), meaning literally 'wealth,' is always used in the sense of real property." L. Finkelstein, "The Pharisees: Their Origin and Their Philosophy," *HTR* 22 (1929), pp. 189–90.
5 M. Clawson, "Land: I. Economic Aspects," D. L. Sills, ed., *International Encyclopedia of the Social Sciences*, vol. 8, New York, 1968, pp. 551–2.
6 M. I. Finley, *Land and Credit in Ancient Athens, 500–200 BC*, New York, 1952, reprinted 1973, p. 13.
7 M. Smith, *Palestinian Parties and Politics that Shaped the Old Testament*, New York, 1971, reprinted London, 1987, p. 58, postulates that the land tenure system of the classical world was characterized by smallholdings of "ordinary citizens," while "in the Hellenistic world it was the large estate of the king, the temple, or the great official" that was prevalent.
8 Clawson, "Land: I: Economic Aspects," p. 552; P. A. Samuelson, *Economics*, New York and Tokyo, 1970, pp. 536–46; for a review of the idea of land and rent through history see Chapter 2 in J. W. McConnell, *The Basic Teachings of the Great Economists*, New York, 1943, pp. 37–63.
9 The minimum crop is discussed in the section on dietary needs. For climate see: F. M. Abel, *Géographie de la Palestine*, vol. I, pp. 108–34; D. Baly, *The Geography of the Bible*, New York, 1957; idem, "The Geography of Palestine and the Levant in Relation to its History," *CHJ*, vol. I, pp. 15–18; Y. Karmon, *Israel: A Regional Geography*, London, 1971, pp. 23–4, 27–8; E. Orni and E. Efrat, *Geography of Israel*, Jerusalem, 1971, pp. 148–9; R. B. Y. Scott, "Palestine, Climate of," G. A. Buttrick, ed., *IDB*, vol. III, Nashville, 1982, p. 625.

10 M.Ta'anit 3:1; I. Arnon, *Crop Production in Dry Regions*, vol. II, London, 1972, pp. 4, 7; G. E. Rickman, "The Grain Trade Under the Roman Empire," J. H. D'Arms and E. C. Kopff, eds, *Roman Seaborne Commerce (Memoirs of the American Academy in Rome*, vol. XXXVI), Rome, 1980, p. 261; Baly, *Geography*, pp. 50–2; *The Encyclopedia of Agriculture*, ed. H. Halperin, Tel-Aviv, 1966–87 (Heb.), vol. II, s.v. "*Hitta*" (Wheat), pp. 51–2, 69, recommends 450–550 mm. for an excellent crop.

11 G. Hamel, *Poverty and Charity in Roman Palestine*, Ph.D. Thesis, Univ. of California, Santa Cruz, 1983, p. 129, believes that droughts occurred every twenty years; see also Scott, "Palestine, Climate of," p. 625, and Orni and Efrat, *Geography of Israel*, pp. 148–9, on the frequency of droughts, with examples. My own examination of the rainfall record of Jerusalem for the period 1846/7–1959/60 indicates that the total annual precipitation fell below the minimum necessary for wheat only nine times in those 113 years. A relevant question is whether the precipitation levels were different in the ancient period than they are in the period since scientific meteorological records have been kept. Baly, *Geography*, pp. 70–6, 120, proposes that the climate was wetter then. Cf. D. Sperber, "Drought, Famine, and Pestilence in Amoraic Palestine," *JESHO* 17 (1974), pp. 272, 283, 293; Y. Wiesl, N. Liphschitz, and S. Lev-Yadun, "Flora in Ancient Eretz-Israel," A. Kasher, A. Oppenheimer, U. Rappaport, eds, *Man and Land in Eretz-Israel in Antiquity*, Jerusalem, 1986 (Heb.), pp. 237, 240.

12 Sibylline Oracles 3, 753–4.

13 Amos 7:1; Joel 1:4.

14 Hag. 2:17.

15 W. Jongman and R. Dekker, "Public Intervention in the Food Supply in Pre-Industrial Europe," P. Halstead and J. O'Shea, eds, *Bad Year Economics: Cultural Responses to Risk and Uncertainty*, Cambridge, 1989, p. 116; J. Drèze and A. Sen, *Hunger and Public Action*, Oxford, 1989, pp. 9–10, 23, 25–7.

16 A. Sen, *Poverty and Famines: An Essay on Entitlement and Deprivation*, Oxford, 1981, p. 38 n. 2; Drèze and Sen, *Hunger and Public Action*, p. 7; P. Garnsey, *Famine and Food Supply in the Graeco-Roman World*, Cambridge, 1988, pp. x, 6.

17 Garnsey, *Famine and Food Supply*, pp. x, 6.

18 K. S. Gapp, *Famine in the Roman World: From the Founding of Rome to the Time of Trajan*, Ph.D. Dissertation, Princeton Univ., 1934, pp. 113, 137; Garnsey, *Famine and Food Supply*, p. 19.

19 R. MacMullen, *Enemies of the Roman Order*, Appendix A: Famines, Harvard, 1967, p. 249, quotes Rostovtzeff on the desirability of compiling a full collection of the evidence on famines in the Roman Empire. MacMullen then provides an admittedly partial collection. Other than these works one should note Gapp's Doctorate of 1934, the collection of articles, P. Garnsey and C. R. Whittaker, eds, *Trade and Famine in Classical Antiquity*, Cambridge, 1983, and Garnsey's own recent and seminal contribution discussed hereon. On Judean famines *per se* the only works are: K. Gapp, "The Universal Famine Under Claudius," *HTR* 28 (1935), pp. 258–65; Sperber, "Drought, Famine, and Pestilence"; and

D. Flusser, "Qumran and the Famine During the Reign of Herod," *IMJ* 6 (1987), pp. 7–15.
20 Garnsey, *Famine and Food Supply.*
21 Ibid. p. 8.
22 Ibid. pp. 20–39.
23 Ibid. p. 21.
24 M. Aymard, "Toward the History of Nutrition: Some Methodological Remarks," R. Forster and O. Ranum, eds, *Food and Drink in History (Selections from the Annales Economies, Societies, Civilizations,* vol. V), Baltimore, 1979, pp. 5–15.
25 C. Clark and M. Haswell, *The Economics of Subsistence Agriculture,* London, 1970, pp. 1–23.
26 Ibid. A comparison of wheat with fish as components of the diet indicates that fish was at best a supplement; see T. W. Gallant, *A Fisherman's Tale: An Analysis of the Potential Productivity of Fishing in the Ancient World,* Miscellanea Graeca, fasciculus 7, Ghent, 1985, pp. 16, 23–4, 31–5.
27 Among the grains mentioned in the Mishnah only the שעורה, חיטה, כוסמת (se'orah = barley, hittah = wheat, kussemet = emmer) were prevalent in the Second Temple period. Of these the *kussemet* is really a wheat. See: N. Jasny, *The Wheats of Classical Antiquity,* Baltimore, 1944, pp. 16, 24, 78, 91, 117, 121, 145, 148; J. Feliks, "The Five Species," *EJ,* vol. 6, pp. 1332–3; J. Feliks, *Agriculture in Palestine in the Period of the Mishna and Talmud,* Jerusalem, 1963 (Heb.), p. 148 n. 178; M. E. Kislev, "*Hitta* and *Kussumet,* Notes on their Interpretation," *Lešonénu* XXXVII (1972–3), pp. 83–95, 243–52 (Heb.).
28 L. Foxhall and H. A. Forbes, "Sitometreia: The Role of Grain as a Staple Food in Classical Antiquity," *Chiron* 12 (1982), pp. 55–6; one Attic *choenix* of wheat could provide 98 percent of the daily energy requirements of a man engaging in moderate physical activity. See Foxhall and Forbes for other examples of wheat's role in meeting dietary demands. Cf. Clark and Haswell, *The Economics of Subsistence Agriculture,* p. 58, for different daily calorie demand figures.
29 M. Feldman, "Wheats," N. W. Simmonds, ed., *Evolution of Crop Plants,* New York and London, 1976, pp. 120–1.
30 Foxhall and Forbes, "Sitometreia," pp. 46–7.
31 Athenians are known to have preferred wheat to barley. Athenaeus III,113A; Aristophanes, *Wasps* 717–18. For relative prices see II Kings 7:1; TBM 9:10; M. Ket. 5:8; Rev. 6:5; Jasny, *Wheats,* p. 145; Gapp, *Famine,* pp. 108–10. See *BJ* 5.427; *Ant.* 5.220 for the preference of the rich for wheat.
32 N. Liphschitz and Y. Waisel, "Dendroarchaeological Investigations in Israel," *IEJ* 23 (1973), p. 35; *The Encyclopedia of Agriculture,* vol. II, s.v. "*se'orah,*" p. 69.
33 Jasny, "The Daily Bread of the Ancient Greeks and Romans," *Osiris* 9 (1950), p. 232; idem, *Wheats,* p. 14; Kislev, "A Barley Store of the Bar-Kochba Rebels (Roman Period)," *Israel Journal of Botany* 35 (1986), pp. 194–5; M. Zohary, *Plants of the Bible,* Cambridge, 1982, p. 74; H. N. Moldenke and A. L. Moldenke, *Plants of the Bible,* New York, 1952, p. 167; but see P. M. Mayerson, "Wheat in the Roman World: An

Addendum," *The Classical Quarterly*, n.s. XXXIV (1984), pp. 243–5, who points out that the evidence from the Nessana papyri indicates that wheat, not barley, was the preferred crop in that desert region. On the other hand D. Rathbone, "The Grain Trade and Grain Shortages in the Hellenistic East," in P. Garnsey and C. R. Whittaker, eds, *Trade and Famine in Classical Antiquity*, Cambridge, 1983, pp. 46–8, infers that in Greece wheat was the preferred grain of the city-folk while the rural population consumed barley. See Z. Safrai, *The Economy of Roman Palestine*, London and New York, 1994, pp. 108–9.

34 M. Broshi, "The Diet of Palestine in the Roman Period," *IMJ* V (1986), p. 42; Foxhall and Forbes, "Sitometreia," p. 62; Garnsey, *Famine and Food Supply*, p. 91; Z. Safrai, *The Galilee in the Time of the Mishna and Talmud*, Ma'alot, Ministry of Education and Culture, Israel, 1985 (Heb.), p. 116. For an overview of diet see L. R. Arrington, "Foods of the Bible," *Journal of the American Dietetic Association* 35 (1959), pp. 816–20; D. Brothwell and P. Brothwell, *Food in Antiquity*, New York, 1969; R. Duncan-Jones, *ERE*, Cambridge, 1982, pp. 50, 146–7; P. Garnsey and R. Saller, *The Roman Empire: Economy, Society, and Culture*, Berkeley and Los Angeles, 1987, pp. 77–92; Hamel, *Poverty and Charity in Roman Palestine*, pp. 67–138; Jasny, "Competition among Grains in Classical Antiquity," *American Historical Review*, XLVII (1941–2), pp. 747–64; idem, "The Daily Bread of the Ancient Greeks and Romans"; idem, *The Wheats of Classical Antiquity*.

35 Clark and Haswell, *The Economics of Subsistence Agriculture*, pp. 58–62. D. E. Oakman, *Jesus and the Economic Questions of His Day*, Lewiston, New York, 1986, p. 72, claims that the farmer was left with only one-fifth to one-third of his produce. See also M. Jameson, "Famine in the Greek World," P. Garnsey and C. R. Whittaker, eds, *Trade and Famine in Classical Antiquity*, Cambridge, 1983, p. 15 n. 21; Foxhall and Forbes, "Sitometreia," p. 68 n. 95; O. Borowski, *Agriculture in Iron Age Israel*, Ph.D. Dissertation, Univ. of Michigan, 1979, Chap. VIII Grain and Food Storage; L. E. Stager, "Appendix: Climate Conditions and Grain Storage in the Persian Period," *HTR* 64 (1971), p. 450; J. D. Currid, "The Beehive Granaries of Ancient Palestine," *Zeitschrift des deutschen Palästina-Vereins* 101 (1985), pp. 97–110; P. Halstead, "The Economy has a Normal Surplus: Economic Stability and Social Change Among Early Farming Communities of Thessaly, Greece," P. Halstead and J. O'Shea, eds, *Bad Year Economics: Cultural Responses to Risk and Uncertainty*, Cambridge, 1989, p. 79; H. Forbes, "Of Grandfathers and Grand Theories: The Hierarchised Ordering of Responses to Hazard in a Greek Rural Community," P. Halstead and J. O'Shea, eds, *Bad Year Economics: Cultural Responses to Risk and Uncertainty*, Cambridge, 1989, p. 93, on the practice of storing two years' supply as hedge against crisis; Varro, *Rust.*,1, 57, 3; Tos. A.Z. 4:1; T. Demai 1:13–14; R. Yankelevitch, "Granaries and Store Buildings in Eretz-Israel," *Milet* 1, S. Ettinger, Y. D. Gilat, S. Safrai, eds, Tel-Aviv, 1983, pp. 107–19 (Heb.).

36 Clark and Haswell, *The Economics of Subsistence Agriculture*; Forbes, "Of Grandfathers and Grand Theories," p. 94: the average minimum household requirement for wheat in Greece is 1,480 kg. per household. Wheat

is considered the preferred crop and calculations of the cost of necessities are done in units of wheat equivalent. See M. Feldman, "Wheats," pp. 120–1; M. Broshi, "The Population of Western Palestine in the Roman–Byzantine Period," *BASOR* 236 (1979), p. 7; Jasny, *The Wheats of Classical Antiquity*, pp. 14, 16; Foxhall and Forbes, "Sitometreia," pp. 46–7.

37 See P. A. Brunt, *Italian Manpower*, Oxford, 1971, esp. pp. 121–30; Duncan-Jones, *ERE*, Part 3 "Population and Demographic Policy," for population estimates of the Roman world.

38 J. Klausner, "How Many Jews Will Be Able to Live in Palestine? Based on an Analysis of the Jewish Population in Palestine in the Days of the Second Temple," *JSS* 11 (1949), pp. 119–28; H. W. Hoehner, *Herod Antipas*, Cambridge, 1972, reprinted Grand Rapids, 1980, pp. 52–3, and "Appendix III, Population," pp. 291–7; A. Byatt, "Josephus and Population Numbers in First Century Palestine," *PEQ* 105 (1973), pp. 51–60.

39 J. Jeremias, *Jerusalem in the Time of Jesus*, London, 1969, pp. 83–4; M. Avi-Yonah, "*Skira al Tzfifut ha-Okhlusim ve-Kamutam be-Eretz-Yisrael ha-Atika*," *Masot u-Mehkarim beYediat ha-Aretz*, Tel-Aviv, 1964 (Heb.).

40 J. Wilkinson, "Ancient Jerusalem and its Water Supply and Population," *PEQ* 106 (1974), pp. 33–51; C. C. McCown, "The Density of Population in Ancient Palestine," *JBL* 66 (1947), pp. 425–36; Broshi, "The Population of Western Palestine in the Roman–Byzantine Period." For a review of different modern approaches see I. Finkelstein, "A Few Notes on Demographic Data from Recent Generations and Ethnoarchaeology," *PEQ* 122 (1990), pp. 47–52.

41 S. Applebaum, "Judaea as a Roman Province: The Countryside as a Political and Economic Factor," *ANRW*, vol. II.8, Berlin, 1977, p. 376; A. Ben-David, *Talmudische Ökonomie: Die Wirtschaft des jüdischen Palästina zur Zeit der Mischna und des Talmud* (Band 1), Hildesheim, 1974, pp. 300–1.

42 S. Baron, "Reflections on Ancient and Medieval Jewish Historical Demography," *Ancient and Medieval Jewish History*, New Brunswick, NJ, 1972, pp. 15–16.

43 Broshi, "The Population of Western Palestine," p. 7.

44 B. Bar-Kochva, "Manpower, Economics, and Internal Strife in the Hasmonean State," *Armées et fiscalité dans le monde antique* (Colloque National du CNRS No. 936, Organisé par H. Van Effentere), Paris, 1977, pp. 167–70; M. Goodman, *The Ruling Class of Judaea*, Cambridge, 1987, pp. 61–2; A. Kasher, "*Hagirah ve-Hityashvut Yehudit be-Tfutzot be-Tekufah ha-Hellenistit–Romit*," A. Shinan, ed., *Emigration and Settlement in Jewish and General History*, Jerusalem, 1982 (Heb.), pp. 77–8.

45 C. M. Cipolla, *The Economic History of World Population*, Harmondsworth, 1978, pp. 88–9.

46 M. Broshi and I. Finkelstein, "The Population of Palestine in 734 BCE," *Cathedra* 58 (1990) (Heb.), p. 21.

47 Using a base figure of 200,000 as the Jewish population of Palestine in the year 400 BCE and an annual growth rate of 0.4 percent, we would arrive at a population of about 1.5 million in the year 100 CE. Over the

same period a growth rate of 0.5 percent would result in a population of 2.4 million. As an illustration of how significant ostensibly small changes in the rate of population growth can be, consider that a population growth of 1 percent over the same period would result in a population of over seventy-eight million people.

48 Brunt, *Italian Manpower*, p. 133.
49 U. Schmeltz, "Population Characteristics of the Jerusalem and Hebron Regions at the Beginning of the Twentieth Century," *Cathedra* 36 (1985) (Heb.), p. 143.
50 Brunt, *Italian Manpower*, p. 153.
51 Hecataeus ap. Diod. 40.3.7; Tacitus, *Hist.* 5.5.3.
52 Goodman, *The Ruling Class*, pp. 61–2.
53 L. E. Stager, "The Archaeology of the Family in Ancient Israel," *BASOR* 260 (1985), p. 20.
54 Finkelstein, "A Few Notes on Demographic Data," pp. 48–9. For comparative data see N. Schur, "The Numerical Relationship Between the Number of Households and the Total Population in the Cities of Eretz Israel During the Ottoman Period," *Cathedra* 17 (1980) (Heb.), pp. 102–6, who shows that families in Ottoman Palestine in 1840 had an average of four persons.
55 J. Feliks, "*Ha-hakla'ut ha-Yehudit beEretz-Yisrael bi-Tkufat ha-Mishna ve-ha-Talmud,*" Z. Baras et al., eds, *Eretz Israel from the Destruction of the Second Temple to the Muslim Conquest*, Jerusalem, 1982 (Heb.), p. 420.
56 The biblical description of a land of milk and honey is a by-word. For the Hellenistic and Roman periods the evidence of the Letter of Aristeas 107, 112–18, and Josephus' glowing description, see *BJ* 3.41–50. See also on the Ginnosar area *BJ* 3.516–17. We also have Hecataeus' statement that the Jews "occupy almost three million *arourae* of the most excellent and fertile soil, productive of every variety of fruits"; *CA* I 195. This figure is problematic since it is equal to c. 8,268 sq. km. which is five times the area of Judah in the Persian period and twice the area of Judea and Idumea. The problem remains unless we include Samaria and the Galilee, but then we have to ask why Hecataeus would include that as Judean area. Perhaps the figure is an example of a later Jewish interpolation: see B. Z. Wacholder, *Eupolemos: A Study of Judaeo-Greek Literature*, Cincinnati and New York, 1974, pp. 269–70.
57 Broshi warns against any attempt to determine the average plot size, or, by analogy to plot sizes, the minimum plot necessary for a family's livelihood. However, his caution is restricted to archaeology as a sole basis for such computations; see M. Broshi, "Agriculture and Economy in Roman Palestine According to Babatha's Papyri," *Zion* LV (1990) (Heb.), pp. 280–1.
58 Oakman, *Jesus and the Economic Questions*, p. 61.
59 Ibid.
60 Eusebius, *HE* 3.20, 1–2; G. Alon, *The Jews in Their Land in the Talmudic Age*, vols I–II, trans. Gershon Levi, Jerusalem, 1980–4, p. 156; Feliks, "*Ha-hakla'ut ha-Yehudit,*" p. 49.
61 Oakman, *Jesus and the Economic Questions*, p. 62.
62 S. Dar, "Agriculture and Agricultural Produce in Eretz-Israel in

the Roman–Byzantian [sic] Period," A. Kasher, A. Oppenheimer, U. Rappaport, eds, *Man and Land in Eretz-Israel in Antiquity*, Jerusalem, 1986 (Heb.), p. 144.

63 Ibid.

64 Ibid. p. 148.

65 Ibid. pp. 144–8.

66 M. Baba Batra 1:6; a *beth kab* is 104 sq.m., hence 9 *kabs* would be almost a *dunam*.

67 Tos. Baba Matzia 11:9, see S. Lieberman's comments in *Tosefta Kifshutah*, part IX, *Order Nezikin*, New York, 1988, p. 309.

68 Dar, "Agriculture and Agricultural Produce," p. 148.

69 Applebaum, "Judaea as a Roman Province," pp. 364–5, 374.

70 D. Orman, "The Economy of Jewish Communities in the Golan in the Mishna and Talmud Period," N. Gross, ed., *Jews in Economic Life*, Jerusalem, 1985 (Heb.), p. 38.

71 B. Golomb and Y. Kedar, "Ancient Agriculture in the Galilee Mountains," *IEJ* 21 (1971), p. 138.

72 D. A. Fiensy, *The Social History of Palestine in the Herodian Period: The Land is Mine, Studies in the Bible and Early Christianity* 20, Lewiston, Queenston, Lampeter, 1991, pp. 23–4.

73 Y. Portugali, "The Settlement Pattern in the Western Jezreel Valley from the 6th Century BCE to the Arab Conquest," A. Kasher, A. Oppenheimer, U. Rappaport, eds, *Man and Land in Eretz-Israel in Antiquity*, Jerusalem, 1986 (Heb.), p. 18.

74 Ibid. pp. 16–18.

75 An indication of the importance and prevalence of flocks and herds can be gained from *Ant.* 15.121–3, which relates that an earthquake destroyed many beasts throughout the country.

76 E. P. Sanders, *Judaism: Practice and Belief 63 BCE–66 CE*, London and Philadelphia, 1992, pp. 121, 136.

77 On 20 July 1994, I had a phone conversation with Mr Joseph Carrasso of the Division of Sheep (מנהל המחלקה לצאן), Dept. of Agriculture, Government of Israel. He stated that to sacrifice 30,000 yearlings annually a national herd of 100,000 head would be sufficient. In order to sacrifice 255,600 a herd of 850,00 would be ample. In Israel, pre-1967 borders, there are 500,000 head; with Judea and Samaria there are approx. 800,000 head. Finally, he related that in a very recent conference held in Greece on the subject of sheep and goats, the Saudi Arabian delegate communicated that for their annual sacrifices in Mecca they sacrificed one million head.

78 Z. Safrai, "The Influence of Demographic Stratification on the Agricultural and Economic Structure During the Mishnaic and Talmudic Periods," A. Kasher, A. Oppenheimer, U. Rappaport, eds, *Man and Land in Eretz-Israel in Antiquity*, Jerusalem, 1986 (Heb.), p. 33.

79 Dar, "Agriculture and Agricultural Produce," p. 144. A cow that caused considerable interest appears in the correspondence between the head of Bar Kokhba's forces in Beth Mashko and some unit which confiscated the unfortunate beast from its more unfortunate owner; see Y. Yadin, *Bar-Kokhba: The Rediscovery of the Legendary Hero of the Second Jewish Revolt against Rome*, London and Jerusalem, 1971, p. 136.

80 Lev. Rabba 30:1.
81 Dar, "Agriculture and Agricultural Produce," p. 149; on the intensification of agriculture see Z. Safrai, "The Influence of Demographic Stratification."
82 According to Pliny, *NH* 12, 118, just the loppings and the shoots alone brought in 800,000 sesterces in five years.
83 Even the king raised dates if he could: see *BJ* 4.467. On dates in Judea see Pliny, *NH* 13.26–49, and see references to other ancient authors in M. Stern, *Greek and Latin Authors on Jews and Judaism (GLAJJ)*, vol. I, Jerusalem, 1976–84, p. 494, note to line 26. See the collection of papyri in N. Lewis, *The Documents from the Bar Kochba Period in the Cave of Letters*, vol. 2, *Greek Papyri*, Jerusalem, 1989, Greek index, s.v. φοινικῶν; see discussion by Broshi, "Agriculture and Economy," pp. 272–4.
84 Dar, *Landscape and Pattern*, pp. 118–19.
85 Ibid. p. 158.
86 Ibid. p. 161.
87 Heronda, II.16–17, quoted by M. Avi-Yonah, *Hellenism and the East: Contacts and Interrelations from Alexander to the Roman Conquest*, Jerusalem, 1978, p. 225.
88 F. Goldmann, "Der Ölbau in Palästina in der tannaitischen Zeit," *MGWJ* 50 (1906), pp. 563–80, 707–28; 51 (1907), pp. 17–40, 129–41; M. Heltzer and D. Eitam, *Olive Oil in Antiquity*, Haifa, 1987; M. Goodman, "Kosher Olive Oil in Antiquity," P. R. Davies and R. T. White, eds, *A Tribute to Geza Vermes: Essays on Jewish and Christian Literature and History*, Sheffield, 1990, pp. 227–45; R. Frankel, *The History of the Processing of Wine and Oil in Galilee in the Period of the Bible, the Mishna and the Talmud*, unpublished Ph.D. Thesis, Univ. of Tel-Aviv, 1984 (Heb.).
89 D. T. Ariel, *Excavations at the City of David 1978–1985*, vol. II, Qedem 30, Jerusalem, 1990, p. 12; M. Broshi, "The Cities of Eretz-Israel in the Herodian Period," *Qadmoniot* XIV (55–6) (1981) (Heb.), pp. 70–9; Z. Maoz, "The City Plan of Jerusalem in the Hasmonean and Herodian Period," *Eretz-Israel* 18 (1985) (Heb.), pp. 46–57.
90 Z. Ron, "Agricultural Terraces in the Judean Mountains," *IEJ* 16 (1966), pp. 33–49, 111–22.
91 L. Stager, "Farming in the Judean Desert During the Iron Age," *BASOR* 221 (1976), p. 157.
92 Ibid.

2 THE PERSIAN PERIOD

1 On the economy of the First Temple period see O. Borowski, *Agriculture in Iron Age Israel*, Ph.D. Dissertation, Univ. of Michigan, 1979, esp. Chap. III "Land Tenure"; M. Silver, *Prophets and Markets: The Political Economy of Ancient Israel*, Boston, The Hague, London, 1983; idem, *Economic Structures of the Ancient Near East*, London, 1985; R. de Vaux, "Economic Life," *Ancient Israel*, vol. I, New York, 1965; K. H. Henrey, "Land Tenure in the Old Testament," *PEQ* 86 (1954), pp. 5–15.

2 Isa. 5:8; I Chron. 27:25–31; II Chron. 26:10; see also de Vaux, *Ancient Israel*, pp. 165–6; Silver, *Prophets and Markets*, pp. 75, 111, 259; L. E. Stager, "The Archaeology of the Family in Ancient Israel," *BASOR* 260 (1985); J. Fager, *Land Tenure and the Biblical Jubilee*, Sheffield, 1993, pp. 27–31, 89–91.

3 II Kings 25:11–12; Jer. 39:9–10; 40:6–12; 52:15–16; Ezek. 11:15; Lam. 5:2; the last verse appears to refer to the loss of lands to foreigners; however, the description of the exiled clearly indicates that an aristocracy has fallen on hard times and we suggest that the זרים (aliens) in the verse are simply the poor who are now the proprietors of the estates. Also see *Ant.* 10.159, 162; J.P. Weinberg, *The Citizen–Temple Community*, trans. D. L. Smith-Christopher, *JSOT* supplement series 151, Sheffield, 1992, pp. 98–9; J. M. Miller and J. H. Hayes, *A History of Ancient Israel and Judah*, Philadelphia, 1986, pp. 420, 424; D. L. Smith, "The Politics of Ezra: Sociological Indicators of Postexilic Judaean Society," P. R. Davies, ed., *Second Temple Studies*, vol. 1, *Persian Period*, p. 93: based on Janssen, the pro-Babylonian "fifth column" within the late pre-exilic community may have had some influence on the redistribution of the land among those left behind on the land (Jer. 40), although as workers and not owners, a view taken also by A. Alt, *Kleine Schriften Zur Geschichte Des Volkes Israel*, vol. II, Munich, 1953, pp. 316–37.

4 See also Ezek. 33:24. According to S. Japhet, "People and Land in the Restoration Period," G. Strecker, ed., *Das Land Israel in Biblischer Zeit*, Göttingen, 1983, pp. 106–7, Ezek. 11:15–21 and 33:23–9 claim proprietary rights to the land for those Jews that remained. Japhet thinks that the claim is rooted in religious concepts and not in any attempt to deprive the exiles of their inheritance; cf. J. Blenkinsopp, "A Jewish Sect of the Persian Period," *CBQ* 52 (1990), p. 9 n. 15, who thinks that Ezek.11:15 is a justification for the expropriation of the land of the exiles.

5 Japhet, "People and Land in the Restoration Period," pp. 113–14; Miller and Hayes, *A History of Ancient Israel and Judah*, p. 445.

6 There is a third possibility proposed by K. C. Hoglund, "The Achaemenid Context," P. R. Davies, ed., *Second Temple Studies*, vol. 1, *Persian Period*, Sheffield, 1991, pp. 57–60. He suggests that many of the rural settlements in the early sixth century were new settlements. This would indicate a deliberate policy of ruralization stimulated by the Persian government. However, this depends on the interpretation of the archaeological findings, which do not support the contention of an empty countryside waiting for settlement.

7 Miller and Hayes, *A History of Ancient Israel and Judah*, p. 445; S. S. Weinberg, "Post-Exilic Palestine, An Archaeological Report," *The Israel Academy of Sciences and Humanities Proceedings* 4 (1969), pp. 79–84, 88; E. Stern, *Material Culture of the Land of the Bible in the Persian Period 538–332 BC*, Warminster and Jerusalem, 1982, pp. 229, 249, 253–5.

8 S. Zeitlin, *The Rise and Fall of the Judaean State*, vol. I, Philadelphia, 1968–78, p. 5.

9 The literature on the Persian period is vast. For discussions on the economic and social questions see Davies, ed., *Second Temple Studies*, vol. 1, *Persian Period*; H. G. Kippenberg, *Religion und Klassenbildung im*

antiken Judäa, Göttingen, 1982; H. Kreissig, *Die Sozialökonomische Situation in Juda zur Achämenidenzeit*, Berlin, 1973; W. Schottroff, "Arbeit und sozialer Konflikt im nachexilischen Juda," L. Schottroff and W. Schottroff, eds, *Mitarbeiter der Schöpfung*, Munich, 1983, pp. 104–48; idem, "Zur Socialgeschichte Israels in der Perserzeit," *Verkuendigung und Forschung* 27 (1982), pp. 46–6.

10 Jer. 40:6–12; *Ant.* 10.159, 163.

11 A. Rofé, "The Vineyard of Naboth: The Origin and Message of the Story," *VT* 38 (1988), pp. 101–2. See Blenkinsopp, "A Jewish Sect of the Persian Period," pp. 18–19; D. L. Smith, "The Politics of Ezra," pp. 93–7. Against this view of conflict is Hoglund, "The Achaemenid Context," pp. 57–60, who holds that it was imperial policy to settle the rural areas and that these new rural settlements militate against the struggle theory proposed by myself and others. We fail to see how the existence of such a policy would by itself ameliorate the resentments caused by an influx of returnees.

12 Ezra 2:3–33; Neh. 7:8–38; M. Heltzer and M. Kochman, *Encyclopedia Olam Ha-Tanach: Ezra ve-Nehemia*, Jerusalem, 1985 (Heb.), p. 28.

13 M. Smith, *Palestinian Parties and Politics that Shaped the Old Testament*, New York, 1971, reprinted London, 1987, p. 187 n. 22.

14 Ezra 1:4, 6–11; 2:68–9; note that approx. 25 percent of the returnees were servants and slaves: Ezra 2:64–5; Neh. 7:66. According to Schottroff, "Arbeit und sozialer Konflikt," pp. 128, 134, the proportion of free to slave was 1 : 6. In Zech. 6:9–15, wealthy members of Zerubbabel's following (returned exiles, verses 10–11) contributed gold and silver crowns to be hung in the Temple treasury; see M. Smith, *Palestinian Parties*, p. 83.

15 Ezra 2:1, 70; Neh.7:6; D. J. Clines, *Ezra, Nehemiah, Esther: The New Century Bible Commentary*, Grand Rapids, 1984, p. 46; F. C. Fensham, *The Book of Ezra, Nehemiah: The New International Commentary on the Old Testament*, Grand Rapids, 1982, p. 48.

16 Neh. 11:20; ‏ושאר ישראל הכהנים הלוים בכל ערי יהודה איש בנחלתו‎ ("And the rest of the Israelites, the priests, and the Levites in all the towns of Judah [lived] each on his own estate"). K. C. Hoglund, *Achaemenid Imperial Administration in Syria–Palestine and the Missions of Ezra and Nehemiah*, Atlanta, 1992, p. 27, demonstrates that the Persian administration pursued a policy of returning deported populations to their original locations.

17 *Ant.* 11.249; P. Briant, "Dons de terres et de villes: L'Asie Mineure dans le contexte Achémenide," *REA* 87 (1985), pp. 54, 55, 69; J.P. Weinberg, *The Citizen–Temple Community*, p. 480; M. Dandamayev, "Achaemenid Babylonia," *Ancient Mesopotamia*, Moscow, 1969, pp. 300–2. Note that the governor himself must have had extensive lands. Nehemiah proudly states that he declined the ‏לחם הפחה‎ (*lehem hapaha* = "governor's food allowance") for twelve years (Neh. 5:14–18); he also voluntarily gave up the debts he was owed (Neh. 5:10). We suggest that he garnered his income from the lands bestowed upon him. See R. N. Frye, *History of Ancient Iran*, p. 117, on the landownership of satraps and other nobles. The king also had lands, as illustrated by Nehemiah's request for a letter to Asaph the guardian of the royal *pardes* (Neh. 2:8). Hoglund,

"The Achaemenid Context," p. 59, presents the argument that the Achaemenids could dispose of all land in the empire at whim. "A classic example of this practice is the Eshmunezzer inscription where the Achaemenid monarch gave the king of Sidon the city of Dor and portions of the Sharon plain." N. V. Sekunda, "Achemenid Colonization in Lydia," *REA* 87 (1985), pp. 19, 27, demonstrates that non-Persians who demonstrated loyalty to Cyrus were rewarded with lands and farms.

18 M. Smith, *Palestinian Parties*, pp. 76, 81, 85–7, 116. Miller and Hayes, *A History of Ancient Israel and Judah*, p. 458, also perceived the return as a cause of conflict between the returnees and the occupants of the land; however, they understood the Israelites who had been left in the land by the Babylonians as the wealthy class.

19 M. Smith, *Palestinian Parties*; Miller and Hayes, *A History of Ancient Israel and Judah*, p. 458.

20 Hag. 1:10 refers to a lack of dew, but it is reasonable to assume that this is a copyist's error. See H. G. Mitchell, J. M. P. Smith, and J. A. Bewer, *ICC: Haggai, Zechariah, Malachi and Jonah*, Edinburgh, 1912, p. 49; it has also been suggested that "dew" represents precipitation of all sorts: see commentary by M. Zer-Kavod, *Haggai, Zechariah, Malachi*, Jerusalem, 1957 (Heb.), p. 17.

21 E. Stern and H. Tadmor, "*Shilton Paras*," I. Epha'al, ed., *Israel and Judah in the Biblical Period: The History of Eretz Israel*, vol. 2, Jerusalem, 1984 (Heb.), pp. 271–2.

22 Neh. 5:1–5. There are textual problems in verse 2: whether the word is רבים (numerous) as in the Masoretic text, or should be emended to ערבים (surety). See L.W. Batten, *The Books of Ezra and Nehemiah, ICC*, Edinburgh, 1913, p. 238; Zer-Kavod, *Ezra ve-Nehemia*, p. 90 n.1; Heltzer and Kochman, *Encyclopedia Olam Ha-Tanach*, p. 131. In any case verses 3 and 5 make it clear that the sons and daughters as well as the mentioned properties were given as security for loans. The word רבים may indicate one of the reasons for the economic crisis.

23 Food: Neh. 5:2, 3, 10, 11; Tax: Neh. 5:4, 14–15, 18.

24 Schottroff, "Arbeit und sozialer Konflikt," p. 109, believes that a famine much like that in Hag. 1:2–11, coinciding with the forced labor on the wall of Jerusalem, created the crisis. Kaufman was convinced that famine was the reason; see Y. Kaufman, *Toldot ha-Emunah ha-Yisraelit*, vol. 4, Book 1, Jerusalem and Tel-Aviv, 1967 (Heb.), p. 320.

25 Widengren, "The Persian Period," p. 509; Heltzer and Kochman, *Encyclopedia Olam Ha-Tanach*, p. 139.

26 Borowski, *Agriculture in Iron Age Israel*, Chap. IV, "The Agricultural Calendar," compares the Gezer calendar with the agricultural year.

27 J. M. Halligan, "Nehemiah 5: By Way of Response to Hoglund and Smith," P. R. Davies, ed., *Second Temple Studies*, vol. 1, *Persian Period*, pp. 149–50, suggests that there was a "chronic" grain shortage, forcing Judean farmers to take loans against the security of their property and children. But he does not address the question of the reasons for a chronic grain shortage.

28 Neh. 5:18: Nehemiah forgoes the bread of the governor because the bondage is heavy on the people, not because they themselves lack food.

29 T. W. Gallant, "Agricultural Systems, Land Tenure, and the Reforms of Solon," *Annual of the British School of Athens* 77 (1982), pp. 112–16.

30 Schottroff, "Zur Socialgeschichte Israels in der Perserzeit," p. 50; J.P. Weinberg, *The Citizen–Temple Community*, pp. 43, 45. According to Ezra 2:64 there were 42,360 returnees; this number is considered an exaggeration by most scholars. It probably represents the population of the province of Judah at the time of Nehemiah. This number of people is very close to the approximate size of the population of Judah and Benjamin in c. 734 BC, just before the Assyrian deportations began to upset the demographic makeup of the Land of Israel. See M. Broshi and I. Finkelstein, "The Population of Palestine in 734 BCE," *Cathedra* 58 (1990) (Heb.), pp. 3, 17.

31 Hecataeus, apud: Diodorus Siculus, *Bibliotheca Historica*, XL, 8; in *GLAJJ*, vol. I, p. 27 and see M. Stern's commentary and other references, idem, pp. 33–4.

32 Borowski, *Agriculture in Iron Age Israel*, Chap. 2 "Land Use," pp. 28–38.

33 Neh. 4:6. For a general discussion of the problems of Jews and gentiles and the available arable land, see U. Rappaport, "The Land Issue as a Factor in Inter-Ethnic Relations in Eretz-Israel During the Second Temple Period," A. Kasher, A. Oppenheimer, U. Rappaport, eds, *Man and Land in Eretz-Israel in Antiquity*, Jerusalem, 1986 (Heb.), pp. 80–6.

34 Gallant, "Agricultural Systems, Land Tenure, and the Reforms of Solon," p. 116.

35 J. Feliks, "*Motivim shel Nof ve-Hakla'ut mi-Yamei Shivat Tzion*," H. Gaveryahu, ed., *Sefer Zer-Kavod*, Haifa, 1968 (Heb.), p. 318.

36 Royal tax: Neh. 5:4; Ezra 4:13; J. Liver, "The Half-Shekel Offering in Biblical and Post-Biblical Literature," *HTR* 56 (1963), pp. 183, 186, suggests that the third of a shekel mandated by Nehemiah was only a temporary measure. He postulates that the royal support for the Temple was not in fact paid.

37 A. T. Olmstead, *History of the Persian Empire*, Chicago, 1948, pp. 297–9; D. L. Smith, "The Politics of Ezra," p. 96; on Persian taxation see Corsaro, "Tassazione Regia" (Eng. abstract).

38 Neh. 5:7; see A. Rofé, "Promises and Desertion: Eretz-Israel and the Beginning of the Second Commonwealth," *Cathedra* 41 (1986) (Heb.), p. 8.

39 M. Smith, *Palestinian Parties*, pp. 99–100.

40 Fager, *Land Tenure and the Biblical Jubilee*, p. 61.

41 In the Elephantine papyrus, Cowley 30, 18–19, it is apparent that the *Horim* are mentioned distinctly from the other classes. This is not to say that some of the priests did not own land, or at least claimed ownership in keeping with some biblical precedent, but we will discuss the possibility of a priestly landowning interest further on; see Neh.11:3, 20. On priestly entitlement to land see Borowski, *Agriculture in Iron Age Israel*, pp. 49–51, with references to OT. Some examples of priests owning land even in First Temple days: Abiathar, the High Priest in David's reign who had land at Anatot (I Kings 2:26) and Amaziah of Bethel owned land (Amos 7:17). R. North, quoted by Fensham, *The Book of Ezra, Nehemiah*, p. 195, thinks that the priests are landowners. A. Rofé, "Isaiah

66:1–14: Judean Sects in the Persian Period as Viewed by Trito-Isaiah," A. Kort and S. Morschauser, eds, *Biblical and Related Studies Presented to Samuel Iwry*, Winona Lake, Ind., 1985, pp. 208, 212, 215, points out that Trito-Isaiah is fervently against the priests, and for the poor and the dispossessed; Isa. 57:16; 58:1–2; 66:2.

42 *Horim* are שרים (*sarim*), *sarim* are ראשי פלכים (heads of counties), therefore *horim* are heads of counties. See also Rofé, "The Vineyard of Naboth," pp. 98–9.

43 B. Mazar, "The Tobiads," *IEJ* 7 (1957), pp. 137–45, 229–38; W. D. Davies and L. Finkelstein, eds, *The Cambridge History of Judaism* (*CHJ*), vol. I, *Introduction: The Persian Period*, Cambridge, 1984, pp. 116–17.

44 J. C. Greenfield, "The Aramaic Legal Texts of the Achaemenian Period," *Transeuphratène* 3 (1990), p. 89. See *Encyclopedia Biblica*, vol. 5, s.v. "סכן". E. Stern and H. Tadmor, "*Shilton Paras*," p. 271. Note also that in Neh. 5:17 it is the *seganim* who are invited to dine at the governor's table, the *horim* are not mentioned. Cf. Heltzer and Kochman, *Encyclopedia Olam Ha-Tanach*, p. 138, who postulate that this is simply a scribal omission.

45 Gallant, "Agricultural Systems, Land Tenure, and the Reforms of Solon," pp. 122–4.

46 Neh. 5:16; note that Nehemiah is especially proud that he resisted the temptation to buy land from impoverished Jews, inferring that the contrary was the common practice. On the wealth of the *horim* and the *Roshei Ha-Avot* ("heads of the clans"), whom we consider as belonging to the same class, or even being identical, see Ezra 2:68–9; Neh. 7:70–1. By way of illustration, in Sparta large Persian grants of gold and silver to a few families led to a concentration of land in their hands; see A. Fuks, "Patterns and Types of Social–Economic Revolution," *Ancient Society* 5 (1974), p. 55. Cf. Halligan, "Nehemiah 5: By Way of Response to Hoglund and Smith," pp. 149–50, who maintains that a class of commodities traders arose in the "sophisticated Persian network of commerce." He sees the *horim* as this class of creditors.

47 Neh. 5:15; 9:36–7; Ezra 4:13; Mal. 1:8; Heltzer and Kochman, *Encyclopedia Olam Ha-Tanach*, pp. 131–4; E. Stern, "The Archaeology of Persian Palestine," *CHJ*, vol. I, pp. 110, 112–13; E. M. Yamauchi, "Two Reformers Compared: Solon of Athens and Nehemiah of Jerusalem," G. Rendsburg et al., eds, *The Bible World*, New York, 1980, pp. 276, 286–7; Dandamayev, "Achaemenid Babylonia," p. 91; M. Heltzer, "The Provincial Taxation in the Achaemenian Empire and 'Forty Shekels of Silver' (Neh. 5:15)," *Michmanim* 6 (1992), pp. 15–25; idem, "The Social and Fiscal Reforms of Nehemiah in Judah and the Attitude of the Achaemenid Kings to the Internal Affairs of the Autonomous Provinces," *Apollinaris* 62 (1989), pp. 339–47; M. Dandamayev and V. G. Lukonin, *The Culture and Social Institutions of Ancient Iran*, Cambridge, 1989, pp. 179–80. Against all of these and others is Hoglund, "The Achaemenid Context," p. 61, who still believes that taxes were usually paid in kind. He further maintains that the crisis was caused by the "shortfall" in crops which made it more difficult to pay taxes in kind: Hoglund, *Achaemenid Imperial Administration*, p. 213.

48 Neh. 3:8, 31–2; 13:16, 20.
49 Ex. 22:24; Lev. 25:35–7; Deut. 23:20–1.
50 Rejecting any idea of interest on loans: Heltzer and Kochman, *Encyclopedia Olam Ha-Tanach*, p. 136; A. van Selms, "The Year of Jubilee in and outside the Pentateuch," *Die ou Testameniest Werkgemeinskop Sud-Afrika* 17s (1974), p. 81; H. Gamoran, "The Biblical Law Against Loans on Interest," *JNES* (1971), p. 134 and n. 55. Among those who assert that there was interest on loans: Miller and Hayes, *A History of Ancient Israel and Judah*, pp. 470–1; M. Smith, *Palestinian Parties*, p. 99; Yamauchi, "Two Reformers Compared," p. 270; E. Neufeld, "The Rate of Interest and the Text of Nehemiah 5.11," *JQR* 44 (1953–4), p. 200 passim.
51 Neh. 5:7, 11; see the commentaries and Heltzer, "The Social and Fiscal Reforms of Nehemiah," pp. 353–4.
52 S. E. Loewenstamm, "נשך and מ/תרבית," *JBL* 88 (1969), pp. 78–80. The terms *neshekh, tarbit,* or *marbit* are interpreted in a number of ways, all of which still mean interest; see *EJ*, vol. 16, s.v. Usury.
53 Halligan, "Nehemiah 5: By Way of Response to Hoglund and Smith," pp. 152–3, simply refuses to believe that such a solution was ever carried out. He claims that it would have wreaked havoc with the essential credit system and wounded the economy. However, he ignores the fact that cancellation of debts has been known in other societies. Furthermore, he ignores the host of problems and questions that arise if he is right.
54 Y. Freund, "*Ve-eten aleyhem Kahala Gedola*," H. Gaveryahu, ed., *Sefer Zer-Kavod*, Haifa, 1968 (Heb.), pp. 330–2.
55 Cf. M. Smith, *Palestinian Parties*, pp. 99–100.
56 Cf. ibid. pp. 98–9.
57 Ibid. pp. 11, 202 n. 108.
58 Ibid. pp. 103–9.
59 Freund, "*Ve-eten aleyhem Kahala Gedola*," p. 331.
60 Yamauchi, "Two Reformers Compared."
61 Van Selms, "The Year of Jubilee"; R. Westbrook, "Jubilee Laws," *Israel Law Review* 6 (1971), pp. 216–19: the Jubilee is irrelevant to Nehemiah's actions. Fager, *Land Tenure and the Biblical Jubilee*, pp. 34–5, cogently comments that "the reform of Neh. 5 is so different from Lev. 25 that they must not have emerged from the same economic milieu." On the *misarum* and Nehemiah see M. Weinfeld, *Social Justice in Ancient Israel and in the Ancient Near East*, Jerusalem and Minneapolis, 1995, pp. 75–96, 168–74. On the *misarum* see J. J. Finkelstein, "Amisaduqa's Edict and the Babylonian 'Law Codes,'" *JCS* 15 (1961), pp. 91–104; N.-P. Lemche, "*Andurarum* and *Mišarum*: Comments on the Problem of Social Edicts and their Application in the Ancient Near East," *JNES* 38 (1979), pp. 11–22; H. Lewy, "The Biblical Institution of *Derôr* in the Light of Akkadian Documents," *Eretz-Israel* 5 (1958), pp. 21–31.
62 B. Z. Wacholder, "The Calendar of Sabbatical Cycles During the Second Temple and the Early Rabbinic Period," *HUCA* 44 (1973), p. 158, proposes that the laws of *Shemitah*, which include a moratorium on debts, were known but neglected until the occasion of the "*Amana.*"
63 V. Tcherikover, *Hellenistic Civilization and the Jews*, Philadelphia, 1966, pp. 122–3.

3 THE EARLY HELLENISTIC PERIOD

1 This view of the situation was already formulated by V. Tcherikover, *"Eretz-Yisrael le-Or ha-Papyrusim shel Zenon,"* *The Jews in the Graeco-Roman World*, Tel-Aviv and Jerusalem (Heb.), 1974, pp. 33–82.

2 This problem is not within the compass of this research; on this subject see S. J. D. Cohen, "Alexander the Great and Jaddus the High Priest According to Josephus," *AJS Review* 7–8 (1982–3), pp. 41–68; A. Momigliano, "Flavius Josephus and Alexander's Visit to Jerusalem," *Athenaeum* 57 (1979), pp. 442–8; D. Golan, "Josephus, Alexander's Visit to Jerusalem, and Modern Historiography," U. Rappaport, ed., *Josephus Flavius: Historian of Eretz-Israel in the Hellenistic–Roman Period*, Jerusalem, 1982 (Heb.), pp. 29–55; A. Kasher, *"Masa Alexander ha-Gadol be-Eretz-Yisrael,"* *Beit Mikra* 2 (1975) (Heb.), pp. 187–208; J. Gutman, "Alexander of Macedonia in Palestine," *Tarbiz* XI (1940) (Heb.), pp. 271–94.

3 F. W. Walbank et al., *The Cambridge Ancient History (CAH)*, vol. 7.1, *The Hellenistic World*, Cambridge, 1984, pp. 122 and n. 5, 296 and n. 238; D. Golan, *The Hellenistic World*, Jerusalem, 1983 (Heb.), pp. 31–2.

4 E. Schürer, *The History of the Jewish People in the Age of Jesus Christ*, vol. II, rev. and ed. G. Vermes and F. Millar, Edinburgh, 1973–87, p. 160; A. Kasher, *Jews and Hellenistic Cities in Eretz-Israel*, Tübingen, 1990, pp. 19–20.

5 See the commentary to I Macc. 10:30 in S. Zeitlin, ed., and S. Tedesche, English translation, *The First Book of Maccabees*, New York, 1950. M. Stern hints at such a possibility: see *The Documents on the History of the Hasmonean Revolt*, Ha-Kibbutz Ha-Meuhad, 1972 (Heb.), p. 110. It is unclear whether these nomes were also converted to royal land at this time. We will argue that they were royal land at the time of their transfer to Jonathan, therefore it is conceivable that their status as crown land initiated with Alexander since this was the most fitting occasion for a major change of status.

6 M. Hengel, *Judaism and Hellenism*, vol. I, Philadelphia, 1981, p. 14; Peridiccas, founder of new Samaria and of Gerasa. Pella, Dion, and some other cities with Macedonian names originate with Antigonus.

7 Ibid. Palestine crossed or occupied seven or eight times in twenty-two years.

8 *Ant.* 12.7; Letter of Aristeas 12.

9 Diod. 40.3.7 and see M. Stern's comment and references in *Greek and Latin Authors on Jews and Judaism*, vol. I, Jerusalem, 1976–84, pp. 20–4, 33.

10 Regarding Syria and Palestine see Tcherikover, *"Eretz-Yisrael le-Or ha-Papyrusim shel Zenon,"* p. 46 n. 25 who refers to Neh. 2:8; Xen. Anab. I.4.9; I.4.10; Diod. XVI.41.5; XIX.12.2; XVIII.39.1; Strabo XVI.756.

11 Diod. 18.39.5; 43.1; 19.105.4; and M. Rostovtzeff, *The Social and Economic History of the Hellenistic World (SEHHW)*, vol. I, Oxford, 1953, p. 267.

12 *CAH*, vol. 7.1, p. 122 n. 5 and p. 148; and C. Préaux, "L'économie Lagide: 1933–1958," L. Amundson and V. Skanland, eds, *Proceedings of the IX International Congress of Papyrology*, Oslo, 1958, p. 219, who comments

that new sources have created a breach in the former schematic concept of total royal control of the land.

13 V. Tcherikover, *Hellenistic Civilization and the Jews* (*HCJ*), Philadelphia, 1966, pp. 55–8.

14 *SEHHW*, vol. I, p. 269; W. W. Tarn and G.T. Griffith, *Hellenistic Civilization*, New York, 1952, reprinted 1975, p. 187; F. W. Walbank, *The Hellenistic World*, Cambridge, Mass., 1981, pp. 107–12; *CAH*, vol. 7.1, pp. 300–3, but cf. p. 148.

15 J. Bingen, *Le Papyrus revenue laws – tradition Grecque et adaption Hellénistique*, Opladen, 1978.

16 D. J. Crawford, *Kerkeosiris*, Cambridge, 1971; Préaux, "L'économie Lagide: 1933–1958," pp. 218–19; idem, *L'économie royale des Lagides*, Brussels, 1939, reprinted New York, 1979; *SEHHW*, vol. I, pp. 267–92; J. Bingen, "Économie Grecque et société Égyptienne au IIIe siècle," H. Maehler and V. M. Strocka, eds, *Das Ptolemäische Ägypten*, Mainz, 1978, pp. 215–16; *CAH*, vol. 7.1, pp. 135, 144, 148–58.

17 *SEHHW*, vol. I, p. 269.

18 Ibid. p. 276.

19 Ibid. p. 277; C. C. Edgar, "Introduction," *Zenon Papyri in the University of Michigan Collection*, Ann Arbor, 1931, p. 8, suggested that land granted to soldiers and officials was in the main poor or unclaimed land on the edge of cultivation.

20 *SEHHW*, vol. I, p. 278.

21 Ibid. pp. 51, 53.

22 Ibid., vol. I, pp. 332–3: "Nothing is known of the Ptolemaic management of the royal land in the provinces we are dealing with. It was based on the same traditional principles as in the Seleucid kingdom, where we have some information on the subject" (p. 338).

23 Ibid. pp. 332–51.

24 Ibid. p. 346.

25 A. Schalit, *König Herodes, Der Mann und Sein Werk*, Berlin, 1969, pp. 702–3.

26 Hengel, *Judaism and Hellenism*, vol. I, p. 22.

27 R. S. Bagnall, *The Administration of the Ptolemaic Possessions Outside Egypt*, Leiden, 1976, p. 23.

28 G. M. Cohen, *The Seleucid Colonies*, Wiesbaden, 1978, p. 53.

29 V. Tcherikover, "Palestine Under the Ptolemies," *Mizraim* 4–5 (1937), p. 43.

30 See Hengel, *Judaism and Hellenism*, vol. I, p. 22; vol. II, p. 20 n. 170, who quotes Alt, *KS*, vol. II, p. 401.

31 See A. Rofé, "The Vineyard of Naboth: The Origin and Message of the Story," *VT* 38 (1988), pp. 89–104, who demonstrates that stories set in the First Temple can be vehicles to air complaints of later periods.

32 The reference is probably to Carmel which is in southern Judah. See commentaries to the verse.

33 M. Hengel, in W. D. Davies and L. Finkelstein, eds, *The Cambridge History of Judaism* (*CHJ*), vol. II: *The Hellenistic Age*, Cambridge, 1989, p. 63, who refers to this as an early Hellenistic work.

34 *KAI* 14, lines 18–19; Alt, *KS*, p. 382 n. 4.

35 Theophrastus, *HP* 9.6.1, and see Hengel, *Judaism and Hellenism*, vol. I, pp. 44–5.

36 Ibid.

37 E. Stern, "The Archaeology of Persian Palestine," *CHJ*, vol. I, p. 109; idem, *Material Culture of the Land of the Bible in the Persian Period 538–332 BC*, Warminster and Jerusalem, 1982, pp. 209, 235; N. Avigad, "New Light on MSH Seal Impressions," *IEJ* 8 (1958), p. 119.

38 Ibid. pp. 203, 209; N. Avigad, "More Evidence on the Judean Post-Exilic Stamps," *IEJ* 24 (1974), p. 58.

39 E. Stern, *Material Culture*, pp. 202–13.

40 S. Dar, *Landscape and Pattern*, BAR International Series, Oxford, 1986, pp. 18–20, 109–14, 120–1, 247.

41 S. Applebaum, Historical Commentary to S. Dar, *Landscape and Pattern*, pp. 257, 259, 260, 310 n. 23.

42 Y. Magen, "Kalandia: A Vineyard Farm and Winery of the Second Temple Times," *Qadmoniot* XVII, 66–7 (1984) (Heb.), pp. 61–71; and see Dar, *Landscape and Pattern*, pp. 120–1.

43 *PCZ* 59004; Tcherikover, "Palestine Under the Ptolemies," p. 48; S. Klein, "Notes on the History of Large Estates in Palestine," *Bulletin of the Jewish Palestine Exploration Society*, I.3 (1933), pt. 1, p. 4; idem, *Eretz-Yehuda*, Tel-Aviv, 1939 (Heb.), p. 40.

44 Klein, *Eretz-Yehuda*, p. 40.

45 Ibid. p. 42.

46 On their location see further on. Regarding the question of the ethnic–religious identity of the inhabitants, Applebaum, "Economic Life in Palestine," S. Safrai and M. Stern, eds, *The Jewish People in the First Century*, Philadelphia, 1976, p. 634, while writing about the farmers on Ptolemy's estate, claimed that "It would be a bold assumption that they included no Jews."

47 *PCZ* 59004 line 11.

48 *PCZ* 59011 line 8. This text is very badly preserved and cannot be deciphered well: see Edgar, *Zenon papyri* I, p. 19; likewise *PSI* 554, see Tcherikover, "Palestine Under the Ptolemies," p. 45; *PSI* 594; *P.London* 1948.

49 See T. C. Skeat, ed., *Greek Papyri in the British Museum*, vol. VII, *The Zenon Archive*, London, 1974, *P.London* 1948, acquired in 1925, but published in 1974, although excerpts were quoted prior to then.

50 *P.London* 1948 lines 7, 9.

51 M. Hengel, "Das Gleichnis von den Weingärten Mc 12: 1–12 im Lichte der Zenonpapyri und der rabbinischen Gleichnisse," *ZNW* 59 (1968), p. 13 and n. 48. In addition to the figures that Hengel obtained, consider that in modern Israel there are 200 to 220 vines planted to the dunam. My thanks to Mr Tuvia Reiss, formerly of the Fruit Production Council of Israel and member of Kibbutz Kfar HaMaccabi.

52 *PSI* 594, col. III; and see Tcherikover, "*Eretz-Yisrael le-Or ha-Papyrusim shel Zenon*," pp. 45–6; G. M. Harper Jr, "A Study in the Commercial Relations Between Egypt and Syria in the Third Century Before Christ," *AJPh* 49 (1928), p. 4, considers the grain that is mentioned in *PSI* 324, 325 a product of Apollonius' estates, specifically including Beth Anath.

53 The whole subject of the *laoi* is as yet unclear and awaits further clarification. See G. E. M. de Ste. Croix, *The Class Struggle in the Ancient Greek World*, Ithaca, NY, 1981, pp. 152–3, 566 nn. 26–32.

54 Walbank, *The Hellenistic World*, pp. 105, 111; P. M. Fraser, *Ptolemaic Alexandria*, vol. I, Oxford, 1971, pp. 136, 150; Hengel, *Judaism and Hellenism*, vol. I, p. 39.

55 Tcherikover, "Palestine Under the Ptolemies," p. 77 n. 26: according to the Revenue Laws 52.26 foreign oil is distinguished from Syrian oil, "thus proving that Syria did not belong to foreign territory."

56 Herondas II, 16–17, quoted by M. Avi-Yonah, *Hellenism and the East: Contacts and Interrelations from Alexander to the Roman Conquest*, Jerusalem, 1978, p. 225; and see Tebtunis Papyrus 869, quoted in A. E. Samuel, "The Money Economy and the Ptolemaic Peasantry," *BASP* 21 (1984), p. 189, indicating that early in the 2nd century BCE Arsinoite Nome vineyard land was valued at 18,000 drachmas, and garden land was valued at 6,000 per *aroura*.

57 See Tcherikover, "Palestine Under the Ptolemies," p. 84 n. 80; A. Alt, "Beth=Anath," *PJB* 22 (1926), pp. 55–9; Orrieux, *Les Papyrus de Zenon*, pp. 47–8, who holds that it was in Lebanon; cf. Klein, "Notes on the History of Large Estates," p. 4. He rejects Galilee and proposes a location on the border between northern Transjordan and southern Syria. For a summary of the different positions and discussion of rabbinic evidence see S. Safrai and Z. Safrai, "*Beth Anath*," *Sinai* 78 (1976) (Heb.), pp. 18–34.

58 Safrai and Safrai, "*Beth Anath*," p. 25.

59 Tcherikover, "Palestine Under the Ptolemies," pp. 45–8.

60 *SEHHW*, vol. III, p. 1403 n. 1409.

61 Hengel, *Judaism and Hellenism*, vol. II, p. 16 n. 134.

62 *SEHHW*, vol. III, p. 1403 n. 149.

63 Tcherikover, "Palestine Under the Ptolemies," p. 46.

64 Hengel, "Das Gleichnis von den Weingärten," p. 14 n. 54.

65 *SEHHW*, vol. I, p. 345.

66 *SEHHW*, vol. I, pp. 344–5.

67 W. L. Westermann, "Enslaved Persons Who Are Free," *AJPh* 59 (1938), p. 9.

68 S. Freyne, *Galilee from Alexander the Great to Hadrian*, Notre Dame, 1980, p. 158, surmises that the villagers who owned their own land are the ones who petitioned the king, and were probably *kleruchs*.

69 Hengel, "Das Gleichnis von den Weingärten," p. 14 n. 54; idem, *Judaism and Hellenism*, vol. I, p. 39.

70 M. Rostovtzeff, *A Large Estate in the Third Century BC*, Madison, Wis., 1922; reprinted Rome, 1967, pp. 9–10; Alt, "Beth=Anath," pp. 55–6.

71 Westermann, *P.Col.* III, document 54, col. I, ll. 2–8. See also Rostovtzeff, *A Large Estate*, pp. 47, 71–3.

72 Y. H. Landau, "A Greek Inscription Found Near Hefzibah," *IEJ* 16 (1966), pp. 54–70; J. and L. Robert, "Skythopolis," *REG* 83 (1970), pp. 469–73; 84 (1971), p. 407; T. Fischer, "Zur Seleukideninschrift von Hefzibah," *ZPE* 33 (1979), pp. 131–8; J. M. Bertrand, "Sur l'inscription d'Hefzibah," *ZPE* 46 (1982), pp. 167–74; J. E. Taylor, *Seleucid Rule in Palestine*, Ph.D. Dissertation, Duke Univ., 1979; S. Sherwin-White,

"Seleucid Babylonia," A. Kuhrt and S. Sherwin-White, eds, *Hellenism in the East*, London, 1987, pp. 22–3; Briant, "Remarques sur 'laoi' et esclaves ruraux en Asie Mineure Hellénistique," *RTP*, Besançon and Paris, 1982, pp. 95–135; M. Stern, ed., *The Hellenistic Period and the Hasmonean State*, *The History of Eretz-Israel*, vol. 3, Jerusalem, 1981 (Heb.), pp. 65–9. The discussion of Seleucid landowning practice follows this section on the Ptolemaic rule.

73 Ibid. p. 67.

74 The Fifth Syrian War was started by Antiochus III in 202 or 201 BCE and hostilities in Palestine were concluded in 198 BCE. The political marriage sealing the status quo was in 193–194 BCE. See Stern, ibid. pp. 63–4.

75 Landau, "A Greek Inscription," p. 66.

76 Ibid. p. 66 n. 14.

77 Lines 23–4 μοι κώ[μ]ας [ἐγ]κτήσει και εἰς [τ]ό πα[τ]ρικὸν καὶ εἰς [ἅς] σὺ προ[σ]έταξας καταγπάψ[αι](?) . . .] ("the villages belonging to me as property and hereditary tenure and those which you ordered to be assigned to me . . . ").

78 Fischer, "Zur Seleukideninschrift," p. 136.

79 Landau, "A Greek Inscription," IIIa, lines 11–13. But we interpret the text according to the corrections and interpretations proposed by Bertrand, "Sur l'inscription d'Hefzibah," pp. 171–2.

80 *C. Ord. Ptol.* 22, lines 17–20.

81 *PCZ* 59003, *CPJ*, vol. I, no. 1.

82 *CPJ*, vol. I, no. 1, lines 6, 7, 8.

83 J. M. Dentzer, F. Villeneuve, and F. Larché, "Iraq el Amir: Excavations at the Monumental Gateway," A. Hadidi, ed., *Studies in the History and Archaeology of Jordan*, vol. I, Amman, 1982, p. 207; *CPJ* I, p. 116; G. M. Cohen, *The Seleucid Colonies*, p. 66.

84 Vincent quoted in *PCZ* I, p. 5; *CPJ* I, p. 116; Dentzer, Villeneuve, and Larché, "Iraq el Amir," p. 207, think that the soldiers were given plots within the agricultural estate in the *paradeisos*; D. Gera, "On the Credibility of the History of the Tobiads," A. Kasher, U. Rappaport, G. Fuks, eds, *Greece and Rome in Eretz Israel*, Jerusalem, 1990, p. 24 and n. 14, p. 30, suggests that the birta was within the boundaries of the "land of Tobiah," and that is where the soldiers were found.

85 B. Mazar, "The Tobiads," *IEJ* 7 (1957), pp. 140–1.

86 *CPJ* I, p. 117.

87 F. M. Abel, *Géographie de la Palestine*, vol. II, Paris, 1933–7, p. 131; cf. M. Avi-Yonah, *The Holy Land from the Persian to the Arab Conquests: A Historical Geography (536 BC to AD 640)*, Grand Rapids, 1966, p. 40, who suggests that the area assigned to Philadelphia was originally under the control of the Tobiads. This made the development of a Jewish-controlled area possible in the region of Amman. E. Will, "L'Urbanisation de la Jordanie aux époques hellénistique et romaine: conditions géographiques et ethniques," A. Hadidi, ed., *Studies in the History and Archaeology of Jordan*, vol. II, Amman, London, and New York, 1985, p. 239 n. 14, maintains that the Birta of Ammanitis is the name of Philadelphia before it received city status.

88 II Macc. 4:26; Hengel, *Judaism and Hellenism*, vol. I, p. 275.
89 In the Fourth Syrian War, Philadelphia was a major fort for the Ptolemies: Polybius 5.71.4–11.
90 Schalit, *König Herodes*, p. 704; Cohen, *The Seleucid Colonies*, p. 51.
91 Aristeas to Philocrates 116.
92 Ex. 12:37; Num. 11:12.
93 Hadas, *Aristeas*, p. 147, note to line 116.
94 Tcherikover, "Palestine Under the Ptolemies," p. 43, mentions a fifth city, also called Arsinoe, but it is placed somewhere in Syria, so we are hesitant at assuming that it was necessarily in Palestine.
95 Fuks, *Scythopolis*, pp. 49–51.
96 Barghouti, "Urbanization of Palestine and Jordan in Hellenistic and Roman Times," p. 213; cf. Rostovtzeff, "Foreign Commerce of Ptolemaic Egypt," *Journal of Economic and Business History* 4 (1931–3), p. 736, who credits political and not commercial considerations as determining Ptolemaic policy toward this area. However, he does stress the value of Ptolemaic Syria to Egyptian commerce, pp. 737–9.
97 S. Applebaum, "Jewish Urban Communities and Greek Influences," *SCI* 5 (1979–80), p. 165.
98 *Ant.* 12.159; see Gera, "On the Credibility of the History of the Tobiads," who calls into question the historical reliability of much of the Tobiad story. He admits, however, that many of the details regarding Ptolemaic policy are correct (p. 35). He does not specifically deal with the alleged threat of expropriation; however, his claim that the tale was concocted after 150 BCE indicates that he would reject the idea. Cf. M. Stern, "Notes on the Story of Joseph the Tobiad," *Tarbiz* 32 (1962/63) (Heb.), pp. 35–47, who tends to see the story as a source of reliable historical information (see esp. pp. 40–1). He interprets the High Priest's action as an outcome of the Third Syrian War (p. 43).
99 Hecataeus, apud: Diod. 40.3.7.
100 The dating of the Letter of Aristeas is crucial to this assumption; if it is a late composition, i.e. after the Seleucid conquest of Palestine, its value as a testament to Ptolemaic rule there is minimal. However, we accept the view of U. Rappaport, "When Was the Letter of Aristeas Written?" A. Gilboa et al., eds, *Studies in the History of the Jewish People and the Land of Israel in Memory of Zvi Avneri*, Haifa, 1970 (Heb.), pp. 37–50, who dates the letter to the late third century BCE.
101 *PCZ* 59006, 59007, 59015.
102 Cf. *SEHHW*, vol. I, pp. 81, 348; Hengel, *Judaism and Hellenism*, vol. I, p. 24. J. Herz, "Grossgrundbesitz in Palästina im Zeitalter Jesu," *PJB* 24 (1928), p. 103, wrote that Temple land was out of the question in the Land of Israel. Unfortunately, he did not explain why.
103 Hengel, *Judaism and Hellenism*, vol. I, p. 24; II, pp. 18–19 n. 160, referring to Diod. 40.3 and the Letter of Aristeas.
104 *SEHHW*, vol. I, pp. 503–5: temples "owned" at least a village, while a temple state had a "large" territory and an organization resembling that of a state.
105 Hengel, *Judaism and Hellenism*. See *OGIS* 56, line 73.
106 Ezra 6:9–10; Neh. 10:33–4; *Ant.* 12.140; see also E. Bickerman, "La

Charte Séleucide de Jérusalem," *Studies in Jewish and Christian History*, vol. II, Leiden, 1980, pp. 72–3.

107 On God's ownership of the land as a theological motif, see W. D. Davies, *The Territorial Dimension of Judaism*, Berkeley, CA and London, 1982, pp. 17–18.

108 Judith 8:7 (*APOT*).

109 On the date of Judith see G. W. E. Nickelsburg, *Jewish Literature Between the Bible and the Mishnah*, Philadelphia, 1987, pp. 108–9, who suggests it is a tale originating in the Persian period that has been rewritten in Hasmonean times. R. Doran, "Judith," R. A. Kraft and G. W. E. Nickelsburg, eds, *Early Judaism and its Modern Interpreters*, Atlanta, 1986, p. 304, holds for a Hellenistic date. Schürer, III.1, pp. 218–19, dates it to the Hasmonean era, but no later than Yannai. M. Delcor in *CHJ*, vol. II, p. 445, considers it post-Septuaginta, maybe c. 245 BCE. Y. M. Grintz, *Sefer Yehudith*, Jerusalem, 1986 (Heb.), p. 15, maintains that it was composed in the Persian period in the middle of the fourth century BCE; C. A. Moore, *Judith* (*AB* 40), Garden City, 1985, pp. 50, 51, 67, holds that the setting may be Persian, but that the book was composed during the Hasmonean period, either in John Hyrcanus' day or during Alexander Yannai's reign.

110 *CPJ*, vol. I, no. 5; *HCJ*, pp. 65–6; Tcherikover, "Palestine Under the Ptolemies," p. 50.

111 J. M. Dentzer et al., "Fouille de la porte monumental à Iraq-al-Amir," *ADAJ* 26 (1982), pp. 301–21; E. Will, "Un Monument Hellénistique de Jordanie: Le Qasr el' abd d'Iraq al Amir," A. Hadidi, ed., *Studies in the History and Archaeology of Jordan*, vol. I, Amman, 1982, pp. 197–200; P. W. Lapp and N. L. Lapp, "Iraq el-Emir," *NEAEHL*, vol. 2, pp. 646–9.

112 Dentzer, Villeneuve, and Larché, "Iraq el Amir: Excavations at the Monumental Gateway," pp. 206–7.

113 *CPJ*, vol. I, nos 2b, 2c, 2d.

114 *CPJ*, vol. I, nos 4, 5.

115 *CPJ*, vol. I, no. 2d, line 15.

116 *CPJ*, vol. I, no. 6.

117 Ibid. p. 129.

118 Ibid.

119 *HCJ*, p. 65.

120 *HCJ*, p. 66.

121 *C.Ord.Ptol.* 21, line 20.

122 Tarn and Griffith, *Hellenistic Civilization*, p. 179.

123 *SEHHW*, vol. I, p. 414; II, pp. 706, 712; III, p. 1420 n. 212.

124 *CAH*, vol. 7.1, pp. 158–67.

125 Quoted by E. Bevan, *A History of Egypt Under the Ptolemaic Dynasty*, London, 1927, pp. 194–5.

126 Mahaffy, quoted by Bevan, *A History of Egypt Under the Ptolemaic Dynasty*, pp. 196–7.

127 *CAH*, vol. 7.1, pp. 158 and n. 115.

128 *CAH*, vol. 7.1, p. 159.

129 Wilcken *Chr.* 198 quoted in *CAH*, vol. 7.1, p. 161 n. 127.

130 Garnsey, *Famine and Food Supply*, p. 76.

131 *CAH*, vol. 7.1, pp. 158–9.
132 M.Stern, "Notes on the Story of Joseph the Tobiad," pp. 42–3; see also *HCJ*, p. 129. J. A. Goldstein, "The Tales of the Tobiads," J. Neusner, ed., *Christianity, Judaism and Other Greco-Roman Cults*, vol. III, Leiden, 1975, pp. 96, 101, rejects this chronology and proposed explanation, maintaining that the Ptolemies had a secure hold on Palestine and would not have made harsh demands on the populace. Goldstein here ignores the cumulative evidence of events in those years.
133 Hengel, *Judaism and Hellenism*, vol. I, pp. 27, 269; II, p. 21 n. 184.
134 Another reason for Onias II to support the Seleucids, if in fact he did so, was that the Seleucid treatment of temples was reputedly more benign and generous than that of Ptolemy.
135 *Ant.* 12.156; U. Rappaport, "The Samaritans in the Hellenistic Period," *Zion* LV (1990) (Heb.), pp. 382–3.
136 *Ant.* 12.156: τήν τε χώραν αὐτῶν τεμόντες καὶ σώματα διαρπάσαντες.
137 Marcus, *Josephus*, vol. VII, p. 81; Liddell and Scott, s.v. τέμνω; διαρπαγή.
138 *C.Ord.Ptol.* 22, lines 20–9.
139 M. Stern, "Notes on the Story of Joseph the Tobiad," pp. 38–9; Goldstein, "The Tales of the Tobiads," pp. 97,104.
140 S. R. Driver, *An Introduction to the Literature of the Old Testament*, New York, 1960, p. 471, dates Ecclesiastes to the Persian or Greek period; Delcor, *CHJ* II, pp. 359, 363, to the Greek period, but no later than the middle of the second century BCE; Ginsberg, *EJ*, vol. 6, p. 352, to the third century BCE; E. Bickerman, *Four Strange Books of the Bible*, New York, 1967, p. 141 – written in the third century; Hengel, *Judaism and Hellenism*, vol. I, p. 115 and n. 58 on pp. 50–1, dates the composition to between 280 and 230 BCE.
141 *SEHHW*, vol. I, p. 350.
142 For a different view, see his discussion in *SEHHW*, vol. III, p. 1403 n. 147.
143 *C.Ord.Ptol.* 22, lines 11, 30.
144 A royal order preventing advocates in Egypt from pleading the case of debtors to the crown is known from *P. Amherst* 33 and *P. Rylands* 577; and see Préaux, "L'économie Lagide: 1933–1958," pp. 204–5.
145 See the Third Book of Maccabees.
146 This is notwithstanding Taeubler's efforts to construct a Jewish messianic movement; see E. Taeubler, "Jerusalem 201 to 199 BCE: On the History of a Messianic Movement," *JQR* 37 (1946–7), pp. 1–30, 125–37, 249–63. Qoheleth probably pre-dates the Fifth Syrian War, and even Taeubler made no use of it in his article.
147 Translation from the Jewish Publication Society edition of Ecclesiastes, and note e.
148 Mandelkern, *Concordantiae*, S.V. נכר.
149 Eccl. 5:10, 12, 13.
150 Polyb. 5.61–2; 70; 71.
151 Polybius' claim (5.86.10) that the populace of Coele-Syria was pro-Ptolemy, is countered by Hengel with the observation that Polybius had

an "anti-Seleucid attitude"; *Judaism and Hellenism*, vol. II, p. 4 n. 15. Regarding the visit of the royal couple see the references, ibid. p. 5 n. 19.

152 Bevan, *A History of Egypt Under the Ptolemies*, Chap. VII.

153 *Ant.* 12.135; Porphyry in *GLAJJ*, vol. II, p. 461, no. 464l, lines 1–3.

154 Ibid. lines 3–4: "et optimates Ptolomaei partium secum abducens in Aegyptum reversus est."

155 Landau, "A Greek Inscription Found Near Hefzibah," lines 24–33.

156 *Ant.* 12.133, 136, 138. It is generally believed that Simon II, called the "Just," was in favor of the arrangement with Antiochus III; see Ben-Sira 50:1–5. Note that John the father of Eupolomos is credited with obtaining privileges from the king. This John was a member of the priestly family of Hakkoz: see II Macc. 4:11.

157 F. M. Heichelheim, "New Light On Currency and Inflation in Hellenistic–Roman Times from Inscriptions and Papyri," *Economic History* 10 (1935), pp. 3–4; M. Reekmans, "Economic and Social Repercussions of the Ptolemaic Copper Inflation," *Chronique d'Égypte* 48 (1949), pp. 324–42; A. Segré, "The Ptolemaic Copper Inflation, Ca. 230–140 BC," *AJPh* 63 (1942), pp. 174–91; *CAH*, vol. 7.1, p. 164.

158 Ibid.

159 Hengel, *Judaism and Hellenism*, vol. I, pp. 27, 43; O. Morkholm, "The Ptolemaic Coinage in Phoenicia and the Fifth War With Syria," E. van't Dack, P. van Dessel, W. van Gucht, eds, *Egypt and the Hellenistic World*, Leuven, 1983, pp. 241–50.

160 Hengel, *Judaism and Hellenism* is the basic work on the interaction between Ptolemaic political and economic policy, and the Jews. See also Applebaum, "Jewish Urban Communities and Greek Influences," pp. 159–61, 166–7.

161 Hengel, *Judaism and Hellenism*, Vol. I, p. 269.

162 Ibid. pp. 27–8; *Ant.* 12.224.

163 Hengel, *Judaism and Hellenism*, vol. I, pp. 23, 49, 50–1: "a strict, indeed harsh administration, which joined the rich in oppressing the poor" (p. 115).

164 *HCJ*, pp. 143–5; Hengel, *Judaism and Hellenism*, vol. I, pp. 131–53; Schürer, vol. III.1, p. 202.

165 See *HCJ*, pp. 145–51; Hengel, *Judaism and Hellenism*, vol. I, pp. 137–8.

166 Author's translation Ben-Sira 8:1–2,12–14; 13:2–8, 9–13; 31:5.

167 It is to be regretted that we do not have many documents actually attesting loans in Ptolemaic Palestine. The only ones we know of are *CPJ*, vol. I, no.6 from the middle of the third century, in which Jeddous is mentioned as owing money to Zenon, and the third-century ostracon from Khirbet el-Kôm, in which 32 drachmas are lent to one Niqeratos. See L. T. Geraty, "The Khirbet El-Kôm Bilingual Ostracon," *BASOR* 220 (1975), pp. 55–61; idem., "Recent Suggestions on the Bilingual Ostracon from Khirbet El-Kôm," *St Andrews University Seminary Studies* 19 (1981), pp. 137–40.

168 See Box and Oesterley in *APOT* I, p. 327; cf. M. Z. Segal, *Sefer Ben-Sira ha-Shalem*, Jerusalem, 1962 (Heb.), p. 25.

169 A quarter of a century into the Seleucid period Hyrcanus is still reckoned one of the influential and wealthy men in the land. See II Macc. 3:11.

4 THE LATE HELLENISTIC PERIOD

1 D. Golan, *A History of the Hellenistic World*, Jerusalem, 1983 (Heb.), pp. 435–8.

2 *Ant.* 12.133–8; see E. Bickerman, "La charte séleucide de Jérusalem," *Studies in Jewish and Christian History*, vol. II, Leiden, 1980, pp. 44–85; E. Will and C. Orrieux, *IOUDAÏSMOS–HELLÈNISMOS: Essai sur la judaïsme judéen à l'époque hellénistique*, Nancy, 1986, pp. 98–100.

3 *Ant.* 12.142–5; M. Hengel, *Judaism and Hellenism*, vol. I, Philadelphia, 1981, p. 271; H. Kreissig, "Der Makkabäeraufstand," *Studii Clasice* 4 (1962), p. 160; V. Tcherikover, *Hellenistic Civilization and the Jews*, Philadelphia, 1966 (*HCJ*), pp. 75–89; but cf. Will and Orrieux, *IOUDAÏSMOS–HELLÈNISMOS*, pp. 99–101, who suggest that there was tension between the High Priest and Antiochus III.

4 Porphyry, *Adversus Christianos apud: Hieronymus Comm. in Dan. 11:13–14*.

5 *Ant.* 12.222, 229–34.

6 *HCJ*, p. 137.

7 *Ant.* 12.387; II Macc. 4: 26; 57–10.

8 This is not to say that Jerusalem was granted full rights as a Greek polis, or that it had the internal structure of a Greek city. This status would come to Jerusalem only with the Hellenistic reform. However, we cannot let the imprecise word "polis" deter us from judging whether the land around the city belonged to it or not.

9 H. Kreissig, "Landed Property in the Hellenistic Orient," *Eirene* 15 (1977), p. 17.

10 E. Neufeld, "Inalienability of Mobile and Immobile Pledges in the Laws of the Bible," *RIDA* 9 (1968), pp. 38–40; R.Westbrook, "Redemption of Land," *Israel Law Review* 6 (1971), pp. 367–75.

11 In addition to references in the previous chapter, see E. Bickerman, "Héliodore au Temple de Jérusalem," *Studies in Jewish and Christian History*, vol. II, Leiden, 1980, p. 167.

12 Cf. Hengel, *Judaism and Hellenism*, vol. I, p. 24.

13 C. Roueché and S. M. Sherwin-White, "Some Aspects of the Seleucid Empire: The Greek Inscriptions from Failaka, in the Arabian Gulf," *Chiron* 15 (1985), pp. 15–16, lines 29–33; p. 35.

14 S. Applebaum, "Economic Life in Palestine," S. Safrai and M. Stern, eds, *The Jewish People in the First Century*, Philadelphia, 1976, p. 633, claims that Kreissig in "Die Landswirtschaftliche Situation in Palästina vor dem Judäischen Krieg" (no page reference) stated that the Seleucids tried to convert rural areas into royal lands (*basilke ge*). But p. 231 (as well as in Kreissig's "Der Makkabäeraufstand," p. 168) states that Kreissig maintained that Judea was being divided into city land, royal land, and gift land, after the hostilities commenced.

15 A. Mittwoch, "Tribute and Land-Tax in Seleucid Judaea," *Biblica* 36 (1955), p. 355.

16 M. Rostovtzeff, *The Social and Economic History of the Hellenistic World* (*SEHHW*), vol. I, Oxford, 1953, pp. 468–9.

17 Grants to Zeus of Baetocaece (date uncertain, but M. Austin, *The*

Hellenistic World from Alexander to the Roman Conquest: A Selection of Ancient Sources in Translation, Cambridge, 1981, p. 291: "it may well belong to the reigns of Antiochus I or II"): land is taken away from someone and granted to the Temple; *IGLS* VII.4028 B and C, *RC* 70; Estates of Achaeus, Austin, *The Hellenistic World*, pp. 241–2; gift of land to Aristodicides by Antiochus I, ibid. pp. 293–4; Mnesimachus inscription; Antiochus II returns to Samos lands held by friends of the king *SEG* I, 366, line 17.

18 Polybius, V,86,7–11; A. Kasher, *Jews and Hellenistic Cities in Eretz-Israel*, Tübingen, 1990, p. 54.

19 *RC* 38, a letter of Antiochus III to Amyzon, 203 BC, demonstrates the generous treatment of a city, including respect for private property, that was Antiochus' policy toward cities which came over to his side from the Ptolemies. See Welles' commentary on pp. 167–8.

20 Scythopolis and Philoteria, see Polybius V.70.3–5; but see Kasher, *Jews and Hellenistic Cities*, pp. 81–2; G. Fuks, *Scythopolis: A Greek City in Eretz-Israel*, Jerusalem (Heb.), 1983, pp. 66–7. Kasher, based on the Hefzibah inscription, concludes that Scythopolis lost much of its *chora*. We reject this view for two reasons. The inscription gives no basis for conclusions as to the extent of the *dorea*, or the proportion of the *chora* this area represented, or even if it ever was a part of the *chora*. Furthermore, Kasher claims that these lands had formerly been *dorea* of senior Ptolemaic officials. Yet Polybius claims that the *chora* was large enough to feed an army, so that it must have been extensive even without the gift-lands. We also reject Fuks' assertion that the cities did not have their own territory because it is not supported by Polybius' text. See also S. Applebaum, "When Did Scythopolis Become a Greek City?" *Judaea in Hellenistic and Roman Times*, *SJLA* 40, Leiden, 1989, pp. 3–5, 7.

21 H. Eshel, "The Prayer of Joseph: A Papyrus from Masada and the Samaritan Temple on ΑΡΓΑΡΙΖΙΝ," *Zion* LVI (1991) (Heb.), pp. 131–3; Y. Magen, "A Fortified Town of the Hellenistic Period on Mount Gerizim," *Qadmoniot* XIX (75–6) (1986) (Heb.), p. 101; idem, "Mount Gerizim: A Temple City," *Qadmoniot* XXIII (91–2) (1990), pp. 83–96.

22 II Macc. 4:11; I Macc. 8:17.

23 *Ant.* 12.142. On the privileges granted to Jerusalem by Antiochus III see Bickerman, "La charte séleucide de Jérusalem"; idem, "Une Proclamation Séleucide relative au temple de Jérusalem," *Studies in Jewish and Christian History*, vol. II, Leiden, 1980, pp. 86–104.

24 M. Stern, *The Documents on the History of the Hasmonean Revolt*, Ha-Kibbutz Ha-Meuhad, 1972 (Heb.), p. 34. See also E. Bickerman, *Institutions des Séleucides*, Paris, 1938, p. 165; see also H. G. Kippenberg, *Religion und Klassenbildung im antiken Judäa*, Göttingen, 1982, pp. 83–4, who suggests that the aristocracy profited most of all from Antiochus III's munificence. This is rejected by Will and Orrieux, *IOUDAÏSMOS–HELLÈNISMOS*, p. 111 n. 9.

25 Bickerman, "La Charte Séleucide de Jérusalem," p. 59.

26 H. Kreissig, *Wirtschaft und Gesellschaft im Seleukidenreich*, Berlin, 1978, pp. 70–4.

27 "Ownership of property rights," which means the full title to a plot of

land. See Kreissig, "Landed Property," p. 17; see Liddell and Scott, s.v. παγκτησία.

28 Bickerman, *Institutions des Séleucides*, pp. 164–5.

29 Ibid. p. 164; and see Kreissig, *Wirtschaft und Gesellschaft im Seleukidenreich*, pp. 70–4, who, despite five pages of discussion on "Land der ἔθνη," hardly gives any documentation. See also J. Goldstein, *I Maccabees* (*AB*, vol. 41), New York, 1976, pp. 196, 212, who discusses the concept of ethnos, but does not add any substantive evidence.

30 Tcherikover, *HCJ*, pp. 153–74; Hengel, *Judaism and Hellenism*, vol. I, pp. 267–72, 277–80; M. Stern, ed., *The Hellenistic Period and the Hasmonean State, The History of Eretz-Israel*, vol. 3, Jerusalem, 1981 (Heb.), pp. 148–53.

31 By Hellenizers we signify all those who approved the Hellenistic reform. It has been noted that the term "Hellenizers" is used by the books of the Maccabees as a condemnatory label for all those who opposed them. See L. L. Grabbe, *Judaism from Cyrus to Hadrian*, vol. I, Minneapolis, 1992, pp. 256–8, 277–81. Indeed, there was never a single organized party self-defined as "Hellenizers"; however, whatever differences might have existed between Jason, Menelaus, Alcimus, their adherents, and unnamed others, we assume that they all were in favor of some form of change which was closer to the content or forms of the Hellenistic world than the Judean society had previously known.

32 Tcherikover, *HCJ*, pp. 167–8.

33 Ibid. pp. 149–50.

34 Ibid. p. 121.

35 Ibid. pp. 123–4.

36 See Bickerman, "Héliodore au Temple de Jérusalem," esp. pp. 169, 171. Bickerman considers the money in the treasury a surplus from the king's own largesse to the Temple. But even he admits that there must have been a significant amount of money on deposit there. He suggests that the money is Hyrcanus' gain from taxing the Arabs. However, is it reasonable to assume that he was the only wealthy man to place his money in the Temple? Furthermore, there must have been an astonishingly large number of wealthy widows and orphans in order to make up a sum tempting enough to bring a royal representative to Jerusalem.

37 II Macc. 3:12–15, 18–19, 22.

38 Bickerman, "Héliodore au Temple de Jérusalem," p. 168; cf. Kreissig, "Der Makkabäeraufstand," p. 161.

39 S. Applebaum, "Jewish Urban Communities and Greek Influences," *SCI* 5 (1979–80), pp. 166–7.

40 Tcherikover, *HCJ*, pp. 83–4; Bickerman, "La charte séleucide de Jérusalem," pp. 69–71.

41 S. Zeitlin, ed., *The Second Book of Maccabees*, New York, 1954, 3:4 and the commentary; Goldstein, *II Maccabees* (*AB* 41A), New York, 1983, p. 203; F. M. Abel, *Les Livres des Maccabées*, Paris, 1949, p. 317.

42 Tcherikover, *HCJ*, p. 157.

43 II Macc. 3:1; Liddell and Scott, s.v. συντηρέω.

44 II Macc. 4:2; Liddell and Scott, s.v. κήδω.

45 We certainly do not know what exactly was the status of the non-citizen

residents of the polis of Antioch-in-Jerusalem. In fact, to quote one of the most exhaustive researches on the subject, "we know too little about systems of land tenure in Asia to be able to describe with confidence the methods by which the working agricultural population was exploited, either before or after they came under the direct control of Greek cities." G. E. M. de Ste. Croix, *The Class Struggle in the Ancient Greek World*, Ithaca, NY, 1981, pp. 157–8.

46 II Macc. 4:9, 12, 14. It is the finest young men who join the Ephebia, and it is the priests who hasten to the palaestra. See Tcherikover, *HCJ*, p. 162; H.-I. Marrou, *Histoire de l'éducation dans l'antiquité*, Paris, 1965, pp. 170–3; Kreissig, "Der Makkabäeraufstand," p. 162.

47 II Macc. 4:27–8, 32, 39. These payments may well have been annual tribute; see Mittwoch, "Tribute and Land-Tax," pp. 352–3; K. Bringmann, *Hellenistische Reform und Religionsverfolgung in Judäa*, Göttingen, 1983, p. 115.

48 Kreissig, "Der Makkabäeraufstand," p. 163.

49 II Macc. 5:5–7; Tcherikover, *HCJ*, pp. 187–8, suggested that Jason was driven out by the enemies of the Hellenizers. We accept his argument, although the text does not explicitly state who drove Jason out. Cf. Hengel, *Judaism and Hellenism*, vol. I, p. 281.

50 I Macc. 1:35–6; see Tcherikover, *HCJ*, p. 189.

51 I Macc. 1:34; 3:45; Dan. 11:39; see Schürer, *The History of the Jewish People*, vol. I, p. 154; *CHJ* II, p. 285; Hengel, *Judaism and Hellenism*, vol. I, p. 281; Kreissig, "Der Makkabäeraufstand," p. 168; Tcherikover, *HCJ*, pp. 188–9; M.Stern, *The Hellenistic Period*, p. 159.

52 I Macc. 1:34; 3:45.

53 Applebaum, "Jewish Urban Communities," p. 167 n. 42.

54 Ibid.

55 Ibid. n. 43.

56 B. Bar-Kochva, *Judas Maccabaeus*, Cambridge, 1988, pp. 432–8; idem, "The Status and Origin of the Garrison at the Akra on the Eve of the Religious Persecutions," *Zion* XXVIII (1973) (Heb.), p. 40.

57 Ibid.

58 Bickerman, *Institutions des Séleucides*, p. 85; M. Stern, *The Hellenistic Period*, p. 159.

59 Bar-Kochva, *Judas Maccabaeus*, pp. 438–9. He takes issue with J. M. Montgomery, *The Book of Daniel*, Edinburgh, 1927, p. 463; E. Bickerman, *Der Gott der Makkabäer*, Berlin, 1937, pp. 85–6; Bickerman, *Institutions des Séleucides*, p. 85; U.Wilcken, *P-W*, Antiochus (4) col. 2474; A.Bentzen, *Daniel*, Tübingen, 1952, p. 83; Tcherikover, *HCJ*, pp. 189–90; Hengel, *Judentum*, pp. 512–13, 515; Fischer, *Seleukiden und Makkabäer*, p. 32.

60 Bar-Kochva, *Judas Maccabaeus*, pp. 438–9; idem, *The Seleucid Army*, p. 216 n. 22.

61 Goldstein, *I Maccabees*, p. 212; Bickerman, *Institutions des Séleucides*, pp. 179–80; Bickerman, *Der Gott der Makkabäer*, p. 72.

62 Cf. Goldstein, *I Maccabees*, p. 124, who first insists that the lemma refers to apostate Jews, and then asserts that Antiochus "now surely sent into the Akra new military settlers, at least some of whom were Gentiles."

NOTES

63 See Abel, *Les Livres des Maccabées*, p. 17.
64 Goldstein, *I Maccabees*, p. 123.
65 Hengel, *Judaism and Hellenism*, vol. I, p. 281. Cf. I. Shatzman, *The Armies of the Hasmoneans and Herod*, Tübingen, 1991, p. 11 n. 1, who suggests that Apollonius' actions against Jason's supporters led to the flight from the city.
66 See Bickerman, *Institutions des Séleucides*, pp. 131, 169–85; Mittwoch, "Tribute and Land-Tax," p. 355; Goldstein, *I Maccabees*, pp. 212, 432; Applebaum, "Economic Life in Palestine," pp. 633–4; *CHJ* II, p. 285; M. Stern, *The Hellenistic Period*, p. 159.
67 Rostovtzeff already suggested that this was unlikely, *SEHHW*, vol. I, p. 468.
68 For a similar view see Kippenberg, *Religion und Klassenbildung im antiken Judäa*, pp. 87–8.
69 II Macc. 11:27–33; cf. M. Stern, *The Documents*, pp. 34, 71, who considers the gerousia the traditional leadership of the ethnos of the Jews, which continued to exist side-by-side with the polis. Goldstein, *II Maccabees*, p. 212, suggests that the term "ethnos" is not used in regard to the Jews between the promulgation of the decrees and their cancellation, because the Jews lost their status as an ethnos. However, the reason for that might just as well be Judea's status as the *chora* of a polis.
70 For the change to Greek "way" see II Macc. 4:11; I Macc. 1:15; *Ant.* 12.240.
71 See I Macc. 1:43; Dan. 11:32; *Ant.* 12.255. J. Sievers, *The Hasmoneans and Their Supporters: From Mattathias to the Death of John Hyrcanus I*, Ithaca, NY, 1990, pp. 21–6, discusses various responses to the decrees.
72 See II Macc. 8:6; I Macc. 2:44–7.
73 Gift land was often granted with a proviso that the new owner could attach his lands to the *chora* of a nearby city. This was to the advantage of the new owner because he now shared whatever benefits accrued to owners of land in the *chora* of the polis, such as tax-easements. The polis, of course, increased its area of influence and gained a well-connected citizen. See the gift of land to Aristodicides by Antiochus I; *RC* 13,10–12; *OGIS* 221; P. Frisch, ed., *Die Inschriften von Ilion*, Bonn, 1975, no. 33; R. S. Bagnall and P. Derow, eds, *Greek Historical Documents: The Hellenistic Period*, Chico, CA, 1981, no. 18 p. 37; and the comments by Austin, *The Hellenistic World*, p. 294. See also a sale of land by Antiochus II to his divorced queen Laodice; *RC* 19, 18, 20.
74 Bar-Kochva, *Judas Maccabaeus*, p. 441.
75 I Macc. 3:36; see Bar-Kochva, *Judas Maccabaeus*, pp. 236–7. Also note that in their complaint to the king (I Macc. 6:22–7) the men of the Akra say that they are hated by their own people (verse 24).
76 G. Le Rider, *Suse sous les Séleucides et les Parthes*, Paris, 1965, pp. 410–11.
77 Applebaum, "Jewish Urban Communities," p. 167 n. 43. But there are no city coins from Scythopolis, Gadara, Iamnia, or Marissa, to name a few.
78 I Macc. 2:1, 6–13.
79 I Macc. 2:70; 9:19; 13:25.
80 Maisler (Mazar), "Topographical Researches II, The Place of Origin of the Maccabeans," *BJPES* VIII (1941) (Heb.), p. 105.

81 Bar-Kochva, *Judas Maccabaeus*, pp. 438–41; idem, "The Status and Origin of the Garrison at the Akra," p. 42.
82 He gives no references. See II Sam. 24:24; I Kings 10:28; Isa. 45:13; Jer. 15:13; Mich. 3:1; Lam. 5:4; II Chr. 1:16.
83 Bar-Kochva, *Judas Maccabaeus*, p. 441.
84 For the usual translation see *HCJ*, p. 482 n. 17. Cf. I Macc. 2:56; Num. 14:6, 24; and in other compositions prior to I Maccabees. In Ben-Sira 22:23 the possession of a friend will be shared if one remains loyal. Furthermore, the association of this word is generally with something granted, as in Num. 26:54, 56.
85 See Polybius 4.17.8; *OGIS* 90.19.
86 On the *idia*, see Bickerman, *Institutions des Séleucides*, p. 178. In II Macc. 12:1 Jews return to their "farming" after the pact between Lysias and Judah was agreed to.

5 THE HASMONEANS

1 Once again we stress that there is a diversity of opinion as to the character of the division in Judean society. See L. L. Grabbe, *Judaism from Cyrus to Hadrian*, vol. I, Minneapolis, 1992, p. 290. We use the term "Hellenizers" to label the Seleucid supporters because by accepting the Seleucid rule they were supporting the regime which for whatever reasons had tried to force Hellenistic pagan religion on Jewish society. It might be argued that the majority of Jews seemed willing to settle with the Seleucids once religious freedom was restored and that the Seleucids were willing to conciliate the Jews. We reject this view. The murder of the sixty Hasideans (I Macc. 7:12–18) indicates how far the Seleucids were willing to be conciliatory. We will show that the majority of Jews, far from condoning the actions of the Hellenizers, demonstrated their feelings by joining the Hasmoneans as soon as the physical conditions made it possible.
2 S. Applebaum, "The Hasmoneans: Logistics, Taxation and Constitution," *Judaea in Hellenistic and Roman Times*, *SJLA* 40, Leiden, 1989, p. 10.
3 I Macc. 6:17–27: the chronological problems are formidable. See J. C. Dancy, *A Commentary on I Maccabees*, Oxford, 1954, pp. 113–14; B. Bar-Kochva, *Judas Maccabaeus*, Cambridge, 1988, pp. 276–82, 300, 543–51; L. L. Grabbe, "Maccabean Chronology: 167–164 or 168–165 BCE," *JBL* 110 (1991), pp. 59–74.
4 V. Tcherikover, *Hellenistic Civilization and the Jews* (*HCJ*), Philadelphia, 1966, p. 213. Bar-Kochva, *Judas Maccabaeus*, pp. 303–4, points out that the word αἱ κληρονομίαι was probably translated from the Hebrew word *nahala*, which he renders into English as "land allotments." He points out that these "estates . . . had been confiscated by the Seleucid authorities and alloted to the Hellenizers."
5 F. M. Abel, *Les Livres des Maccabées*, Paris, 1949, p. 115, based on another manuscript, reads "all of your (the King's) domains." Dancy, *Commentary on I Maccabees*, p. 114, interprets the verse as referring to Judas' campaigns against the gentiles in Palestine. So do J. A. Goldstein,

I Maccabees (*AB*, 41), New York, 1976, p. 319 and Bar-Kochva, *Judas Maccabaeus*, pp. 297, 303.

6 See J. V. A. Fine, *Horoi: Studies in Mortgage, Real Security, and Land Tenure in Ancient Athens* (*Hesperia*, suppl. IX), Athens, 1951, pp. 41–60, and the review by P. B. R. Forbes in *The Classical Review* 3 (1953), pp. 109–11.

7 Translation by Goldstein, *I Maccabees*, p. 327.

8 Applebaum, "The Hasmoneans: Logistics," p. 10.

9 Ibid. p. 11.

10 "The foreigners who were in the strongholds that Bacchides had built fled; each one left his place, and went back to his own country": I Macc. 10:12–13, translation by Tedesche. On military settlers see B. Bar-Kochva, *The Seleucid Army*, Cambridge, 1976, pp. 36–7, but cf. G. M. Cohen, *The Seleucid Colonies*, Wiesbaden, 1978, pp. 4, 21, 29–30.

11 P. Garnsey, *Famine and Food Supply in the Graeco-Roman World*, Cambridge, 1988, pp. 31–2, 58–63.

12 Book of Jubilees 23:18–19 may also refer to the famine, but it is difficult to determine the precise historical framework intended by the verses. They belong to a passage which is thought to be relevant to the period of Judah the Maccabee. See *OTP*, vol. 2, pp. 43–4 and bibliography there.

13 Bar-Kochva, *Judas Maccabaeus*, pp. 44, 192–3; Dancy, *Commentary on I Maccabees*, pp. 30–1; M. Stern, *The Documents on the History of the Hasmonean Revolt*, Ha-Kibbutz Ha-Meuhad, 1972 (Heb.), pp. 25–75.

14 Basic works on the Maccabean period that do not even mention this famine: Bar-Kochva, *Judas Maccabaeus*; E. Schürer, *The History of the Jewish People in the Age of Jesus Christ*, vols I–III, rev. and ed. G. Vermes and F. Millar, Edinburgh, 1973–87; S. Zeitlin, *The Rise and Fall of the Judaean State*, vols I–III, Philadelphia, 1968–78; Tcherikover, *HCJ*; U. Rappaport, "The Hasmonean State," M. Stern, ed., *The Hellenistic Period and the Hasmonean State, The History of Eretz-Israel*, vol. 3, Jerusalem, 1981 (Heb.), pp. 191–273; A. Schalit, ed., *The Hellenistic Age: Political History of Jewish Palestine from 332 BCE to 67 BCE, World History of the Jewish People*, series 1, vol. 6, Jerusalem, 1972; J. Klausner, *Ha-Historia Shel ha-Bayit ha-Sheni*, Jerusalem (Heb.), 1958. Two exceptions to the prevailing standpoint are C. Préaux, *Le Monde Hellénistique*, vol. II, Paris, 1978, p. 582; and very recently J. Sievers, *The Hasmoneans and Their Supporters: From Mattathias to the Death of John Hyrcanus I*, Ithaca, NY, 1990, p. 73, who suggests the famine was caused by the war, and credits it with forcing "country dwellers to make what terms they could with the city people and the government who controlled most of the imported and – probably more important – stored food."

15 *Septuaginta I*, ed. A. Rahlfs, Stuttgart, 1935; *Maccabaeorum liber I*, ed. W. Kappler, Göttingen, 1967.

16 W. O. E. Oesterley, *APOT*, vol. I, p. 98 n. 24.

17 A. Kahana, *Ha-Sefarim ha-Hitzonim*, vol. II, Tel-Aviv, 1959 (Heb.), p. 140.

18 Abel, *Les Livres des Maccabées*, pp. 164–5.

19 S. Zeitlin, ed., *The First Book of Maccabees*, New York, 1950, pp. 158–9.

20 Dancy, *Commentary on I Maccabees*, p. 134.

21 Goldstein, *I Maccabees*, pp. 376–7.
22 K. D. Schunck, *Historische und legendarische Erzählungen: I Makkabäerbuch* (Jüdische Schriften aus hellenistisch–römischer Zeit, I, 4), Gütersloh, 1980, p. 334.
23 I Maccabees uses *chora* at least twice in the sense of the "people" (9:53; 14:28).
24 I Macc. 7:25, 46–50; 9:1; and see Bar-Kochva, *Judas Maccabaeus*, pp. 348, 359, 376.
25 See note 35 in Chap. 1, "Dietary Needs." Note also the verses in Lev. 25:20–2 which state that after the Sabbatical Year the farmer will eat of his stored produce until the new crop bears fruit.
26 I Macc. 6:49–53; *Ant.* 12.378; 13.40, 234; 14.475; *BJ* 3.181; 4.137; 5.24–6; *Vita* 71,117–18; Tacitus, *Hist.* V, 12, 3. See R. North, "Maccabaean Sabbath Years," *Biblica* 34 (1953), p. 506; G. Hamel, *Poverty and Charity in Roman Palestine*, Ph.D. Thesis, Univ. of California, Santa Cruz, 1983, pp. 124–5, 414 n. 354, 415 n. 355.
27 I Macc. 5:23, 45, 53.
28 See Bar-Kochva, *Judas Maccabaeus*, pp. 544–5, who elaborates this point.
29 B. Isaac, "A Seleucid Inscription from Jamnia-on-the-Sea: Antiochus V Eupator and the Sidonians," *IEJ* 41 (1991), pp. 132–44. My thanks to Prof. Benjamin Isaac of the University of Tel-Aviv who gave me an early opportunity to study this inscription. See also A. Kasher, "A Second-Century BCE Greek Inscription from Iamnia," *Cathedra* 63 (1992) (Heb.), pp. 3–21.
30 Ibid.
31 For a very full discussion and resolution of the chronological problems involved in the Sabbath Year, see Bar-Kochva, *Judas Maccabaeus*, pp. 339–40, 341–2, 543–51. Cf. Grabbe, "Maccabean Chronology," pp. 69–70, who agrees with the determination of the Sabbatical Year, but not with the dating of the siege of Beth Zur. Cf. Schürer, vol. I, p. 167 n. 14 and bibliography there. However, cf. B. Z. Wacholder, "The Calendar of Sabbatical Cycles During the Second Temple and the Early Rabbinic Period," *HUCA* 44 (1973), pp. 160–3, who suggests autumn 163 to autumn of 162.
32 Bar-Kochva, *Judas Maccabaeus*, p. 385.
33 As a subsistence-farming society approaches harvest time a pre-harvest hunger occurs as the stocks of food from the previous harvests dwindle. The society is dependent on the new crop to increase the amount of food available for consumption. The failure of the new crop causes a food crisis at the very least, and depending upon the availability and efficiency of famine protection institutions, the situation can deteriorate into famine. See C. Clark and M. Haswell, *The Economics of Subsistence Agriculture*, London, 1970, pp. 22–3.
34 Wacholder's proposal if correct would only strengthen our case, indicating that there was no crop at all immediately before Judah's defeat; Wacholder, "The Calendar of Sabbatical Cycles," pp. 162–3.
35 *Leket* = gleanings, *Shikhhah* = forgotten produce, *Pe'ah* = corners of the field, *Ma'aser sheni* = second or poor tithe. See *EJ*, vol. 13, s.v. Poor, Provision for the; M. Haran, "*Matanot Aniim*," *Encyclopedia Biblica*,

vol. V, p. 758 (Heb.); M. Weinfeld, *Social Justice in Ancient Israel and in the Ancient Near East*, Jerusalem and Minneapolis, 1995, pp. 215–17, 218, 222–30.

36 Garnsey, *Famine and Food Supply*, pp. xi, 82.

37 Ibid. pp. 82–3; Heichelheim, "Sitos," *P-W* suppl. VI, col. 819–92, Stuttgart, 1935; A. R. Hands, *Charities and Social Aid in Greece and Rome*, Ithaca, NY, 1968, pp. 77–81; L. Robert, "Une Epigramme d'Automedon," *REG* 94 (1981), pp. 341–4.

38 Liddell and Scott, s.v. αὐτομόλεω.

39 Hands, *Charities and Social Aid in Greece and Rome*, pp. 35, 56, 156 n. 40 and bibliography there. Also W. W. Tarn and G. T. Griffith, *Hellenistic Civilization*, New York, 1952, reprinted 1975, p. 53. On Hellenistic kingship see F. W. Walbank, "Monarchies and Monarchic Ideas" in *The Cambridge Ancient History*, vol. 7.1, *The Hellenistic World*, Cambridge, 1984; and Préaux, *Le Monde Hellénistique*, pp. 181–294.

40 *SIG* 344, 81–101; *RC* 3; and Tarn's comment that the Seleucid king received enough taxes in kind to make him a great corn merchant: Tarn and Griffith, *Hellenistic Civilization*, p. 142.

41 *Ant.* 12.138, 142–5; E. Bickerman, "La charte séleucide de Jérusalem," *Studies in Jewish and Christian History*, vol. II, Leiden, 1980, pp. 44–85.

42 The actual location of some of these forts is a matter of considerable discussion. See S. Dar, *Landscape and Pattern*, Oxford, 1986, p. 221 and S. Applebaum's comments on p. 260 there. But compare comments of I. Shatzman, *The Armies of the Hasmoneans and Herod*, Tübingen, 1991, pp. 42–3, 68; F. M. Abel, *Géographie de la Palestine*, vol. II, pp. 475–6, 481–2; G. Galil, "Parathon, Timnatha, and the Fortifications of Bacchides," *Cathedra* 63 (1992) (Heb.), pp. 22–31; M. Avi-Yonah, *The Holy Land from the Persian to the Arab Conquests: A Historical Geography (536 BC to AD 640)*, Grand Rapids, 1966, pp. 53–4. It is also noteworthy that according to regional geographic studies administrative and market centers exist on the periphery of a city region. This is a natural development of the need for a local center as a nearby alternative to the main metropolis. Bacchides' forts would fit this description. See I. W. J. Hopkins, "The City Region in Roman Palestine," *PEQ* 112 (1980), pp. 19–32.

43 P. Briant, "Contrainte militaire, dépendance rurale et exploitation des territoires en Asie Achéménide," *RTP*, Paris, 1982, p. 180.

44 Ibid. pp. 192–3.

45 Ostraca from the late Persian period at Tel Beer-sheba and Tel Arad are thought to be receipts for grain handed into government storage, as well as receipts for government grain provided to horsemen, horses, and donkeys; see J. Naveh, "The Aramaic Ostraca from Tel Beer-sheba," *Tel-Aviv* 6 (1979), pp. 182–98.

46 Briant, "Contrainte militaire," p. 212; idem, "Des Achéménides aux rois Hellénistiques: continuités et ruptures," *RTP*, Paris, 1982, pp. 291–330; S. Sherwin-White, "Seleucid Babylonia," A. Kuhrt and S. Sherwin-White, eds, *Hellenism in the East*, London, 1987, pp. 17, 22–3; cf. F. Millar, "The Problem of Hellenistic Syria," pp. 110–33.

47 I Macc. 10:29, 30, 36; and see B. Bar-Kochva, "Manpower, Economics, and Internal Strife in the Hasmonean State," *Armées et fiscalité dans le*

monde antique (Colloque National du CNRS no. 936, Organisé par H. Van Effentere), Paris, 1977, p. 169, who suggests that Demetrius I offered to hire 30,000 Judean soldiers in order to ease their economic plight. On Simon see I Macc. 14:8, 10, 32, 34.

48 D. Rathbone, "The Grain Trade and Grain Shortages in the Hellenistic East," P. Garnsey and C. R. Whittaker, eds, *Trade and Famine in Classical Antiquity*, Cambridge, 1983, pp. 46, 50.

49 Even if the reckoning is not exact to the month, two years after spring 160 BCE would not be later than the beginning of the civil year in autumn of 158 BCE. For chronological questions on the months and years see Schürer, *The History of the Jewish People*, vol. I, p. 18.

50 The question whether Jonathan really did control the countryside might be raised because of the lack of any detail for the period from 157 BCE to 152 BCE. The situation in 152 BCE is the best indication that Jonathan was the major, perhaps the only, significant force in Judea. The Seleucid contenders solicit his support, not the support of the occupants of the Akra. Demetrius' action is particularly revealing since by offering recognition to Jonathan he in effect abandoned dedicated supporters.

51 Hengel points out that "The suggestion in the letter of protection from the consul L. Calpurnius Piso for the Jewish embassy to Rome that a whole series of Greek states should hand over Jewish fugitives to the high priest Simon 'so that he might punish them according to the law' may refer above all to Jewish apostates who had fled abroad (I Macc. 15:21–4)." M. Hengel, *Judaism and Hellenism*, Philadelphia, 1981, vol. I, p. 291. Sievers, *The Hasmoneans and Their Supporters*, pp. 82–3, suggests that the Jews in the Akra held out for so long because they did not want to leave land which they may have owned and which would have been lost to them had they left Judea. This seems a bit far-fetched in light of the relations between the apostates and their opponents. It also contradicts what he himself said about the Maccabeans confiscating the lands of the Hellenizers.

52 *Ant.* 13.394, 427; 14.6, 10.

53 On the subject of Hasmonean Hellenization see U. Rappaport, "The Hellenization of the Hasmoneans," M. Mor, ed., *Jewish Assimilation, Acculturation and Accommodation: Past Traditions, Current Issue and Future Prospects, Proceedings of the Second Annual Symposium of the Philip M. and Ethel Klutznick Chair in Jewish Civilization*, Sept. 24–5 1989, Center for the Study of Religion and Society, Creighton University, pp. 1–13.

54 I Macc. 5:18, 56: Judah left Zechariah and Azariah as leaders of the people. I Macc. 8:17: Eupolomus son of Johanan son of Hakkoz and Jason son of Eleazar. I Macc. 11:70: Mattathias son of Absalom and Judah son of Chalpi. I Macc. 13:11: Jonathan son of Absalom.

55 I Macc. 10:20–1 relates that some of the leaders of the people betrayed their trust out of avarice.

56 See M. Stern, *The Documents*, pp. 107–10. There is also the possibility that the Perea was added to Judea during the time of Jonathan; see Avi-Yonah, *The Holy Land*, p. 57.

57 The word is used to indicate a distribution of land and it may be

significant that it is used in the LXX in connection with Psalm 77:55, where the heathen is cast out of his land and the Lord divides it for an inheritance for Israel, who will now dwell there. See also Avi-Yonah, *The Holy Land*, p. 55.

58 Bar-Kochva, "Manpower, Economics."
59 I Macc. 10:36; Bar-Kochva, *The Seleucid Army*, p. 186; idem, "Manpower, Economics," pp. 167–70; idem, *Judas Maccabaeus*, pp. 53–5. See A. Kasher, "The Changes in Manpower and Ethnic Composition of the Hasmonean Army (167–63 BCE)," *JQR* LXXXI (1991), p. 342, who credits the influx of Jewish refugees from the gentile areas also as a cause of the distress.
60 Applebaum, "The Hasmoneans: Logistics," pp. 9–11, 18 n. 38.
61 Shatzman, *The Armies*, pp. 18 and n. 41, 28–9 and n. 81.
62 See U. Rappaport, "The Land Issue as a Factor in Inter-Ethnic Relations in Eretz-Israel During the Second Temple Period," A. Kasher, A. Oppenheimer, U. Rappaport, eds, *Man and Land in Eretz-Israel in Antiquity*, Jerusalem, 1986 (Heb.), pp. 80–1, and the references there.
63 Applebaum, "The Hasmoneans: Logistics," p. 23.
64 I Macc. 5:58–60; 10:69.
65 M. Stern, *GLAJJ*, vol. I, p. 293.
66 Zeitlin, *The First Book of Maccabees*, p. 239 n. 39; Goldstein, *I Maccabees*, map 13, p. 537; cf. Abel, *Les Livres des Maccabées*, p. 274 n. 41; S. Klein, *Eretz-Yehuda*, Tel-Aviv, 1939 (Heb.), pp. 71–2.
67 C. Möller and G. Schmitt, *Siedlungen Palästinas Nach Flavius Josephus* (*Beihefte Zum Tübinger Atlas des Vordern Orients* 14), Wiesbaden, 1976, p. 10.
68 Applebaum, "The Hasmoneans: Logistics," pp. 11, 14. For Dar's primary work see Dar, *Landscape and Pattern*.
69 We do not count the actions of the Hasideans as "rejection." For an up-to-date discussion and survey of the literature see J. Kampen, *The Hasideans and the Origin of Pharisaism: A Study of 1 and 2 Maccabees*, Ithaca, NY, 1990.
70 IQpHab 8:11–12; translation by W.H. Brownlee, *The Midrash Pesher of Habakkuk*, Missoula, MT, 1979, p. 131. In the following learned commentary Brownlee does not relate the verses to a specific Hasmonean. See Brownlee, "The Wicked Priest, the Man of Lies, and the Righteous Teacher," *JQR* 73 (1982–3), pp. 1–37, in which he suggests that the "wicked priest" is to be identified with a succession of Hasmonean rulers. M. P. Horgan, *Pesharim: Qumran Interpretations of Biblical Books*, Washington DC, 1979, pp. 7–8 and n. 16, summarizes the points of view, which in the main support Hengel, i.e. Jonathan is the wicked priest. But cf. B. Nitzan, *Pesher Habakkuk: A Scroll from the Wilderness of Judaea (1QpHab)*, Jerusalem, 1986 (Heb.), p. 178, who interprets this passage to refer to Alexander Yannai, but her view depends on the assumption that the passage refers to the confiscation of the property of the Pharisees, not of the Hellenizers.
71 Hengel, *Judaism and Hellenism*, vol. I, p. 290 and n. 217.
72 Gift of land to Aristodicides by Antiochus I: *RC* 13,10–12; *OGIS* 221; P. Frisch, ed., *Die Inschriften von Ilion*, Bonn, 1975, no. 33. Samos decree

for Boulagoras (c. 246–243): *SEG* 1.366. For Ptolemy Thraseas in the Hefzibah inscription, see the references in Chapter 3, note 72. Bacchides appoints people as lords of the country, I Macc. 9:25.

73 Megillat Ta'anit 14(17)th of Sivan, see H. Lichtenstein, "Die Fastenrolle: Eine Untersuchung zur Juedisch–Hellenistischen Geschichte," *HUCA* 89 (1931), pp. 281–2, 319, 327.

74 The scholion of Megillat Ta'anit refers to Beth Zur as part of Edom, but the geographical information is so misleading that some scholars believed that Caesarea was intended. See Lichtenstein, "Die Fastenrolle," pp. 281–2, 319, 327; B. Z. Lurie, *Megillath Ta'anith*, Jerusalem, 1964 (Heb.), pp. 117–19.

75 See the summary of scholarly points of view on I Maccabees in H. W. Attridge, "Jewish Historiography," R. A. Kraft and G. W. E. Nickelsburg, eds, *Early Judaism and its Modern Interpreters*, Atlanta, 1986, p. 318.

76 H. W. Attridge, "Historiography," M. E. Stone, ed., *Jewish Writings of the Second Temple Period*, Assen and Philadelphia, 1984, p. 175 n. 51: "Thus conditions under Simon parallel those under Solomon as described in I Kgs. 5:5 and as predicted for the latter days in Mic. 4:4, cf. Zech. 3:10." See also Goldstein, *I Maccabees*, p. 491, commentary to verses 8–14.

77 Gezer, the Pampras inscription, *CIJ*, vol. I, p. 225, nos 1,183, 1,184. For archaeological evidence of the Hasmonean strata of Gezer, see W. G. Dever, *Gezer* I, Jerusalem, 1970, pp. 6–7 and n. 31, pp. 10, 68 and n. 17; idem, *Gezer* II, Jerusalem, 1974, pp. 4–5 (table); J. D. Seager, "The Search for Maccabean Gezer," *BA* 39 (1976), pp. 142–4; idem, "The Search for Maccabean Gezer," *Proceedings of the Sixth World Congress of Jewish Studies* (English section), vol. I, Jerusalem, 1977, p. 395. R. Reich, "Archaeological Evidence of the Jewish Population at Hasmonean Gezer," *IEJ* 31 (1981), pp. 48–52.

78 I Kings 5:5; Mic. 4:4; Zech. 3:10. For other biblical parallels in this song of praise see the commentary of Abel, *Les Livres des Maccabées*, pp. 249–52.

79 I Macc. 14:6: καί ἐπλάτυνεν τὰ ὅρια τῷ ἔθνει αὐτοῦ καὶ ἐκράτησεν τῆς χώρας. Additional proof of Hasmonean control of Gezer can be seen in the Roman document *Ant.* 13.261, in which the senate demands the return of Gezer to the Jews. On this document see M. Stern, *The Documents*, pp. 159–65; idem, "The Relations Between Judaea and Rome During the Rule of John Hyrcanus," *Zion* XXVI (1961) (Heb.), pp. 7–11.

80 Cf. *Ant.* 14.74, καί τὸ σύμπαν ἔθνοσ . . . , ἐντὸς τῶν ἰδίων ὅρον συνέστειλεν ("and the entire nation . . . he confined within its own borders"). This refers to the liberation of the Hellenistic gentile areas from Judean rule by Pompey, and is assumed to indicate that the Jews who lived in these areas were now forced to return to the Jewish areas.

81 Food: I Macc. 14:10. The poor: I Macc.14:14, καὶ ἐστήρισε πάντας τοὺς ταπεινοὺς τοῦ λαοῦ αυτοῦ ("He strengthened all the lowly of his people"). Goldstein, *I Maccabees*, pp. 491–2, interprets the poor as the humble; Zeitlin sees them as the "pious": *The First Book of Maccabees*, p. 225 n. 14; Abel, *Les Livres des Maccabées*, p. 252 n. 14, likewise views them as the humble, with the added remark that they are

often associated with the poor; Dancy, *A Commentary on I Maccabees*, pp. 181–2, identifies them with the humble. It appears that all these commentaries are strongly influenced by the metaphorical meaning of the word and its use as a synonym for the pious. The text does not support such a view, rather it suggests that the poor in the material sense are intended. Note that two of the readings are τῆς γῆς: see Kappler's edition.

82 For a review of the points of view on the document see Sievers, *The Hasmoneans and Their Supporters*, p. 121.

83 Applebaum, "The Hasmoneans: Logistics," pp. 14–16.

84 Goldstein, *I Maccabees*, p. 504 nn. 32–4.

85 Bar-Kochva, "Manpower, Economics," p. 171. See also Kasher, "The Changes in Manpower and Ethnic Composition of the Hasmonean Army," p. 343.

86 Applebaum, "The Hasmoneans: Logistics," p. 15.

87 Sievers, *The Hasmoneans and Their Supporters*, p. 123, thinks that the decree was in the third year, but it was accepted by the people at some later date.

88 Applebaum, "The Hasmoneans: Logistics," p. 17.

89 Gezer is considered a royal estate by B. Z. Rosenfeld in "The 'Boundary of Gezer': Inscriptions and the History of Gezer at the End of the Second Temple Period," *IEJ* 38 (1988), pp. 243–4; but cf. J. Schwartz, "Once More on the 'Boundary of Gezer': Inscriptions and the History of Gezer and Lydda at the End of the Second Temple Period," *IEJ* 40 (1990), p. 55, who claims that he cannot find any reference to Gezer as a Hasmonean estate. Indeed, there is no specific proof-text, but the following facts suggest that Gezer was an estate. (1) The distribution of land to Jewish settlers. (2) Of all the conquered areas this is the only one in which a residence of Simon was reportedly built. (3) The boundary stones suggest personal property. (4) A town should have prospered; only the conversion to a private estate can explain why the place was steadliy eclipsed by Emmaus.

90 His sons were field commanders; his own experience was of family members taking positions of responsibility.

91 See Schürer, *The History of the Jewish People*, vol. I, p. 200.

92 For discussions on the problems involved see Kasher, *Jews and Hellenistic Cities*, pp. 120–31; idem, *Jews, Idumaeans, and Ancient Arabs*, Tübingen, 1988, pp. 44–78; Rappaport, "The Hasmonean State," pp. 214–18.

93 Kasher, *Jews and Hellenistic Cities*, p. 121.

94 See G. Fuks, *Scythopolis: A Greek City in Eretz-Israel*, Jerusalem, 1983 (Heb.), pp. 14, 29, 36.

95 Prov. 22:28.

96 *Ant.* 13.257–8. See U. Rappaport, "The Hellenistic Cities and the Judaization of Eretz Israel," Y. Perlman and B. Shimron, eds, *Doron: Mehkarim be-Tarbut Klassit Mugashim le-Professor Ben-Zion Katz*, Tel-Aviv, 1967, pp. 219–30 (Heb.). See also Kasher, *Jews, Idumaeans, and Ancient Arabs*, pp. 46–77, who discusses in exhaustive detail the conversion of the Idumeans to Judaism. He argues that the conversion was voluntary.

97 J. Goldstein suggests that Idumea presented a particular religious dilemma; see *CHJ*, vol. II, p. 326.

98 For example, see G. Fuks, *Scythopolis*, p. 63: "In accordance with the accepted policy of the Hasmoneans the residents of the city were given the choice of conversion or exile." For the case of Scythopolis Fuks seems to be relying on *Megillat Taanit*, a problematical source. See also Kasher's comments in *Jews and Hellenistic Cities*, p. 128 n. 42. Also, Goldstein, *CHJ*, vol. II, p. 326: "Once the option had been devised for the Idumeans, it could be offered to other pagan peoples as the Hasmoneans reconquered more and more of the Promised Land."

99 Hengel, *Judaism and Hellenism*, vol. I, pp. 61–2; Rappaport, "The Hellenistic Cities and the Judaization of Eretz Israel," pp. 220, 222–4.

100 U. Rappaport, "Les Iduméens en Egypte," *Revue de philologie de littérature et d'histoire ancienne* XLIII (1969), p. 81.

101 That would have been an unnecessary step if the indigenous population had emigrated. See *BJ* 1.123; *Ant.* 14.10 and I. Ronen, "Formation of Jewish Nationalism Among the Idumaeans," Appendix B, in Kasher, *Jews, Idumaeans, and Ancient Arabs.*

102 *Ant.* 14.74.

103 See A. Kloner, "Mareshah (Marisa)," *NEAEHL*, vol. 3, p. 953.

104 Applebaum, "The Hasmoneans: Logistics," pp. 12–14.

105 Kasher, *Jews and Hellenistic Cities*, p. 125. Cf. U. Rappaport, "The Samaritans in the Hellenistic Period," *Zion* LV (1990) (Heb.), pp. 382–3, for a different interpretation of the text.

106 Bar-Kochva, "Manpower, Economics," p. 174.

107 See I. L. Levine, "The Political Struggle between Pharisees and Sadducees in the Hasmonean Period," A. Oppenheimer, U. Rappaport, M. Stern, eds, *Jerusalem in the Second Temple Period: Abraham Schalit Memorial Volume*, Jerusalem, 1980 (Heb.), pp. 61–83.

108 Bar-Kochva, "Manpower, Economics," p. 175.

109 For the borders of Jewish settlement in the heyday of the Davidic empire see II Sam. chap. 24; and see the discussion in Y. Aharoni, *The Land of the Bible: A Historical Geography*, A. F. Rainey, ed., Philadelphia, 1979, pp. 296–7.

110 Probably the Jezreel Valley. See *Josephus* vol. VII, Marcus' note a, p. 558, which refers to *Ant.* 12.348. Rappaport, "La Judée et Rome," p. 331, demonstrates the connection between conditions in Hyrcanus I's reign and the Roman recognition in Caesar's day.

111 *Ant.* 14.207, English translation by Marcus.

112 Applebaum, "The Hasmoneans: Logistics," p. 23; B. Z. Lurie, *Mi-Yannai Ad Hordos*, Jerusalem, 1974 (Heb.), pp. 36–42; S. Lieberman, "The Three Abrogations of Johanan the High Priest," *Hellenism in Jewish Palestine*, New York, 1962, p. 143 n. 28. The declaration stated that the farmer had brought his offering from his own land, a false declaration in the case of tenant farmers. Although this edict appears in a relatively late source, the Mishnah, it is considered to be an authentic record of an enactment made by John Hyrcanus. The declaration was relevant to the period before the destruction of the Temple, and no other High Priest is identified as "the High Priest Yohanan" other than John Hyrcanus. See

H. Danby, *The Mishnah*, Oxford, 1933, p. 82 n. 3; E. E. Urbach, *The Halakha: Its Sources and Developments*, Yad Le-Talmud, 1986, pp. 44–9.

113 English translation by Marcus; but note that the Greek verb used is καρπόω, which is better translated as "to reap the fruits of."

114 D. R. Schwartz, "Josephus and Nicolaus on the Pharisees," *JStJ* XIV (1983), pp. 158–9.

115 *Ant.* 13.301–19; *BJ* 1.70–84; see Schürer, *The History of the Jewish People*, vol. I, pp. 216–18; *GLAJJ*, vol. I, pp. 224–6, 307.

116 A. Schalit, *König Herodes: Der Mann und Sein Werk*, Berlin, 1969, p. 172 n. 92.

117 On Aristobolus' foreign policy see Kasher, *Jews and Hellenistic Cities*, pp. 133–6.

118 The question of whether Aristobolus was the first Hasmonean to wear a royal crown, or if it was Alexander Yannai, is beyond the purview of this investigation. Nevertheless, in order to remain faithful to scientific accuracy we will enumerate the basic points of the problem. Josephus writes that Aristobolus transformed the government into a monarchy (*Ant.* 13.301), while Strabo ascribes this change to Yannai (Strabo 16.2.40). Those who consider that Josephus is correct claim that he was closer to the facts and had no reason to knowingly mislead his readers. Those who accept Strabo's view base their case on the fact that Aristobolus did not mint any coins with the title "king," while Yannai still had coins with the title "High Priest" and later "king." See Stern, *GLAJJ*, vol. I, p. 307, commentary to line 40.

119 Schürer, *The History of the Jewish People*, vol. I, p. 217.

120 Kasher, *Jews and Hellenistic Cities*, pp. 133–6.

121 See Schürer, *The History of the Jewish People*, vol. I, pp. 219–28; G. Alon, "Did the Jewish People and its Sages Cause the Hasmoneans to be Forgotten?" *Jews, Judaism and the Classical World*, Jerusalem, 1977, pp. 1–17; J. Efron, "Simon ben Shetah and Alexander Jannaeus," *Studies on the Hasmonean Period*, Leiden, 1987, pp. 143–218; B. Z. Lurie, *Yannai ha-Melekh*, Jerusalem, 1960 (Heb.); Klausner, *Ke-she-Euma Nilchemet al Heruta*, pp. 93–116.

122 On Yannai's wars see Shatzman, *The Armies*, passim; Kasher, *Jews and Hellenistic Cities*; idem, *Jews, Idumaeans*; A. Schalit, "Die Eroberungen des Alexander Jannäus," *Theokratia* 1 (1967/9), pp. 3–50; Kanael, "Notes on Alexander Jannaeus' Campaigns in the Coastal Region," *Tarbiz* XXIV (1956) (Heb.), pp. 9–15; U. Rappaport, "La Judée et Rome pendant le règne d'Alexandre Jannée," *REJ* 127 (1968), pp. 329–45; A. Kasher, "Alexander Yannai's Wars with the Nabateans," *Zion* L (1985) (Heb.), pp. 107–20; M. Stern, "The Relations between the Hasmonean Kingdom and Ptolemaic Egypt in View of the International Situation during the 2nd and 1st Centuries BCE," *Zion* L (1985) (Heb.), pp. 81–106; M. Stern, "Judea and her Neighbors in the Days of Alexander Jannaeus," *The Jerusalem Cathedra* 1 (1981), pp. 22–46.

123 On the order of Yannai's wars see Schürer, *The History of the Jewish People*, vol. I, pp. 219–28; Kasher, *Jews and Hellenistic Cities*, pp. 137–69; Kasher, *Jews, Idumaeans*, pp. 86–105; M. Stern, "Judea and her Neighbors in the Days of Alexander Jannaeus." On the chronology of the

war with Acco see G. Cohen, *The Judean–Syrian–Egyptian Conflict of 103–101 BC*, Brussels, 1989; cf. G. Fuks, "On the Reliability of a Reference in Josephus," U. Rappaport, ed., *Josephus Flavius: Historian of Eretz-Israel in the Hellenistic–Roman Period*, Jerusalem, 1982 (Heb.), pp. 131–8.

124 U. Rappaport, "Akko-Ptolemais and the Jews in the Hellenistic Period," *Cathedra* 50 (1988) (Heb.), pp. 31–48.

125 Klausner, *Ke-she-Euma Nilchemet al Heruta.*

126 Kasher, *Jews and Hellenistic Cities*, p. 140; Kasher, *Jews, Idumaeans*, p. 86.

127 Schalit, "Die Eroberungen des Alexander Jannaeus in Moab"; Kanael, "Notes on Alexander Jannaeus' Campaigns in the Coastal Region"; Kasher, "Alexander Yannai's Wars with the Nabataeans"; idem., *Jews and Hellenistic Cities*, pp. 145,154; idem, *Jews, Idumaeans*, pp. 89, 99–101.

128 Kasher, *Jews and Hellenistic Cities*, pp. 141–2, 163–5, demonstrates that the gentile population was probably not expelled. See Rappaport, "The Hellenization of the Hasmoneans," p. 5: the existence of Yannai coins with Greek inscriptions indicates that there was a Greek population in Hasmonean Judea.

129 Kasher, *Jews and Hellenistic Cities*, p. 167.

130 *Ant.* 14.74: "the entire nation, which had before raised itself so high, he confined within in its own borders" (translation by Marcus, LCL). The latter verb συστέλλω has the meaning of "to condense," or "to compact," but also has the metaphorical meaning of "to abase"; this parallels well with the previous verb αἴρω which means "to raise," but also "to exalt." So we can understand that on the one hand the Judeans had exalted themselves by their rule over these areas, but were now abased by being confined to their own lands. See also *BJ* 1.155.

131 See *Ant.* 14.77 which amplifies Josephus' earlier remarks.

132 Bar-Kochva, "Manpower, Economics," p. 174; cf. U. Rappaport, "The Galilee between the Hasmonean Revolt and the Roman Conquest," I. Gafni, A. Oppenheimer, M. Stern, eds, *Jews and Judaism in the Second Temple, Mishna, and Talmud Period*, Jerusalem, 1993 (Heb.), p. 23 n. 27, who holds that the Jewish population of the Galilee was a mix of earlier Jewish settlers, with converted Semites predisposed to sympathize with Judaism, and new settlers introduced by the Hasmoneans.

133 In Pompey's list of freed cities (*Ant.* 14.75–6; *BJ* 1.156) Adora is totally lacking; in the list of Gabinius' restorations (*Ant.* 14.87–8; *BJ* 1.166) Adora appears but perhaps Gadara is meant; see Möller and Schmitt, *Siedlungen*, p. 7. See also Avi-Yonah, *The Holy Land*, p. 184; Kasher, *Hellenistic Cities*, p. 179, who raises the possibility that if it is the Idumean Adora, then this may have been an attempt by Gabinius to curtail Jewish Idumea.

134 Conquest, see *Ant.* 13.394, 396; Jewish identity in 6 CE, see *Ant.* 18.4; activity during the revolt, see *BJ* 2.568; 4.2–10.

135 See S. Freyne, *Galilee from Alexander the Great to Hadrian*, Notre Dame, 1980, p. 63; S. Applebaum, "The Struggle for the Soil and the Revolt of 66–73 CE," *Eretz-Israel* 12 (1975) (Heb.), p. 125. Schalit, *König Herodes*, p. 326, suggests that the turmoil in Judea between 63 BCE till 37 BCE was partly the result of the dislodgement of Jewish farmers by Pompey.

See also Y. Shahar, "Clashes Between Jewish and Non-Jewish Settlements During the War of Destruction," *Cathedra* 51 (1989) (Heb.), pp. 3–20, who demonstrates that in the Galilee the proximity of Jewish areas to Hellenistic centers led to the extreme levels of violence in the region during the Great Revolt.

136 M. Stern, *"Divrei Strabon al ha-Yehudim,"* M. Dorman, S. Safrai, M. Stern, eds, *Essays in Jewish History and Philology in Memory of Gedaliahu Alon*, Ha-Kibbutz Ha-Meuhad, 1970 (Heb.), p. 177; and see his comments in *GLAJJ*, I, p. 293.

137 Dor: *Ant.* 19.300; Caesarea: *BJ* 2.266; Scythopolis: *BJ* 2.466; Gerasa: *BJ* 2.480; Iamnia: *BJ* 4.130, 444.

138 See I. L. Levine, "The Hasmonean Conquest of Strato's Tower," *IEJ* 24 (1974), pp. 62–9.

139 *Ant.* 20.173.

140 Avi-Yonah, *The Holy Land*, p. 76; I. Shatzman, "The Hasmoneans in Greco-Roman Historiography," *Zion* vol. LVII (1991) (Heb.), pp. 39, 57; Kasher, *Jews and Hellenistic Cities*, p. 165.

141 See the list in Applebaum, "The Hasmoneans: Logistics," p. 21 and n. 51. Also Applebaum, "Hellenistic Cities of Judaea and its Vicinity: Some New Aspects," B. Levick, ed., *The Ancient Historian and His Materials: Essays in Honor of C. E. Stevens*, Farnborough, 1975, p. 63; idem, "Jewish Urban Communities and Greek Influences," *SCI* 5 (1979–80), pp. 158–77. However, Applebaum's interpretation of the archaeological evidence is not really solid. It is notoriously difficult to determine whether a site was inhabited by Jews. For example, the finding of eighteen coins of Yannai proves nothing.

142 *Geographica* 16.2,20–7 = *GLAJJ*, vol. I, no. 114. But Shatzman, "The Hasmoneans in Greco-Roman Historiography," p. 36 and n. 115, thinks that Strabo got Alexander the Great confused with Alexander Yannai.

143 A. Kasher, *"Temurot Demographiot ve-Mediniot be-Arei ha-Hof Me-Az Ha-Kibush Ha-Helenisti ve-Ad Ha-Kibush Ha-Romi,"* Sh. Bonimovitz, M. Kochavi, A. Kasher, eds, *Yishuvim, Okhlusiah, ve-Kalkala be-Eretz-Yisrael beEt HaAtika*, Tel-Aviv, 1988 (Heb.), p. 188, suggests that Antipas, Herod's grandfather, was appointed governor of Gaza in order to renew the economic activity of the port with the Nabateans. Cf. G. Fuks, "On the Reliability of a Reference in Josephus," who claims the whole story is an attempt by Nicolaus to glorify Herod's antecedents.

144 M. Dothan, "Ashdod," *NEAEHL*, vol. 1, pp. 101–2; and see also Applebaum, "Jewish Urban Communities and Greek Influences," pp. 169–70, who bases his statement on Josephus.

145 R. Gophna and E. Ayalon, "History of Settlement in the Tel Michal Region," Z. Herzog, G. Rapp Jr, O. Negbi, eds, *Excavations at Tel Michal, Israel*, Minneapolis and Tel-Aviv, 1989, p. 23; I. Roll and E. Ayalon, *Apollonia and Southern Sharon*, Tel-Aviv, 1989 (Heb.), pp. 34, 128–9, 239.

146 *Ant.* 13.332; J. Elgavish, "Shiqmona," *NEAEHL*, vol. 4, pp. 1373, 1376, suggests the remains of fortresses.

147 *Geog.* 16.2.27 = *GLAJJ*, vol. I, pp. 290–2.

148 Gadara: *Ant.* 13.356; Gaza: *Ant.* 13.362; Avi-Yonah, *The Holy Land*, pp. 74–6.

149 R.H.Smith, "Trade in the Life of Pella of the Decapolis," A. Hadidi, ed., *Studies in the History and Archaeology of Jordan*, vol. III, Amman, London, and New York, 1987, p. 55: "Although probably obliged to pay tribute to Hasmonean kings during the latter part of that period, Pella maintained a strongly Hellenistic, anti-Hasmonean stance."

150 The city was probably captured by Yannai about 100 BCE. See E. Stern, *Dor: Ruler of the Seas*, Jerusalem, 1994, pp. 203, 260, who notes that only during the Hasmonean period was there an apparent lack of development.

151 G. Fuks, "Tel Anafa: A Proposed Identification," *SCI* 5 (1979–80), p. 180.

152 Syncellus, *Chronographia* 559,3. Z. Safrai and M. Lin, "Geva in the Hasmonean Period," *Cathedra* 69 (1993) (Heb.), pp. 29–30, admit that there is no visible sign of destruction, but the ceramic evidence, as well as the level of maintenance of the aqueduct, indicate that the city was captured. The house of Abdagon was damaged, probably because he was a leading figure in the Hellenistic polis and a priest of a pagan cult.

153 Rappaport, "The Galilee between the Hasmonean Revolt and the Roman Conquest," pp. 28–9.

154 A. Segal and Y. Naor, "Four Seasons of Excavations at a Hellenistic Site in the Area of Kibbutz Sha'ar Ha-Amakim," D. H. French and C. S. Lightfoot, eds, *The Eastern Frontier of the Roman Empire*, BAR International Series 553 (ii), London, 1989, pp. 431, 433, 434.

155 J. Pecirka, "Homestead Farms in Classical and Hellenistic Hellas," M. I. Finley, ed., *Problèmes de la terre en Grèce*, Paris, 1973, pp. 115–17, 120–1.

156 D. W. Roller, "The Northern Plain of Sharon in the Hellenistic Period," *BASOR* 247 (1982), p. 48.

157 Y. Portugali, "The Settlement Pattern in the Western Jezreel Valley from the 6th Century BCE to the Arab Conquest," A. Kasher, A. Oppenheimer, U. Rappaport, eds, *Man and Land in Eretz-Israel in Antiquity*, Jerusalem, 1986 (Heb.), pp. 7–19.

158 See the commentary of Nitzan, *Pesher Habakkuk*, p. 178.

159 See Brownlee, *The Midrash Pesher of Habakkuk*, pp. 132–43, for an exhaustive discussion of the various candidates for Evil Priest, and the reasons for the criticism of their actions.

160 *BJ* 1.105; *Ant.* 13.394.

161 Y. Yadin, "Pesher Nahum Reconsidered," *IEJ* 21 (1971), pp. 1–12. Yadin's interpretation has been challenged; see J. M. Baumgarten, "Does *tlh* in the Temple Scroll Refer to Crucifixion?" *JBL* 91 (1972), pp. 472–81. Cf. J. D. Amusin, "The Reflection of Historical Events in the First Century BC in Qumran Commentaries (4Q161; 4Q169; 4Q166)," *HUCA* 48 (1977), p. 136.

162 E. Eshel, H. Eshel, and A. Yardeni, "A Qumran Composition Containing Part of Ps. 154 and a Prayer for the Welfare of King Jonathan and His Kingdom," *IEJ* 42 (1992), pp. 199–229.

163 Freyne, *Galilee from Alexander*, p. 63; S. Applebaum, "Hasmonean

Internal Colonization: Problems and Motives," A. Kasher, A. Oppenheimer, U. Rappaport, eds, *Man and Land in Eretz-Israel in Antiquity*, Jerusalem, 1986 (Heb.), p. 79. Cf. M. Goodman, *The Ruling Class of Judaea*, Cambridge, 1987, p. 38: "Late Hasmonean monarchs had no reason to grant great estates to their Jewish supporters, except when they required them as border troops for the expanded kingdom in Idumaea and Galilee, for most of the soldiers in the field armies on which the kings relied were probably non-Jewish mercenaries." This conclusion ignores the fact that most of the army was Jewish even in Yannai's blackest hour: see *BJ* 1.93; *Ant.* 14.377. See also Kasher, "The Changes in Manpower and Ethnic Composition of the Hasmonean Army," pp. 346–7, who notes that Yannai depended mainly on mercenaries for political reasons, but in *Jews and Hellenistic Cities*, p. 138, he makes the observation about the relative number of mercenaries to Jewish soldiers.

164 Gophna and Ayalon, "History of Settlement in the Tel Michal Region," p. 23; Roll and Ayalon, *Apollonia and Southern Sharon*, pp. 34, 128–9, 239.

165 R. Frankel and I. Finkelstein, "The Northwest Corner of Eretz-Israel in the Baraita Boundaries of Eretz-Israel," *Cathedra* 27 (1983) (Heb.), pp. 39–46.

166 R. Frankel and N. Gazov, "Tefen, a Hellenistic Stronghold in Galilee," E. Schiller, ed., *Zev Vilnay's Jubilee Volume*, part II, Jerusalem, 1987, (Heb.) pp. 163–5.

167 M. Aviam, "Large-Scale Production of Olive Oil in Galilee," *Cathedra* 73 (1994) (Heb.), pp. 32–4.

168 Schürer, *The History of the Jewish People*, vol. I, p. 222.

169 M. Stern, "Trachides: Surname of Alexander Yannai in Josephus and Syncellus," *Tarbiz* XXIV (1956) (Heb.), pp. 9–15.

170 G. Alon, "The Attitude of the Pharisees to Roman Rule and the House of Herod," *Jews, Judaism and the Classical World*, trans. I. Abrahams, Jerusalem, 1977, p. 24.

171 Levine, "The Political Struggle between Pharisees and Sadducees."

172 *CHJ*, vol. II, p. 338. For a survey of the problem see D. R. Schwartz, "On Pharisaic Opposition to the Hasmonean Monarchy," *Studies in the Jewish Background of Christianity*, Tübingen, 1992, pp. 44–56. See also M. Hengel, J. H. Charlesworth, and D. Mendels, "The Polemical Character of 'On Kingship' in the Temple Scroll: An Attempt at Dating 11Q Temple," *JJS* 37 (1986), pp. 31, 37.

173 Zeitlin, *The Rise and Fall of the Judaean State*, vol. I, p. 321.

174 Schalit, *König Herodes*, pp. 171–2, esp. n. 92, 259–60; idem, *The Hellenistic Age*, pp. 280–2; Applebaum, "Hasmonean Internal Colonization," pp. 78–9; idem, "The Hasmoneans: Logistics"; idem., "Judaea as a Roman Province: The Countryside as a Political and Economic Factor," *ANRW*, vol. II.8, Berlin, 1977, pp. 358–9. Lurie, *Mi-Yannai Ad Hordos*, p. 40, suggested that the conversion of farmers into tenants began with Hyrcanus I who allegedly cancelled the "avowal" because it was valid only for direct owners of land, and not tenants.

175 *Ant.*14.41; Diod. *Hist.* 40, 2 = *GLAJJ* I, pp. 185–7; Schalit, *König Herodes*, p. 172 n. 92.

176 Alon, "The Attitude of the Pharisees," p. 29.
177 Applebaum, "Hasmonean Internal Colonization," p. 78; idem, "The Hasmoneans: Logistics," pp. 18, 24, 28; idem, "Judaea as a Roman Province," pp. 359, 386.
178 Lurie, *Mi-Yannai Ad Hordos*, pp. 53–4; idem, "*Har ha-Melekh.. Ma-Hu?*" *The Hasmonean Kings*, Tel-Aviv, 1985 (Heb.), pp. 169–76.
179 Bar-Kochva, "Manpower, Economics," p. 175.
180 Avi-Yonah, *The Holy Land*, p. 95. Jerusalem was the central toparchy of Judea called Orine. Dalman came to this conclusion even earlier; see Klein, *Eretz-Yehuda*, p. 240.
181 Goodman, *Ruling Class*, p. 37 n. 13.
182 Klein, "Βεμσελις – Βαιθομμις, Βαιθομμη," *Tarbiz* I (1930) (Heb.), pp. 137–44; idem, *Eretz-Yehuda*, pp. 41–2, 239–47.
183 G. Alon, *The Jews in Their Land in the Talmudic Age*, Vol, II Jerusalem, 1980–4, p. 741. Z. Safrai, *The Economy of Roman Palestine*, London and New York, 1994, p. 325; idem, *Gevulot ve-Shilton be-Eretz Yisra'el bi-Tekufat ha-Mishna ve-ha-Talmud*, Tel-Aviv, 1980 (Heb.), pp. 156–7, gives a very good summary of the main points as to the geographical location, but very little, if anything at all, on the actual meaning of the word or its significance. He rejects the theory of Luria that northwestern Samaria was *Har ha-Melekh*. See also J. Schwartz, *Jewish Settlement in Judaea*, Jerusalem, 1986 (Heb.), pp. 40 n. 44; 193 n. 6: the meaning of *Har ha-Melekh* has changed, and it may refer to different areas at different times. R. Yankelevitch, "*Herodium: Har ha-Melekh*," *Cathedra* 20 (1981) (Heb.), pp. 23–8, thinks Herodion is *Har ha-Melekh*.
184 J. Efron, "Simon ben Shetah and Alexander Jannaeus," *Studies on the Hasmonean Period*, Leiden, 1987, pp. 203–5; idem, "Bar-Kokhva in the Light of the Palestinian and Babylonian Talmudic Traditions," *Studies on the Hasmonean Period*, pp. 84–5; and see Kasher, *Jews and Hellenistic Cities*, p. 168.
185 Schürer, *The History of the Jewish People*, vol. I, pp. 229–32; and see J. Sievers, "The Role of Women in the Hasmonean Dynasty," L. H. Feldman and G. Hata, eds, *Josephus, the Bible and History*, Detroit, 1989, pp. 135–40.
186 BT Taan 23a; Siphra be-Hukkotai I,1.
187 *Ant.* 13.410–17; *BJ* 1.113–14.
188 Except Hyrcania, Alexandreion, Machaerus, *Ant.* 13.417.
189 *Ant.* 14.19–34. For references to the talmudic versions of the story, which do not refer to a food crisis, but rather to an earthquake, see Schürer, *The History of the Jewish People*, vol. I, p. 236. Marcus, *Josephus* VII (LCL), p. 462 note b, refers the reader to Graetz, who tied the talmudic story of an earthquake to the earthquake recorded in 64 BCE which destroyed cities in Asia Minor. The events mentioned happened too far north to be relevant to Judea, unless one claims the whole Middle East was rocked. The timing is also wrong: the quake struck after Pompey was in Syria (64 BCE at the earliest), but the siege of Jerusalem by Hyrcanus was in 65 BCE. The earthquake version of events is problematic. Earthquakes may cause social dislocations leading to economic consequences, but not necessarily. If there was a quake, Josephus' silence on the subject is strange (cf. *Ant.* 15.121–3).

190 Horgan, *Pesharim*, p. 139.

191 The similarity in phrasing of 4QpHos[a] 2:12–17, 1QpHab 2:1–15, 4QpIsa[b] 2:1, 4QpPs[a] 2:1, 20, was pointed out by Horgan, *Pesharim*, p. 140.

192 Psalms of Solomon 17:18–19; see D. Flusser, "Qumran and the Famine During the Reign of Herod," *IMJ* 6 (1987), pp. 9, 15 n. 25. However, the Psalm speaks of drought, not of wind. Flusser does not notice the distinction. The drought cannot be the drought of Onia's day because supposedly his righteousness ended the drought, while the Psalmist here emphasizes that the drought took its course since there were no righteous people. Unless perhaps the Josephean and Mishnaic stories are in a Pharisee tradition but the Psalms of Solomon are in another tradition, perhaps Essene.

193 Horgan, *Pesharim*, pp. 11, 87, 138.

194 "Josephus stresses the anger of god [sic] as a cause of famine when addressing Jews, and refers to natural causes when writing for gentiles (cf. Jos. *Ant.* 15.299ff; *BJ* 1.377)," K. S. Gapp, *Famine in the Roman World: From the Founding of Rome to the Time of Trajan*, Ph.D. Dissertation, Princeton Univ., 1934, p. 182 n. 75.

195 I. Rosensohn, "*Eymatay Shibolim Omrot Shira be-Nisan*," *Teva ve-Aretz* XXXI (1989) (Heb.), pp. 38–40.

196 Ezek. 19:12; Ps. 11:6;148:8; Job 1:19; Ben-Sira 38:28–9.

197 D. Baly, *The Geography of the Bible*, New York, 1957, p. 66; D. Nir, "Whirlwinds in Israel in the Winters 1954/5 and 1955/6," *IEJ* 7 (1957), pp. 109–17.

198 E. C. Dos Santos, *An Expanded Hebrew Index for the Hatch–Redpath Concordance to the Septuaginta*, Jerusalem, n.d., s.v. סופה.

199 Dos Santos, *Hebrew Index*, indicates that there is one such occurrence, in Ben-Sira 48:12.

200 Baly, *Geography*, p. 65; Schürer, *The History of the Jewish People*, vol. I, p. 236 n. 7.

201 A. Ben-David, *Jerusalem und Tyros*, Tübingen, 1969, pp. 5–9; idem., "Jewish and Roman Bronze and Copper Coins: Their Reciprocal Relations in Mishnah and Talmud from Herod the Great to Trajan and Hadrian," *PEQ* 103 (1971), p. 120; Schürer, *The History of the Jewish People*, vol. II, pp. 62–3 and nn. 193–5, pp. 266, 272.

202 Jeremias, *Jerusalem in the Time of Jesus*, p. 123.

203 Ibid. pp. 122–3, obtains the "normal price" from M.Peah 8:7, and confirms it by comparison to Mark 6:37,44, and Cicero, *2 Verrem* III 81, no. 188–9. D. E. Oakman accepts his reckoning: *Jesus and the Economic Questions of His Day*, Lewiston, New York, 1986, p. 60. Heichelheim at first glance appears to differentiate between his various sources: *ESAR*, IV, pp. 181–8, but a careful reading of the text shows that he too uses late sources to learn about early situations: "It is recorded that Hillel had to satisfy his own needs and those of his family with half a victoriatus a day" (p. 180). Here he bases his estimate of the income of a first century BCE figure on information gleaned from the Babylonian Talmud, circa 500 CE. See also Freyne, *Galilee*, p. 182.

204 J. T. Milik, "Le Couvercle de Bethpage," *Hommages à André Dupont-Sommer*, Paris, 1971, pp. 92–4.

205 There is one unusual entry of three tetradrachmas of which Milik is unsure; see ibid. pp. 80, 93.
206 Both D. Sperber, *Costs of Living in Roman Palestine*, Leiden, 1965, p. 251 and Heichelheim, "Roman Syria," *ESAR*, vol. IV, p. 183, listed Josephus' evidence with question marks. On effects of famine on working men see Sen, *Poverty and Famines: An Essay on Entitlement and Deprivation*, Oxford, 1981 pp. 96–100.
207 There are about 24,800 calories in the bread yielded by one modius (derived from computations we made on the basis of data given in *ERE*, p. 147 n. 2). A man needs 2,852–3,822 calories a day (L. Foxhall and H. A. Forbes, "Sitometreia: The Role of Grain as a Staple Food in Classical Antiquity," *Chiron* 12 (1982), p. 48). Clark and Haswell, *The Economics of Subsistence Agriculture*, p. 17 table V, give substantially lower estimates of the daily needs of agricultural workers, i.e. 1,625–2,012 calories per day. Therefore, taking 1,625 as a minimum, a man could manage on 48,750 calories a month, about two modii. Hence, all those earning about 5 *obols* daily would be able to manage the purchase of grain. The others would have to resort to charity, eat famine foods, or starve.
208 Applebaum, "Judaea as a Roman Province," p. 370; M. Goodman, "The First Jewish Revolt: Social Conflict and the Problem of Debt," *JJS* 33 (1982), pp. 417–27; D. E. Oakman, "Jesus and Agrarian Palestine: The Factor of Debt," H. Richards, ed., *SBL Seminar Papers*, Atlanta, 1985, pp. 57–73; D. A. Fiensy, *The Social History of Palestine in the Herodian Period: The Land Is Mine, Studies in the Bible and Early Christianity* 20, Lewiston, Queenston, and Lampeter, 1991, p. 78; H. Moxnes, *The Economy of the Kingdom*, Philadelphia, 1988, p. 73.
209 Unfortunately, the only documentation we have for the amounts paid by tenant farmers and lessors is from the beginning of the first century CE, i.e. the Babatha archive and the Bar Kokhba documents.

6 THE EARLY ROMAN PERIOD

1 *BJ* 1.155; *Ant.* 14.73–7; Strabo 16.2.46.
2 E. Schürer, *The History of the Jewish People in the Age of Jesus Christ*, vol. I, rev. and ed. G. Vermes and F. Millar, Edinburgh, 1973–87, p. 240, ignores the question but implies that Judea became a client state. E. M. Smallwood, *The Jews Under Roman Rule: From Pompey to Diocletian*, Leiden, 1981, p. 2 ("client-kingdom"); L. L. Grabbe, *Judaism from Cyrus to Hadrian*, vol. II, Minneapolis, 1992, p. 321 ("separate identity and its own rule"). I. L. Levine, *The Roman Period from the Conquest to the Ben Kozba War (63 BCE–135 CE)*, M. Stern, ed., *The History of Eretz Israel*, vol. 4: *The Roman Byzantine Period*, Jerusalem, 1984 (Heb.), ignores the issue. A. Schalit, "The Fall of the Hasmonean Dynasty," M. Avi-Yonah and Z. Baras, eds, *The Herodian Period: World History of the Jewish People*, vol. 7, Jerusalem, 1975, p. 36: although fitting the description of a *civitas stipendiaria* ("tributary town") for all intents and purposes it was practically a province. E. R. Bevan, in S. A. Cook, F. E. Adcock, and M. P.

Charlesworth, eds, *The Cambridge Ancient History (CAH)*, vol. IX: *The Roman Republic*, Cambridge, 1951, p. 403: "under control of the Roman pro-consul of Syria." A. N. Sherwin-White, *Roman Foreign Policy in the East: 168 BC to 1 AD*, London, 1984, p. 218: autonomous, under the supervision of the governor of Syria. The imprecise nature of Judea's status confused ancient authors as well; see Ammianus Marcellinus, *Res Gestae* 14.8.12.

3 Sherwin-White, *Roman Foreign Policy in the East*, p. 218. Cf. L. Goldschmid, "Impôts et droits de douane en Judée," *REJ* 34 (1897), p. 192, who claims that Pompey considered Judea subjugated, as demonstrated by its inclusion in his triumph.

4 M. S. Ginsburg thought that the tribute indicated that Judea had been converted into *ager publicus*; quoted in H. G. Kippenberg, *Religion und Klassenbildung im antiken Judäa*, Göttingen, 1982, p. 112 n. 33.

5 Cicero, *De Leg. Agr.* I,6; cf. *in Verrem* II, 21, 37, quoted in W. T. Arnold, *Roman Provincial Administration*, rev. by E. S. Bouchier, Oxford, 1914, reprinted Chicago, 1974, p. 20. See also G. H. Stevenson, *Roman Provincial Administration*, New York, 1939, reprinted Westport, Conn., 1975, pp. 137–9, who rejects the idea that the Roman government at this time "made any claim to be the legal owner of provincial soil" and in our case Judea was not even a province.

6 Sherwin-White, *Roman Foreign Policy in the East*, p. 232.

7 τῇ τε χώρᾳ καὶ τοῖς Ἱεροσολύμοις ἐπιτάσσει φόρον ("The country and Jerusalem were laid under tribute.") *BJ* 1.154; see also *Ant.* 14.74; Cicero, *Pro Flacco* 28.69: "illa gens (Judaeorum) . . . quam cara dis immortalibus esset docuit, quod est victa, quod elocata, quod serva facta" ("That nation . . . how dear it was to the immortal gods is shown by the fact that it has been conquered, let out for taxes, made a slave"). Cf. Cassius Dio, *Historia Romana* 39:6.

8 Goldschmid, "Impôts et droits de douane en Judée," p. 192, assumes that there were various taxes, the imposition of which demonstrates that Rome looked upon Judea as a possession.

9 On publicani see M. Rostovtzeff, *The Social and Economic History of the Hellenistic World (SEHHW)*, vol. II, Oxford, 1953, pp. 965–76; A. H. M. Jones, "Taxation in Antiquity," P. A. Brunt, ed., *The Roman Economy*, Oxford, 1974, p. 163; E. Badian, *Publicans and Sinners*, Oxford, 1972. Kippenberg, *Religion und Klassenbildung*, pp. 112–13, maintains that the publicani, based in Sidon, collected the tribute.

10 See Plutarch, *Lucullus* 20.1–5, on the destructive actions of the publicani in Asia. Their tax burden was unusually heavy because of the fine imposed by Sulla on Asia. While the situation may be particular, it nevertheless demonstrates how ruinous the publicani could be.

11 Cicero, *De Prov. Cons.* 5.10.

12 A. H. M. Jones, *The Greek City*, Oxford, 1940, reprinted New York, 1984, pp. 125–6, postulates that the tax farmers levied taxes from client kingdoms and public land, while cities paid a block sum without the services of the tax farmers. This interpretation of the situation does not materially change our understanding of the conditions because Judea would have been in the former category, with only Jaffa in the latter.

13 *SEHHW*, vol. II, p. 982.
14 *Kleine Pauly* 5. 1150; *OCD*, s.v. *Vectigal*.
15 *SEHHW*, vol. II, p. 1,000. See also *OCD*, s.v. *Stipendium*, which states that the stipendium was a direct tax on a province equal to the tributum.
16 *SEHHW*, vol. III, n. 103: the reference to I Macc. 11:34; 10:30, which do not use the word *phoros*, refers to the taxes on land and other fruits which were paid to the crown.
17 *SEHHW*, vol. II, p. 967; III, p. 1,573 n. 73; Jones, "Taxation in Antiquity," p. 163 nn. 71, 180.
18 *SEHHW*, vol. II, p. 1,000.
19 A. Schalit, *Roman Administration in Palestine, Library of Palestinology of the Jewish Palestine Exploration Society*, vols V/VI, Jerusalem, 1937 (Heb.), p. 35.
20 Pompey's actions may be compared to those of his predecessor and rival Lucullus, who re-established the city of Amisus, settled Greeks in it, and added to its *chora*. See Plutarch, *Lucullus* 19. Furthermore, Pompey himself established cities in Bithynia in areas formerly under Mithridates' control. See J. Leach, *Pompey the Great*, London, 1978, pp. 98–9.
21 See S. Freyne, *Galilee from Alexander the Great to Hadrian*, Notre Dame, 1980, p. 63; S. Applebaum, "The Struggle for the Soil and the Revolt of 66–73 CE," *Eretz-Israel* 12 (1975) (Heb.), p. 125. A. Schalit, *König Herodes: Der Mann und Sein Werk*, Berlin, 1969, p. 326, suggests that the turmoil in Judea between 63 BCE till 37 BCE was partly the result of the dislodgement of Jewish farmers by Pompey. M. Hengel, *The Zealots*, Edinburgh, 1989, p. 315, suggests that Hezekias was a man of "rank and influence" who was one of the settlers of the Galilee from the days of Yannai.
22 Strabo, *Geo.* 16.2.28, and see M. Stern's comments, *GLAJJ*, vol. I, p. 292 and Marcus' notes to *Ant.* 14.334 in *Josephus*, vol. VII (LCL), pp. 626–7.
23 I. Shatzman, *The Armies of the Hasmoneans and Herod*, Tübingen, 1991, p. 131, surmises that Hyrcanus could only maintain a force a "fraction" of what once was the Hasmonean army.
24 T. Frank, "Dominium in Solo Provinciali" and "Ager Publicus," *JRS* 17 (1927), p. 152, claims that land called by the Romans *agri regii* was not *chora basilike*, but rather only the personal estates of the kings. Hence, as part of the punishment meted out to Aristobolus, some of the royal land was expropriated. Unfortunately for Hyrcanus, they were also his lands.
25 Frank, "Dominium in Solo Provinciali" and "Ager Publicus," p. 144.
26 Schalit, *König Herodes*, pp. 48–51.
27 Schalit proposed that the publicani received their golden opportunity only when Gabinius created his scheme of five sanhedria; see Schalit, *Roman Administration in Palestine*, p. 35. His suggestion seems illogical because he ignored the fact that Gabinius was known for his policies against the publicani. We would subscribe to the idea that Pompey's conquest gave the publicani their chance because of his ties to them. See Badian, *Publicans and Sinners*, pp. 99, 109. However, this view is contradicted by A. N. Sherwin-White, *Roman Foreign Policy in the East*, pp. 216, 232–3, who maintains that the Pompeian settlement eliminated the power of the publicani in the new areas.

28 *BJ* 1.160; *Ant.* 14.87–8. Smallwood, *The Jews Under Roman Rule*, p. 31. Schalit, *König Herodes*, p. 31 n. 80a, argues that Gabinius provoked Alexander's uprising by embarking upon the renewal of the poleis. Shatzman points out that Gabinius was not physically rebuilding the cities, but rather restoring Hellenistic populations to their cities. In this connection one should note *BJ* 1.106, that settlers gladly went to each city.

29 *BJ* 1.91; *Ant.* 14.169–70.

30 A. Schalit, "The Fall of the Hasmonean Dynasty," p. 41, thought it was based on the model of Roman administration in Macedonia. If so, one should note that the Macedonian kingdom was dismembered and divided into four autonomous districts that paid tribute to Rome, but were not subject to military occupation or the supervision of a Roman governor. On this see A. N. Sherwin-White, *Roman Foreign Policy in the East*, pp. 30, 274–5. B. Kanael, "The Partition of Judea by Gabinius," *IEJ* 7 (1957), pp. 101–2, thought the partition was intended to compensate for Hyrcanus' weak leadership; see also E. Bammel, "The Organization of Palestine by Gabinius," *JJS* 12 (1961), pp. 159–62; D. C. Braund, "Gabinius, Caesar, and the publicani of Judaea," *Klio* 65 (1983), pp. 241–4; E. M. Smallwood, "Gabinius' Organization of Palestine," *JJS* 18 (1967), pp. 89–92; Shatzman, *The Armies*, p. 137 n. 24.

31 *SEHHW*, vol. II, pp. 982–3; S. J. De Laet, *Portorium*, Bruges, 1949, reprinted New York, 1975, p. 87; *GLAJJ*, vol. I, p. 204.

32 Cicero, *De Prov. Cons.* 5.10.

33 Smallwood, *The Jews Under Roman Rule*, pp. 32–3.

34 A similar suggestion was put forth by Kippenberg, *Religion und Klassenbildung*, pp. 114–15.

35 Smallwood, *The Jews Under Roman Rule*, pp. 32–3, also notes that Gabinius probably personally profited from the arrangement. This, however, is of no interest to us here.

36 Braund, "Gabinius, Caesar, and the publicani of Judaea," p. 243.

37 *GLAJJ*, vol. I, p. 204; note that in connection with Gabinius' victories there is no mention of the mass crucifixions or slave-markets characteristic of later Roman governors. See *BJ* 1.163,173; *Ant.* 14.85, 96–7.

38 See p. 495 n. g in *Josephus* vol.VII (LCL). Kippenberg, *Religion und Klassenbildung*, p. 113 n. 43, rejects this, but does not explain.

39 *BJ* 1.172: it is possible to see this merely as a military rank, i.e. deputy commander. However, Peitholaus was apparently more than just a military man, otherwise Antipater would not have sought his death later on; see *BJ* 1.180; *Ant.* 14.120; Schalit, *König Herodes*, p. 35 n. 103; Kanael, "The Partition of Judea," p. 103.

40 The text variants indicate that the word could be "most."

41 *BJ* 1.172; *Ant.* 14.93–4; possession of arms and armor was always associated with financial well-being. The social–economic division in Greece and in the Roman republic till Marius' reforms demonstrate this clearly.

42 *BJ* 1.178 and *Ant.* 14.103 state that Gabinius arranged affairs in Jerusalem in accordance with Antipater's wishes. However, as Shatzman pointed out, Antipater is called ἐπιμελητής (supervisor) even before Julius Caesar rewarded him; see Shatzman, *The Armies*, p. 138 and n. 26.

43 Bammel, "The Organization of Palestine by Gabinius," pp. 161–2; Schalit, *König Herodes*, pp. 36, 750–3.

44 *BJ* 1.179; *Ant.* 14.105–9.

45 Seleucus IV: II Macc. 3:6, 13; Menelaus: II Macc. 4:32, 39; Antiochus Epiphanes: II Macc. 5:16, 21; Strabo, apud Josephus: *CA* 2.83–4; Sabinus: *BJ* 2.50; Pilatus: *BJ* 2.175; Florus: *BJ* 2.293.

46 *BJ* 1.179; *Ant.*14.105–9. He further claims that 8,000 talents worth of gold ornaments were also looted. Smallwood, *The Jews Under Roman Rule*, p. 36 n. 51, claims that the amounts "belong to the realm of legend." E. P. Sanders, *Judaism: Practice and Belief 63 BCE – 66 CE*, London and Philadelphia, 1992, p. 84, agrees with her. He points out the disproportion between the sum of 2,000 talents and the annual revenue of Herod's heirs, i.e. 960 talents. However, as Sanders himself notes, there is evidence that the "temple tax provided a great deal of money." Cicero, *Pro Flacco* 28.66–9 (*GLAJJ*, vol. I, pp. 196–201), relates that the Romans confiscated some of the Temple tax in gold from Asia Minor: Apamea 100 pounds, Laodicea 20 pounds, Adramyttium 100 pounds, Pergamum a small amount. Strabo, apud: Josephus, *Ant.* 14.111–13, relates that 800 talents of the Jews were seized by Mithridates in 88 BCE. Although M. Stern suggests that not all of this could have been Temple tax, it does indicate large amounts of gold intended for the Temple. If we consider that the places mentioned are only a small part of the total diaspora, and that until Crassus money had been accumulating in the Temple, we can assume that the figure of 2,000 talents is not all that legendary.

47 Add to the documents on taxes and gifts to the Temple: *BJ* 5.417; *Philo de spec.leg* 1.76–8; see also E. Gabba, "The Finances of King Herod," A. Kasher, U. Rappaport, G. Fuks, eds, *Greece and Rome in Eretz-Israel*, Jerusalem, 1990, p. 167; M. Broshi, "The Cardinal Elements of the Economy of Palestine during the Herodian Period," N. Gross, ed., *Jews in Economic Life*, Jerusalem, 1985 (Heb.), pp. 31–2.

48 M. Shek, 4:2. Gabba, "Finances of King Herod," p. 168, claims that the High Priest Simon the Righteous used the Temple funds for reconstruction after the Fifth Syrian War. However his evidence, Ben-Sira, does not say specifically where the money came from. We cannot rule out the testimony of *Ant.* 12.138–42 that Antiochus III paid for the restoration.

49 Broshi, "The Cardinal Elements of the Economy of Palestine during the Herodian Period," p. 33.

50 On this aspect and others see Y. Tsafrir, "The Desert Fortresses of Judaea in the Second Temple Period," *The Jerusalem Cathedra* 2 (1982), pp. 120–45.

51 Shatzman, *The Armies*, p. 135.

52 *Ant.* 14.143–4,190–216. These documents are discussed from various aspects in A. Büchler, "The Priestly Dues and the Roman Taxes in the Edicts of Caesar," *Studies in Jewish History*, New York, 1956, pp. 1–23; A. Momigliano, *Ricerche Sull'Organizzazione Della Giudea Sotto Il Domino Romano (63 a.C.–70 d.C.)*, Annali della R. Scuola Normale Superiore di Pisa, series II, vol. III (1934, XII); reprinted Amsterdam, 1967, pp. 21–3; A. H. M. Jones, "Review of Arnaldo Momigliano," in

JRS 25 (1935), pp. 228–9; Smallwood, *The Jews Under Roman Rule*, pp. 40–1; Schürer, *The History of the Jewish People*, vol. I, pp. 272–5; Schalit, *König Herodes*, pp. 753–9.

53 *Ant.* 14.195, 204, 205. Examples of such actions are the activities of Crassus and Cassius. For the former see *Ant.* 14.105–9; *BJ* 1.179; for the latter see *Ant.* 14.272; *BJ* 1.220.

54 The text reporting on this particular benefit is difficult to understand. *Ant.* 14.202, 205–6 can be read so that the inhabitants of Jerusalem pay a tax for the city of Jaffa; or that the inhabitants of Jaffa pay a tax to the city of Jerusalem. See Marcus' translation, *Josephus*, vol. VII, pp. 555, 557, but see the Latin on p. 555 n. g. F. M. Heichelheim, "Roman Syria," *ESAR*, vol. IV, p. 232; Schalit, *König Herodes*, pp. 777–81.

55 See Manuscript "V."

56 Schalit, *König Herodes*, pp. 779–80.

57 Ibid. and Marcus' translation, *Josephus*, vol. VII, p. 556.

58 Marcus rejected this because the Greek would have needed emendation. Schalit, *König Herodes*, p. 780, pointed out that Heichelheim's version does not lack validity. Schalit's translation into Hebrew is nevertheless significantly different from Heichelheim's. See Schalit, *Flavii Josephi, Antiquitates Judaicae*, Libri XI–XX, p. 136. Furthermore, he mistranslated the amount to 20,665, although in *König Herodes*, pp. 149, 780, he got it right.

59 Smallwood, *The Jews Under Roman Rule*, p. 41 n. 62.

60 Ibid. Smallwood lists the varied and ingenious ways it is possible to interpret the rate of the tribute. We consider that the general evidence for a *tributum soli* of 12.5 percent is preponderant. For the determination of 12.5 percent see A. Mittwoch, "Tribute and Land-Tax in Seleucid Judaea," *Biblica* 36 (1955), p. 354 n. 3; Büchler, "The Priestly Dues and the Roman Taxes in the Edicts of Caesar," p. 17, agreeing with Graetz, refers to one-fourth every second year, i.e. 12.5 percent annually. So also for Judaea; however, R. Duncan-Jones, *Structure and Scale in the Roman Economy*, Cambridge, 1990, p. 189, includes the Sabbatical Year exemption in his calculations, thus arriving at 10.7 percent annually. While arithmetically correct this is misleading as Caesar exempted the Sabbatical Year because there was no crop to tax. Actually, the tax remains 25 percent per biennium. Jones, "Review of Arnaldo Momigliano," p. 229, proposed 5 percent annually, but we cannot understand how he justifies that conclusion.

61 The text refers to the Great Plain, but Marcus, *Josephus*, vol. VII, p. 558 n. a, based on *Ant.* 12.348, demonstrated that the intention is the Esdraelon Valley, now more frequently referred to as the Jezreel Valley.

62 De Laet, *Portorium*, pp. 87–8.

63 *Ant.* 13.261; B. Z. Rosenfeld, "The 'Boundary of Gezer': Inscriptions and the History of Gezer at the End of the Second Temple Period," *IEJ* 38 (1988), pp. 243–5.

64 J. Schwartz, "Once More on the 'Boundary of Gezer' Inscriptions and the History of Gezer and Lydda at the End of the Second Temple Period," *IEJ* 40 (1990), pp. 54–5.

65 Ibid. p. 55.

66 Büchler, "The Priestly Dues and the Roman Taxes in the Edicts of Caesar," pp. 4–6.

67 Bar-Kochva, "Manpower, Economics, and Internal Strife in the Hasmonean State," *Armées et fiscalité dans le monde antique* (Colloque National du CNRS no. 936, Organisé par H. Van Effentere), Paris, 1977, pp. 185–7.

68 *Ant.* 14.163 (Marcus' trans. in LCL).

69 Shatzman, *The Armies*, p. 142.

70 On the position of ἐπιμελητής see *Ant.* 14.128 and Marcus' note d, p. 514. Also Schalit, *König Herodes*, pp. 750–3; Bammel, "The Organization of Palestine by Gabinius"; Smallwood, *The Jews Under Roman Rule*, p. 36 n. 49. On ἐπίτροπος (procurator) see *BJ* 1.199; *Ant.* 14.143; Smallwood, *The Jews Under Roman Rule*, p. 39 n. 60.

71 *BJ* 1.220–2; *Ant.* 14.272–6.

72 Hyrcanus' income from his estates, and whatever was due him as Ethnarch, must have been considerable if he could pay a sum equal to the tribute of the Galilee.

73 Schalit, *König Herodes*, pp. 49–50 nn. 174–5. Cf. Shatzman, *The Armies*, p. 144, who suggests that Malichus was responsible for Idumea.

74 *Ant.* 17.318–20; Herod's finances will be discussed in greater detail further on in this work.

75 Marcus, *Josephus*, p. 611 n. c, refers to *Ant.* 14.297f., which relates that Marion of Tyre conquered three fortresses in the Galilee and that Antigonus led an offensive into the Galilee at that time.

76 *Ant.*14. 309.

77 U. Rappaport, "The Land Issue as a Factor in Inter-Ethnic Relations in Eretz-Israel During the Second Temple Period," A. Kasher, A. Oppenheimer, U. Rappaport, eds, *Man and Land in Eretz-Israel in Antiquity*, Jerusalem, 1986, pp. 83–4.

7 THE HERODIAN PERIOD

1 See A. Schalit, *König Herodes: Der Mann und Sein Werk*, Berlin, 1969; E. Schürer, *The History of the Jewish People in the Age of Jesus Christ*, vol. I, rev. and ed. G. Vermes and F. Millar, Edinburgh, 1973, pp. 287–329.

2 S. Applebaum, "Judaea as a Roman Province: The Countryside as a Political and Economic Factor," *ANRW*, vol. II.8, Berlin, 1977, p. 378; idem, "Josephus and the Economic Causes of the Jewish War," L. H. Feldman and G. Hata, eds, *Josephus, the Bible and History*, Detroit, 1989, pp. 241–2; G. W. Edwards, "The Maladjustment of Palestinian Economy Under Herod," *Journal of Bible and Religion* 17 (1949), pp. 116–19; A. H. M. Jones, "Review of Arnaldo Momigliano, *Ricerche Sull'Organizzazione Della Guidea Sotto Il Domino Romano (63 a.C.–70 d.C.), Annali della R. Scuola Normale Superiore di Pisa*, series II, vol. III (1934: XII)," *JRS* 25 (1935), p. 230; S. Zeitlin, *The Rise and Fall of the Judaean State*, vol. II, Philadelphia, 1969, p. 97; G. Theissen, *The First Followers of Jesus*, London, 1978, pp. 35, 41; J. Klausner, *Ha-Historia Shel ha-Bayit ha-Sheni*, vol. 4, Jerusalem, 1958 (Heb.), pp. 101–10; I. Ben-Shalom, *The*

School of Shamai and the Zealot's Struggle against Rome, Jerusalem, 1993 (Heb.), pp. 54–5.

3 This version of events is particularly proposed by D. A. Fiensy, *The Social History of Palestine in the Herodian Period: The Land is Mine, Studies in the Bible and Early Christianity* 20, Lewiston, Queenston, Lampeter, 1991, esp. pp. 77–90. His suggestion is that "Probably the best explanation for the loss of peasant plots is the entrepreneurial investment in land by the aristocracy in Judea and Galilee." Much can be said in favor of that argument during the procuratorial period, but for the reign of Herod we have not been able to find a single source to substantiate his theory.

4 E. Gabba, "The Finances of King Herod," A. Kasher, U. Rappaport, G. Fuks, eds, *Greece and Rome in Eretz-Israel*, Jerusalem, 1990, pp. 162–3, 166; Fiensy, *The Social History of Palestine*, pp. 21–3; an ambivalent view is expressed by M. Broshi, "The Role of the Temple in the Herodian Economy," *JJS* 38 (1987), p. 31, who on the one hand states that the country "experienced unprecedented prosperity and that considerable surpluses were available," and on the other hand asserts: "There is no doubt that he oppressed his subjects and extracted heavy taxes."

5 Gabba, "The Finances of King Herod"; L. L. Grabbe, *Judaism from Cyrus to Hadrian*, vol. I, Minneapolis, 1992, p. 19; Schalit, *König Herodes*, pp. 645–75.

6 Most of our knowledge of Herod and his kingdom comes from Nicolaus of Damascus via Josephus; see M. Stern, "Nicolaus of Damascus as a Source of Jewish History in the Herodian and Hasmonean Age," B. Uffenheimer, ed., *Bible and Jewish History: Studies in Bible and Jewish History Dedicated to the Memory of Jacob Liver*, Tel-Aviv, 1971 (Heb.), pp. 374–94.

7 Schalit suggested that the family owned land in Maresha, and that is the reason the Parthians sacked the city in 40 BCE. See Schalit, *König Herodes*, pp. 257–8 n. 382.

8 *Ant.* 16.291; Schalit, *König Herodes*, p. 258, asserts that the land was in Nabatea and came to Herod by way of his mother; S. Applebaum, "Economic Life in Palestine," S. Safrai and M. Stern, eds, *The Jewish People in the First Century*, Philadelphia, 1976, p. 657 with n. 15, thinks the grazing land was in Idumea, although this seems less likely. We feel that there is no evidence supporting the contention that these grazing areas were personal land; they could just as well have been royal land.

9 See A. Gulak, *Yesodei ha-Mishpat ha-Ivri*, vol. 3, Berlin, 1922, reprinted Tel-Aviv, 1967 (Heb.), pp. 86–8.

10 The word πρόσοδος can indicate tax revenues, or rent revenues; Liddell and Scott, s.v. πρόσοδος, ii.

11 Ein Gedi is held by most authors to be a royal estate since Hasmonean times; N. Lewis, *The Documents from the Bar Kochba Period in the Cave of Letters*, vol. 2, *Greek Papyri*, Jerusalem, 1989, p. 42; Phasaelis: *Ant.* 16.145; *BJ* 1.418; 2.167. Ein Boqeq: M. Fisher, "*Naveh ha-Midbar Ein Boqeq: Yihidah Ta'asiyatit be-tekufat Beit Hordos: Skirah Arkhiologit-Historit*," *Nofim* 11–12 (1979) (Heb.), pp. 21–38; M. Gichon, "En Boqeq," *NEAEHL*, vol. 2, pp. 395, 396.

12 *BJ* 1.396; *Ant.* 15.217. On the problem of how Jaffa and Samaria could

be included in this list see I. Shatzman, *The Armies of the Hasmoneans and Herod*, Tübingen, 1991, p. 169 n.177.

13 D. Barag, "King Herod's Royal Castle at Samaria-Sebaste," *PEQ* 125 (1993), pp. 3–18.

14 E. Netzer, "Tulul Abu el 'Alayiq," *NEAEHL*, vol. 2, pp. 682–91.

15 Horace, *Epistulae* II, 2, 184 = *GLAJJ*, vol. I, p. 326.

16 *Ant.* 15.296; *BJ* 1.403; G. M. Cohen, *The Seleucid Colonies*, Wiesbaden, 1978, p. 21; Shatzman, *The Armies*, p. 169. Applebaum, "Economic Life," p. 658, questions whether the land belonged to Herod, or whether he simply used his royal authority to "do as he liked."

17 Antipatris, *Ant.* 16.142–3; see S. Applebaum, "The Question of Josephus' Historical Reliability in the Two Test Cases: Antipatris of Kefar-Saba and Antipatris of Caesarea," U. Rappaport, ed., *Josephus Flavius: Historian of Eretz-Israel in the Hellenistic–Roman Period*, Jerusalem, 1982 (Heb.), pp. 13–19. On Gaba: *Ant.* 15.294; *BJ* 3.36; see G. M. Cohen, *The Seleucid Colonies*, p. 45; Z. Safrai and M. Lin, "Geva in the Hasmonean Period," *Cathedra* 69 (1993) (Heb.), p. 25. Idumeans in Trachonitis: *Ant.* 16.285, 292. S. Applebaum, "The Troopers of Zamaris," *Judaea in Hellenistic and Roman Times*, *SJLA* 40, Leiden, p. 48, argues convincingly that the Idumean settlement was not withdrawn, but continued its presence in the area. On Zamaris: *Ant.* 16.285; 17.23–5. There are questions regarding the exact status of the land granted by Herod. G. Cohen suggests that the land was granted by Herod to Zamaris in full ownership, while Applebaum, "Zamaris," pp. 49–50, asserts that it was state domain leased to the settlers.

18 See the texts in S. Dar, "*Ktovot mi-Tekufat Beit Hordos – be-Bashan, be-Trachon, ube-Horan,*" S. Applebaum et al., eds, *Ha-Hermon uMargalotav, Ha-Mador le-Yidiat ha-Aretz shel Brit ha-Tnuah Ha-Kibbutzit*, 1978 (Heb.), pp. 42–8, and others discussed by Applebaum in "Zamaris," p. 50.

19 This latter site was later established as the city of Livias (*Ant.* 18.27), which had its own district; see P. Yadin 37, line 4; B. Isaac, "The Babatha Archive: A Review Article," *IEJ* 42 (1992), p. 69.

20 *Ant.* 14.450; cf. 415, 432; *BJ* 1.325.

21 S. Freyne, *Galilee from Alexander the Great to Hadrian*, Notre Dame, 1980, p. 164.

22 On the development of a new elite for Herodian society see M. Stern, "Aspects of Jewish Society: The Priesthood and Other Classes," S. Safrai and M. Stern, eds, *The Jewish People in the First Century*, Philadelphia, 1976, pp. 570–2; idem, "Social and Political Realignments in Herodian Judaea," *The Jerusalem Cathedra* 2 (1982), pp. 40–62.

23 *BJ* 2.69; *Ant.* 17.289. Recently S. Dar, "The Estate of Ptolemy, Senior Minister of Herod," I. Gafni, A. Oppenheimer, M. Stern, eds, *Jews and Judaism in the Second Temple, Mishna, and Talmud Period*, Jerusalem, 1993 (Heb.), pp. 38–50, claimed that Aris in Samaria is the Arous (Haris) given to Ptolemy. He finds a connection between the Arabic names and the Herodian period. He asserts that the archaeological finds strengthen the likelihood that this is Ptolemy's estate. Unfortunately, none of the material evidence is conclusive. He claims that this area is an excellent

example of Herodian confiscations of Hasmonean land. He brings no conclusive proof that these lands were Hasmonean, were expropriated, or were Herodian.

24 *Ant.* 16.250 relates that Antipater received 200 talents from this area, but as Marcus, *Josephus*, vol. VIII, p. 309 n. a, points out, *Ant.* 17.96 states that Antipater had an annual income of 50 talents. If we consider that all of Herod's territories yielded about 1,000 talents annually, and Herod paid 200 talents for the lease of the valuable balsam-producing areas, it is evident that Antipater could not have received the higher sum.

25 Shatzman, *The Armies*, pp. 170–6, 190; B. Mazar, *Geva: Archaeological Discoveries at Tell Abu-Shusha, Mishmar ha-'Emeq*, Ha-Kibbutz Ha-Meuhad, 1988 (Heb.); Z. Safrai, "Shechem in the Days of Mishna and Talmud 63 BC–637 CE," S. Dar and Z. Safrai, eds, *Shomron Studies*, Tel-Aviv, 1986 (Heb.), pp. 83–126; I. Shatzman, "Herod's Kingdom: Army and Security Problems," *Milet* 1 (1983) (Heb.), pp. 75–98; Schalit, *König Herodes*, pp. 174–82.

26 Freyne, *Galilee*, p. 164.

27 Applebaum, "Judaea as a Roman Province," p. 367.

28 See Safrai and Lin, "Geva in the Hasmonean Period." Gaba Hippeon was on the border of the Jezreel Valley, irrespective of whether it was in Shaar Ha-Amakim or Mishmar Ha-Emek.

29 With due caution regarding late sources, we read in the Babatha documents that in Ein Gedi, the village of "the Lord Caesar," people own private property: *P. Yadin* 11, 16, 19, 20. Similarly, there is a document from Nabatea indicating that a person owned property adjoining that of the Nabatean king: B. Isaac, "Judaea after AD 79," *JJS* 35 (1984), p. 70.

30 A. Kasher, *Jews and Hellenistic Cities in Eretz-Israel*, Tübingen, 1990, p. 208, maintains that Geba was not a polis; Safrai and Lin, "Geva in the Hasmonean Period," pp. 30–1, suggest that it became a polis from Herod's time on.

31 Applebaum, "Judaea as a Roman Province," p. 368.

32 *Ant.* 17.305, 307; cf. *BJ* 1.358; 2.86.

33 Gabba, "The Finances of King Herod," p. 162.

34 Ibid.; W. Otto, "Herodes," *P-W*, suppl. 2 (1913), cell. 68–9. The suggestion that two-thirds of the country was royal land served as a basis for a discussion of taxes in J. Dinur, *Taxation System of Palestine in the Roman Age as Reflected in Talmudic Literature (63 BC–395 AD)*, Ph.D. Thesis, Hebrew University of Jerusalem, 1982 (Heb.), p. 7.

35 Luke 12:16–21: a rich landowner has abundant crops; 14:12: Jesus urges that the poor, and not the rich, should be invited to supper; 15:11–32: the father of the prodigal son has fields, hired servants, and cattle; 16:19: a rich man with fine clothes fares sumptuously.

36 A. N. Sherwin-White, *Roman Society and Roman Law in the New Testament*, Oxford, 1963, p. 139. Applebaum, "Josephus and the Economic Causes of the Jewish War," p. 244: "Of the twenty references to landowners . . . that I have discovered in the three books [the synoptic gospels] . . . only three refer to cultivators who are not described as big proprietors; the rest most decidedly are." Many other historians and New Testament commentators adopt the gospel version of a society consisting

of a few wealthy landowners, and many poverty-struck unfortunates. We would suggest caution before adopting this version of events as totally accurate. The didactic and ethical message of the gospels would not be as effective if society was portrayed less starkly.

37 Acts 4:34, 37: people who have land and houses sell them and give the proceeds to the church; 5:1ff.: a man called Ananias sold his possessions, but kept back the price.

38 The question arises as to the ultimate legal status of the land. Was it *dominium*, i.e. did it belong to the Roman people? *Dominium* referred to the status of the lands of a province. In this period Judea was the land of *Rex socius et amicus* ("Ally and Friend"), and not a province. An indication of this state of affairs is that Herod could and did cancel and reduce taxes at his discretion. See Schürer, *The History of the Jewish People*, vol. 1, pp. 316–17.

39 A. J. Avery-Peck, *Mishnah's Division of Agriculture: A History and Theology of Seder Zeraim*, Chico, CA, 1985, p. 341: "Anonymous law holds that in order to bring first fruits, the individual must own the land upon which the produce grew."

40 Applebaum, "Judaea as a Roman Province," p. 367.

41 Applebaum, "Economic Life," p. 643.

42 Ibid.

43 S. Applebaum, "Historical Commentary" to S. Dar, *Landscape and Pattern*, Oxford, 1986, p. 263, claims that Hirbet Hamad, Hirbet Shehadah, and Qarawat bene Hassan are examples of separate individual holdings which in the Herodian era became consolidated as the property of one. We fail to see how the archaeological record is so definitive.

44 Schalit, *König Herodes*, pp. 262–98, has an exhaustive discussion of all the possible taxes in Herod's realm.

45 *Ant.* 15.94–6; 16.106–7, 132; *BJ* 1.361–2; Cassius Dio 49.32.4–5; Plutarch, *Vita Antonii* 36.3–4.

46 Schalit, *König Herodes*, pp. 274–5, thinks that the tax cuts were on the eve of periodic censuses and were intended to ease the sting.

47 Applebaum, "Judaea as a Roman Province," pp. 375–8, makes a valiant effort to reckon tax figures. The weakness in his system is that all the factors are uncertain, i.e. population and total revenue. An indication of the multifaceted nature of the Roman taxation can be found in R. Duncan-Jones, *Structure and Scale in the Roman Economy*, Cambridge, 1990, pp. 187–91.

48 D. E. Oakman, *Jesus and the Economic Questions of His Day*, Lewiston, NY, 1986, p. 71.

49 See the discussion in M. Broshi, "Agriculture and Economy in Roman Palestine According to Babatha's Papyri," *Zion* LV (1990) (Heb.), pp. 269–82.

50 Gabba, "The Finances of King Herod," p. 163.

51 Andocides, *De Mysteriis* 133, in F. Meijer and O. van Nijf, eds, *Trade, Transport and Society in the Ancient World*, London and New York, 1992, pp. 37–8.

52 *SEG* XI, 1,026.

53 Engelmann and Knibbe, "Das Zollgesetz der Provinz Asia. Eine neue

Inschrift aus Ephesos," paras 1–9 and 25; in Meijer and van Nijf, *Trade, Transport and Society*, pp. 80–1.

54 Duncan-Jones also finds that the usual rate was 2–5 percent, although he notes that there are some exceptions, up to as much as 25 percent. See *Structure and Scale*, p. 194. However, Schalit, *König Herodes*, pp. 293–5, drawing on comparisons from the Red Sea trade, suggests a customs of 25 percent. This seems too high and extraordinary when compared to the Mediterranean trade.

55 Papyri from the Babatha archive reveal that the 50 percent tax on fruit with which we are acquainted from Seleucid times was in effect during Hadrian's day; see Broshi, "Agriculture and Economy," p. 278.

56 Polybius XXX.31.10–12.

57 S. J. De Laet, *Portorium*, Bruges, 1949, reprinted New York, 1975, pp. 87–8. In the most approximate calculation, and with due caution, 20,675 modii are worth about 6 talents, at least.

58 Cf. *Ant.* 15.370: they are excused and no fine is mentioned.

59 Shatzman, *The Armies*, p. 299, thinks the 60 talents were one payment in a series which added up to 500.

60 Broshi, "Agriculture and Economy," p. 280, shows that 12 percent was a permanent legal rate; he refers to Cicero, *Ad Atticum*, VI:1, 2, 3; Pliny the Younger, *Epistles*, X, 54, 55.

61 *Ant.* 16.145; *BJ* 1.418; 2.167. Applebaum, "Judaea as a Roman Province," p. 378, maintains that Herod's agricultural developments in the Jordan Valley did little to aid the suffering Jewish peasantry. However, if they provided one more significant source of income they would have done much to lighten their own tax burden. We have seen that Herod did cut taxes when his situation demanded it, but also when he could afford to do so; *Ant.* 16.64.

62 J. Porath, "The Development of the Arid Regions of Judea During Herod's Reign," *Cathedra* 53 (1989) (Heb.), pp. 13–23.

63 Gabba, "The Finances of King Herod," p. 163, assumes that Herod got half the income.

64 Applebaum, "Judaea as a Roman Province," pp. 375–7, estimates more than 900 talents; F. M. Heichelheim, "Roman Syria," *ESAR*, vol. IV, p. 235, estimates total income as 1,000–1,300 Tyrian talents; J. Jeremias, *Jerusalem in the Time of Jesus*, London, 1969, p. 91, believes about 900 talents.

65 The Cyprian copper was worth at least 300 talents. The balsam is hard to estimate; however, there is a line in Pliny, *NH* 12.118, that just the loppings and shoots alone were worth 800,000 sestertii (HS), which are by our reckoning over 30 talents.

66 *Ant.* 17.189–91. In *BJ* 1.646 the figures are 500 and 1,000 talents. The proportion is obvious: 10,000 drachmas to the talent. Therefore, Josephus is probably referring to the Tyrian talent.

67 On senatorial census see Dio 54.26.3; Tac. *Ann.* 1.75.5; 2.37.2. Four HS equal one denatius, which is considered equal to the Attic drachma. There are 6,000 Attic drachmas in a talent. Herod left 15.5 million Tyrian drachmas (1,550 talents). If these were figured in Attic drachmas then he bequeathed at least 62 million HS. The two largest recorded

personal fortunes in Rome in the first century CE were in the order of 400,000 HS. See R. Duncan-Jones, *The Economy of the Roman Empire* (*ERE*), Cambridge, 1982, pp. 4–5. Oakman, *Jesus and the Economic Questions*, pp. 69–71, used wheat equivalents and came to the same conclusion.

68 *Bella Civilia* 5.75.318–19; see *GLAJJ*, vol. II, pp. 188–9.
69 *GLAJJ*, vol. II, pp. 189–90.
70 Ibid. p. 190.
71 Applebaum, "Judaea as a Roman Province," p. 373.
72 D. C. Braund, *Rome and the Friendly King: The Character of Client Kingship*, New York and London, 1984, pp. 65–6.
73 Braund, *Rome and the Friendly King*, pp. 63–6; Schürer, *The History of the Jewish People*, vol. I, pp. 317, 416 n. 85; Gabba, "The Finances of King Herod," p. 164.
74 Braund, *Rome and the Friendly King*, pp. 63–6; P. C. Sands, *The Client Princes of the Roman Empire Under the Republic*, Cambridge, 1908, reprinted New York, 1975, pp. 57, 129, 133–4, and Appendix A, pp. 163–228, esp. pp. 222, 226.
75 *BJ* 1.394–5; *Ant.* 15.196–200.
76 Gabba, "The Finances of King Herod," pp. 164–5.
77 *Ant.* 17.300, 304–10. Cf. *BJ* 1.358; 2.86.
78 See M. Stern, "Nicolaus of Damascus."
79 BT Baba Batra 3b–4a; Assump. of Moses 6:2–6; Matt. 2:16.
80 M. Broshi, "The Cities of Eretz-Israel in the Herodian Period," *Qadmoniot* XIV, 55–6 (1981) (Heb.), pp. 72–3; Z. Maoz, "The City Plan of Jerusalem in the Hasmonean and Herodian Period," *Eretz-Israel* 18 (1985) (Heb.), pp. 46–57.
81 Applebaum, "Judaea as a Roman Province," p. 367.
82 Z. Safrai, "Samaria: From the Hellenistic to Byzantine Periods, in Light of Numismatic–Quantitative Finds," Z. H. Erlich and Y. Eshel, eds, *Judea and Samaria Research Studies*, Proceedings of the Second Annual Meeting, Ariel, 1992 (Heb.), pp. 177–8.
83 Applebaum, "The Question of Josephus' Historical Reliability," pp. 13–15.
84 E. Netzer, "Herod's Building Projects: State Necessity or Personal Necessity?" *The Jerusalem Cathedra*, vol. 1 (1981), pp. 48–61, 73–80.
85 See Shatzman, *The Armies*, pp. 266, 270, 273–4; Netzer, "Herod's Building Projects."
86 John 2:20 says 46 years. On the building of the Temple see Schürer, *The History of the Jewish People*, vol. I, p. 292 and n. 12; Smallwood, *The Jews Under Roman Rule*, p. 92 n.112.
87 A. Warszawski and A. Peretz, "Building the Temple Mount: Organization and Execution," *Cathedra* 66 (1992) (Heb.), pp. 3–46.
88 The figures are very approximate and the room for error is too great.
89 M. Goodman, *The Ruling Class of Judaea*, Cambridge, 1987, pp. 53, 64.
90 P. A. Brunt, "Free Labour and Public Works at Rome," *JRS* 80 (1980), p. 92.
91 According to I. Finkelstein, "A Few Notes on Demographic Data from Recent Generations and Ethnoarchaeology," *PEQ* 122 (1990), pp. 48–9,

the average size of the nuclear family is 4.3–4.75 per family. There is of course a problem relative to the size of the population of Jerusalem. If we ignore the incredible figures of A. Byatt, "Josephus and Population Numbers in First Century Palestine," *PEQ* 105 (1973), pp. 51–60, and remain with the more realistic estimates of Broshi, "La Population de l'ancienne Jérusalem," *RB* 82 (1975), p. 13, we arrive at a population of about 40,000. Obviously the whole population of Jerusalem was not directly supported by the project. The options are that Broshi's estimate is too low by far, or that the Technion engineers cannot compute man-hours for a project, or that many of the workers came from the surrounding countryside, from villages and farms. We would accept the last as the correct option. The population living around the city is not figured in to the population estimates of Jerusalem. One would have to reckon the reasonable distance for a laborer to travel to work in a day (c. 15 km) and the number of villages in the vicinity. The raw information for the latter is just slowly being compiled. See the works surveyed in J. J. Price, *Jerusalem Under Siege*, Leiden, 1992, p. 247, the Survey of Israel for the Judea region, and I. W. J. Hopkins, "The City Region in Roman Palestine," *PEQ* 112 (1980), pp. 19–32.

92 J. M. Keynes, *General Theory of Employment, Interest and Money*, p. 129, quoted in M. K. Thornton, "Julio-Claudian Building Programs: Eat, Drink, and Be Merry," *Historia* 35 (1986), p. 40. There is an academic argument whether public works were intended to solve social and economic ills, or whether they were built without any thought of the benefits to be gained. Those in the first camp: Brunt, "Free Labour and Public Works at Rome," p. 97; M. K. Thornton, "The Augustan Tradition and Neronian Economics," *ANRW*, vol. II.2, Berlin, 1977, pp. 150–2; idem, "Julio-Claudian Building Programs: Eat, Drink, and Be Merry." In the opposite camp: L. Casson, "Unemployment, the Building Trade, and Suetonius Vesp. 18," *Ancient Trade and Society*, Detroit, 1984, pp. 117–29.

93 *OGIS*, p. 599; *SEG* VIII 200; N. Haas, "Anthropological Observations on the Skeletal Remains from Giv'at HaMivtar," *IEJ* 20 (1970), pp. 38–59; J. Naveh, "The Ossuary Inscriptions from Giv'at HaMivtar," *IEJ* 20 (1970), pp. 33–7. On the secondary effects of this prosperity, i.e. the development of a "funereal" economic branch, see J. F. Strange, "Late Hellenistic and Herodian Ossuary Tombs, French Hill," *BASOR* 219 (1975), pp. 39–67.

94 Thornton, "Julio-Claudian Building Programs," p. 39.

95 Shatzman, *The Armies*, pp. 273–4, has a list of projects in chronological sequence of work. He lists them by the decade in which they started. The Temple is listed in the 30–20 BCE column and in the 20–10 BCE period. He also notes that the work continued throughout most of Herod's reign.

96 B. Isaac, "A Donation for Herod's Temple in Jerusalem," *IEJ* 33 (1983), pp. 86–93; F. Hüttenmeister and G. Reeg, *Die antiken Synagogen in Israel*, Wiesbaden, 1977, pp. 192–5.

97 H. M. Cotton and J. Geiger, *Masada, The Yigael Yadin Excavations 1963–1965: Final Reports*, vol. II, *The Latin and Greek Documents*, Jerusalem, 1989, p. 180.

98 Ibid. pp. 180–1. The editors suggest that a similar expression is found in *Midrash Rabbah to Genesis*, ed. Theodor-Albeck, pp. 290, 314, 585.

99 Cotton and Geiger, *Masada*, p. 182.

100 Grabbe, *Judaism*, vol. I, p. 19.

101 K. S. Gapp, *Famine in the Roman World: From the Founding of Rome to the Time of Trajan*, Ph.D. Dissertation, Princeton Univ., 1934, pp. 63–6, 262 n.14.

102 D. Flusser, "Qumran and the Famine During the Reign of Herod," *IMJ* 6 (1987), p. 10 and n.28.

103 Ibid. pp. 9–10.

104 D. Baly, *The Geography of the Bible*, New York, 1957, pp. 50, 52. The ancients were well aware of the importance of the timing of the rain; M. Ta'anit 3:1 states that forty days between rains is a drought. The climax of the Honi HaMaagel story is that he saves the crop at the last minute. Rains also save the crop when Petronius makes his promise to write to the emperor (*Ant.* 18.285).

105 E. Orni and E. Efrat, *Geography of Israel*, Jerusalem, 1971, pp. 148–9; R. B. Y. Scott, "Palestine, Climate of," G. A. Buttrick, ed., *IDB*, vol. III, Nashville, 1982, p. 625; Y. Karmon, *Israel: A Regional Geography*, London, 1971, pp. 23–4, 27–8.

106 P. Garnsey, *Famine and Food Supply in the Graeco-Roman World*, Cambridge, 1988, p. 21.

107 See also C. Siegfried and H. Gelzer, *Eusebii Canonum Epitome ex Dionysii Telmaharensis petita*, p. 42: "Magna et vehemens fames erat in Iudea et Syria, et homines e regione (hac) dissipati sunt et discesserunt" ("A great and violent famine occurred in Judea and Syria, and people from this region dispersed and departed"), quoted by Gapp, *Famine*, pp. 63–4, 158 n. 21.

108 E. Huntington, *Palestine and its Transformation*, London, 1911, p. 320.

109 This famine is discussed in Chapter XIII.

110 M. Finley, *The Ancient Economy*, London, 1985, p. 127; Garnsey, *Famine and Food Supply*, pp. 22–3.

111 N. Hohlwein, "Le Blé d'Egypte," *Études de papyrologie* 4 (1938), pp. 62–7; J. Vandier, *La Famine dans l'Egypte ancienne*, Cairo, 1936, pp. 45–8; M. Schnebel, *Die Landwirtschaft im Hellenistischen Aegypten*, vol. I, *Der Betrieb der Landwirtschaft*, Munich, 1925, reprinted Milan, 1977, pp. 29–30.

112 "Going down to Egypt" is a frequent theme in the Bible. For the post-biblical period see: C. Préaux, *L'economie royale des Lagides*, Brussels, 1939, reprinted New York, 1979, pp. 148–52; D. Sperber, "Objects of Trade Between Palestine and Egypt in Roman Times," *JESHO* 19 (1976), pp. 117–19; A. C. Johnson, "Roman Egypt," *ESAR*, vol. II, pp. 346–7; M. Rostovtzeff, *The Social and Economic History of the Roman Empire* (*SEHRE*), vol. II, rev. by P. M. Fraser, Oxford, 1957, p. 700 n. 21; Garnsey, *Famine and Food Supply*, pp. 98–100; G. E. Rickman, *The Corn Supply of Ancient Rome*, pp. 70, 233–4.

113 *OGIS* 56.14–18; Herondas, *Pornoboskos* 16–20; Herondas, *The Mimes and Fragments*, pp. 76–7 n. 17.

114 The statement above is an accepted view. The economics of Hellenistic and Roman Egypt are not the subject of this volume. See P. M. Fraser,

Ptolemaic Alexandria, vol. I (Ch.4, "Industry and Trade"), Oxford, 1971; Casson, "The Grain Trade of the Hellenistic World," *Ancient Trade and Society*, Detroit, 1984, pp. 70–95; D. J. Thompson, "Nile Grain Transport Under the Ptolemies," P. Garnsey, K. Hopkins, C. R. Whittaker, eds, *Trade in the Ancient Economy*, Berkeley, CA, 1983, pp. 64–75; Johnson, *ESAR*, vol. II.

115 J. H. D'Arms and E. C. Kopff, eds, *Roman Seaborne Commerce: Memoirs of the American Academy in Rome*, vol. XXXVI, Rome, 1980; K. Hopkins, "Models, Ships, and Staples," P. Garnsey and C. R. Whittaker, eds, *Trade and Famine in Classical Antiquity*, Cambridge, 1983, pp. 92–105. Hopkins has challenged the prevailing opinion crystalized by Finley, *The Ancient Economy*, pp. 128–31. He admits that water-borne transport is cheaper than land transport, but he disagrees as to how much cheaper it really was.

116 J. K. Evans, "Wheat Production and its Social Consequences in the Roman World," *Classical Quarterly* n.s. 31 (1981), p. 429, points out that "Given the prohibitive cost of land transport every community and district without direct access to the sea was necessarily dependent on its own food," an observation based on Gregory of Nazianzus, *Or.* 43.34. However, Evans also presents the view of some scholars that access to the sea did not guarantee immediate relief from famine (note 6). We do not claim that access to the sea guaranteed immediate relief from famine, but that it made famine relief easier and that sea transport was preferred to land transport when bringing in supplies.

117 F. M. Abel, *Géographie*, vol. II, pp. 207–22; Y. Aharoni, *The Land of the Bible: A Historical Geography* (Ch. 3 "Roads"), A. F. Rainey, ed., Philadelphia, 1979. Now see a detailed study and summary of the subject: D. A. Dorsey, *The Roads and Highways of Ancient Israel*, Baltimore and London, 1991.

118 Abel, *Géographie*, vol. I., pp. 222–31; B. Isaac and I. Roll, *Roman Roads in Judea*, vol. I, Oxford, 1982; G. H. Stevenson, "Communications and Commerce," C. Bailey, ed., *The Legacy of Rome*, Oxford, 1923, pp. 146, 156; Dorsey, *The Roads and Highways*, pp. 54–5.

119 *PCZ* 2, and see the commentary in W. L. Westermann and E. S. Hasenoehrl, *Zenon Papyri: Business Papers of the Third Century BC Dealing with Palestine and Egypt*, vol. I, New York, 1934, pp. 3–10.

120 D. V. Sippel, "Some Observations on the Means and Cost of the Transport of Bulk Commodities in the Late Republic and Early Empire," *Ancient World* 16 (1987), p. 38, claims that for distances under 200 miles it was economically feasible to transport bulk cereals; Rickman, *The Corn Supply*, p. 121; Préaux, *L'Economie*, p. 144.

121 Hopkins, "Models, Ships, and Staples," pp. 102–5; Sippel, "Some Observations on the Means and Cost of the Transport of Bulk Commodities," p. 38; Garnsey and Whittaker, *Trade and Famine*, pp. 1–3. K. Greene, *The Archaeology of the Roman Economy*, London, 1986, p. 40, after confirming the point that water-borne trade was substantially cheaper than land transport, summarizes: "However, land transport in the less mountainous parts of the empire may have been substantially cheaper than the ancient figures imply." See also p. 169.

122 *BJ* 1.175, 388; 5.520; *Ant.* 16.80, 99.

123 I Macc. 14:5; Aristeas 114–15.

124 Strabo, *Geographica* XVI, 2, 27–8.

125 *Ant.* 15.330–3. Note that Caesarea was not built till after the famine; see Schürer, *The History of the Jewish People*, vol. I, pp. 291, 293.

126 I am grateful for the highly elucidating comments of Dr Avner Raban of the University of Haifa on the subject of Palestine's coastal cities.

127 See the comments by Marcus, *Josephus* VIII (LCL), p. 143 n. e; Schürer, *The History of the Jewish People*, vol. I, p. 290 n.9, p. 291. See O. Edwards, "Herodian Chronology," *PEQ* 114 (1982), p. 38: this year could be either from Tishri 25 to Tishri 24, or Nisan 24 to Nisan 25, depending on whether Josephus is referring to the civil calendar or the ecclesiastical calendar. See W. L. Westermann, "Aelius Gallus and the Reorganization of the Irrigation System in Egypt," *Classical Philology* XII (1917), pp. 242–3.

128 *Res Gestae* 5, 1; 15, and see the comments by P. A. Brunt and J. M. Moore, *Res Gestae Divi Augusti: The Achievements of the Divine Augustus*, Oxford, 1967, pp. 44–5; Suetonius, *Tib.* 8; Dio LIII 33, 4; LIV 1, 1–4; Gapp, *Famine*, pp. 66, 67, 159 n. 28; Garnsey, *Famine and Food Supply*, pp. 219–20.

129 Westermann, "Aelius Gallus and the Reorganization of the Irrigation System in Egypt," pp. 242–3.

130 W. Otto, "Herodes," *P-W*, suppl. II, p. 67, and see the comment by Marcus, *Josephus*, p. 145 n. c.

131 This creates another chronological problem, which can only be solved by assuming that the regnal years began in Nisan 37 BCE; cf. Edwards, "Herodian Chronology."

132 Garnsey, *Famine and Food Supply*, p. 77; Gapp, *Famine*, pp. 118, 135, 141; A. Sen, *Poverty and Famines: An Essay on Entitlement and Deprivation*, Oxford, 1981, pp. 76, 80; Duncan-Jones, *ERE*, pp. 38, 146, 252, esp. n. 3.

133 Garnsey, *Famine and Food Supply*, p. 24.

134 Sen, *Poverty and Famines*, pp. 101–2, 121.

135 Galen VI 749; Garnsey, *Famine and Food Supply*, pp. 26, 28; Brunt, *Italian Manpower*, p. 135.

136 Sen, *Poverty and Famines*, pp. 203–6; M. Livi-Bacci, "The Nutrition–Mortality Link in Past Times," R. I. Rotberg and T. K. Rabb, eds, *Hunger and History*, Cambridge, 1985, p. 100; A. G. Carmichael, "Infection, Hidden Hunger, and History," R. I. Rotberg and T. K. Rabb, eds, *Hunger and History*, Cambridge, 1985, pp. 52, 54, 56; R. M. Suskind, "Characteristics and Causation of Protein–Calorie Malnutrition in the Infant and Pre-school Child," L. S. Greene, ed., *Malnutrition, Behavior, and Social Organization*, New York, 1977, p. 16; D. V. Sippel, "Dietary Deficiency Among the Lower Classes of Late Republican and Early Imperial Rome," *Ancient World* 16 (1987), pp. 52–4.

137 Sippel, "Dietary Deficiency," p. 53; C. Clark and M. Haswell, *The Economics of Subsistence Agriculture*, London, 1970, p. 21.

138 Garnsey, *Famine and Food Supply*, p. xi; see also pp. 82–6, 272; Gapp, *Famine*, pp. 130–1.

139 A. R. Hands, *Charities and Social Aid in Greece and Rome*, Ithaca, NY, 1968, pp. 56, 156 n. 40; W. L. Westermann, "The Ptolemies and the Welfare of their Subjects," *American Historical Review* 43 (1938), p. 282; Walbank, *CAH*, vol. 7.1, pp. 83–4; M. M. Austin, "Hellenistic Kings, War, and the Economy," *Classical Quarterly* 36 (1986), p. 459; D. M. Jacobson, "King Herod's 'Heroic' Public Image," *RB* 95 (1988), pp. 389–91.

140 *CA* 2.60; see also U. Wilcken, "Zum Germanicus Papyrus," *Hermes* 63 (1928), p. 52.

141 *Euergetes*: see Y. Meshorer, "A Stone Weight from the Reign of Herod," *IEJ* 20 (1970), p. 97.

142 Dio LIII.2.1–2; see Garnsey, *Famine and Food Supply*, p. 218.

143 Tacitus, *Annales*, 3.54.6–8.

144 See M. Weinfeld, *Social Justice in Ancient Israel and in the Ancient Near East*, Jerusalem and Minneapolis, 1995, pp. 45–56, 145–51.

145 The rebuilding of Samaria may be meant: see Marcus, *Josephus* VIII, p. 143 n. e.

146 Meshorer, *Ancient Jewish Coinage*, vol. II, pp. 5–9, proposes a not widely accepted theory that Tyrian shekels were coined in Jerusalem. Note also his remarks on *Ant.* 17.189 regarding coins formed from metals which had previously been vessels: pp. 6, 201 n. 7.

147 L. Casson, "The Role of the State in Rome's Grain Trade," *Ancient Trade and Society*, Detroit, 1984, pp. 98–101, reviews the evidence and the scholarly opinions. He rejects the idea.

148 Rickman, *The Corn Supply*, pp. 70, 232–4; P. Garnsey, K. Hopkins, C. R. Whittaker, eds, "Grain for Rome," in *Trade in the Ancient Economy*, Berkeley, 1983, p. 120; S. E. Sidebotham, *Roman Economic Policy in the Erythra Thalassa*, Leiden, 1986, p. 124; P. Garnsey and R. Saller, *The Roman Empire: Economy, Society, and Culture*, Berkeley and Los Angeles, 1987, pp. 98–100; Garnsey, *Famine and Food Supply*, p. 227.

149 Gapp, *Famine*, p. 66; idem, "The Universal Famine," p. 262 n.14. See also Braund, *Rome and the Friendly King*, pp. 84–5, who argues that client kings were very much also Roman officials.

150 S. Jameson, "Chronology of the Campaigns of Aelius Gallus and C. Petronius," pp. 77–8; cf. Sidebotham, *Roman Economic Policy in the Erythra Thalassa*, p. 124.

151 The size of the *kor* is a problem. However, since Josephus first noted the amount in *kors* we will assume that that is the quantity that he found recorded, and that the conversion to Attic figures represents a later confusion. The most accepted value of the *kor* is 390 liters to the *kor*; but there is sufficient reason, we think, to consider measuring the *kor* as 465 liters. See the appendix on weights and measures.

152 Gapp, *Famine*, p. 64, thinks 3,690,000 modii, which at 8.6 liters to the modius equal 31,734,000 liters. Jeremias, *Jerusalem in the Time of Jesus*, p. 129 n.17, presents the figure of 31,500,000; 1 liter of wheat equals c. 782.1 gr. See also L. Foxhall and H. A. Forbes, "Sitometreia: The Role of Grain as a Staple Food in Classical Antiquity," *Chiron* 12 (1982), pp. 43, 76.

153 K. D. White, *Greek and Roman Technology*, Ithaca, NY, 1984, p. 145.

154 Aurelius Victor, *Caes.* 1.6; cf. Casson, "The Role of the State," pp. 96–7.
155 Rickman, "The Grain Trade," pp. 263, 267.
156 Garnsey, "Grain for Rome," p. 118.
157 *ERE*, p. 50.
158 Ibid. p. 146.
159 He imported 90,000 *kor* but 10,000 were intended for use outside the kingdom.
160 Garnsey, "Grain for Rome," p. 118, uses 200 kg. per annum as a basic figure. Rickman, "The Grain Trade," uses 3.33 modii per month at 9 liters per modii, which are c. 280 kg. per annum. D. J. Crawford, *Kerkeosiris*, Cambridge, 1971, p. 129, found the average annual amount of wheat available per head to be 223 liters or 890 liters per family. Crawford's and Garnsey's figures are close to Clark and Haswell's subsistence minimum of 210 kg.: *The Economics of Subsistence Agriculture*, p. 59.
161 Unfortunately, we have no way of knowing how much land was under cultivation, hence we cannot be more precise on the effectiveness of this program. For example, if we calculate a maximum figure of 381,000 hectares available for production at the accepted seeding rate of 150 kg. per hectare, we would use more seed than twice the amount of grain Herod brought into the country. See Oakman, *Jesus and the Economic Questions*, p. 28.
162 Based on J. C. Russell, *Late Ancient and Medieval Population, Transactions of the American Philosophical Society*, n.s. 48, 3, Philadelphia, 1958, p. 64.
163 Flusser, "Qumran and the Famine During the Reign of Herod," p. 11.
164 Ibid. p. 13.
165 R. Duncan-Jones, "The Price of Wheat in Roman Egypt Under the Principate," *Chiron* 6 (1976), pp. 241–62. The *artaba* in question is equal to 4.5 Roman modii at 8.6 liters per modius: see Duncan-Jones, "The Choenix, the Artaba, and the Modius," p. 52, and *Structure and Scale*, pp. 142, 146–8. The price is almost certainly in Egyptian drachmas which are one-fourth the Attic drachma.
166 Duncan-Jones, *Structure and Scale*, pp. 144–6.
167 Gabba, "The Finances of King Herod," p. 161.
168 A. Hamburger, "Surface Finds from Caesarea Maritima – Tesserae," L. I. Levine and E. Netzer, eds, *Excavations at Caesarea Maritima 1975, 1976, 1979: Final Report* (Qedem 21), Jerusalem, 1986, p. 188. *Tesserae* are tokens that were used for a variety of purposes, such as admission to gladiatorial games. In Rome there were *tesserae frumentariae* (tokens of grain distribution). Citizens presented the tokens to receive a ration of grain.
169 Rickman, *The Corn Supply*, pp. 187, 197.
170 N. Jasny, "Wheat Prices and Milling Costs in Classical Rome," *Wheat Studies of the Food Research Institute* 20 (1944), p. 154. For indications that bread was sometimes baked and delivered, see Y. Yadin and J. Naveh, *Masada*, vol. I, *The Yigael Yadin Excavations 1963–1965: Final Reports: The Aramaic and Hebrew Ostraca and Jar Inscriptions*, Jerusalem, 1989, pp. 52–7, nos 557–84; and A. Yardeni, "New Jewish Aramaic Ostraca," *IEJ* 40 (1990), pp. 135–40, no. 2.
171 Sen, *Poverty and Famines*, pp. 71–2, 79, 96–100, 103. Gabba, "The Finances of King Herod," pp. 165–6 and n. 29, postulates that the

intensive public works program embarked on by Herod from 24/23 BCE was related to the famine and epidemic.

172 Sen, *Poverty and Famines*, pp. 49, 96–100.
173 Garnsey, *Famine and Food Supply*, pp. 28–9.
174 Thackeray, *Josephus* IV, p. 247 note b.
175 K. D. White, "Food Requirements and Food Supplies in Classical Times," *Progress in Food and Nutrition Science*, Oxford, 1976, pp. 172–4.
176 Garnsey, *Famine and Food Supply*, pp. 29–31.
177 Ibid. pp. 31–2.
178 A. Kasher, "*Hagirah ve-Hityashvut Yehudit be-Tfutzot be-Tekufah ha-Hellenistit-Romit*," A. Shinan, ed., *Emigration and Settlement in Jewish and General History*, Jerusalem, 1982 (Heb.), pp. 64–91.
179 Gapp, *Famine*, p. 65.
180 The Theatre, Amphitheatre, Official Games, high visibility of Greeks in public life.
181 *Ant.* 17.317–21; see Schürer, *The History of the Jewish People*, vol. I, pp. 333–5, 336–8, 341–2, 354.
182 *BJ* 2.111–13; *Ant.* 17.339–55; Strabo, *Geo.* 12.2.46; Cassius Dio, *Hist.* 55.27.6.
183 Smallwood, *The Jews Under Roman Rule*, p. 114; Grabbe, *Judaism*, vol. II, p. 368.
184 *BJ* 2.4–13; *Ant.* 17.200–18. Nicolaus' version of events only mentions the fact of the revolt and not its causes; see *GLAJJ*, vol. I, p. 252, line 53. On the episode of the golden eagle see *BJ* 1.648–55; *Ant.* 17.149–64.
185 For example, we have seen tax breaks given by the Seleucids to Jerusalem to encourage recovery: *Ant.* 12.144; to Iamnia in return for naval service: B. Isaac, "A Seleucid Inscription from Jamnia-on-the-Sea: Antiochus V Eupator and the Sidonians," *IEJ* 41 (1991), pp. 132–44; A. Kasher, "A Second-Century BCE Greek Inscription from Iamnia," *Cathedra* 63 (1992) (Heb.), pp. 3–21; and to the Judeans to buy their loyalty: I Macc. 10:25–45.
186 It is curious that almost no scholar has remarked on the contrast between the ambiguous description of Sabinus' activities and the ferocity of the reaction which he provoked. For example, see Schürer, *The History of the Jewish People*, vol. I, p. 331: Sabinus "oppressed the people in every sort of way, and generally behaved most recklessly." Cf. A. Kasher, "*Mavo: ha-Reka ha-Sibati ve-ha-Nisibati le-Milhamet ha-Yehudim be-Romayim*," A. Kasher, ed., *The Great Jewish Revolt: Factors and Circumstances Leading to its Outbreak*, Jerusalem, 1983, p. 13.
187 *BJ* 2.80; *Ant.* 17.300; Ben-Shalom, *The School of Shamai*, p. 120, suggests that the embassy to Augustus from the people represented the old aristocracy of Hyrcanus II, which was anti-Herodian and yet willing and able to cooperate with Rome. The rebels were of a different mind.
188 *BJ* 2.41; *Ant.* 17.253. *Ant.* 17.252 makes it appear that Sabinus harassed the Jewish people with his own armed slaves, but that explanation strains credulity, loaded as it is with contradictions and irrationalities.
189 *BJ* 2.55; *Ant.* 17.270.
190 For a recent discussion on this aspect see Ben-Shalom, *The School of Shamai*, pp. 110–18.

191 *Ant.* 15.353 trans. by Marcus and Wikgren; see Shatzman, *The Armies*, p. 190, who claims that they were probably not poor because of low salaries, but were poor before joining. He states that the wages were reasonable, even generous. But why would soldiers be ripe for treason for economic reasons which no longer applied to them? The only solution is to totally disregard this evidence, although there is no reason to assume that it is fabricated.

192 G. M. Cohen, "The Hellenistic Military Colony: A Herodian Example," *TAPA* 103 (1972), pp. 90–1, explains that the Samaritan colony probably enjoyed very fertile soil.

193 Nicolaus, *GLAJJ*, vol. I, pp. 252 lines 53–5; 259–60.

194 On the ethnic make-up of the auxilia in Judea and their hatred for the Jews see U. Rappaport, "Jewish–Pagan Relations and the Revolt Against Rome in 66–70 CE," *Jerusalem Cathedra* 1 (1981), pp. 81–95; and A. Kasher, "The Connection Between the Hellenistic Cities in Eretz-Israel and Gaius Caligula's Rescript to Install an Idol in the Temple," *Zion* LI (1986) (Heb.), pp. 135–52.

195 *BJ* 2.55; *Ant.* 17.271–2. This incident is usually mentioned in the seemingly inexhaustible number of studies of the Jewish revolutionary movements. The salient studies referred to by us: M. Hengel, *The Zealots*, Edinburgh, 1989; D. M. Rhoads, *Israel in Revolution: 6–74 CE*, Philadelphia, 1976; H. Kreissig, *Die Sozialen Zusammenhänge des Judäischen Krieges*, Berlin, 1970, pp. 113–17; R. A. Horsley, "Ancient Jewish Banditry and the Revolt against Rome, AD 66–70," *CBQ* 43 (1981), pp. 409–32; idem, "Josephus and the Bandits," *JStJ* 10 (1979), pp. 37–62; and the articles by M. Stern collected in *Studies in Jewish History: The Second Temple Period*, M. Amit, I. Gafni, M. D. Herr, eds, Jerusalem, 1991 (Heb.), pp. 277–343.

196 *BJ* 2.60, 62; *Ant.* 17.278, 282.

197 Applebaum, "Judaea as a Roman Province," p. 368.

198 The Jezreel Valley is considered to have been part of the Galilee; see M. Avi-Yonah, *The Holy Land from the Persian to the Arab Conquests: A Historical Geography (536 BC to AD 640)*, Grand Rapids, 1966, pp. 25, 67, 82; Z. Safrai, *The Galilee in the Time of the Mishna and Talmud*, Ma'alot, Ministry of Education and Culture, Israel, 1985 (Heb.), pp. 25–32.

199 *Ant.* 17.281. On the royal pretensions of the rebels see Hengel, *The Zealots*, p. 328.

200 Cohen, "The Hellenistic Military Colony," p. 90, discusses the reasons the Bathyrians received tax immunity and the Sebastians did not. The claim that they lived on fertile soil may be true, but the Herodian tenants of Jericho and Perea also lived in a productive region.

201 *Ant.* 27.281: Athronges slaughtered the king's men "because of the arrogance they had shown during the reign of Herod."

202 This description is repeated in the following verse. The figure of the rich man who "takes up what he did not store and reaps what he did not sow" is also found in Matt.25: 24–6, but without the obvious hint concerning Archelaus.

203 Smallwood, *The Jews Under Roman Rule*, pp. 115–16, suggests that

Archelaus failed to initiate the widespread economic activity which was one of his father's strong points. She proposes that the consequent "economic stagnation" contributed to the discontent of his subjects. It is difficult to see Caesar's severe action as a reaction to nothing more than economic malaise.

204 See Yadin, "Expedition D: The Cave of the Letters," *IEJ* 12 (1962), p. 243. In Ein Gedi the irrigation arrangements were also very carefully allocated: ibid. p. 249. On the total use of the water potential by the Hasmoneans and Herod see Porath, "Development of the Arid Regions," pp. 18–20.

205 Recent archaeological research at Khirbet el Beiyudat indicates that this may have been the village of Archelais, with the remains of one monumental building from our period. It is suggested that the building served as storage for agricultural products, or as living quarters. See Hizmi, "Beiyudat, Khirbet el-", *NEAEHL*, vol. 1, pp. 181–2.

206 *Ant.* 18.31; Pliny, *NH* 13.44 = *GLAJJ*, vol. I, pp. 491, 494.

207 *BJ* 2.96; *Ant.* 17.319. See Jeremias, *Jerusalem*, p. 91, for a discusson of whether Archelaus received 600 talents as in *Ant.* or 400 as in *BJ*. One is tempted to suggest that the difference can be explained by assuming that the *Ant.* version recorded the total possible income, while the lower figure in *BJ* represents the income after Augustus' kindness to the Samaritans.

208 καί τοῦ ᾽Αρωελάου ἀποδωσόμενος οἶκον ("and to sell the estate of Archelaus") *Ant.* 17.355; καί ἀποδωσόμενος τὰ ᾽Αρωελάου χρήματα ("to liquidate the estate of Archelaus") *Ant.* 18.2; Κυρίνιος δὲ τὰ ᾽Αρωελάου χρήματα ἀποδωσόμενος ἤδη ("Quirinius had now liquidated the estate of Archelaus") *Ant.* 18.26.

209 See H. W. Hoehner, *Herod Antipas*, Cambridge, 1972, reprinted Grand Rapids, 1980; Schürer, *The History of the Jewish People*, vol. I, pp. 340–53.

210 Freyne, *Galilee*, p. 68. For Varus' repression in Galilee see *BJ* 2.68; *Ant.* 17.288–9; in Judea see *BJ* 2.71–5; *Ant.* 17.295–8; *Ascension of Moses* 6:7–9.

211 *Ant.* 18.27; *BJ* 2.168. See Hoehner, *Herod Antipas*, pp. 84–100; Schürer, *The History of the Jewish People*, vol. II, pp. 172–83.

212 Hoehner, *Herod Antipas*, pp. 86–7.

213 *Ant.* 14.452–3; *BJ* 1.329–30.

214 The date of the founding of Tiberias is debated by scholars. Hoehner, *Herod Antipas*, pp. 93–5, summarizes some of the points. He opts for 23 CE, while M. Avi-Yonah, "The Foundation of Tiberias," *IEJ* 1 (1950), pp. 54–60, proposes 18 CE.

215 G. M. Harper Jr, "Village Administration in the Roman Province of Syria," *YCS* 1 (1928), pp. 113–14.

216 A. H. M. Jones, *The Greek City*, Oxford, 1940, reprinted New York, 1984, p. 171.

217 Because of Josephus' feud with Justus we must be cautious regarding his version of events. However, the information which Josephus provides was in the framework of a controversy waged by publications. Josephus' accusations and descriptions were subject to contradiction and verification by his readers. We assume that even if there are exaggerations the

basic story is significantly correct. On Justus see T. Rajak, "Justus of Tiberias," *Classical Quarterly* 23 (1973), pp. 345–68.

218 Lewis, *The Documents from the Bar-Kokhba Period*, pp. 6–10.

219 PT Ta'anit 4:5, 69a, with a parallel story in Lam. R. (ed. Buber, p. 103). This Aggada ostensibly recounts the tensions between Jerusalem and Bethar sometime before the revolt of Bar-Kochva. The source of the tale is difficult to date. Most scholars credit it with some seed of truth reflecting the period before the Great Revolt; see P. Mendel, *Ha-Sipur be-Midrash Eikha – Nusakh ve-Signon*, M.A. Thesis, Hebrew University of Jerusalem, 1983 (Heb.), pp. 121–45. For our purposes it illustrates the prevalence of forgery in landownership deeds. The story would have been pointless if it had not rung familiar to the audience. For a brief summary of the scholarship on this pericope see M. Mor, "Bar Kochba: Was it a Farmers' Uprising?" A. Kasher, A. Oppenheimer, U. Rappaport, eds, *Man and Land in Eretz-Israel in Antiquity*, Jerusalem, 1986 (Heb.), pp. 109–10.

8 JUDEA UNDER DIRECT ROMAN RULE

1 On the establishment of the province of Judea see M. Stern, "The Status of Provincia Judaea and its Governors in the Roman Empire under the Julio-Claudian Dynasty," *Eretz Israel* 10 (1971), pp. 274–82.

2 H. Kreissig, "Die Landswirtschaftliche Situation in Palästina vor dem Judäischen Krieg," *Acta Antiqua Academiae Scientiarum Hungaricae* 17 (1969), pp. 223–54; idem, "A Marxist View of Josephus' Account of the Jewish War," L. H. Feldman and G. Hata, eds, *Josephus, the Bible and History*, Detroit, 1989, pp. 265–77; idem, *Die Sozialen Zusammenhänge des Judäischen Krieges*, Berlin, 1970.

3 Kreissig, "A Marxist View of Josephus' Account of the Jewish War," p. 275.

4 M. Goodman, *The Ruling Class of Judaea*, Cambridge, 1987, p. 51.

5 Goodman, *The Ruling Class*, pp. 53–4; idem, "The First Jewish Revolt: Social Conflict and the Problem of Debt," *JJS* 33 (1982), pp. 417–27.

6 J. J. Price, *Jerusalem Under Siege*, Leiden, 1992.

7 Ibid. p. 47.

8 A point of view similar to Price's is expressed by E. P. Sanders, *Judaism: Practice and Belief 63 BCE–66 CE*, London and Philadelphia, 1992, p. 168, who rejects the contention that there were particularly remarkable levels of poverty and unemployment in Judea, and likewise rejects that taxation was administered unreasonably, or that conditions were in relentless deterioration, or that ordinary people were significantly more hard pressed in Palestine than were their counterparts in Syria or Anatolia.

9 On the Fourth Philosophy and other rebel groups see M. Hengel, *The Zealots*, Edinburgh, 1989; D. M. Rhoads, *Israel in Revolution: 6–74 CE*, Philadelphia, 1976; M. Stern, *Studies in Jewish History: The Second Temple Period*, M. Amit, I. Gafni, M. D. Herr, eds, Jerusalem, 1991 (Heb.), pp. 277–343, and the articles in A. Kasher, ed., *The Great Jewish Revolt: Factors and Circumstances Leading to its Outbreak*, Jerusalem, 1983.

10 Census information was also collected by military officers in other provinces, notably Britain, according to the evidence from the Babatha archive and on the basis of Tacitus, *Annales* 14.31; see B. Isaac, "The Babatha Archive: A Review Article," *IEJ* 42 (1992), pp. 65–6.

11 The officers of the auxilia, which was known for its antipathy to Jews.

12 Dio 54.36.2–3.

13 Dio 56.18.4; Brunt and Moore, *Res Gestae*, p. 70, commentary to 26.2.

14 J. Dinur, *Taxation System of Palestine in the Roman Age as Reflected in Talmudic Literature (63 BC–395 AD)*, Ph.D. Thesis, Hebrew University of Jerusalem, 1982 (Heb.); L. Goldschmid, "Impôts et droits de douane en Judée," *REJ* 34 (1897), pp. 192–217; M. Hadas-Lebel, "La Fiscalité romaine dans la littérature rabbinique jusqu'à la fin du IIIᵉ siècle," *REJ* 143 (1984), pp. 5–29.

15 *Ant.* 14.206; the taxes raised by Herod; the royal granaries in the Galilee, *Vita* 71, 73.

16 The confusion on the two basic taxes *tributum soli* and *tributum capitis* is astonishing. In A. H. M. Jones, "Taxation in Antiquity," P. A. Brunt, ed., *The Roman Economy*, Oxford, 1974, pp. 164–5, *tributum soli* was assessed not only on land, but also on houses, slaves, and ships. "The tax was a percentage of the assessed value; it is known to have been 1 percent in Cilicia and Syria (Appian, *Bell. Syr.* 50). The *tributum capitis* was a poll tax levied at a flat rate." Dinur, *Taxation System of Palestine in the Roman Age*, pp. 234–5, asserts that it was not uniform, but in the "developed" provinces related to income, property, and source of livelihood. In the undeveloped provinces it was uniform. Hengel, *The Zealots*, p. 135, claims it was imposed on incomes which were not based on the possession of land and that it was paid in money. Schürer, *The History of the Jewish People*, vol. I, pp. 401–2, claims that it was various kinds of personal taxes, namely a property tax which varied according to a person's capital valuation as well as a proper poll tax levied at a flat rate for all capita. E. M. Smallwood, *The Jews Under Roman Rule*, Leiden, 1981, p. 151, holds that the conversion of Judea to a province resulted in the addition of *tributum capitis* in the form, apparently, of a flat-rate tax, which by c. 30 was one Roman denarius per head. Stern, *GLAJJ* II, p. 180, states it was the assessed value of a man's property. He is referring to Appian, *Syriacus Liber* 50.253, which is a late source. Our own view is that the *tributum capitis* was levied on assets based on the census. We base this on Josephus, who uses the expression κεφαλὴν εἰσφορας (*BJ* 2.385) for the returns in Egypt, where it has been shown this meant an assessed non-uniform tax; and Mark 12:14, which has ἐπικεφάλαιον in some versions, and κῆνσος in others. See Smallwood, *The Jews Under Roman Rule*, p. 151 n. 35; Schürer, *The History of the Jewish People*, p. 402 n. 10.

17 *Ant.* 18.90; 17.205.

18 Mark 2:14–15; we assume that John the τελώνης ("tax official") in Caesarea was a customs official (*BJ* 2.287).

19 F. C. Grant, *The Economic Background of the Gospels*, Oxford, 1926; G. Theissen, *The First Followers of Jesus*, London, 1978, p. 44.

20 Grant, *Economic Background*, pp. 104–5: 30–40 percent.

21 Sanders, *Judaism: Practice and Belief*, pp. 146–9. See the discussion in Schürer, *The History of the Jewish People*, vol. II, pp. 257–74.

22 Sanders, *Judaism: Practice and Belief*, p. 168.

23 Ibid. For example, the remittal of tax during the Sabbatical Year.

24 S. Applebaum, "The Zealots: The Case for Revaluation," *JRS* 61 (1971), p. 158 n. 27a, rejects the possibility that the land was sold because he feels "the wholesale selling up of crown domains would not have been in harmony with his policy."

25 P. Brunt, "Charges of Provincial Maladministration Under the Early Principate," *Historia* 10 (1961), pp. 189–227, deals primarily with the law of *repetundae* which penalized senatorial magistrates, but it is clear that equestrians were no better; see p. 201. Indeed, throughout the article Brunt freely cites cases of equestrian governors who abused their power; see pp. 208, 210, 214, and the appendices to the article.

26 The pay of equestrian procurators as listed in *ERE*, p. 4 n.5: HS60,000, 100,000, 200,000, and 300,000. See M. Stern, "The Status of Provincia Judaea and its Governors," p. 277, who reckons HS100,000 as the salary of the Judean prefect.

27 *Ant.* 18.172–6; Suetonius, *Tib.* 32.

28 Dio 56.16.3.

29 S. L. Dyson, "Native Revolt Patterns in the Roman Empire", *ANRW*, vol. II.3, Berlin, 1975, pp. 155, 157.

30 Philo, *Legatio ad Gaium* 199; *Ant.* 18.158, 163, 164.

31 *Ant.* 18.60–2; *BJ* 2.175–7.

32 M. Shekalim 4:2.

33 Philo, *Legatio ad Gaium* 302.

34 Tacitus, *Annales* 2.42: "per idem tempus . . . et provinciae Syria atque Iudaea, fessae oneribus deminutionem tributi orabant" ("About the same time . . . the provinces, too of Syria and Judaea, were pressing for a diminution of the tribute").

35 *Ant.* 18.155–7. Agrippa I, through his freedman Marsyas, borrowed money from a freedman of his deceased mother, now a retainer of Antonia (the younger). Marsyas was forced to draw up a bond for 20,000 Attic drachmas, but to accept 2,500 less. This means a rate of 12.5 percent off the top; this is significant evidence that 12.5 percent was the current rate of interest on loans. Agrippa borrowed astonishing sums of money: 200,000 drachmas from Alexander the Abalarch (*Ant.* 18.159–61), one million from a Samaritan (*Ant.* 18.167).

36 S. Applebaum, "The Struggle for the Soil and the Revolt of 66–73 CE," *Eretz-Israel* 12 (1975) (Heb.), pp. 125–8; U. Rappaport, "The Land Issue as a Factor in Inter-Ethnic Relations in Eretz-Israel During the Second Temple Period," A. Kasher, A. Oppenheimer, U. Rappaport, eds, *Man and Land in Eretz-Israel in Antiquity*, Jerusalem, 1986 (Heb.), pp. 80–6; idem, "Jewish–Pagan Relations and the Revolt Against Rome in 66–70 CE," *Jerusalem Cathedra* 1 (1981), pp. 81–95.

37 Tacitus, *Annales* 12.54.1, and in *Historia* 5.9.3 his remarks are more cutting, but less clear.

38 *BJ* 2.277–9; *Ant.* 20.252–8; Tacitus, *Historia* 5.10.1.

39 If this figure is accurate, and we will never know if it is, it would equal

about twice the procurator's annual pay. Eight talents = 48,000 Attic Dr. = HS192,000.

40 *BJ* 2.293; Thackeray, *Josephus* II, n. a, p. 439, based on Reinach, suggests that this was the arrears of the tribute.

41 *BJ* 2.383, referring to all of North Africa: "besides their annual produce . . . pay tribute (*phoros*) of all kinds . . . and devote their contributions (*eisphoros*)."

42 Meg. Taan. 9 = Lichtenstein, pp. 302ff.

43 There is a parallel version in the Tosefta, but it is seriously garbled: T. Men. 13:21–2.

44 S. Lieberman, *Greek in Jewish Palestine*, New York, 1965, p. 182 n.195, suggests that he was nicknamed ben Nadbai, the "generous one," in irony, but Feldman, *Josephus* X, pp. 110–11 n. c, takes the nickname literally.

45 *BJ* 2.425–9, 441.

46 Another example: the second tithe which the cultivator is supposed to consume in Jerusalem can be converted to cash and then the pilgrim may buy food in the same value when he arrives in Jerusalem; see Schürer, *The History of the Jewish People*, vol. II, p. 264 n. 23.

47 Goodman, *The Ruling Class*, p. 55 n.10, suggests that NT parables do not reflect Judean reality, but Diaspora conditions. Frankly, I do not see what elements in these stories would lead to this supposition.

48 S. Applebaum, "The Roman Villa in Judaea: A Problem," *Judaea in Hellenistic and Roman Times*, *SJLA* 40, Leiden, 1989, pp. 128, 130, suggests that there may be as many as forty-two sites in the grid between Jerusalem–Beth Shemesh–Shechem–Qalqilyah. Although these have not been properly investigated, he suggests that Givat Ram and Beth Hakerem may contain farm houses.

49 E. Damati, "The Palace of Hilkiya," *Qadmoniot* XV (60) (1982) (Heb.), pp. 117–21.

50 G. Edelstein, Y. Gat, and S. Gibson, "Food Production and Water Storage in the Jerusalem Region," *Qadmoniot* XVI (61) (1983) (Heb.), pp. 16–23.

51 Y. Hirschfeld and R. Birger-Calderon, "Early Roman and Byzantine Estates near Caesarea," *IEJ* 41 (1991), pp. 81–111.

52 Y. Magen, "Kalandia: A Vineyard Farm and Winery of the Second Temple Times," *Qadmoniot* XVII (66–7) (1984) (Heb.), pp. 61–71; idem, "Qalandiyeh," *NEAEHL*, vol. 4, pp. 1,197–1,200.

53 R. Hachlili, "The Goliath Family in Jericho: Funerary Inscriptions from a First Century AD Jewish Monumental Tomb," *BASOR* 235 (1979), pp. 32–47. In a study of bones found in the Jericho tombs it was found that the deceased had lower infant mortality, a longer life-span, healthier vertebrae and joints, and better general health than the comparable remains from Jerusalem. The researchers postulate that the better climate of Jericho is responsible for the difference: B. Arensburg and P. Smith, "Appendix: The Jewish Population of Jericho 100 BC–70 AD," *PEQ* 115 (1983), pp. 133–9. We wonder if it is not because rich people work less, and eat more.

54 *DJD* 2 (Mur.18), pp. 100–4; J. A. Fitzmyer and D. J. Harrington, *A*

Manual of Palestinian Aramaic Texts, Rome, 1978, no. 39; see also M. R. Lehmann, "Studies in the Murabba'at and Nahal Hever Documents," *Revue de Qumran* 4 (1963), pp. 53–81, who has a few different readings; and compare a different translation by J. Naveh, *On Sherd and Papyrus*, Jerusalem, 1992 (Heb.), pp. 84–9, who sees it as a debt incurred by a purchase.

55 Ibid. p. 27.

56 The question whether there was Jewish slavery in Second Temple times is difficult to answer. There are those who deny it existed, e.g. G. Alon, *The Jews in Their Land in the Talmudic Age*, vol. I, Jerusalem, 1980–4, p. 160, and J. Gutman, "*Shiabud Gufo shel Adam be-Hovotav be-Torat Yisrael*," Y. Baer, J. Gutman, M. Schwabe, eds, *Sefer Dinaburg*, Jerusalem, 1949, pp. 76, 81. E. E. Urbach, *The Laws Regarding Slavery as a Source for Social History of the Period of the Second Temple, the Mishnah, and Talmud*, reprint edition New York, 1979; originally published as *Papers of the Institute of Jewish Studies*, vol. I, London, 1964, pp. 3–5, based on the frequent mention of slavery in talmudic sources, believes it did. We believe that slavery existed, but not of Jews by Jews for debt. There were Jews enslaved as punishment, captives in war and rebellion, and perhaps those who were in debt either to the crown, or to gentiles. Goodman, "The First Jewish Revolt," p. 424, asserts that Bar Giora's emancipations (*BJ* 4.508) are proof of Jewish debt slavery. The slaves may have been Jews, but were their masters? Where does it indicate that they were enslaved for debt?

57 Fitzmyer and Harrington, *Palestinian Aramaic Texts*, pp. 217–18.

58 Goodman, *The Ruling Class*, pp. 55–7; idem, "The First Jewish Revolt."

59 Goodman, *The Ruling Class*, p. 55; he goes on to explain that the "elsewhere" was the "pilgrimage business" (p. 58).

60 Goodman, *The Ruling Class*, pp. 117, 126. But did it have respect for large landholdings? Isa. 5:8; Micah 2:2: "adding field to field"; Test. of Judah 21:7–10: "Those who rule shall be like sea monsters. . . . Free sons and daughters they shall enslave; houses, fields, flocks, goods they shall seize. . . . They shall make progress in evil; they shall be exalted in avarice." Enoch 97:8–10: "Woe to you, who acquire silver and gold, but not in righteousness, and say: We have become very rich, and have possessions . . . for we have gathered silver, and filled our store houses, and as many as water are the husbandmen of our houses" (trans. *OTP*).

61 Ibid., p. 58.

62 Howgego, "The Supply and Use of Money," p. 14.

63 Goodman, *The Ruling Class*, pp. 61–2. We have examined this thesis in the introduction, in the section on population.

64 We have mentioned the stoneware industry of Jerusalem. There are indications that the Galilee had a pottery industry; however, all the surveys indicate that the product did not reach beyond the Galilee and the Golan. See D. Adan-Bayewitz and I. Perlman, "The Local Trade of Sepphoris in the Roman Period," *IEJ* 40 (1990), pp. 152–72.

65 According to J. F. Strange, "Late Hellenistic and Herodian Ossuary Tombs, French Hill," *BASOR* 219 (1975), pp. 63–4, "The specialization in terms of tomb-cutting and ossuary manufacture suggests a division of

the economy in early Palestine that supported the whole cultural enterprise associated with burial. That is, we have professional mourners, tomb-cutters, ossuary builders, and flutists, plus those who precede and follow the bier, and the coffin-bearers, though the latter need not be paid." This is all probably true, but burials are not a growth industry.

66 S. J. De Laet, "Une dévaluation dans l'antiqité: la réforme monétaire de l'année 64 après Jésus-Christ," *La Revue de la banque* 7 (1943), pp. 1–8, 54–61. In 33 CE, there was a financial crisis of a different sort that led to rising interest rates and falling values of land. The pressure forced Tiberius to increase the coinage. The problem seems to be tied to the decline in government investment after Augustus' reign. See also T. Frank, "The Financial Crisis of 33 AD," *AJPh* 56 (1935), pp. 336–41; S. J. De Laet, "La Crise monétaire de l'année 33 après Jésus-Christ," *La Revue de la banque* 5 (1941), pp. 245–52, 297–304.

67 M. K. Thornton, "Julio-Claudian Building Programs: Eat, Drink, and Be Merry," *Historia* 35 (1986), pp. 32–3.

68 Caligula's blasphemous attempt is not at issue here. On that see Schürer, *The History of the Jewish People*, vol. I, pp. 389–97, and others. The question here is what effects did the crisis have on the landholding system and the economy in general?

69 Philo, *Leg. ad Gaium* 249, states that the field crops and the harvest of fruit trees were in danger. Smallwood (in her commentary to Philo, pp. 280–3) notes that Philo was referring only to the grain harvest and not to the fruit harvest because these cannot be at the same time, therefore Philo must have been referring to demonstrations in the early summer. But Josephus (*Ant.* 18.272, 274; *BJ* 2.200) dates the demonstrations in Tiberias to the seed time (autumn). Smallwood simply rejects his evidence as inaccurate.

70 *Ant.* 18.272. Fifty days in *BJ* 2.200.

71 The question is why would Philo describe wheat harvests in the wrong season? On the chronological question see Smallwood, *The Jews Under Roman Rule*, and D. R. Schwartz, *Agrippa I*, Tübingen, 1990, pp. 78–80, who sides with Schürer and Jones. Schwartz, pp. 84–5, suggests a framework of: autumn 39, Petronius travels to Acco; spring 40, Jews make protest in Acco and threaten to destroy harvest, Petronius delays matters by writing to Caligula; late summer/autumn 40, he moves to Tiberias, Jews threaten not to sow, Petronius writes Caligula. This would fit Philo, i.e. he is referring to the spring of 40, and the reference to the fruit harvest is a future threat, as interpreted by Smallwood.

72 *BJ* 2.200. Petronius claims that the country is unsown.

73 M. Stern comments to Tacitus, *Hist.* 5.9.2, *GLAJJ* II, p. 51, that he "stresses, probably with much justification, that armed resistance was offered by the Jews." See Philo, *Leg. ad Gaium* 208, 215.

74 *Ant.* 3.320–1; 20.51–3; Acts 11:27–31; Eusebius, *EH* II, 12; *Chron. Can.* ed. Schoene, p. 152; Orosius VII 6, 9–17. On the time of the famine see Thackeray, *Josephus*, vol. IV, pp. 472–5; L. H. Feldman, *Josephus*, vol. X, pp. 28–9; Schürer, *The History of the Jewish People*, vol. I, p. 457 n. 8; T. Rajak, *Josephus: The Historian and His Society*, London, 1983, pp. 124–5; Goodman, *The Ruling Class*, p. 142 n. 5; Gapp, "The Universal Famine,"

pp. 259–61; F. J. Foakes Jackson and K. Lake, *The Beginnings of Christianity*, part I, V, Grand Rapids, 1966 (reprint), pp. 454–5; D. R. Schwartz, "Ishmael ben Phiabi and the Chronology of Provincia Judaea," *Studies in the Jewish Background of Christianity*, Tübingen, 1992, pp. 220–1, 236–7.

75 *Ant.* 20.101 mentions only the grain from Alexandria, and adds that the famine occurred during the procuratorship of Tiberius Alexander.

76 L. Feldman, *Josephus* X, p. 28 n. a.

77 Schürer, *The History of the Jewish People*, vol. I, p. 457 n. 8.; Gapp, "The Universal Famine," p. 260.

78 L. Feldman, *Josephus* X, p. 29 n. c.

79 D. R. Schwartz, "Ishmael ben Phiabi and the Chronology of Provincia Judaea," discusses the literature on the chronological problem at length and concludes that Ishmael was appointed in 49 CE.

80 Schwartz, ibid., tries to maintain the talmudic tradition that Ishmael ben Phiabi served as High Priest for a decade; Jeremias, *Jerusalem in the Time of Jesus*, p. 143, suggests that Josephus substituted Ishmael for Joseph or Ananias; Foakes-Jackson and Lake, *The Beginnings of Christianity*, p. 455, propose that the High Priest Cantheras was called Ishmael.

81 Gapp, *Famine*, p. 166 n. 73.

82 See also D. R. Schwartz, "Ishmael ben Phiabi and the Chronology of Provincia Judaea," p. 220 n. 9.

83 Foakes-Jackson and Lake, *The Beginnings of Christianity*, pp. 454–5.

84 Jeremias, *Jerusalem in the Time of Jesus*, pp. 142–3.

85 Schürer, *The History of the Jewish People*, vol. I, p. 457 n. 8.

86 Feldman, *Josephus* X, p. 28 n. a.

87 Gapp, "The Universal Famine," p. 262.

88 Tacitus, *Annales* 2, 59; Suetonius, *Tib.* 52, 2; U. Wilcken, "Zum Germanicus Papyrus," *Hermes* 63 (1928), pp. 48–65; Pliny, *Pan.* 29–32; Gapp, *Famine*, pp. 74–9, 110.

89 Johnson, *ESAR*, vol. II, pp. 310–11.

90 Gapp, "The Universal Famine," pp. 259–60.

91 *P. Mich.* 123 V. XI; Tebtynis: Johnson, *ESAR*, vol. II, p. 310.

92 Agrippa died in the spring of 44 CE; see Schürer, *The History of the Jewish People*, vol. I, pp. 452–3 n. 43. "Thus Tiberius Alexander must have been procurator not earlier than 45 and not later than 47–48 . . . though part of 45 and part of 47 may also belong to Tiberius Alexander": Foakes-Jackson and Lake, *The Beginnings of Christianity*, p. 453.

93 Cf. Feldman, *Josephus* X, p. 29 n. e.

94 Garnsey, *Famine and Food Supply*, pp. 254–66.

95 Ibid. pp. 218, 230–1, 237. On the whole question of cash distribution as a preventive and alleviative measure in food shortages, see Drèze and Sen, *Hunger and Public Action*, pp. 95–102.

96 Figs are a respectable source of needed nutrients and were used by Philip V to feed his troops when grain was unavailable; see Polyb. 16.24.9. Evidence for consumption of fig cakes in our period can be found in A. Yardeni, "New Jewish Aramaic Ostraca," *IEJ* 40 (1990), pp. 130–3, which record deliveries of dried pressed fig cakes.

97 Goodman, *The Ruling Class*, pp. 126–8.

98 BT Gittin 56a, also Gen. R. 42.1, Lam. R. 1.32; BT Ket. 66b–67a.

99 A. Fuks, "Notes on the Archive of Nicanor," *Social Conflict in Ancient Greece*, Leiden, 1984, pp. 211, 214–15; idem, "Marcus Julius Alexander (Relating to the History of Philo's Family)," *Zion* XIII–XIV (1948–9) (Heb.), pp. 10–17.

100 Nakdimon Ben-Guryon, Ben Kalba Savu'a, Ben Tzitzit HaKassat: councilors of Jerusalem who provided wheat, barley, wine, oil, salt, and wood for Jerusalem. See BT Gittin 56a; Avot de-Rabi Natan 13 (Schecter, p. 16). The latter states that Nakdimon had enough grain for all of Jerusalem for three years, but that the sicarii burned it. The parallel versions in the rabbinic literature have variants as to the number of years: see G. Alon, "Rabban Johanan B. Zakkai's Removal to Jabneh," *Jews, Judaism and the Classical World*, Jerusalem, 1977, p. 304 n. 71.

101 In an unpublished M.A. thesis, *Josephus and Jewish Society: Joseph Ben-Mattityahu's Attitudes Toward the Various Social Strata in Jewish Society and Social Questions of His Age*, Univ. of Haifa, 1985 (Heb.), we demonstrated that Josephus refers to the "respectable" people by the word "demos," and the common people by the word "plethos."

102 U. Rappaport, "On the Factors Leading to the Great Revolt Against Rome," *Cathedra* 8 (1978) (Heb.), p. 46.

103 R. A. Horsley, "Ancient Jewish Banditry and the Revolt against Rome, AD 66–70," *CBQ* 43 (1981), pp. 409–32; idem, "Josephus and the Bandits," *JStJ* 10 (1979), pp. 37–62.

104 Price, *Jerusalem Under Siege*, pp. 46–7: "that the brigands were the Robin Hoods of Palestinian society is refuted by all good evidence." It all depends on what you expect from your Robin Hoods. B. D. Shaw, "Bandits in the Roman Empire," *Past and Present* 105 (1984), pp. 3–52, also rejects the immediate connection between economic deprivation and banditry. However, we are not saying that all poor people became bandits, but that banditry was an option when few options existed. Even Josephus saw the connection between economic conditions and banditry, when he wrote that without a harvest, banditry would blossom (*Ant.* 18.274).

105 Goodman, *The Ruling Class*, p. 18.

106 Goodman, "The First Jewish Revolt," p. 418.

107 Isaac, "Babatha Archive," pp. 66–7.

108 Price, *Jerusalem Under Siege*, pp. 93–4.

109 *BJ* 4.353; G. Fuks, "Simon Bar Giora, *Gerasenos*," *Zion* LII (1987) (Heb.), pp. 147–8, claims that Simon had no particular brief for the poor.

110 Some examples of his rancor: *BJ* 4.540–1; 5.535–6; 7.265.

111 *Vita* 375, 384, 99. See J. R. Armenti, "On the Use of the Term Galileans in the Writings of Josephus Flavius," *JQR* 72 (1981), pp. 45–9; L. H. Feldman, "The Term 'Galileans' in Josephus," *JQR* 72 (1981), pp. 50–3: the term refers to the peasants; Freyne, *Galilee*, p. 166: the Galileans are the village people and probably free landowners.

9 EPILOGUE: FROM YAVNEH TO BAR KOKHBA

1 G. Alon, *The Jews in Their Land in the Talmudic Age*, vol. I, trans. G. Levi, Jerusalem, 1980–4, p. 56. Figures for destruction: Josephus 1,100,000 dead, *BJ* 6.420; Tacitus 600,000, *Hist.* 5.1.13. From Josephus, Alon collects another 106,000, from all over the country, plus 37,500 from the mob attacks in the mixed cities. Josephus adds 97, 000 prisoners taken in Jerusalem and another 41,000 all over the country and disposed of as slaves.

2 A. Büchler, *The Economic Conditions of Judaea after the Destruction of the Second Temple*, London, 1912, concentrates all the literary information on the places and population at the end of the war.

3 D. Goodblatt, "*Yehudei Eretz-Yisrael be-Shanim 70–132*," U. Rappaport, ed., *Judea and Rome: The Jewish Revolts*, Ramat Gan, 1983 (Heb.), pp. 155–6, makes the point that many of the Jewish communities surrendered without a fight, some actively cooperated with the Romans, and even some devastated settlements were soon rebuilt and resettled (*BJ* 4.442). While certainly some of this is true, it ignores the large numbers of inhabitants who were killed, enslaved, or fled the area, and the communities which were not rebuilt.

4 *BJ* 4.81; S. Gutman, "Gamala," *NEAEHL*, vol. 2, p. 459.

5 E. Damati, "The Palace of Hilkiya," *Qadmoniot* XV (60) (1982) (Heb.), p. 121.

6 A. Zertal, "Hammam, Khirbet el-," *NEAEHL*, vol. 2, p. 565.

7 *BJ* 4.135, 138, 419–39, 451.

8 We do not have specific details regarding collaborators, but we know some of them were around years after the war; Julius Archelaus, a Herodian aristocrat, was in contact with Josephus (*CA* 1.51).

9 B. Isaac, "Judaea after AD 79," *JJS* 35 (1984), pp. 46–7.

10 The assumption made by some authors that the Jezreel Valley is meant is unwarranted. The "plain" could refer to any one of the lowland areas in Palestine.

11 *BJ* 7.216–17; E. Schürer, *The History of the Jewish People in the Age of Jesus Christ*, vol. I, Edinburgh, 1973–87, p. 512; Büchler, *The Economic Conditions*, pp. 29–30; Alon, *The Jews in Their Land*, p. 60; M. Stern, "*Ha-Mishtar ha-Romi be-Provintzia Yudeia min ha-Hurban ve-ad le-Mered Bar-Kokhva*," Z. Baras et al., eds, *Eretz Israel from the Destruction of the Second Temple to the Muslim Conquest*, Jerusalem, 1982 (Heb.), pp. 12–14.

12 Isaac, "Judaea after AD 79," pp. 44–6.

13 The city enjoyed a territory stretching to Mt. Tabor according to Eusebius; see Schürer, *The History of the Jewish People*, vol. II, p. 176.

14 *BJ* 7.217. For attempts to locate the colony see Schürer, *The History of the Jewish People*, vol. I, p. 512 n.141; C. Möller and G. Schmitt, *Siedlungen Palästinas Nach Flavius Josephus (Beihefte Zum Tübinger Atlas des Vordern Orients* 14), Wiesbaden, 1976, pp. 16–17. The prevailing view places it in Motza.

15 Pliny, *NH* 5.69.

16 See G. Alon, "Rabban Johanan B. Zakkai's Removal to Jabneh," *Jews, Judaism and the Classical World*, Jerusalem, 1977, pp. 269–313.

17 *P. Yadin* 19 and 20: the editor supposes that this is an indication of the build-up contingent to the Trajanic wars. That may be so; however, we see it as an indication that the Romans could use an area for their purposes on a temporary basis.

18 Alon, *The Jews in Their Land*, pp. 60–3; cf. S. Safrai, *"Sikarikon," Zion* XVII (1952) (Heb.), pp. 56–64.

19 The sources are concentrated in M. Mor, *The Bar-Kochba Revolt: Its Extent and Effect*, Jerusalem, 1991 (Heb.), pp. 59–79.

20 S. Applebaum, "Judaea as a Roman Province: The Countryside as a Political and Economic Factor," *ANRW*, vol. II.8, Berlin, 1977, pp. 385–95; idem, "The Agrarian Question, and the Revolt of Bar Kokhba," *Eretz-Israel* 8 (1967) (Heb.), pp. 283–7.

21 See D. Sperber, *Roman Palestine 200–400: The Land*, Ramat-Gan, 1978, for a detailed examination of the agrarian situation in Palestine as reflected in the rabbinic sources.

22 Applebaum, "Judaea as a Roman Province," p. 386.

23 Ibid. p. 285.

24 Ibid. p. 284.

25 Mor, "Bar Kochba: Was it a Farmers' Uprising?" See the same comments more recently in Mor, *The Bar-Kochba Revolt: Its Extent and Effect*, pp. 59–79.

26 Mor, *The Bar-Kochba Revolt: Its Extent and Effect*, p. 66.

27 Eusebius, *HE* 4.6.1. "Tinius Rufus under the law of war enslaved their land" indicates that the land could not have been all Roman.

28 Eusebius, *HE* 3.20.1–3.

29 Applebaum, "The Agrarian Question, and the Revolt of Bar Kokhba."

30 See the legends, Mor, *The Bar-Kochba Revolt: Its Extent and Effect*, pp. 74–5.

31 *DJD* II (Mur. 24); Y. Yadin, "Expedition D: The Cave of the Letters," *IEJ* 12 (1962), documents 42–6.

32 *DJD* II, p. 123.

33 Translation by J. P. Yadin, *Bar Kokhba*, p. 133 = Yadin, "Expedition D," papyrus 12.

34 *Neches* originally meant sheep for slaughter, and because sheep were the major form of property it became a word denoting property in goods; see Josh. 22:8; Eccles. 5:18; 6:2; I Chron. 2:11, 12. In talmudic literature it has been used to indicate an inheritance, in the sense of a *nahala*. M. A. Jastrow, *A Dictionary of the Targumim, the Talmud Babli and Yerushalmi, and the Midrashic Literature*, New York, 1950, s.v. נכס: BT Bekh.48a "Has not the estate been made responsible for the debt?" "Does not a person's property take the place of a guarantor?" BT Baba.Bathra.58a "All my property shall go to one son of mine." "All the property goes to the son."

35 See also M. Broshi, "Agriculture and Economy in Roman Palestine According to Babatha's Papyri," *Zion* LV (1990) (Heb.), p. 271 n. 15, which discusses Dead Sea ports.

36 *DJD* II (Mur. 22): property sold for 40 zuz. Yadin, "Expedition D," Hevdoc. 42, p. 249: Jonathan son of . . . and Horin son of Ishmael, administrators of Bar Kokhba, lease a plot of land to Eliezer son of

Shmuel for a monetary payment of 650 zuzim a year. *DJD* II (Mur. 30): in 135 CE Dostes sold a piece of property including building, grounds, figs, olives, trees, for 88 zuz. J. T. Milik, "Un contrat juif de l'an 134 après J-C," *RB* 61 (1954), pp. 182–90 (= Fitzmyer and Harrington, *A Manual of Palestinian Aramaic Texts* 51; Naveh, *On Sherd and Papyrus*, pp. 98–100): sales contract of a house in Kefar Bero (previously thought Bebyahu). The price is 8 zuz, which are 2 sela. Payment in full, 36 zuz. M. Broshi and E. Qimron, "A House Sale Deed from Kefar Baru from the Time of Bar Kokhba," *IEJ* 36 (1986), pp. 201–14.

BIBLIOGRAPHY

OLD TESTAMENT, NEW TESTAMENT, AND APOCRYPHA

A New Translation of the Holy Scriptures according to the Masoretic Text, Philadelphia, 1967–82.
Biblia Hebraica Stuttgartensia, Stuttgart, 1968.
The Greek New Testament, K. Aland et al., eds, Munster, 1975.
Maccabaeorum liber I, ed. W. Kappler, Göttingen, 1967.
Maccabaeorum liber II, ed. W. Kappler, Göttingen, 1967.
Septuaginta I, ed. A. Rahlfs, Stuttgart, 1935.

RABBINICAL SOURCES

The Babylonian Talmud, Vilna, 1882–6.
The Mishnah, with commentary by H. Albeck, Jerusalem, 1958.
The Palestinian Talmud, Vilna, 1922.
Siphra, ed. I. H. Weiss, Vienna, 1862, facsimile New York, 1947.
The Tosephta, ed. M. S. Zuckermandel, Jerusalem, 1970.
The Tosephta, ed. S. Lieberman, New York, 1962–88.

ANCIENT SOURCES

Epigraphical and papyrological sources are listed under the names of editors

Appian, *Roman History*, vols I–IV, Eng. trans. H. White, LCL, London and Cambridge, Mass., 1912.
Aristophanes, *Wasps*, Eng. trans. A. H. Sommerstein, Warminster, 1983.
Aristotle, *Oeconomica*, Eng. trans. G. C. Armstrong, London and Cambridge, Mass., 1935.
Athenaeus of Naucratis, *The Deipnosophists*, Eng. trans. C. B. Gulick, LCL, 1957.
Cato, *On Agriculture*, Eng. trans. W. D. Hooper, rev. H. B. Ash, LCL, 1934.
Cicero, *The Verrine Orations*, vols I–II, trans. L. H. G. Greenwood, LCL, 1935.
Columella, *On Agriculture*, vols I–III, Eng. trans. H. B. Ash et al., LCL, 1941.

Diodorus Siculus, vols I–XII, Eng. trans. F. R. Walton et al., LCL, 1936–47.

Dio's Roman History, Eng. trans. E. Cary, LCL, 1917.

Eupolemus, in C. R. Holladay, *Fragments from Hellenistic Jewish Authors*, vol. I: *Historians*, Chico, CA, 1983.

Eusebius, *Chronicorum Canonum*, ed. A. Schoene, Dublin, 1967.

—— *The Ecclesiastical History*, trans. K. Lake and J. E. L. Oulton, LCL, 1980.

Herodas (Herondas), *The Mimes and Fragments*, ed. A. D. Knox, with notes by W. Headlam, Cambridge, 1966.

Josephus, *The Life, Against Apion, The Jewish War, Jewish Antiquities*, vols I–X, Eng. trans. H. St. J. Thackeray et al., LCL, 1926–65.

Orosius, *CSEL, Pauli Orosii Historiarum Adversus Paganos*, ed. C. Zangemeister, Vindobonae, 1882.

Philo, vols I–XII, Eng. trans. F. H. Colson, LCL, 1967.

Philonis Alexandrini, *Legatio ad Gaium*, ed. E. M. Smallwood, Leiden, 1970.

Plutarch, *The Parallel Lives*, vols I–XII, Eng. trans. B. Perrin, LCL, 1959.

Polybius, *The Histories*, vols I–IV, Eng. trans. W. R. Paton, LCL, 1968.

Porphyry, *Adversus Christianos* apud: Hieronymus *Comm. in Dan.*, in *GLAJJ*, vol. II, no. 464l.

Strabo, *The Geography of Strabo*, vols I–VIII, Eng. trans. H. L. Jones, LCL, 1917.

Suetonius, vols I–II, Eng. trans. J. C. Rolfe, LCL, 1965.

Tacitus, Eng. trans. C. H. Moore et al., LCL, 1965.

Theophrastus, *Enquiry into Plants*, vols I–II, Eng. trans. A. Hart, LCL, 1961.

Varro, *On Agriculture*, Eng. trans. W. D. Hooper, rev. H. B. Ash, LCL, 1935.

SCHOLARLY LITERATURE

Abel, F. M., *Géographie de la Palestine*, vols I–II, Paris, 1933–7.

—— *Les Livres des Maccabées*, Paris, 1949.

Ackroyd, P. R., "The Written Evidence for Palestine," eds H. Sancisi-Weedenburg and A. Kuhrt, *Achaemenid History*, vol. IV: *Centre and Periphery*, Leiden, 1990, pp. 207–20.

Adan-Bayewitz, D. and Perlman, I., "The Local Trade of Sepphoris in the Roman Period," *IEJ* 40, 1990, pp. 152–72.

Aharoni, Y., *The Land of the Bible: A Historical Geography*, A. F. Rainey, ed., Philadelphia, 1979.

Alon, G., "The Attitude of the Pharisees to Roman Rule and the House of Herod," *Jews, Judaism and the Classical World*, trans. I. Abrahams, Jerusalem, 1977, pp. 18–47.

—— "Did the Jewish People and its Sages Cause the Hasmoneans to be Forgotten?" *Jews, Judaism and the Classical World*, Jerusalem, 1977, pp. 1–17.

—— *The Jews in Their Land in the Talmudic Age*, vols I–II, trans. G. Levi, Jerusalem, 1980–4.

—— "Rabban Johanan B. Zakkai's Removal to Jabneh," *Jews, Judaism and the Classical World*, Jerusalem, 1977, pp. 269–313.

Alt, A., "Beth=Anath," *PJB* 22, 1926, pp. 55–9.

—— *Kleine Schriften Zur Geschichte Des Volkes Israel*, vol. II, Munich, 1953.

Amusin, J. D., "The Reflection of Historical Events in the First Century BC in Qumran Commentaries (4Q161; 4Q169; 4Q166)," *HUCA* 48, 1977, pp. 123–52.

Anderson, A. J., "A Note on Wages in the First Century AD," *The Voice of the Turtle, The North American Journal of Numismatics* 5, 1966, pp. 177–8.

Applebaum, S., "The Agrarian Question, and the Revolt of Bar Kokhba," *Eretz-Israel* 8, 1967, pp. 283–7, (Heb.).

—— "Economic Life in Palestine," S. Safrai and M. Stern, eds, *The Jewish People in the First Century*, Philadelphia, 1976, pp. 631–700.

—— "Hasmonean Internal Colonization: Problems and Motives," A. Kasher, A. Oppenheimer, U. Rappaport, eds, *Man and Land in Eretz-Israel in Antiquity*, Jerusalem, 1986, pp. 75–9, (Heb.).

—— "The Hasmoneans: Logistics, Taxation and Constitution," *Judaea in Hellenistic and Roman Times, SJLA* 40, Leiden, 1989, pp. 9–29.

—— "Hellenistic Cities of Judaea and its Vicinity: Some New Aspects," B. Levick, ed., *The Ancient Historian and His Materials: Essays in Honor of C. E. Stevens*, Farnborough, 1975, pp. 59–73.

—— "Historical Commentary" to S. Dar, *Landscape and Pattern*, Oxford, 1986, pp. 259–69.

—— "Jewish Urban Communities and Greek Influences," *SCI* 5, 1979–80, pp. 158–77.

—— "Josephus and the Economic Causes of the Jewish War," L. H. Feldman and G. Hata, eds, *Josephus, the Bible and History*, Detroit, 1989, pp. 237–64.

—— "Judaea as a Roman Province: The Countryside as a Political and Economic Factor," *ANRW*, vol. II.8, Berlin, 1977, pp. 355–96.

—— "The Question of Josephus' Historical Reliability in the Two Test Cases: Antipatris of Kefar-Saba and Antipatris of Caesarea," U. Rappaport, ed., *Josephus Flavius: Historian of Eretz-Israel in the Hellenistic–Roman Period*, Jerusalem, 1982, pp. 13–19, (Heb.).

—— "The Roman Villa in Judaea: A Problem," *Judaea in Hellenistic and Roman Times, SJLA* 40, Leiden, 1989, pp. 124–31.

—— "The Struggle for the Soil and the Revolt of 66–73 CE," *Eretz-Israel* 12, 1975, pp. 125–8, (Heb.).

—— "The Towers of Samaria," *PEQ* 110, 1978, pp. 91–100.

—— "The Troopers of Zamaris," *Judaea in Hellenistic and Roman Times, SJLA* 40, Leiden, 1989, pp. 47–65.

—— "When Did Scythopolis Become a Greek City?" *Judaea in Hellenistic and Roman Times, SJLA* 40, Leiden, 1989, pp. 1–8.

—— "The Zealots: The Case for Revaluation," *JRS* 61, 1971, pp. 155–70.

Arensburg, B. and Smith, P., "Appendix: The Jewish Population of Jericho 100 BC–70 AD," *PEQ* 115, 1983, pp. 133–9.

Ariel, D. T., *Excavations at the City of David 1978–1985*, vol. II, Qedem 30, Jerusalem, 1990.

Armenti, J. R., "On the Use of the Term Galileans in the Writings of Josephus Flavius," *JQR* 72, 1981, pp. 45–9.

Arnold, W. T., *Roman Provincial Administration*, rev. by E. S. Bouchier, Oxford, 1914, reprinted Chicago, 1974.

Arnon, I., *Crop Production in Dry Regions*, vols I–II, London, 1972.

Arrington, L. R., "Foods of the Bible," *Journal of the American Dietetic Association* 35, 1959, pp. 816–20.

Atkinson, K. T. M., "A Hellenistic Land-Conveyance: The Estate of Mnesimachus in the Plain of Sardis," *Historia* 21, 1972, pp. 45–74.

Attridge, H. W., "Historiography," M. E. Stone, ed., *Jewish Writings of the Second Temple Period*, Assen and Philadelphia, 1984, pp. 171–6.

—— "Jewish Historiography," R. A. Kraft and G. W. E. Nickelsburg, eds, *Early Judaism and its Modern Interpreters*, Atlanta, 1986, pp. 311–23.

Austin, M., "Hellenistic Kings, War, and the Economy," *Classical Quarterly* 36, 1986, pp. 450–66.

—— *The Hellenistic World from Alexander to the Roman Conquest: A Selection of Ancient Sources in Translation*, Cambridge, 1981.

Avery-Peck, A. J., *Mishnah's Division of Agriculture: A History and Theology of Seder Zeraim*, Chico, CA, 1985.

Aviam, M., "Large-Scale Production of Olive Oil in Galilee," *Cathedra* 73, 1994, pp. 26–35, (Heb.).

Avigad, N., "More Evidence on the Judean Post-Exilic Stamps," *IEJ* 24, 1974, pp 52–7.

—— "New Light on MSH Seal Impressions," *IEJ* 8, 1958, pp. 113–19.

Avi-Yonah, M., "The Foundation of Tiberias," *IEJ* 1, 1950, pp. 54–60.

—— *Hellenism and the East: Contacts and Interrelations from Alexander to the Roman Conquest*, Jerusalem, 1978.

—— *The Holy Land from the Persian to the Arab Conquests: A Historical Geography (536 BC to AD 640)*, Grand Rapids, 1966.

—— "*Skira al Tzfifut ha-Okhlusim ve-Kamutam be-Eretz-Yisrael ha-Atika*," *Masot u-Mehkarim beYediat ha-Aretz*, Tel-Aviv, 1964, (Heb.).

Aymard, M., "Toward the History of Nutrition: Some Methodological Remarks," R. Forster and O. Ranum, eds, *Food and Drink in History* (*Selections from the Annales Economies, Societies, Civilizations*), vol. V, Baltimore, 1979, pp. 1–16.

Badian, E., *Publicans and Sinners*, Oxford, 1972.

Bagnall, R. S., *The Administration of the Ptolemaic Possessions Outside Egypt*, Leiden, 1976.

Bagnall, R. S. and Derow, P., eds, *Greek Historical Documents: The Hellenistic Period*, Chico, CA, 1981.

Baly, D., *The Geography of the Bible*, New York, 1957.

—— "The Geography of Palestine and the Levant in Relation to its History," *CHJ*, vol. I, 1984, pp. 1–24.

Bammel, E., "The Organization of Palestine by Gabinius," *JJS* 12, 1961, pp. 159–62.

Bar-Kochva, B., *Judas Maccabaeus*, Cambridge, 1988.

—— "Manpower, Economics, and Internal Strife in the Hasmonean State," *Armées et fiscalité dans le monde antique* (Colloque National du CNRS No. 936, Organisé par H. Van Effentere), Paris, 1977, pp. 167–95.

—— *The Seleucid Army*, Cambridge, 1976.

—— "The Status and Origin of the Garrison at the Akra on the Eve of the Religious Persecutions," *Zion* XXVIII, 1973, pp. 32–47, (Heb.).

Barag, D., "King Herod's Royal Castle at Samaria-Sebaste," *PEQ* 125, 1993, pp. 3–18.

Barghouti, A. N., "Urbanization of Palestine and Jordan in Hellenistic and Roman Times," A. Hadidi, ed., *Studies in the History and Archaeology of Jordan*, vol. I, Amman, 1982, pp. 209–29.

Baron, S., "Reflections on Ancient and Medieval Jewish Historical Demography," *Ancient and Medieval Jewish History*, New Brunswick, NJ, 1972, pp. 10–22.

Batten, L. W., "The Books of Ezra and Nehemiah," *ICC*, Edinburgh, 1913.

Baumgarten, J. M., "Does *tlh* in the Temple Scroll Refer to Crucifixion?" *JBL* 91, 1972, pp. 472–81.

Ben-David, A., *Jerusalem und Tyros*, Tübingen, 1969.

—— "Jewish and Roman Bronze and Copper Coins: Their Reciprocal Relations in Mishnah and Talmud from Herod the Great to Trajan and Hadrian," *PEQ* 103, 1971, pp. 109–28.

—— *Talmudische Ökonomie: Die Wirtschaft des jüdischen Palästina zur Zeit der Mischna und des Talmud*, vol. 1, Hildesheim, 1974.

Ben-Shalom, I., *The School of Shamai and the Zealot's Struggle against Rome*, Jerusalem, 1993, (Heb.).

Benoit, P., Milik, J. T., and de Vaux, R., eds, *Discoveries in the Judean Desert*, vol. II, *Les Grottes de Murabba'at*, Oxford, 1961.

Bertrand, J. M., "Sur l'inscription d'Hefzibah," *ZPE* 46, 1982, pp. 167–74.

Bevan, E., *A History of Egypt Under the Ptolemaic Dynasty*, London, 1927.

Bickerman, E., "La charte séleucide de Jérusalem," *Studies in Jewish and Christian History*, vol. II, Leiden, 1980, pp. 44–85.

—— *Four Strange Books of the Bible*, New York, 1967.

—— "Héliodore au Temple de Jérusalem," *Studies in Jewish and Christian History*, vol. II, Leiden, 1980, pp. 159–91.

—— *The Jews in the Greek Age*, Cambridge, 1988.

—— "Une Proclamation Séleucide relative au temple de Jérusalem," *Studies in Jewish and Christian History*, vol. II, Leiden 1980, pp. 86–104.

Bickerman (Bickermann), E., *Der Gott der Makkabäer*, Berlin, 1937.

Bickerman (Bikerman), E., *Institutions des Séleucides*, Paris, 1938.

Bingen, J., "Économie Grecque et société Égyptienne au IIIe siècle," H. Maehler and V. M. Strocka, eds, *Das Ptolemäische Ägypten*, Mainz, 1978, pp. 211–19.

—— *Le Papyrus revenue laws: tradition Grecque et adaption Hellénistique*, Opladen, 1978.

Blenkinsopp, J., "A Jewish Sect of the Persian Period," *CBQ* 52, 1990, pp. 5–20.

—— "Temple and Society in Achaemenid Judah," in P. R. Davies, ed., *Second Temple Studies*, vol. 1, *Persian Period*, *JSOT* 117, Sheffield, 1991, pp. 22–53.

Borowski, O., *Agriculture in Iron Age Israel*, Ph.D. Dissertation, University of Michigan, 1979.

Braund, D. C., "Gabinius, Caesar, and the publicani of Judaea," *Klio* 65, 1983, pp. 241–4.

—— *Rome and the Friendly King: The Character of Client Kingship*, New York and London, 1984.

Briant, P., Des Achéménides aux rois Hellénistiques: continuités et ruptures," *RTP*, Paris, 1982, pp. 291–330.

—— "Contrainte militaire, dépendance rurale et exploitation des territoires en Asie Achéménide," *RTP*, Besançon and Paris, 1982, pp. 175–223.

—— "Dons de terres et de villes: L'Asie Mineure dans le contexte Achéménide," *REA* 87, 1985, pp. 53–72.

—— "Remarques sur "laoi" et esclaves ruraux en Asie Mineure Hellénistique," *RTP*, Besançon and Paris, 1982, pp. 95–135.

Bringmann, K., *Hellenistische Reform und Religionsverfolgung in Judäa*, Göttingen, 1983.

Broshi, M., "Agriculture and Economy in Roman Palestine According to Babatha's Papyri," *Zion* LV, 1990, pp. 269–82, (Heb.).

—— "The Cardinal Elements of the Economy of Palestine during the Herodian Period," N. Gross, ed., *Jews in Economic Life*, Jerusalem, 1985, pp. 27–35, (Heb.).

—— "The Cities of Eretz-Israel in the Herodian Period," *Qadmoniot* XIV, 55–6, 1981, pp. 70–9, (Heb.).

—— "The Diet of Palestine in the Roman Period," *IMJ* V, 1986, pp. 41–56.

—— "La Population de l'ancienne Jérusalem," *RB* 82, 1975, pp. 5–14.

—— "The Population of Western Palestine in the Roman–Byzantine Period," *BASOR* 236, 1979, pp. 1–10.

—— "The Role of the Temple in the Herodian Economy," *JJS* 38, 1987, pp. 31–7.

Broshi, M. and Finkelstein, I., "The Population of Palestine in 734 BCE," *Cathedra* 58, 1990, pp. 3–24, (Heb.).

Broshi, M. and Qimron, E., "A House Sale Deed from Kefar Baru from the Time of Bar Kokhba," *IEJ* 36, 1986, pp. 201–14.

Brothwell, D. and Brothwell, P., *Food in Antiquity*, New York, 1969.

Brownlee, W. H., *The Midrash Pesher of Habakkuk*, Missoula, Mont., 1979.

—— "The Wicked Priest, the Man of Lies, and the Righteous Teacher," *JQR* 73, 1982–3, pp. 1–37.

Brunt, P. A., "Charges of Provincial Maladministration Under the Early Principate," *Historia* 10, 1961, pp. 189–227.

—— "Free Labour and Public Works at Rome," *JRS* 80, 1980, pp. 81–100.

—— *Italian Manpower*, Oxford, 1971.

—— "Josephus on Social Conflicts in Roman Judaea," *Klio* 59, 1977, pp. 149–53.

Brunt, P. A. and Moore, J. M., *Res Gestae Divi Augusti: The Achievements of the Divine Augustus*, Oxford, 1967.

Büchler, A., *The Economic Conditions of Judaea after the Destruction of the Second Temple*, London, 1912.

—— "On the Provisioning of Jerusalem in the Year 69–70 CE," *Studies in Jewish History*, New York, 1956, pp. 99–125.

—— "The Priestly Dues and the Roman Taxes in the Edicts of Caesar," *Studies in Jewish History*, New York, 1956, pp. 1–23.

Byatt, A., "Josephus and Population Numbers in First Century Palestine," *PEQ* 105, 1973, pp. 51–60.

Carmichael, A. G., "Infection, Hidden Hunger, and History," R. I. Rotberg and T. K. Rabb, eds, *Hunger and History*, Cambridge, 1985, pp. 52–66.

Cary, M. et al., *Oxford Classical Dictionary*, Oxford, 1970.

Casson, L., "The Grain Trade of the Hellenistic World," *Ancient Trade and Society*, Detroit, 1984, pp. 70–95.

—— "The Role of the State in Rome's Grain Trade," *Ancient Trade and Society*, Detroit, 1984, pp. 96–116.

—— "Unemployment, the Building Trade, and Suetonius Vesp. 18," *Ancient Trade and Society*, Detroit, 1984, pp. 117–29.

Charles, R. H., *The Apocrypha and Pseudepigrapha of the Old Testament*, vols I–II, Oxford, 1913.

Charlesworth, J. H., *The Old Testament Pseudepigrapha*, vols I–II, New York, 1983–5.

Childe, V. G., *Man Makes Himself*, New York, 1951.

—— *What Happened in History*, New York, 1946.

Cipolla, C. M., *The Economic History of World Population*, Harmondsworth, 1978.

Clark, C. and Haswell, M., *The Economics of Subsistence Agriculture*, London, 1970.

Clawson, M., "Land: I. Economic Aspects," D. L. Sills, ed., *International Encyclopedia of the Social Sciences*, vol. 8, New York, 1968, pp. 550–6.

Clines, D. J., *Ezra, Nehemiah, Esther: The New Century Bible Commentary*, Grand Rapids, 1984.

Cohen, G., "The Beginning of the reign of Jannaeus" *The Judean–Syrian–Egyptian Conflict of 103–101 BC*, E. van't Dack et al., eds, pp. 118–21, Brussels, 1989.

Cohen, G. M., "Colonization and Population Transfer in the Hellenistic World," E. van't Dack, P. van Dessel, W. van Gucht, eds, *Egypt and the Hellenistic World*, Leuven, 1983, pp. 63–74.

—— "The Hellenistic Military Colony: A Herodian Example," *TAPA* 103, 1972, pp. 81–95.

—— *The Seleucid Colonies*, Wiesbaden, 1978.

Cohen, S. J. D., "Alexander the Great and Jaddus the High Priest According to Josephus," *AJS Review* 7–8, 1982–3, pp. 41–68.

Cook, S. A., Adcock, F. E., and Charlesworth, M. P., eds, *The Cambridge Ancient History*, vol. IX: *The Roman Republic*, Cambridge, 1951.

—— eds, *The Cambridge Ancient History*, vol. X: *The Augustan Empire*, Cambridge, 1952.

Cook, T. H., "Hellenistic Administration in Rural Palestine," *Near East Archaeological Bulletin* 20, 1982, pp. 15–32.

Corbier, M., "Propriété et gestion de la terre: grand domaine et économie paysanne," G. A. Ritter and R. Vierhaus, eds, *Aspekte der historischen forschung in Frankreich und Deutschland*, Göttingen, 1981, pp. 11–29.

Corsaro, M., "Tassazione Regia e Tassazione Cittadina Dagli Achemendi Ai Re Ellenistici: Alcune Osservazioni," *REA* 87, 1985, pp. 73–95.

Cotton, H. M. and Geiger, J., *Masada II, The Yigael Yadin Excavations 1963–1965: Final Reports, The Latin and Greek Documents*, Jerusalem, 1989.

Cowley, A. E., *Aramaic Papyri of the Fifth Century BC*, Oxford, 1923.

Crawford, D. J., *Kerkeosiris*, Cambridge, 1971.

Currid J. D., "The Beehive Granaries of Ancient Palestine," *Zeitschrift des deutschen Palästina-Vereins* 101, 1985, pp. 97–110.

Damati, E., "The Palace of Hilkiya," *Qadmoniot* XV (60), 1982, pp. 117–21.

Danby, H., *The Mishnah*, Oxford, 1933.

Dancy, J. C. *A Commentary on I Maccabees*, Oxford, 1954.

Dandamayev, M., "Achaemenid Babylonia," *Ancient Mesopotamia*, Moscow, 1969, pp. 296–310.

Dandamayev, M. A. and Lukonin, V. G., *The Culture and Social Institutions of Ancient Iran*, Cambridge, 1989.

Dar, S., "Agriculture and Agricultural Produce in Eretz-Israel in the Roman–Byzantian [sic] Period," A. Kasher, A. Oppenheimer, U. Rappaport, eds, *Man and Land in Eretz-Israel in Antiquity*, Jerusalem, 1986, pp. 142–69, (Heb.).

—— "The Estate of Ptolemy, Senior Minister of Herod," I. Gafni, A. Oppenheimer, M. Stern, eds, *Jews and Judaism in the Second Temple, Mishna, and Talmud Period*, Jerusalem, 1993, pp. 38–50, (Heb.).

—— "The History of the Hermon Settlements," *PEQ*, vol. 120 1988, pp. 26–44.

—— "*Ktovot mi-Tekufat Beit Hordos – be-Bashan, be-Trachon, ube-Horan*," S. Applebaum et al., eds, *Ha-Hermon uMargalotav, Ha-Mador le-Yidiat ha-Aretz shel Brit ha-Tnuah Ha-Kibbutzit*, 1978, pp. 42–8, (Heb.).

—— *Landscape and Pattern*, BAR International Series, Oxford, 1986.

D'Arms, J. H. and Kopff, E. C., eds, *Roman Seaborne Commerce: Memoirs of the American Academy in Rome*, vol. XXXVI, Rome, 1980.

Davies, P. R., ed., *Second Temple Studies*, vol. 1, *Persian Period*, Sheffield, 1991.

Davies, W. D., *The Territorial Dimension of Judaism*, Berkeley, Los Angeles, London, 1982.

Davies, W. D. and Finkelstein, L., eds, *The Cambridge History of Judaism*, vol. I, *Introduction; The Persian Period*, Cambridge, 1984.

—— eds, *The Cambridge History of Judaism*, vol. II, *The Hellenistic Age*, Cambridge, 1989.

Davisson, W. I. and Harper, J. E., *European Economic History*, vol. I, *The Ancient World*, New York, 1972.

De Laet, S. J., "La Crise monétaire de l'année 33 après Jésus-Christ," *La Revue de la banque* 5, 1941, pp. 245–52, 297–304.

—— "Une dévaluation dans l'antiqité: la réforme monétaire de l'année 64 après Jésus-Christ," *La Revue de la banque* 7, 1943, pp. 1–8, 54–61.

—— *Portorium*, Bruges, 1949, reprinted New York, 1975.

Dentzer, J. M., Villeneuve, F., and Larché, F., "Iraq el Amir: Excavations at the Monumental Gateway," A. Hadidi, ed., *Studies in the History and Archaeology of Jordan*, vol. I, Amman, 1982, pp. 201–7.

Dentzer, J. M. et al., "Fouille de la porte monumental à Iraq-al-Amir," *ADAJ* 26, 1982, pp. 301–21.

Descat, R., "Mnesimachos, Herodote, et le système tributaire Achéménide," *REA* 87, 1985, pp. 97–112.

Dever, W. G., *Gezer* vol. I, Jerusalem, 1970.

—— *Gezer* vol. II, Jerusalem, 1974.

Dinur, J., *Taxation System of Palestine in the Roman Age as Reflected in Talmudic Literature (63 BC–395 AD)*, Ph.D. Thesis, Hebrew University of Jerusalem, 1982, (Heb.).

Dittenberger, W., ed., *Orientis Graeci Inscriptiones Selectae*, Leipzig, 1903–5.

—— ed., *Sylloge Inscriptionum Graecarum*, Leipzig, 1915–24.

Donner, H. and Röllig, W., *Kanaanäische und aramäische Inschriften*, Wiesbaden, 1962.

Doran, R., "Judith," R. A. Kraft and G. W. E. Nickelsburg, eds, *Early Judaism and its Modern Interpreters*, Atlanta, 1986, pp. 302–4.

Dorsey, D. A., *The Roads and Highways of Ancient Israel*, Baltimore and London, 1991.

Dos Santos, E. C., *An Expanded Hebrew Index for the Hatch–Redpath Concordance to the Septuaginta*, Jerusalem, n.d.

Dothan, M., "Ashdod," *NEAEHL*, vol. 1, pp. 93–102.

Drèze, J. and Sen, A., *Hunger and Public Action*, Oxford, 1989.

Driver, S. R., *An Introduction to the Literature of the Old Testament*, New York, 1960.

Duncan-Jones, R., "The Choenix, the Artaba, and the Modius," *ZPE* 21, 1976, pp. 43–52.

—— *The Economy of the Roman Empire* (ERE), Cambridge, 1982.

—— "The Price of Wheat in Roman Egypt Under the Principate," *Chiron* 6, 1976, pp. 241–62.

—— *Structure and Scale in the Roman Economy*, Cambridge, 1990.

Dyson, S. L., "Native Revolt Patterns in the Roman Empire," *ANRW*, vol. II.3, Berlin, 1975, pp. 138–75.

—— "Native Revolts," *Historia* 20, 1971, pp. 239–74.

Edelstein, G., Gat, Y., and Gibson, S., "Food Production and Water Storage in the Jerusalem Region," *Qadmoniot* XVI (61), 1983, pp. 16–23, (Heb.).

Edgar, C. C., "Introduction," *Zenon Papyri in the University of Michigan Collection*, Ann Arbor, 1931, pp. 1–55.

—— ed., *Zenon papyri, catalogue général des antiquités égyptiennes du musée du Caire*, vols I–V, Cairo, 1925–40.

Edwards, G. W., "The Maladjustment of Palestinian Economy Under Herod," *Journal of Bible and Religion* 17, 1949, pp. 116–19.

Edwards, O., "Herodian Chronology," *PEQ* 114, 1982, pp. 29–42.

Efron, J., "Bar-Kokhva in the Light of the Palestinian and Babylonian Talmudic Traditions," A. Oppenheimer and U. Rappaport, eds, *The Bar-Kokhva Revolt: A New Approach*, Jerusalem, 1984, pp. 47–106, (Heb.).

—— "Simon ben Shetah and Alexander Jannaeus," *Studies on the Hasmonean Period*, Leiden, 1987, pp. 143–218.

Elgavish, J., "Shiqmona," *NEAEHL*, vol. 4, 1993, pp. 1,373–6.

Encyclopedia of Agriculture, The, ed. H. Halperin, Tel-Aviv, 1966–87, (Heb.).

Encyclopedia Biblica, Jerusalem, 1955–88, (Heb.).

Eshel, E., Eshel, H., and Yardeni, A., "A Qumran Composition Containing Part of Ps. 154 and a Prayer for the Welfare of King Jonathan and His Kingdom," *IEJ* 42, 1992, pp. 199–229.

Eshel, H., "The Prayer of Joseph: A Papyrus from Masada and the Samaritan Temple on ΑΡΓΑPIZIN," *Zion* LVI, 1991, pp. 125–36, (Heb.).

Evans, J. K., "Wheat Production and its Social Consequences in the Roman World," *Classical Quarterly* n.s. 31, 1981, pp. 428–42.

Fager, J., *Land Tenure and the Biblical Jubilee*, Sheffield, 1993.

Feldman, L., "The Term 'Galileans' in Josephus," *JQR* 72, 1981, pp. 50–3.

Feldman, M., "Wheats," N. W. Simmonds, ed., *Evolution of Crop Plants*, New York and London, 1976, pp. 120–8.

Feliks, J., *Agriculture in Palestine in the Period of the Mishna and Talmud*, Jerusalem, 1963.

—— "The Five Species," *EJ*, vol. 6, pp. 1,332–3.

—— "*Ha-hakla'ut ha-Yehudit beEretz-Yisrael bi-Tkufat ha-Mishna ve-ha-Talmud*," Z. Baras et al., eds, *Eretz Israel from the Destruction of the Second Temple to the Muslim Conquest*, Jerusalem, 1982, pp. 420–41, (Heb.).

—— "*Motivim shel Nof ve-Hakla'ut mi-Yamei Shivat Tzion*," H. Gaveryahu, ed., *Sefer Zer-Kavod*, Haifa, 1968, pp. 315–22, (Heb.).

Fensham, F. C., *The Book of Ezra, Nehemiah: The New International Commentary on the Old Testament*, Grand Rapids, 1982.

Fiensy, D. A., *The Social History of Palestine in the Herodian Period: The Land is Mine, Studies in the Bible and Early Christianity* 20, Lewiston, Queenston, Lampeter, 1991.

Fine, J. V. A., *Horoi: Studies in Mortgage, Real Security, and Land Tenure in Ancient Athens* (*Hesperia*, suppl. IX), Athens, 1951.

Finkelstein, I., "A Few Notes on Demographic Data from Recent Generations and Ethnoarchaeology," *PEQ* 122, 1990, pp. 47–52.

Finkelstein, J. J., "Amisaduqa's Edict and the Babylonian 'Law Codes,'" *JCS* 15, 1961, pp. 91–104.

Finkelstein, L., "The Pharisees: Their Origin and Their Philosophy," *HTR* 22, 1929, pp. 189–90.

Finley, M. I., "The Ancient City: From Fustel De Coulanges to Max Weber and Beyond," *Economy and Society in Ancient Greece*, New York, 1982, pp. 3–23, 250–3.

—— *The Ancient Economy*, London, 1985.

—— "Debt-Bondage and the Problem of Slavery," *Economy and Society in Ancient Greece*, New York, 1982, pp. 150–66, 267–71.

—— *Land and Credit in Ancient Athens, 500–200 BC*, New York, 1952, reprinted 1973.

Fischer, T., "Zur Seleukideninschrift von Hefzibah," *ZPE* 33, 1979, pp. 131–8.

Fisher, M., "*Naveh ha-Midbar Ein Boqeq: Yihidah Ta'asiyatit be-tekufat Beit Hordos: Skirah Arkhiologit-Historit*," *Nofim* 11–12, 1979, pp. 21–38, (Heb.).

Fitzmyer, J. A. and Harrington, D. J., *A Manual of Palestinian Aramaic Texts*, Rome, 1978.

Flusser, D., "Qumran and the Famine During the Reign of Herod," *IMJ* 6, 1987, pp. 7–15.

Foakes-Jackson, F. J. and Lake, K., *The Beginnings of Christianity*, part I, V, Grand Rapids, 1966 (reprint).

Forbes, H., "Of Grandfathers and Grand Theories: The Hierarchised Ordering of Responses to Hazard in a Greek Rural Community," P. Halstead and J. O'Shea, eds, *Bad Year Economics: Cultural Responses to Risk and Uncertainty*, Cambridge, 1989, pp. 87–97.

Forbes, P. B. R., review of Fine, *Horoi*, in *The Classical Review* 3, 1953, pp. 109–11.

Foxhall, L. and Forbes, H. A., "Sitometreia: The Role of Grain as a Staple Food in Classical Antiquity," *Chiron* 12, 1982, pp. 41–90.

Frank, T., "Dominium in Solo Provinciali" and "Ager Publicus," *JRS* 17, 1927, pp. 141–61.

—— ed., *An Economic Survey of Ancient Rome*, vols I–V, Baltimore, 1938, reprinted Paterson, NJ, 1959.

—— "The Financial Crisis of 33 AD," *AJPh* 56, 1935, pp. 336–41.

Frankel, R., *The History of the Processing of Wine and Oil in Galilee in the Period of the Bible, the Mishna and the Talmud*, unpublished Ph.D. Thesis, University of Tel-Aviv, 1984.

BIBLIOGRAPHY

Frankel, R. and Finkelstein, I., "The Northwest Corner of Eretz-Israel in the Baraita Boundaries of Eretz-Israel," *Cathedra* 27, 1983, pp. 39–46, (Heb.).
Frankel, R. and Gazov, N., "Tefen, a Hellenistic Stronghold in Galilee," E. Schiller, ed., *Zev Vilnay's Jubilee Volume*, part II, Jerusalem, 1987, pp. 163–5.
Fraser, P. M., *Ptolemaic Alexandria*, Oxford, 1971.
Freund, Y., "*Ve-eten aleyhem Kahala Gedola*," H. Gaveryahu, ed., *Sefer Zer-Kavod*, Haifa, 1968, pp. 323–32, (Heb.).
Frey, J. B., *Corpus Inscriptionum Judaicarum*, vols I–II, Rome, 1936–52.
Freyne, S., "The Galileans in the Light of Josephus' Vita," *NTS* 26, 1980, pp. 397–413.
—— *Galilee from Alexander the Great to Hadrian*, Notre Dame, 1980.
Frisch, P., ed., *Die Inschriften von Ilion*, Bonn, 1975.
Frye, R. N., *History of Ancient Iran*, Berlin and New York, 1984.
Fuks, A., "Marcus Julius Alexander (Relating to the History of Philo's Family)," *Zion* XIII–XIV, 1948–9, pp. 10–17, (Heb.).
—— "Notes on the Archive of Nicanor," *Social Conflict in Ancient Greece*, Leiden, 1984, pp. 207–16.
—— "Patterns and Types of Social–Economic Revolution," *Ancient Society* 5, 1974, pp. 51–81.
—— "Τοῖς ἀπορουμένοις κοινωνεῖν: in the Sharing of Property by the Rich with the Poor in Greek Theory and Practice," *SCI* 5, 1979–80, pp. 46–63.
Fuks, G., "On the Reliability of a Reference in Josephus," U. Rappaport, ed., *Josephus Flavius: Historian of Eretz-Israel in the Hellenistic–Roman Period*, Jerusalem, 1982, pp. 131–8, (Heb.).
—— *Scythopolis: A Greek City in Eretz-Israel*, Jerusalem, 1983, (Heb.).
—— "Simon Bar Giora, *Gerasenos*," *Zion* LII, 1987, pp. 141–52, (Heb.).
—— "Tel Anafa: A Proposed Identification," *SCI* 5, 1979–80, pp. 178–84.
Funck, B., "Zu den Landschenkungen hellenistischer Könige," *Klio* 60, 1978, pp. 45–55.
Gabba, E., "The Finances of King Herod," A. Kasher, U. Rappaport, G. Fuks, eds, *Greece and Rome in Eretz-Israel*, Jerusalem, 1990, pp. 160–8.
Galil, G., "Parathon, Timnatha, and the Fortifications of Bacchides," *Cathedra* 63, 1992, pp. 22–31, (Heb.).
Gallant, T. W., "Agricultural Systems, Land Tenure, and the Reforms of Solon," *Annual of the British School of Athens* 77, 1982, pp. 111–24.
—— *A Fisherman's Tale: An Analysis of the Potential Productivity of Fishing in the Ancient World*, Miscellanea Graeca, fasciculus 7, Ghent, 1985.
Gamoran, H., "The Biblical Law Against Loans on Interest," *JNES*, vol. 30, 1971, pp. 127–34.
Gapp, K. S., *Famine in the Roman World: From the Founding of Rome to the Time of Trajan*, Ph.D. Dissertation, Princeton University, 1934.
—— "The Universal Famine Under Claudius," *HTR* 28, 1935, pp. 258–65.
Garnsey, P., *Famine and Food Supply in the Graeco-Roman World*, Cambridge, 1988.
—— "Famine in Rome," P. Garnsey and C. R. Whittaker, eds, *Trade and Famine in Classical Antiquity*, Cambridge, 1983, pp. 56–64.
—— "Grain for Rome," P. Garnsey, K. Hopkins, C. R. Whittaker, eds, *Trade in the Ancient Economy*, Berkeley, 1983, pp. 118–38.

—— "Non-Slave Labour in the Roman World," *Non-Slave Labour in the Greco-Roman World*, Cambridge, 1980, pp. 34–47.

Garnsey, P. and Morris, I., "Risk and the Polis: The Evolution of Institutionalised Responses to Food Supply Problems in the Ancient Greek State," P. Halstead and J. O'Shea, eds, *Bad Year Economics: Cultural Responses to Risk and Uncertainty*, Cambridge, 1989, pp. 98–105.

Garnsey, P. and Saller, R., *The Roman Empire: Economy, Society, and Culture*, Berkeley and Los Angeles, 1987.

Garnsey, P. and Whittaker, C. R., eds, *Trade and Famine in Classical Antiquity*, Cambridge, 1983.

Garnsey, P., Hopkins, K., and Whittaker, C. R., eds, *Trade in the Ancient Economy*, Berkeley, 1983.

Gera, D., "On the Credibility of the History of the Tobiads," A. Kasher, U. Rappaport, G. Fuks, eds, *Greece and Rome in Eretz Israel*, Jerusalem, 1990, pp. 21–38.

Geraty, L. T., "The Khirbet El-Kôm Bilingual Ostracon," *BASOR* 220, 1975, pp. 55–61.

—— "Recent Suggestions on the Bilingual Ostracon from Khirbet El-Kôm," *St Andrews University Seminary Studies* 19, 1981, pp. 137–40.

Gichon, M., "En Boqeq," *NEAEHL*, vol. 2, pp. 395–9.

Gil, M., "Land Ownership in Palestine Under Roman Rule," *Revue internationale des droits de l'antiquité*, 17, 1970, pp. 11–53.

Golan, D., *A History of the Hellenistic World*, Jerusalem, 1983, (Heb.).

—— "Josephus, Alexander's Visit to Jerusalem, and Modern Historiography," U. Rappaport, ed., *Josephus Flavius: Historian of Eretz-Israel in the Hellenistic–Roman Period*, Jerusalem, 1982, pp. 29–55, (Heb.).

Goldmann, F., "Der Ölbau in Palästina in der tannaitischen Zeit," *MGWJ* 50, 1906, pp. 563–80, 707–28; 51, 1907, pp. 17–40, 129–41.

Goldschmid, L., "Impôts et droits de douane en Judée," *REJ* 34, 1897, pp. 192–217.

Goldstein, J. A., *I Maccabees*, AB, vol. 41, New York, 1976.

—— *II Maccabees*, AB, vol. 41A, New York, 1983.

—— "The Tales of the Tobiads," J. Neusner, ed., *Christianity, Judaism and Other Greco-Roman Cults*, vol. III, Leiden, 1975, pp. 85–123.

Golomb, B. and Kedar, Y., "Ancient Agriculture in the Galilee Mountains," *IEJ* 21, 1971, pp. 136–140.

Goodblatt, D., "*Yehudei Eretz-Yisrael be-Shanim 70–132*," U. Rappaport, ed., *Judea and Rome: The Jewish Revolts*, Ramat Gan, 1983, pp. 155–84, (Heb.).

Goodman, M., "The First Jewish Revolt: Social Conflict and the Problem of Debt," *JJS* 33, 1982, pp. 417–27.

—— "Kosher Olive Oil in Antiquity," P. R. Davies and R. T. White, eds, *A Tribute to Geza Vermes: Essays on Jewish and Christian Literature and History*, Sheffield, 1990, pp. 227–45.

—— "The Origins of the Great Revolt: A Conflict of Status Criteria," A. Kasher, U. Rappaport, G. Fuks, eds, *Greece and Rome in Israel*, Jerusalem, 1990, pp. 39–53.

—— *The Ruling Class of Judaea*, Cambridge, 1987.

Gophna, R. and Ayalon, E., "History of Settlement in the Tel Michal Region,"

Z. Herzog, G. Rapp Jr, O. Negbi, eds, *Excavations at Tel Michal, Israel*, Minneapolis and Tel-Aviv, 1989.

Grabbe, L. L., *Judaism from Cyrus to Hadrian*, vols I–II, Minneapolis, 1992.

—— "Maccabean Chronology: 167–164 or 168–165 BCE," *JBL* 110, 1991, pp. 59–74.

Grant, F. C., *The Economic Background of the Gospels*, Oxford, 1926.

—— "The Economic Significance of Messianism," *Anglican Theological Review* 6, 1923, pp. 196–213; 7, 1924, pp. 281–9.

Greene, K., *The Archaeology of the Roman Economy*, London, 1986.

Greenfield, J. C., "The Aramaic Legal Texts of the Achaemenian Period," *Transeuphratène* 3, 1990, pp. 85–92.

Grintz, Y. M., *Sefer Yehudith*, Jerusalem, 1986, (Heb.).

Gulak, A., *Yesodei ha-Mishpat ha-Ivri*, Berlin, 1922, reprinted Tel-Aviv, 1967, (Heb.).

Gutman, J., "Alexander of Macedonia in Palestine," *Tarbiz* XI, 1940, pp. 271–94, (Heb.).

—— "*Shiabud Gufo shel Adam be-Hovotav be-Torat Yisrael*," Y. Baer, J. Gutman, M. Schwabe, eds, *Sefer Dinaburg*, Jerusalem, 1949, pp. 68–82.

Gutman, S., "Gamala," *NEAEHL*, vol. 2, pp. 459–63.

Haas, N., "Anthropological Observations on the Skeletal Remains from Giv'at HaMivtar," *IEJ* 20, 1970, pp. 38–59.

Hachlili, R., "The Goliath Family in Jericho: Funerary Inscriptions from a First Century AD Jewish Monumental Tomb," *BASOR* 235, 1979, pp. 32–47.

Hadas, M., *Aristeas to Philocrates (Letter of Aristeas)*, New York, 1973.

Hadas-Lebel, M., "La Fiscalité romaine dans la littérature rabbinique jusqu'à la fin du IIIᵉ siècle," *REJ* 143, 1984, pp. 5–29.

Hahn, I., "Königsland und königliche Besteuerung im hellenistischen Osten," *Klio* 60, 1978, pp. 11–34.

Halligan, J. M., "Nehemiah 5: By Way of Response to Hoglund and Smith," P. R. Davies, ed., *Second Temple Studies*, vol. 1, *Persian Period*, pp. 146–53.

Halstead, P., "The Economy Has a Normal Surplus: Economic Stability and Social Change Among Early Farming Communities of Thessaly, Greece," P. Halstead and J. O'Shea, eds, *Bad Year Economics: Cultural Responses to Risk and Uncertainty*, Cambridge, 1989, pp. 68–80.

Halstead, P. and O'Shea, J., "Introduction: Cultural Responses to Risk and Uncertainty," P. Halstead and J. O'Shea, eds, *Bad Year Economics: Cultural Responses to Risk and Uncertainty*, Cambridge, 1989, pp. 1–7.

Hamburger, A., "Surface Finds from Caesarea Maritima–Tesserae," L. I. Levine and E. Netzer, eds, *Excavations at Caesarea Maritima 1975, 1976, 1979: Final Report* (Qedem 21), Jerusalem, 1986, pp. 187–204.

Hamel, G., *Poverty and Charity in Roman Palestine*, Ph.D. Thesis, University of California, Santa Cruz, 1983.

Hands, A. R., *Charities and Social Aid in Greece and Rome*, Ithaca, NY, 1968.

Haran, M., "*Matanot Aniim*," *Encyclopedia Biblica*, vol. V, p. 758.

Harper, G. M., Jr, "A Study in the Commercial Relations Between Egypt and Syria in the Third Century Before Christ," *AJPh* 49, 1928, pp. 1–35.

—— "Village Administration in the Roman Province of Syria," *YCS* 1, 1928, pp. 105–68.

Heichelheim, F. M., "New Light on Currency and Inflation in Hellenistic–Roman Times from Inscriptions and Papyri," *Economic History* 10, 1935, pp. 1–11.
—— "Roman Syria," *ESAR*, vol. IV, pp. 121–257, 927–9.
—— "Sitos," *P-W* suppl. VI, col. 819–92, Stuttgart, 1935.
—— *Wirtschaftliche Schwankungen der Zeit von Alexander bis Augustus*, Jena, 1930.
Heltzer, M., "The Provincial Taxation in the Achaemenian Empire and 'Forty Shekels of Silver' (Neh. 5:15)," *Michmanim* 6, 1992, pp. 15–25.
—— "The Social and Fiscal Reforms of Nehemiah in Judah and the Attitude of the Achaemenid Kings to the Internal Affairs of the Autonomous Provinces," *Apollinaris* 62, 1989, pp. 333–54.
Heltzer, M. and Eitam, D., *Olive Oil in Antiquity*, Haifa, 1987.
Heltzer, M. and Kochman, M., *Encyclopedia Olam Ha-Tanach: Ezra ve-Nehemia*, Jerusalem, 1985, (Heb.).
Hengel, M., "Das Gleichnis von den Weingärten Mc 12: 1–12 im Lichte der Zenonpapyri und der rabbinischen Gleichnisse," *ZNW* 59, 1968, pp. 1–39.
—— *Judaism and Hellenism*, Philadelphia, 1981.
—— *The Zealots*, Edinburgh, 1989.
Hengel, M., Charlesworth, J. H., and Mendels, D., "The Polemical Character of 'On Kingship' in the Temple Scroll: An Attempt at Dating 11Q Temple," *JJS* 37, 1986, pp. 28–38.
Henrey, K. H., "Land Tenure in the Old Testament," *PEQ* 86, 1954, pp. 5–15.
Herbert, S., "Tel Anafa," *IEJ* 23, 1973, pp. 113–17.
—— "Tel Anafa," *IEJ* 28, 1978, pp. 271–4.
Herz, J., "Grossgrundbesitz in Palästina im Zeitalter Jesu," *PJB* 24, 1928, pp. 98–113.
Hirschfeld, Y. and Birger-Calderon, R., "Early Roman and Byzantine Estates near Caesarea," *IEJ* 41, 1991, pp. 81–111.
Hizmi, H., "Beiyudat, Khirbet el-," *NEAEHL*, vol. 1, pp. 181–2.
Hoehner, H. W., *Herod Antipas*, Cambridge, 1972, reprinted Grand Rapids, 1980.
Hoglund, K. C., "The Achaemenid Context," P. R. Davies, ed., *Second Temple Studies*, vol. 1, *Persian Period*, Sheffield, 1991, pp. 54–73.
—— *Achaemenid Imperial Administration in Syria–Palestine and the Missions of Ezra and Nehemiah*, Atlanta, 1992.
Hohlwein, N., "Le Blé d'Égypte," *Études de papyrologie* 4, 1938, pp. 3–120.
Hopkins, I. W. J., "The City Region in Roman Palestine," *PEQ* 112, 1980, pp. 19–32.
Hopkins, K., "Economic Growth and Towns in Classical Antiquity," P. Abrams and E. A. Wrigley, eds, *Towns in Societies*, Cambridge, 1978, pp. 35–77.
—— "Models, Ships, and Staples," P. Garnsey and C. R. Whittaker, eds, *Trade and Famine in Classical Antiquity*, Cambridge, 1983, pp. 84–109.
Horgan, M. P., *Pesharim: Qumran Interpretations of Biblical Books*, Washington DC, 1979.
Horsley, R. A., "Ancient Jewish Banditry and the Revolt against Rome, AD 66–70," *CBQ* 43, 1981, pp. 409–32.

—— "Josephus and the Bandits," *JStJ* 10, 1979, pp. 37–62.

Howgego, C., "The Supply and Use of Money in the Roman World 200 BC to AD 300," *JRS* 82, 1992, pp. 1–31.

Hugo, G. J., "The Demographic Impact of Famine: A Review," B. Currey and G. Hugo, eds, *Famine as a Geographical Phenomenon*, Dordrecht, Boston, Lancaster, 1984, pp. 7–31.

Huntington, E., *Palestine and its Transformation*, London, 1911.

Hüttenmeister, F. and Reeg, G., *Die antiken Synagogen in Israel*, Wiesbaden, 1977.

Isaac, B., "The Babatha Archive: A Review Article," *IEJ* 42, 1992, pp. 62–75.

—— "A Donation for Herod's Temple in Jerusalem," *IEJ* 33, 1983, pp. 86–93.

—— "Judaea after AD 79," *JJS* 35, 1984, pp. 44–50.

—— "A Seleucid Inscription from Jamnia-on-the-Sea: Antiochus V Eupator and the Sidonians," *IEJ* 41, 1991, pp. 132–44.

Isaac, B. and Roll, I., *Roman Roads in Judea*, vol. I, Oxford, 1982.

Jacobson, D. M., "King Herod's 'Heroic' Public Image," *RB* 95, 1988, pp. 386–403.

Jalabert, L. and Mouterde, R., *Inscriptions Grecques et Latines de la Syrie*, Paris, 1929–82.

Jameson, M., "Famine in the Greek World," P. Garnsey and C. R. Whittaker, eds, *Trade and Famine in Classical Antiquity*, Cambridge, 1983, pp. 6–16.

Jameson, S., "Chronology of the Campaigns of Aelius Gallus and C. Petronius," *JRS* 58, 1968, pp. 77–8.

Japhet, S., "People and Land in the Restoration Period," G. Strecker, ed., *Das Land Israel in Biblischer Zeit*, Göttingen, 1983.

Jasny, N., "Competition among Grains in Classical Antiquity," *American Historical Review* XLVII, 1941–2, pp. 747–64.

—— "The Daily Bread of the Ancient Greeks and Romans," *Osiris* 9, 1950, pp. 227–253.

—— "Wheat Prices and Milling Costs in Classical Rome," *Wheat Studies of the Food Research Institute* 20, 1944, pp. 137–70.

—— *The Wheats of Classical Antiquity*, Baltimore, 1944.

Jastrow, M., *A Dictionary of the Targumim, the Talmud Babli and Yerushalmi, and the Midrashic Literature*, New York, 1950.

Jeremias, J., *Jerusalem in the Time of Jesus*, London, 1969.

Jeselsohn, D., "Hever Yehudim: A New Jewish Coin," *PEQ* 112, 1980, pp. 11–17.

Johnson, A. C., "Roman Egypt," *ESAR*, vol. II, 1938.

Jones, A. H. M., "Ancient Empires and the Economy: Rome," P. A. Brunt, ed., *The Roman Economy*, Oxford, 1974, pp. 114–39.

—— "The Cities of the Roman Empire," P. A. Brunt, ed., *The Roman Economy*, Oxford, 1974, pp. 1–34.

—— *The Greek City*, Oxford, 1940, reprinted New York, 1984.

—— "Review of Arnaldo Momigliano, *Ricerche Sull'Organizzazione Della Guidea Sotto Il Domino Romano (63 a.C.–70 d.C.)*, *Annali della R. Scuola Normale Superiore di Pisa*, series II, vol. III (1934 – XII)," *JRS* 25, 1935, pp. 228–31.

—— "Taxation in Antiquity," P. A. Brunt, ed., *The Roman Economy*, Oxford, 1974, pp. 151–86.

Jongman, W. and Dekker, R., "Public Intervention in the Food Supply in Pre-Industrial Europe," P. Halstead and J. O'Shea, eds, *Bad Year Economics: Cultural Responses to Risk and Uncertainty*, Cambridge, 1989, pp. 114–22.

Kahana, A., *Ha-Sefarim ha-Hitzonim*, Tel-Aviv, 1959, (Heb.).

Kampen, J., *The Hasideans and the Origin of Pharisaism: A Study of 1 and 2 Maccabees*, Ithaca, NY, 1990.

Kanael, B., "Notes on Alexander Jannaeus' Campaigns in the Coastal Region," *Tarbiz* XXIV, 1956, pp. 9–15, (Heb.) .

—— "The Partition of Judea by Gabinius," *IEJ* 7, 1957, pp. 98–106.

Karmon, Y., *Israel: A Regional Geography*, London, 1971.

Kasher, A., "Alexander Yannai's Wars with the Nabataeans," *Zion* L, 1985, pp. 107–20, (Heb.).

—— "The Changes in Manpower and Ethnic Composition of the Hasmonean Army, 167–63 BCE," *JQR* LXXXI, 1991, pp. 325–52.

—— "The Connection Between the Hellenistic Cities in Eretz-Israel and Gaius Caligula's Rescript to Install an Idol in the Temple," *Zion* LI, 1986, pp. 135–52, (Heb.).

—— ed., *The Great Jewish Revolt: Factors and Circumstances Leading to its Outbreak*, Jerusalem, 1983, (Heb.).

—— "*Hagirah ve-Hityashvut Yehudit be-Tfutzot be-Tekufah ha-Hellenistit–Romit*," A. Shinan, ed., *Emigration and Settlement in Jewish and General History*, Jerusalem, 1982, pp. 64–91, (Heb.).

—— *Jews and Hellenistic Cities in Eretz-Israel*, Tübingen, 1990.

—— *Jews, Idumaeans and Ancient Arabs*, Tübingen, 1988.

—— "*Masa Alexander ha-Gadol be-Eretz-Yisrael*," *Beit Mikra* 2, 1975, pp. 187–208, (Heb.).

—— "*Mavo: ha-Reka ha-Sibati ve-ha-Nisibati le-Milhamet ha-Yehudim be-Romayim*," A. Kasher, ed., *The Great Jewish Revolt: Factors and Circumstances Leading to its Outbreak*, Jerusalem, 1983, pp. 9–90, (Heb.).

—— "A Second-Century BCE Greek Inscription from Iamnia," *Cathedra* 63, 1992, pp. 3–21, (Heb.).

—— "*Temurot Demographiot ve-Mediniot be-Arei ha-Hof Me-Az Ha-Kibush Ha-Helenisti ve-Ad Ha-Kibush Ha-Romi*," Sh. Bonimovitz, M. Kochavi, A. Kasher, eds, *Yishuvim, Okhlusiah, ve-Kalkala be-Eretz-Yisrael beEt HaAtika*, Tel-Aviv, 1988, pp. 166–204, (Heb.).

Kaufman, Y., *Toldot ha-Emunah ha-Yisraelit*, Jerusalem and Tel-Aviv, 1967, (Heb.).

Kindler, A. and Klimowsky, E. W., *The Function and Pattern of the Jewish Coins and the City-Coins of Palestine and Phoenicia*, Jerusalem, 1968.

Kippenberg, H. G., *Religion und Klassenbildung im antiken Judäa*, Göttingen, 1982.

Kislev, M. E., "A Barley Store of the Bar-Kochba Rebels (Roman Period)," *Israel Journal of Botany* 35, 1986, pp. 183–96.

—— "*Hitta* and *Kussumet*, Notes on their Interpretation," *Lešonénu* XXXVII, 1972–3, pp. 83–95, 243–52, (Heb.).

Klausner, J., *Ha-Historia Shel ha-Bayit ha-Sheni*, Jerusalem, 1958, (Heb.).

—— "How Many Jews Will Be Able to Live in Palestine? Based on an Analysis of the Jewish Population in Palestine in the Days of the Second Temple," *JSS* 11, 1949, pp. 119–28.

—— *Ke-she-Euma Nilchemet al Heruta*, Tel-Aviv, 1951, pp. 93–116, (Heb.).

Klein, S., "Βεμσελις – Βαιθομμις, Βαιθομμη," *Tarbiz* I, 1930, pp. 137–44, (Heb.).

—— *Eretz-Yehuda*, Tel-Aviv, 1939, (Heb.).

—— "Notes on the History of Large Estates in Palestine," *Bulletin of the Jewish Palestine Exploration Society* I.3, 1933, Pt. 1 pp. 3–9; III.4, 1936, pp. 109–16, (Heb.).

Kloner, A., "Maresha," *Qadmoniot* XXIV, 1995–6, pp. 70–85, (Heb.).

—— "Mareshah (Marisa)," *NEAEHL*, vol. 3, 1993, pp. 948–57.

Kreissig, H., "Eine beachtenswerte Theorie zur Organization altvorderorientalischer Tempelgemeinden im Achämenidenreich: Zur J. P. Weinberg's 'Bürger-Tempel-Gemeinde' in Juda," *Klio* 66, 1984, pp. 35–9.

—— "Landed Property in the Hellenistic Orient," *Eirene* 15, 1977, pp. 5–26.

—— "Die Landswirtschaftliche Situation in Palästina vor dem Judäischen Krieg," *Acta Antiqua Academiae Scientiarum Hungaricae* 17, 1969, pp. 223–54.

—— "Der Makkabäeraufstand," *Studii Clasice* 4, 1962, pp. 143–75.

—— "A Marxist View of Josephus' Account of the Jewish War," L. H. Feldman and G. Hata, eds, *Josephus, the Bible and History*, Detroit, 1989, pp. 265–77.

—— *Die Sozialen Zusammenhänge des Judäischen Krieges*, Berlin, 1970.

—— *Die Sozialökonomische Situation in Juda zur Achämenidenzeit*, Berlin, 1973.

—— *Wirtschaft und Gesellschaft im Seleukidenreich*, Berlin, 1978.

Landau, Y. H., "A Greek Inscription Found Near Hefzibah," *IEJ* 16, 1966, pp. 54–70.

Lapp, P. W. and Lapp, N. L., "'Iraq el-Emir," *NEAEHL*, vol. 2, 1993, pp. 646–9.

Leach, J., *Pompey the Great*, London, 1978.

Lehmann, M. R., "Studies in the Murabba'at and Nahal Hever Documents," *Revue de Qumran* 4, 1963, pp. 53–81.

Lemche, N.-P., "*Andurarum* and *Mišarum*: Comments on the Problem of Social Edicts and their Application in the Ancient Near East," *JNES* 38, 1979, pp. 11–22.

Lenger, M.-T., *Corpus des Ordonnances des Ptolemées*, Brussels, 1980.

Le Rider, G., *Suse sous les Séleucides et les Parthes*, Paris, 1965.

Levine, L. I., "The Hasmonean Conquest of Strato's Tower," *IEJ* 24, 1974, pp. 62–9.

—— "The Political Struggle between Pharisees and Sadducees in the Hasmonean Period," A. Oppenheimer, U. Rappaport, M. Stern, eds, *Jerusalem in the Second Temple Period: Abraham Schalit Memorial Volume*, Jerusalem, 1980, pp. 61–83, (Heb.).

—— *The Roman Period from the Conquest to the Ben Kozba War (63 BCE–135 CE)*, M. Stern, ed., *The History of Eretz Israel*, vol. 4, *The Roman Byzantine Period*, Jerusalem, 1984, (Heb.).

Lewis, N., *The Documents from the Bar Kochba Period in the Cave of Letters*, vol. 2, *Greek Papyri*, Jerusalem, 1989.

Lewy, H., "The Biblical Institution of *Dᵉrôr* in the Light of Akkadian Documents," *EI* 5, 1958, pp. 21–31.

Lichtenstein, H., "Die Fastenrolle: Eine Untersuchung zur Juedisch–Hellenistischen Geschichte," *HUCA* 89, 1931, pp. 257–351.

Liddell, H. G. and Scott, R., *A Greek–English Lexicon*, with supplement, Oxford, 1968.

Lieberman, S., "Misunderstood Expressions and Words," *Greek in Jewish Palestine*, New York, 1965, pp. 161–85.

—— "The Three Abrogations of Johanan the High Priest," *Hellenism in Jewish Palestine*, New York, 1962, pp. 139–43.

—— *Tosefta Ki-fshutah*, part IX, *Order Nezikin*, New York, 1988.

Liphschitz, N. and Waisel, Y., "Dendroarchaeological Investigations in Israel," *IEJ* 23, 1973, pp. 30–6.

Liver, J., "The Half-Shekel Offering in Biblical and Post-Biblical Literature," *HTR* 56, 1963, pp. 173–98.

Livi-Bacci, M., "The Nutrition–Mortality Link in Past Times," R. I. Rotberg and T. K. Rabb, eds, *Hunger and History*, Cambridge, 1985, pp. 95–100.

Loewenstamm, S. E., "נשד and מ/תרבית," *JBL* 88, 1969, pp. 78–80.

Luria, B. Z., "*Har ha-Melekh .. Ma-Hu?*" *The Hasmonean Kings*, Tel-Aviv, 1985, pp. 169–76, (Heb.).

—— *Megillath Ta'anith*, Jerusalem, 1964, (Heb.).

—— *Mi-Yannai Ad Hordos*, Jerusalem, 1974, (Heb.).

—— *Yannai ha-Melekh*, Jerusalem, 1960, (Heb.).

MacAdam, H. I., "Some Aspects of Land Tenure and Social Development in the Roman Near East: Arabia, Phoenicia and Syria," T. Khalidi, ed., *Land Tenure and Social Transformation in the Middle East*, Beirut, 1984, pp. 45–62.

McConnell, J. W., *The Basic Teachings of the Great Economists*, New York, 1943.

McCown, C. C., "The Density of Population in Ancient Palestine," *JBL* 66, 1947, pp. 425–36.

MacMullen, R., "Appendix A: Famines," *Enemies of the Roman Order*, Harvard, 1967.

Magen, Y., "A Fortified Town of the Hellenistic Period on Mount Gerizim," *Qadmoniot* XIX (75–6), 1986, pp. 91–101, (Heb.).

—— "Kalandia: A Vineyard Farm and Winery of the Second Temple Times," *Qadmoniot* XVII (66–7), 1984, pp. 61–71, (Heb.).

—— "Mount Gerizim: A Temple City," *Qadmoniot* XXIII (91–2), 1990, pp. 70–96, (Heb.).

—— "Qalandiyeh," *NEAEHL*, vol. 4, 1993, pp. 1,197–1,200.

Maisler (Mazar), B., "Topographical Researches II, The Place of Origin of the Maccabeans," *BJPES* VIII, 1941, pp. 105–7, (Heb.).

Maloney, R. P., "Usury and Restrictions on Interest-taking in the Ancient Near East," *CBQ* 36, 1974, pp. 1–20.

—— "Usury in Greek, Roman and Rabbinic Thought," *Traditio* 27, 1971, pp. 79–109.

Mandelkern, S., *Veteris Testamenti Concordantiae*, Jerusalem and Tel-Aviv, 1964, (Heb.).

Maoz, Z., "The City Plan of Jerusalem in the Hasmonean and Herodian Period," *Eretz-Israel* 18, 1985, pp. 46–57, (Heb.).

Marrou, H.-I., *Histoire de l'éducation dans l'antiquité*, Paris, 1965.

Mayerson, P. M., "Wheat in the Roman World: An Addendum," *The Classical Quarterly*, n.s. XXXIV, 1984, pp. 243–5.

Mazar, B., *Geva: Archaeological Discoveries at Tell Abu-Shusha, Mishmar ha-'Emeq, Ha-Kibbutz Ha-Meuhad*, Jerusalem, 1988, (Heb.).

—— "The Tobiads," *IEJ* 7, 1957, pp. 137–45, 229–38.

Meijer, F. and van Nijf, O., eds, *Trade, Transport and Society in the Ancient World*, London and New York, 1992.

Mendel, P., *Ha-Sipur be-Midrash Eikha – Nusakh ve-Signon*, M.A. Thesis, Hebrew University of Jerusalem, 1983, (Heb.).

Meshorer, Y., *Ancient Jewish Coinage*, Dix Hills, NY, 1982.

—— "A Stone Weight from the Reign of Herod," *IEJ* 20, 1970, pp. 97–8.

Michel, O., "τελώνης," G. Friedrich, ed., trans. and ed. G. W. Bromiley, *TDNT*, vol. 8, Grand Rapids, 1972, pp. 88–105.

Milik, J. T., "Un contrat juif de l'an 134 après J-C," *RB* 61, 1954, pp. 182–190.

—— "Le Couvercle de Bethpage," *Hommages à André Dupont-Sommer*, Paris, 1971.

—— "Deux documents inédits du désert de Juda," *Biblica* 38, 1957, pp. 245–68.

Millar, F., "The Mediterranean and the Roman Revolution: Politics, War and the Economy," *Past and Present* 102, 1984, pp. 3–24.

—— "The Problem of Hellenistic Syria," A. Kuhrt and S. Sherwin-White, eds, *Hellenism in the East*, London, 1987, pp. 110–33.

Miller, J. M. and Hayes, J. H., *A History of Ancient Israel and Judah*, Philadelphia, 1986.

Mitchell, H. G., Smith, J. M. P., and Bewer, J. A., *ICC: Haggai, Zechariah, Malachi and Jonah*, Edinburgh, 1912.

Mittwoch, A., "Tribute and Land-Tax in Seleucid Judaea," *Biblica* 36, 1955, pp. 352–61.

Moldenke, H. N. and Moldenke, A. L., *Plants of the Bible*, New York, 1952.

Möller, C. and Schmitt, G., *Siedlungen Palästinas Nach Flavius Josephus* (*Beihefte Zum Tübinger Atlas des Vordern Orients* 14), Wiesbaden, 1976.

Momigliano, A., "Flavius Josephus and Alexander's Visit to Jerusalem," *Athenaeum* 57, 1979, pp. 442–8.

—— *Ricerche Sull'Organizzazione Della Guidea Sotto Il Domino Romano (63 a.C.–70 d.C.)*, Annali della R. Scuola Normale Superiore di Pisa, series II, vol. III, 1934: XII; reprinted Amsterdam, 1967.

Moore, C. A., *Judith* (*AB* 40), Garden City, NY, 1985.

Mor, M., *The Bar-Kochba Revolt: Its Extent and Effect*, Jerusalem, 1991, (Heb.).

—— "Bar Kochba: Was it a Farmers' Uprising?" A. Kasher, A. Oppenheimer, U. Rappaport, eds, *Man and Land in Eretz-Israel in Antiquity*, Jerusalem, 1986, pp. 7–19, (Heb.).

Morkholm, O., "The Ptolemaic Coinage in Phoenicia and the Fifth War with Syria," E. van't Dack, P. van Dessel, W. van Gucht, eds, *Egypt and the Hellenistic World*, Leuven, 1983, pp. 241–50.

Moxnes, H., *The Economy of the Kingdom*, Philadelphia, 1988.

Naveh, J., "The Aramaic Ostraca from Tel Beer-Sheba," *Tel Aviv* 6, 1979, pp. 182–98.

—— *On Sherd and Papyrus*, Jerusalem, 1992, (Heb.).

—— "The Ossuary Inscriptions from Giv'at HaMivtar," *IEJ* 20, 1970, pp. 33–7.

Netzer, E., "Herod's Building Projects: State Necessity or Personal Necessity?" *The Jerusalem Cathedra*, vol. 1, 1981, pp. 48–61, 73–80.

—— "Tulul Abu el 'Alayiq," *NEAEHL*, vol. 2, 1993, pp. 682–91.

Neufeld, E., "Inalienability of Mobile and Immobile Pledges in the Laws of the Bible," *RIDA* 9, 1968, pp. 33–44.

—— "The Prohibition Against Loans at Interest in Ancient Hebrew Loans," *HUCA* 26, 1955, pp. 355–412.

—— "The Rate of Interest and the Text of Nehemiah 5.11," *JQR* 44, 1953–4, pp. 147–204.

—— "Socio-economic Background of Yobel and Semitta," *Rivista Degli Studi Orientali* 33, 1958, pp. 53–124.

Nickelsburg, G. W. E., *Jewish Literature Between the Bible and the Mishnah*, Philadelphia, 1987.

Nir, D., "Whirlwinds in Israel in the Winters 1954/5 and 1955/6," *IEJ* 7, 1957, pp. 109–17.

Nitzan, B., *Pesher Habakkuk: A Scroll from the Wilderness of Judaea (1QpHab)*, Jerusalem, 1986, (Heb.).

North, R., "Maccabaean Sabbath Years," *Biblica* 34, 1953, pp. 501–15.

Oakman, D. E., "Jesus and Agrarian Palestine: The Factor of Debt," H. Richards, ed., *SBL Seminar Papers*, Atlanta, 1985, pp. 57–73.

—— *Jesus and the Economic Questions of His Day*, Lewiston, NY, 1986.

Oesterley, W. O. E., *I Maccabees*, *APOT*, Oxford, 1913.

Olmstead, A. T., *History of the Persian Empire*, Chicago, 1948.

Orman, D., "The Economy of Jewish Communities in the Golan in the Mishna and Talmud Period," N. Gross, ed., *Jews in Economic Life*, Jerusalem, 1985, pp. 35–66, (Heb.).

Orni, E. and Efrat, E., *Geography of Israel*, Jerusalem, 1971.

Orrieux, C., *Les Papyrus de Zenon*, Paris, 1983.

O'Shea, J. and Halstead, P., "Conclusions: Bad Year Economics," *Bad Year Economics: Cultural Responses to Risk and Uncertainty*, Cambridge, 1989, pp. 123–5.

Otto, W., "Herodes," *P-W*, suppl. II, pp. 1–159.

Pecirka, J., "Homestead Farms in Classical and Hellenistic Hellas," M. I. Finley, ed., *Problèmes de la terre en Grèce*, Paris, 1973, pp. 112–47.

Polotsky, H. J., "The Greek Papyri from the Cave of the Letters," *IEJ* 12, 1962, pp. 258–62.

Porath, J., "The Development of the Arid Regions of Judea During Herod's Reign," *Cathedra* 53, 1989, pp. 13–23, (Heb.).

Portugali, Y., "The Settlement Pattern in the Western Jezreel Valley from the 6th Century BCE to the Arab Conquest," A. Kasher, A. Oppenheimer, U. Rappaport, eds, *Man and Land in Eretz-Israel in Antiquity*, Jerusalem, 1986, pp. 7–19, (Heb.).

Preaux, C., *L'économie royale des Lagides*, Brussels, 1939, reprinted New York, 1979.

—— "L'économie Lagide: 1933–1958," L. Amundson and V. Skanland, eds, *Proceedings of the IX International Congress of Papyrology*, Oslo, 1958, pp. 200–32.

—— *Le Monde Hellénistique*, Paris, 1978.

Price, J. J., *Jerusalem Under Siege*, Leiden, 1992.

Rajak, T., *Josephus: The Historian and His Society*, London, 1983.

—— "Justus of Tiberias," *Classical Quarterly* 23, 1973, pp. 345–68.

Rappaport, U., "Akko-Ptolemais and the Jews in the Hellenistic Period," *Cathedra* 50, 1988, pp. 31–48, (Heb.).

—— "The Galilee between the Hasmonean Revolt and the Roman Conquest," I. Gafni, A. Oppenheimer, M. Stern, eds, *Jews and Judaism in the Second Temple, Mishna, and Talmud Period*, Jerusalem, 1993, pp. 16–30, (Heb.).

—— "The Hasmonean State," M. Stern, ed., *The Hellenistic Period and the Hasmonean State, The History of Eretz-Israel*, vol. 3, Jerusalem, 1981, pp. 191–273, (Heb.).

—— "The Hellenistic Cities and the Judaization of Eretz Israel," Y. Perlman and B. Shimron, eds, *Doron: Mehkarim be-Tarbut Klassit Mugashim le-Professor Ben-Zion Katz*, Tel-Aviv, 1967, pp. 219–30, (Heb.).

—— "The Hellenization of the Hasmoneans," M. Mor, ed., *Jewish Assimilation, Acculturation and Accommodation: Past Traditions, Current Issues and Future Prospects, Proceedings of the Second Annual Symposium of the Philip M. and Ethel Klutznick Chair in Jewish Civilization*, Sept. 24–5 1989, Center for the Study of Religion and Society, Creighton University, pp. 1–13.

—— "Les Iduméens en Egypte," *Revue de philologie de littérature et d' histoire ancienne* XLIII, 1969, pp. 73–82.

—— "Jewish–Pagan Relations and the Revolt Against Rome in 66–70 CE," *Jerusalem Cathedra* 1, 1981, pp. 81–95.

—— "La Judée et Rome pendant le règne d'Alexandre Jannée," *REJ* 127, 1968, pp. 329–45.

—— "The Land Issue as a Factor in Inter-Ethnic Relations in Eretz-Israel During the Second Temple Period," A. Kasher, A. Oppenheimer, U. Rappaport, eds, *Man and Land in Eretz-Israel in Antiquity*, Jerusalem, 1986, pp. 80–6, (Heb.).

—— "On the Factors Leading to the Great Revolt Against Rome," *Cathedra* 8, 1978, pp. 42–6, (Heb.).

—— "The Samaritans in the Hellenistic Period," *Zion* LV, 1990, pp. 373–96, (Heb.).

—— "When Was the Letter of Aristeas Written?" A. Gilboa et al., eds, *Studies in the History of the Jewish People and the Land of Israel in Memory of Zvi Avneri*, Haifa, 1970, pp. 37–50, (Heb.).

Rathbone, D., "The Grain Trade and Grain Shortages in the Hellenistic East," P. Garnsey and C. R. Whittaker, eds, *Trade and Famine in Classical Antiquity*, Cambridge, 1983, pp. 45–55.

Reekmans, M., "Economic and Social Repercussions of the Ptolemaic Copper Inflation," *Chronique d'Égypte* 48, 1949, pp. 324–42.

Reich, R., "Archaeological Evidence of the Jewish Population at Hasmonean Gezer," *IEJ* 31, 1981, pp. 48–52.

—— "The 'Boundary of Gezer' Inscriptions Again," *IEJ* 40, 1990, pp. 44–6.

Rhoads, D. M., *Israel in Revolution: 6–74 CE*, Philadelphia, 1976.

Rickman, G. E., *The Corn Supply of Ancient Rome*, Oxford, 1980.

—— "The Grain Trade Under the Roman Empire," J. H. D'Arms and E. C. Kopff, eds, *Roman Seaborne Commerce* (*Memoirs of the American Academy in Rome*, vol. XXXVI), Rome, 1980, pp. 261–75.

—— *Roman Granaries and Storebuilding*, Cambridge, 1971.

Robert, J. and Robert, L., "Skythopolis," *REG* 83, 1970, pp. 469–73; 84, 1971, p. 407.

Robert, L., "Une Epigramme d'automedon," *REG* 94, 1981, pp. 341–4.

Rofé, A., "Isaiah 66:1–14: Judean Sects in the Persian Period as Viewed by Trito-Isaiah," A. Kort and S. Morschauser, eds, *Biblical and Related Studies Presented to Samuel Iwry*, Winona Lake, Ind., 1985, pp. 205–17.

—— "Promises and Desertion: Eretz-Israel and the Beginning of the Second Commonwealth," *Cathedra* 41, 1986, pp. 3–10, (Heb.).

—— "The Vineyard of Naboth: The Origin and Message of the Story," *VT* 38, 1988, pp. 89–104.

Roll, I. and Ayalon, E., *Apollonia and Southern Sharon*, Tel-Aviv, 1989, (Heb.).

Roller, D. W., "The Northern Plain of Sharon in the Hellenistic Period," *BASOR* 247, 1982, pp. 43–52.

Ron, Z., "Agricultural Terraces in the Judean Mountains," *IEJ* 16, 1966, pp. 33–49, 111–22.

Rosenfeld, B. Z., "The 'Boundary of Gezer': Inscriptions and the History of Gezer at the End of the Second Temple Period," *IEJ* 38, 1988, pp. 235–45.

Rosensohn, I., "*Eymatay Shibolim Omrot Shira be-Nisan,*" *Teva ve-Aretz* XXXI, 1989, pp. 38–40, (Heb.).

Rostovtzeff, M., "Foreign Commerce of Ptolemaic Egypt," *Journal of Economic and Business History* 4, 1931–3, pp. 728–69.

—— *A Large Estate in the Third Century BC*, Madison, 1922, reprinted Rome, 1967.

—— *The Social and Economic History of the Hellenistic World*, Oxford, 1953.

—— *The Social and Economic History of the Roman Empire*, rev. by P. M. Fraser, Oxford, 1957.

Rotberg, R. I. and Rabb, T. K., eds, *Hunger and History*, Cambridge, 1985.

Roth, C., ed., *Encyclopedia Judaica*, Jerusalem, 1972.

Roueché, C. and Sherwin-White, S. M., "Some Aspects of the Seleucid Empire: The Greek Inscriptions from Failaka, in the Arabian Gulf," *Chiron* 15, 1985, pp. 1–39.

Russell, J. C., *Late Ancient and Medieval Population, Transactions of the American Philosophical Society*, n.s. 48, 3, Philadelphia, 1958.

Safrai, S., "*Sikarikon,*" *Zion* XVII, 1952, pp. 56–64, (Heb.).

Safrai, S. and Safrai, Z., "*Beth Anath,*" *Sinai* 78, 1976, pp. 18–34, (Heb.).

Safrai, Z., *The Economy of Roman Palestine*, London and New York, 1994.

—— *The Galilee in the Time of the Mishna and Talmud*, Ma'alot, Ministry of Education and Culture, Israel, 1985, (Heb.).

—— *Gevulot ve-Shilton be-Eretz Yisra'el bi-Tekufat ha-Mishna ve-ha-Talmud*, Tel-Aviv, 1980.

—— "The Influence of Demographic Stratification on the Agricultural and Economic Structure During the Mishnaic and Talmudic Periods," A. Kasher, A. Oppenheimer, U. Rappaport, eds, *Man and Land in Eretz-Israel in Antiquity*, Jerusalem, 1986, pp. 20–48, (Heb.).

—— "Samaria: From the Hellenistic to Byzantine Periods, in Light of Numismatic–Quantitative Finds," Z. H. Erlich and Y. Eshel, eds, *Judea and Samaria Research Studies*, Proceedings of the Second Annual Meeting, Ariel, 1992, pp. 167–83, (Heb.).

—— "Shechem in the Days of Mishna and Talmud 63 BC–637 CE," S. Dar and Z. Safrai, eds, *Shomron Studies*, Tel-Aviv, 1986, pp. 83–126, (Heb.).

Safrai, Z. and Lin, M., "Geva in the Hasmonean Period," *Cathedra* 69, 1993, pp. 18–36, (Heb.).

Samuel, A. E., "The Money Economy and the Ptolemaic Peasantry," *BASP* 21, 1984, pp. 187–206.

Samuelson, P. A., *Economics*, New York and Tokyo, 1970.

Sanders, E. P., *Judaism: Practice and Belief 63 BCE–66 CE*, London and Philadelphia, 1992.

Sands, P. C., *The Client Princes of the Roman Empire Under the Republic*, Cambridge, 1908, reprinted New York, 1975.

Sarkisian, G. Kh., "City Land in Seleucid Babylonia," *Ancient Mesopotamia*, Moscow, 1969, pp. 312–34.

Schalit, A., "Die Eroberungen des Alexander Jannäus in Moab," *Theokratia* 1, 1967/9, pp. 3–50.

—— "The Fall of the Hasmonean Dynasty," M. Avi-Yonah and Z. Baras, eds, *The Herodian Period: World History of the Jewish People*, vol. 7, Jerusalem, 1975, pp. 30–42.

—— *Flavii Josephi, Antiquitates Judaicae, in linguam hebraicam vertit, Libri XI–XX*, Jerusalem, 1973.

—— ed., *The Hellenistic Age: Political History of Jewish Palestine from 332 BCE to 67 BCE*, World History of the Jewish People, series 1, vol. 6, Jerusalem, 1972.

—— *König Herodes, Der Mann und Sein Werk*, Berlin, 1969.

—— "The Letter of Antiochus III to Zeuxis Regarding the Establishment of Military Colonies in Phrygia and Lydia," *JQR* 50, 1960, pp. 289–318.

—— *Roman Administration in Palestine, Library of Palestinology of the Jewish Palestine Exploration Society*, vol. V/VI, Jerusalem, 1937, (Heb.).

Schmeltz, U., "Population Characteristics of the Jerusalem and Hebron Regions at the Beginning of the Twentieth Century," *Cathedra* 36, 1985, pp. 123–64, (Heb.).

Schnebel, M., *Die Landwirtschaft im Hellenistischen Aegypten*, vol. I, *Der Betrieb der Landwirtschaft*, Munich, 1925, reprinted Milan, 1977.

Schottroff, W., "Arbeit und sozialer Konflikt im nachexilischen Juda," L. Schottroff and W. Schottroff, eds, *Mitarbeiter der Schöpfung*, Munich, 1983, pp. 104–48.

—— "Zur Socialgeschichte Israels in der Perserzeit," *Verkuendigung und Forschung* 27, 1982, pp. 46–68.

Schunck, K. D., *Historische und legendarische Erzählungen: I Makkabäerbuch*, Jüdische Schriften aus hellenistisch–römischer Zeit, I, 4, Gütersloh, 1980.

Schur, N., "The Numerical Relationship Between the Number of Households and the Total Population in the Cities of Eretz Israel During the Ottoman Period," *Cathedra* 17, 1980, pp. 102–6, (Heb.).

Schürer, E., *The History of the Jewish People in the Age of Jesus Christ*, vols I–III, rev. and ed. G. Vermes and F. Millar, Edinburgh, 1973–87.

Schwartz, D. R., *Agrippa I*, Tübingen, 1990.

—— "Ishmael ben Phiabi and the Chronology of Provincia Judaea," *Studies in the Jewish Background of Christianity*, Tübingen, 1992, pp. 218–42.

—— "Josephus and Nicolaus on the Pharisees," *JStJ* XIV, 1983, pp. 157–71.

—— "On Pharisaic Opposition to the Hasmonean Monarchy," *Studies in the Jewish Background of Christianity*, Tübingen, 1992, pp. 44–56.

Schwartz, J., *Jewish Settlement in Judaea*, Jerusalem, 1986, (Heb.).

—— "Once More on the 'Boundary of Gezer' Inscriptions and the History of Gezer and Lydda at the End of the Second Temple Period," *IEJ* 40, 1990, pp. 47–57.

—— "On Priests and Jericho in the Second Temple Period," *JQR* LXXIX, 1988, pp. 23–48.

Scott, R. B. Y., "Palestine, Climate of," G. A. Buttrick, ed., *IDB*, vol. III, Nashville, 1982.

Seager, J. D., "The Search for Maccabean Gezer," *BA* 39, 1976, pp. 142–4.

—— "The Search for Maccabean Gezer," in *Proceedings of the Sixth World Congress of Jewish Studies* (English section), vol. I, Jerusalem, 1977, p. 395.

Segal, A. and Naor, Y., "Four Seasons of Excavations at a Hellenistic Site in the Area of Kibbutz Sha'ar Ha-Amakim," D. H. French and C. S. Lightfoot, eds, *The Eastern Frontier of the Roman Empire*, BAR International Series 553 (ii), London, 1989, pp. 421–35.

Segal, M. Z., *Sefer Ben-Sira ha-Shalem*, Jerusalem, 1962, (Heb.).

Segré, A., "The Ptolemaic Copper Inflation, Ca. 230–140 BC," *AJPh* 63, 1942, pp. 174–91.

Sekunda, N. V., "Achaemenid Colonization in Lydia," *REA* 87, 1985, pp. 7–29.

Sen, A., "The Economics of Life and Death," *Scientific American*, May 1993, pp. 18–24.

—— *Poverty and Famines: An Essay on Entitlement and Deprivation*, Oxford, 1981.

Shahar, Y., "Clashes Between Jewish and Non-Jewish Settlements During the War of Destruction," *Cathedra* 51, 1989, pp. 3–20, (Heb.).

Shatzman, I., *The Armies of the Hasmoneans and Herod*, Tübingen, 1991.

—— "The Hasmoneans in Greco-Roman Historiography," *Zion*, Vol. LVII, 1991, pp. 5–64, (Heb.).

—— "Herod's Kingdom: Army and Security Problems," *Milet* 1, 1983, pp. 75–98, (Heb.).

Shaw, B. D., "Bandits in the Roman Empire," *Past and Present* 105, 1984, pp. 3–52.

Sherwin-White, A. N., *Roman Foreign Policy in the East: 168 BC to 1 AD*, London, 1984.

—— *Roman Society and Roman Law in the New Testament*, Oxford, 1963.

Sherwin-White, S., "Seleucid Babylonia," A. Kuhrt and S. Sherwin-White, eds, *Hellenism in the East*, London, 1987, pp. 1–31.

Sidebotham, S. E., *Roman Economic Policy in the Erythra Thalassa*, Leiden, 1986.

Sievers, J., *The Hasmoneans and Their Supporters: From Mattathias to the Death of John Hyrcanus I*, Ithaca, NY, 1990.

—— "The Role of Women in the Hasmonean Dynasty," L. H. Feldman and G. Hata, eds, *Josephus, the Bible and History*, Detroit, 1989, pp. 132–46.

Silver, M., *Economic Structures of the Ancient Near East*, London, 1985.

—— *Prophets and Markets: The Political Economy of Ancient Israel*, Boston, The Hague, London, 1983.

Sippel, D. V., "Dietary Deficiency Among the Lower Classes of Late Republican and Early Imperial Rome," *Ancient World* 16, 1987, pp. 47–54.

—— "Some Observations on the Means and Cost of the Transport of Bulk Commodities in the Late Republic and Early Empire," *Ancient World* 16, 1987, pp. 35–45.

Skeat, T. C., ed., *Greek Papyri in the British Museum*, vol. VII, *The Zenon Archive*, London, 1974.

Smallwood, E. M., "Gabinius' Organization of Palestine," *JJS* 18, 1967, pp. 89–92.

—— *The Jews Under Roman Rule: From Pompey to Diocletian*, Leiden, 1981.

Smith, D. L., "The Politics of Ezra: Sociological Indicators of Postexilic Judaean Society," P. R. Davies, ed., *Second Temple Studies*, vol. 1, *Persian Period, JSOT* 117, Sheffield, 1991, pp. 73–97.

Smith, G. A., *The Historical Geography of the Holy Land*, Jerusalem, n.d., reprint of Fontana Library edition, Lord Balerno, 30th edition, 1966.

Smith, M., *Palestinian Parties and Politics that Shaped the Old Testament*, New York, 1971, reprinted London, 1987.

Smith, P. and Tau, S., "Dental Pathology in the Period of the Roman Empire: A Comparison of Two Populations," *OSSA* 5, 1978, pp. 35–41.

Smith, P. and Zias, J., "Skeletal Remains from the Late Hellenistic French Hill Tomb," *IEJ* 30, 1980, pp. 109–15.

Smith, R. H., "The Southern Levant in the Hellenistic Period," *Levant* XXII, 1990, pp. 123–30.

—— "Trade in the Life of Pella of the Decapolis," A. Hadidi, ed., *Studies in the History and Archaeology of Jordan*, vol. III, Amman, London, New York, 1987, pp. 53–8.

Sperber, D., *Costs of Living in Roman Palestine*, Leiden, 1965.

—— "Drought, Famine, and Pestilence in Amoraic Palestine," *JESHO* 17, 1974, pp. 272–98.

—— "Objects of Trade Between Palestine and Egypt in Roman Times," *JESHO* 19, 1976, pp. 113–47.

—— *Roman Palestine 200–400: The Land*, Ramat-Gan, 1978.

Stager, L. E., "Appendix: Climate Conditions and Grain Storage in the Persian Period," *HTR* 64, 1971, pp. 448–50.

—— "The Archaeology of the Family in Ancient Israel," *BASOR* 260, 1985, pp. 1–35.

—— "Farming in the Judean Desert During the Iron Age," *BASOR* 221, 1976, pp. 145–58.

Ste. Croix, G. E. M. de, *The Class Struggle in the Ancient Greek World*, Ithaca, NY, 1981.

Stein, S., "The Laws on Interest in the Old Testament," *Journal of Theological Studies* 4, 1953, pp. 161–70.

Stern, E. "The Archaeology of Persian Palestine," *CHJ*, vol. I, pp. 88–114.

—— *Dor: Ruler of the Seas*, Jerusalem, 1994.

—— *Material Culture of the Land of the Bible in the Persian Period 538–332 BC*, Warminster and Jerusalem, 1982.

——— ed., *New Encyclopedia of Archaeological Excavations in the Holy Land*, Jerusalem, 1993.

Stern, E. and Tadmor, H., "*Shilton Paras*," I. Epha'al, ed., *Israel and Judah in the Biblical Period: The History of Eretz Israel*, vol. 2, Jerusalem, 1984, (Heb.).

Stern, M., "Aspects of Jewish Society: The Priesthood and Other Classes', S. Safrai and M. Stern, eds, *The Jewish People in the First Century*, Philadelphia, 1976, pp. 561–630.

——— "*Divrei Strabon al ha-Yehudim*," M. Dorman, S. Safrai, M. Stern, eds, *Essays in Jewish History and Philology in Memory of Gedaliahu Alon*, Ha-Kibbutz Ha-Meuchad, 1970, pp. 169–91, (Heb.).

——— *The Documents on the History of the Hasmonean Revolt*, Ha-Kibbutz Ha-Meuhad, 1972, (Heb.).

——— *Greek and Latin Authors on Jews and Judaism*, vols I–III, Jerusalem, 1976–84.

——— "*Ha-Mishtar ha-Romi be-Provintzia Yudeia min ha-Hurban ve-ad le-Mered Bar-Kokhva*," Z. Baras et al., eds, *Eretz Israel from the Destruction of the Second Temple to the Muslim Conquest*, Jerusalem, 1982, pp. 1–17, (Heb.).

——— ed., *The Hellenistic Period and the Hasmonean State, The History of Eretz-Israel*, vol. 3, Jerusalem, 1981, (Heb.).

——— "Judea and her Neighbors in the Days of Alexander Jannaeus," *The Jerusalem Cathedra* 1, 1981, pp. 22–46.

——— "Nicolaus of Damascus as a Source of Jewish History in the Herodian and Hasmonean Age," B. Uffenheimer, ed., *Bible and Jewish History: Studies in Bible and Jewish History Dedicated to the Memory of Jacob Liver*, Tel-Aviv, 1971, pp. 374–94, (Heb.).

——— "Notes on the Story of Joseph the Tobiad," *Tarbiz* 32, 1962/63, pp. 35–47, (Heb.).

——— "The Relations Between Judaea and Rome During the Rule of John Hyrcanus," *Zion* XXVI, 1961, pp. 1–22, (Heb.).

——— "The Relations between the Hasmonean Kingdom and Ptolemaic Egypt in View of the International Situation during the 2nd and 1st Centuries BCE," *Zion* L, 1985, pp. 81–106, (Heb.).

——— "Social and Political Realignments in Herodian Judaea," *The Jerusalem Cathedra* 2, 1982, pp. 40–62.

——— "The Status of Provincia Judaea and its Governors in the Roman Empire under the Julio-Claudian Dynasty," *Eretz Israel* 10, 1971, pp. 274–82.

——— *Studies in Jewish History: The Second Temple Period*, M. Amit, I. Gafni, M. D. Herr, eds, Jerusalem, 1991, (Heb.).

——— "Trachides: Surname of Alexander Yannai in Josephus and Syncellus," *Tarbiz* XXIV, 1956, pp. 9–15, (Heb.).

Stevenson, G. H., "Communications and Commerce," C. Bailey, ed., *The Legacy of Rome*, Oxford, 1923, pp. 141–72.

——— *Roman Provincial Administration*, New York, 1939, reprinted Westport, Conn., 1975.

Strange, J. F., "Late Hellenistic and Herodian Ossuary Tombs, French Hill," *BASOR* 219, 1975, pp. 39–67.

Suskind, R. M., "Characteristics and Causation of Protein–Calorie Malnutrition in the Infant and Pre-school Child," L. S. Greene, ed.,

Malnutrition, Behavior, and Social Organization, New York, 1977, pp. 1–18.

Taeubler, E. "Jerusalem 201 to 199 BCE: On the History of a Messianic Movement," *JQR* 37, 1946–7, pp. 1–30, 125–37, 249–63.

Tarn, W. W. and Griffith, G. T., *Hellenistic Civilization*, New York, 1952, reprinted 1975.

Taubenschlag, R., "Papyri and Parchments from the Eastern Provinces of the Roman Empire Outside Egypt," *Journal of Juristic Papyrology* 3, 1949, pp. 49–62.

Taylor, J. E., *Seleucid Rule in Palestine*, Ph.D. Dissertation, Duke University, 1979.

Tcherikover, V., *"Eretz-Yisrael le-Or ha-Papyrusim shel Zenon," The Jews in the Graeco-Roman World*, Tel-Aviv and Jerusalem, 1974, pp. 33–82, (Heb.).

—— *Hellenistic Civilization and the Jews*, Philadelphia, 1966.

—— "Palestine Under the Ptolemies," *Mizraim* 4–5, 1937, pp. 9–90.

Tcherikover, V. and Fuks, A., *Corpus Papyrorum Judaicarum*, vols I–III, Cambridge, Mass., 1957–64.

Tcherikover, V. and Heichelheim, F. M., "Jewish Religious Influence in the Adler Papyri?" *HTR* 35, 1942, pp. 25–44.

Theissen, G., *The First Followers of Jesus*, London, 1978.

Thompson, D. J., "Imperial Estates," J. Wacher, ed., *The Roman World*, vol. II, London and New York, 1990, pp. 555–67.

—— "Nile Grain Transport Under the Ptolemies," P. Garnsey, K. Hopkins, C. R. Whittaker, eds, *Trade in the Ancient Economy*, Berkeley, 1983, pp. 64–75.

Thornton, M. K., "The Augustan Tradition and Neronian Economics," *ANRW* vol. II.2, Berlin, 1977, pp. 149–71.

—— "Julio-Claudian Building Programs: Eat, Drink, and Be Merry," *Historia* 35, 1986, pp. 28–44.

Tov, E., *The Text-Critical Use of the Septuaginta in Biblical Research*, Jerusalem, 1981.

Treggiari, S. M., "Urban Labour in Rome: Mercennarii and Tabernarii," P. Garnsey, ed., *Non-Slave Labour in the Greco-Roman World*, Cambridge, 1980, pp. 48–64.

Tsafrir, Y., "The Desert Fortresses of Judaea in the Second Temple Period," *The Jerusalem Cathedra* 2, 1982, pp. 120–45.

Tuma, E. H., *Economic History and the Social Sciences: Problems of Methodology*, Berkeley and Los Angeles, 1971.

Urbach, E. E., *The Halakha: Its Sources and Developments*, Yad Le-Talmud, 1986.

—— *The Laws Regarding Slavery as a Source for Social History of the Period of the Second Temple, the Mishnah, and Talmud*, reprint edition New York, 1979; originally published in *Papers of the Institute of Jewish Studies*, vol. I, London, 1964.

Van der Spek, R. J., "Varia," *Bibliotheca Orientalis* 37, 1980, pp. 253–9; 38, 1981, pp. 212–19.

Van Selms, A., "The Year of Jubilee in and outside the Pentateuch," *Die ou Testameniest Werkgemeinskop Sud-Afrika* 17s, 1974, pp. 74–85.

Vandier, J., *La Famine dans l'Egypte ancienne*, Cairo, 1936.

Vaux, R. de, *Ancient Israel*, vols I–II, New York, 1965.

Vermes, G., *The Dead Sea Scrolls in English*, Harmondsworth, 1987.

Villeneuve, F., "L'Economie rurale et la vie des campagnes dans le Hauran antique (Ier siècle avant J.-C.–VIe siècle après J.-C.)," J. M. Dentzer, ed., *Hauran*, vol. I, Paris, 1985, pp. 63–136.

Wacholder, B. Z., "The Calendar of Sabbatical Cycles During the Second Temple and the Early Rabbinic Period," *HUCA* 44, 1973, pp. 153–96.

—— *Eupolemos: A Study of Judaeo-Greek Literature*, Cincinnati and New York, 1974.

Walbank, F. W., *The Hellenistic World*, Cambridge, Mass.,1981.

Walbank, F. W. et al., *The Cambridge Ancient History*, vol. 7.1, *The Hellenistic World*, Cambridge, 1984.

Warszawski, A. and Peretz, A., "Building the Temple Mount: Organization and Execution," *Cathedra* 66, 1992, pp. 3–46, (Heb.).

Weber, M., *The Agrarian Sociology of Ancient Civilizations*, trans. R. I. Frank, London, 1976.

Weinberg, J. P., *The Citizen–Temple Community*, trans. D. L. Smith-Christopher, *JSOT*, supplement series 151, Sheffield, 1992.

Weinberg, S. S., "Post-Exilic Palestine, An Archaeological Report," *The Israel Academy of Sciences and Humanities Proceedings* 4, 1969, pp. 78–97.

—— "Tel Anafa: The Hellenistic Town," *IEJ* 21, 1971, pp. 86–109.

Weinfeld, M., *The Organizational Pattern and the Penal Code of the Qumran Sect*, Göttingen, 1986.

—— *Social Justice in Ancient Israel and in the Ancient Near East*, Jerusalem and Minneapolis, 1995.

Welles, C. B., ed., *Royal Correspondence in the Hellenistic Period*, New Haven, 1934.

Westbrook, R., "Jubilee Laws," *Israel Law Review* 6, 1971, pp. 209–26.

—— "Redemption of Land," *Israel Law Review* 6, 1971, pp. 367–75.

Westermann, W. L., "Aelius Gallus and the Reorganization of the Irrigation System in Egypt," *Classical Philology* XII, 1917, pp. 237–43.

—— "Enslaved Persons Who Are Free," *AJPh* 59, 1938, pp. 1–30.

—— "The Ptolemies and the Welfare of their Subjects," *American Historical Review* 43, 1938, pp. 270–87.

Westermann, W. L. and Hasenoehrl, E. S., *Zenon Papyri: Business Papers of the Third Century BC Dealing with Palestine and Egypt*, vol. I, New York, 1934 (= P.Col.III).

Westermann, W. L., Keyes, C. W., and Liebesny, H., eds, *Zenon Papyri: Business Papers of the Third Century BC Dealing with Palestine and Egypt*, Columbia, NY, 1940 (= P.Col.Zen. II)

White, K. D., "Food Requirements and Food Supplies in Classical Times," *Progress in Food and Nutrition Science*, Oxford, 1976, pp. 172–4.

—— *Greek and Roman Technology*, Ithaca, NY, 1984.

Widengren, G., "The Persian Period," J. Hayes and J. Miller, eds, *Israelite and Judaean History*, Philadelphia, 1977, pp. 489–538.

Wiesl, Y., Liphschitz, N., and Lev-Yadun, S., "Flora in Ancient Eretz-Israel," A. Kasher, A. Oppenheimer, U. Rappaport, eds, *Man and Land in Eretz-Israel in Antiquity*, Jerusalem, 1986, pp. 231–43, (Heb.).

Wilcken, U., "Zum Germanicus Papyrus," *Hermes* 63, 1928, pp. 48–65.

Wilkinson, J., "Ancient Jerusalem and its Water Supply and Population," *PEQ* 106, 1974, pp. 33–51.

Will, E., "L'Urbanisation de la Jordanie aux époques hellénistique et romaine: conditions géographiques et ethniques," A. Hadidi, ed., *Studies in the History and Archaeology of Jordan*, vol. II, Amman, London, New York, 1985, pp. 237–41.

—— "Un Monument Hellénistique de Jordanie: Le Qasr el 'abd d"Iraq al Amir," A. Hadidi, ed., *Studies in the History and Archaeology of Jordan*, vol. I, Amman, 1982, pp. 197–200.

Will, E. and Orrieux, C., *IOUDAÏSMOS–HELLÈNISMOS: Essai sur la judaïsme judéen à l'époque hellénistique*, Nancy, 1986.

Yadin, Y., *Bar-Kokhba: The Rediscovery of the Legendary Hero of the Second Jewish Revolt against Rome*, London and Jerusalem, 1971.

—— "Expedition D: The Cave of the Letters," *IEJ* 12, 1962, pp. 227–57.

—— "Pesher Nahum Reconsidered," *IEJ* 21, 1971, pp. 1–12.

Yadin, Y. and Naveh, J., *Masada*, vol. I, *The Yigael Yadin Excavations 1963–1965: Final Reports: The Aramaic and Hebrew Ostraca and Jar Inscriptions*, Jerusalem, 1989.

Yamauchi, E. M., "Two Reformers Compared: Solon of Athens and Nehemiah of Jerusalem," G. Rendsburg et al., eds, *The Bible World*, New York, 1980, pp. 269–92.

Yankelevitch, R., "Granaries and Store Buildings in Eretz-Israel," *Milet* 1, S. Ettinger, Y. D. Gilat, S. Safrai, eds, Tel-Aviv, 1983, pp. 107–19, (Heb.).

—— "Herodium: Har ha-Melekh," *Cathedra* 20, 1981, pp. 23–8, (Heb.).

Yardeni, A., "New Jewish Aramaic Ostraca," *IEJ* 40, 1990, pp. 130–52.

Yaron, R., "Note on a Judean Deed of Sale of a Field," *BASOR* 150, 1958, pp. 26–8.

Zeitlin, S., *The Rise and Fall of the Judaean State*, vols I–III, Philadelphia, 1968–78.

Zeitlin, S., ed., and Tedesche, S., English trans., *The First Book of Maccabees*, New York, 1950.

—— *The Second Book of Maccabees*, New York, 1954.

Zer-Kavod, M., *Ezra ve-Nehemia*, with commentary, Jerusalem, 1980, (Heb.).

—— *Haggai, Zechariah, Malachi*, Jerusalem, 1957, (Heb.).

Zertal, A., "Hammam, Khirbet el-," *NEAEHL*, vol. 2, 1993, pp. 563–5.

Ziegler, K., Sontheimer, W., and Gärtner, H., *Der Kleine Pauly Lexikon der Antike*, Munich, 1979.

Zohary, M., *Plants of the Bible*, Cambridge, 1982.

INDEX